Patents, Citations, and Innovations

Patents, Citations, and Innovations

A Window on the Knowledge Economy

Adam B. Jaffe and Manuel Trajtenberg

The MIT Press
Cambridge, Massachusetts
London, England

This book was set in Palatino on 3B2 by Asco Typesetters, Hong Kong, and was printed and bound in the United States of America.

First printing, 2002

Library of Congress Cataloging-in-Publication Data

Jaffe, Adam B.
  Patents, citations, and innovations : a window on the knowledge economy / Adam B. Jaffe, Manuel Trajtenberg.
      p.   cm.
  Includes bibliographical references and index.
  ISBN 0-262-10095-9 (hc.)
  1. Patents. 2. Inventions. 3. Technological innovations. I. Trajtenberg, Manuel.
T211 .J34   2002
608—dc21   2001056257

To the memory of Zvi Griliches, *moreinu ve-rabeinu*—teacher, mentor, beacon of wisdom

Contents

Foreword

Paul Romer

The study of economic growth is constrained by a shortage of data. Economists have known for decades (and suspected for centuries) that such intangibles as ideas, knowledge, technology, scientific discoveries—call them whatever you want—drive the process of growth. We have learned that it is relatively easy to build theoretical models that capture this dynamic. The difficulty comes in finding empirical counterparts for the variables that stand for the intangibles.

When Robert Solow wrote his pioneering papers on growth in the 1950s, he could build on decades of work on the empirical foundations of macroeconomics. Its system of national accounts and its summary measures of output, capital, labor, and factor shares in income made sense of a bewildering array of information about the tangible inputs and outputs of economic activity. This empirical foundation turned a model that might otherwise have been a one-trick pony into a powerful workhorse.

Adam Jaffe and Manuel Trajtenberg have built a comparable base that a new generation of theorists can use when they are ready to put their models to work. They have carried to completion a program outlined by Simon Kuznets and set into motion by Zvi Griliches—using patents to create systematic measures of the intangibles that drive economic growth. In the process, they have turned the massive body of data collected by the U.S. Patent Office into a resource that any economist can use. Together with their coauthors, they have organized the raw data; created new measures of the importance, generality, and originality of patents; checked the validity of these measures; and addressed the subtle econometric problems that arise along the way. In a series of applications, they have also demonstrated how to use these data to answer important economic questions. Best of all, Jaffe and Trajtenberg have packaged everything up in a user-friendly form. An economist working anywhere in the world will be able to study how two experts formulated and attacked important economic questions, then read about the mechanics of using the data, insert the CD-ROM, and get to work.

As a thesis advisor, my most difficult challenge has been to help students connect formal abstractions about ideas, knowledge, technology, or science to concrete questions that they might have some hope of answering. Next time I face this problem, I know what I'll do: have them study this book.

Acknowledgments

It is indicative of the cooperative and collaborative nature of the NBER Productivity Program that almost half of the papers in this book have been written with additional co-authors. Our debt to Bruce Banks, Ricardo Caballero, Michael Fogarty, Bronwyn Hall, Rebecca Henderson and Josh Lerner goes far beyond the particular papers that bear their names. There are also other individuals, including Ernie Berndt, Iain Cockburn, Sam Kortum, Jenny Lanjouw, Ariel Pakes, Sam Petuchowski, Mark Schankerman, and Scott Stern, whose names don't appear on any of these papers, but whose countless comments, insights and suggestions have nonetheless had an enormous cumulative impact.

Rebecca Henderson played a key role in the original conception of this line of research. Many cups of tea and coffee were consumed in the course of endless discussions about how to conceptualize the process of innovation and technological change, in ways that could be captured by the patent-based measures that we were then toying with. To the extent that this line of work is ultimately judged either "original" or "general" (to paraphrase our own patent-based measures), Rebecca certainly deserves her fair share of the credit.

Bronwyn Hall's name appears as co-author only on chapter 13, but her role in bringing the overall data project to fruition has been fundamental. From the time of our first NSF proposal in 1993, it was clear that one of the largest payoffs to the project depended on being able to match the patent data at the firm level to financial reporting data. This was a difficult and tedious task, the kind that is tempting to do sloppily and hard to do right. Bronwyn did a spectacular job, despite the lack of immediate professional payoff to this type of data drudgery. More generally, Bronwyn has been involved in patent-related research since the early days of the NBER productivity program, and has contributed to it continuously with her wide range of professional skills. She has supported us throughout with her accumulated wisdom, enthusiasm and good will.

Had it not been for Mike Fogarty, there would be no comprehensive patent citations dataset today. It was Mike, at the time the Director of the Center for Regional Economic Issues at Case-Western Reserve University, who was convinced that the investment in time, attention and money necessary to construct the database of *all* U.S. patents would pay off in the long run. Despite major bouts of inattention and procrastination by the current authors, his faith in and enthusiasm for the project never waned. He was instrumental in putting together our first NSF proposal, and his ingenuity in finding ways to get things done allowed the project to survive its grossly inadequate official budget. Finally, it was Mike, with his knowledge of and contacts with "real" inventors, who conceived and pushed the survey reported in chapter 12, which greatly enriches our understanding of what these data mean.

We have benefited over the years from the help of exceptionally talented and dedicated research assistants. We are grateful to Meg Fernando, Michael Katz, Guy Michaels, Adi Raz, and Abi Rubin for their hard work and tolerance of our outbursts.

Financial support was provided by the National Science Foundation via Grants SBR 9320973 and SBR-9413099. By providing funding for the development of data of this kind, the NSF helps to foster the social science infrastructure. We hope that the dataset that we offer with this book will spur research and demonstrate the wisdom of such support. Additional support came from the Alfred P. Sloan Foundation, via a grant to the NBER Industrial Technology and Productivity Program. We thank Martin Feldstein, the president of the NBER, for his support of our work through both the NBER Productivity Program and the NBER/Sloan Project.

Finally, words are inadequate to express the magnitude and significance of our debt to Zvi Griliches, our beloved teacher and mentor. With the exception of the introduction and last two chapters (written after he became ill), every paper in this book benefited directly from Zvi's profound criticism and suggestions. More important, he taught us—on a continuing basis until his death—how to think about economic phenomena and how to do empirical research. He nurtured our interest in technical change and its measurement, he instilled in us the intellectual values that should govern good, honest scientific research, he provided continuous support in every conceivable way, and he was an inexhaustible source of inspiration and wisdom. It is a source of deep sadness and regret that Zvi did not live to see the publication of this book, which we dedicate to his memory.

The Data Disk

These data comprise detailed information on almost 3 million U.S. patents granted between January 1963 and December 1999, all citations made to these patents between 1975 and 1999 (over 16 million), and a reasonably broad match of patents to Compustat (the data set of all firms traded on the U.S. stock market).

The data are in several files described in detailed in chapter 13. Each file appears on the disk in both dBase ("dbf") format and SAS-transport ("tpt") format, along with a text file containing documentation. The data files are zipped to fit them all on the disk. The files are as follows:

		Data	
Description	Documentation	.tpt	.dbf
Overview	Overview.txt		
Pairwise citations data	Cite75_99.txt	Cite75_99.tpt.zip	Cite75_99.dbf.zip
Patent data, including constructed variables	Pat63_99.txt	Pat63_99.tpt.zip	Pat63_99.dbf.zip
Assignee names	Coname.txt	Coname.tpt.zip	Coname.dbf.zip
Matches to CUSIP numbers	Compustat.txt	Compustat.tpt.zip	Compustat.dbf.zip
Individual inventor records	Inventor.txt	Inventor.tpt.txt	Inventor.dbf.txt
Class codes with corresponding class names	Class.txt		
Country codes with corresponding country names	List_of_countries.txt		

Patents, Citations, and Innovations

1 Introduction

Adam B. Jaffe and Manuel Trajtenberg

For more than two centuries now, the economies of the western world have grown at a pace that greatly exceeds anything previously known in the long sweep of human history. In the last few decades, we have experienced what have come to be called the "information age" and the "knowledge economy." Hype aside, these labels do reflect a very real transformation: it is now "knowledge"—not labor, machines, land or natural resources—that is the key economic asset that drives long-run economic performance.

At the heart of this phenomenon lies a complex, multifaceted process of continuous, widespread and far-reaching innovation and technical change. Yet "knowledge," "innovation," and "technical change" are elusive notions, difficult to conceptualize and even harder to measure in a consistent, systematic way. Thus, while economists from Adam Smith on have amply recognized their crucial role in shaping the process of economic growth, our ability to study these phenomena has been rather limited.

The last several decades have seen a number of pioneering efforts to overcome these measurement problems and gather data that can be used for the systematic empirical analysis of technological change. This volume describes our contribution to this tradition, based on the massive use of detailed patent data. Patent records contain a wealth of information on each patented invention, including the identity and location of the inventors and the inventors' employer, and the technological area of the invention. Moreover, they contain citations to previous patents, which open the possibility of tracing multiple links across inventions.

We have compiled a highly detailed dataset on all US patents granted between 1963 and 1999, and the citations they made. The sheer volume of these data (3 million patents, 16 million citations), combined with the rich detail that they provide on each invention, make them indeed a promising "window" on the "knowledge economy."

Ever since we started along this path over a decade ago, our goal has been to throw that window wide open, so as to make empirical research on the economics of innovation and technical change a viable, exciting and fruitful enterprise. Together with a number of co-authors, we have used the patent data to get an empirical handle on quantifying the "importance" or "value" of innovations, measuring flows of technological knowledge, and characterizing the technological development and impact of particular institutions and countries. This volume lays out the conceptual and methodological foundations of this line of research, shows a range of interesting findings that give initial credence to the approach, and provides tools to tackle many of the thorny issues that arise along the way. Moreover, we include with this volume a CD with the complete data on patents and citations, encompassing both data items from the source records, and a range of novel measures that we have developed and computed. We hope that this will stimulate further work in this area, and provide a broader and deeper measurement base upon which research on the economics of technical change can flourish.

The rest of this introduction provides an overview of the patent data, some historical background on the origins of this line of research, and a summary of the main themes of the book. Part I contains three papers from the early 1990s that provide the conceptual foundations of our research approach. Part II describes the use of citations data to explore geographic patterns of spillovers across regions and countries. Part III deploys patent-based data to look at some policy-motivated issues regarding recent changes in the performance and technological impact of universities and government research labs, and to characterize the evolution of innovation in a particular high-tech economy, that of Israel. The final part of the book contains two chapters focused on the patent data themselves. One is a survey of inventors that provides a first-hand perspective on the inferences that can be drawn from citation data, and the other is a detailed overview and "users' guide" to the complete patent database itself, including discussion of statistical problems that arise in the use of the data.

1 Overview of the Data

Patents have long been recognized as a very rich and potentially fruitful source of data for the study of innovation and technical change.[1] The number of patents is very large: the "stock" of patents is currently in excess of 6 million, and the flow is over 150,000 patents per year (as of 1999–2000). Our database contains the approximately 3 million patents granted between 1963 and 1999. Each patent granted produces a highly structured public document containing detailed information on the innovation itself, the technological area to which it belongs, the inventors (e.g., their geographical location), and the organization (if any) to which the inventors assign the patent property right. The data used in this book are the computerized data items that appear on the "front page" of a granted patent, an example of which is reproduced in the appendix.

Patent data include references or citations to previous patents and to the scientific literature. Unlike bibliographic citations, patent citations perform an important legal function, in helping to delimit the patent grant by identifying "prior art" that is not covered by a given patent grant. Our data base contains the 16.5 million citations made by patents granted between 1975 and 1999. These citations open up the possibility of tracing multiple linkages between inventions, inventors, scientists, firms, locations, etc. In particular, patent citations allow one to study spillovers, and to create indicators of the "importance" or technological impact of individual patents, thus introducing a way of capturing the enormous heterogeneity in the value of patents. In addition to the "raw" patent and citations information, our data include a number of citations-based measures that are meant to capture different aspects of the patented innovations, such as "generality," "originality," and citations time lags. The measures are explored in several of the chapters, and described in detail for the complete dataset in chapter 13.

There are, of course, important limitations to the use of patent data, the most glaring being the fact that not all inventions are patented. First, not all inventions meet the patentability criteria set by the USPTO, the United States Patent and Trademark Office (the invention has to be novel and nontrivial, and has to have commercial

---

1. For a broader and more detailed survey of the use of patent statistics in empirical research prior to 1990, see Griliches (1990).

application). Second, the inventor has to make a strategic decision to patent, as opposed to rely on secrecy or other means of appropriability. Exploring the extent to which patents are indeed representative of the wider universe of inventions is an important, wide-open area for future research.

Another problem that used to be a serious hindrance stemmed from the fact that the patent file was not entirely computerized. Furthermore, until not long ago it was extremely difficult to handle those "chunks" that were computerized, because of the very large size of the data. The practical significance of the difficulty of dealing with large datasets was exacerbated by what we call the "inversion" problem. This refers to the fact that, in order to count the number of citations *received* by any given patent, one has to look at the citations made by *all* subsequent patents. Thus, any study using citations received, however small the sample of patents is, requires in fact access to the whole citations data, in a way that permits efficient search and extraction of citations. Indeed, when we started in the late 1980s, it was only possible to analyze relatively small samples of the data, and the feasibility of economic analyses routinely incorporating all patents was dubious. Today, however, rapid progress in computer technology has virtually eliminated these difficulties. Our complete patent data reside in personal computers and can be analyzed with the aid of standard PC software.

2   The Broad Shoulders on Which We Stand[2]

Our conception of the role of patent citations is predicated on a cumulative view of the process of technological development, by which each inventor benefits from the work of those before, and in turn contributes to the base of knowledge upon which future inventors build. Analogously, this book builds upon a broad and deep foundation of previous work. The origins of the quantitative analysis of technological change lie in the immediate post–WW II period. The

---

2. We confine the discussion in this brief subsection to a small number of key research programs that we perceive as *direct* antecedents to our own. The work presented in this volume obviously "stands (also) on the shoulders" of prominent scholars in this field such as Bob Evenson, Edwin Mansfield, Nathan Rosenberg, and Mike Scherer, to mention just the most notable omissions. However, this is not intended as a survey of the literature, and hence we chose not to expand on them simply because the methodological connection between their work and the current volume is somewhat less direct.

path-breaking findings of Abramovitz (1956) and Solow (1957) that there was a large "residual" of aggregate productivity growth that could not be explained by capital accumulation opened up a whole new and exciting research frontier. In parallel, and responding to the challenge posed by the productivity black box identified in those studies, empirical microeconomic analysis of the underlying phenomena of invention and innovation were also undertaken. A conference held in the spring of 1960 brought together these early lines of inquiry, and set the agenda for future work in this area. The resulting volume, edited by Richard Nelson (1962), *The Rate and Direction of Inventive Activity*, went on to became a landmark, and constitutes to this day a source of inspiration and guidance.[3]

Nelson's volume, best known perhaps for the classic paper by Kenneth Arrow that formalized the market failure inherent in research, contains also a less-cited but visionary paper by Simon Kuznets on the difficulties of measuring the results of the inventive process. Kuznets's paper raised many of the issues that permeate later research, including many of the papers in the present volume. He discussed the problems of defining and measuring the magnitude of inventions; the relationship between the technological and economic significance of an invention; the distinction between the cost of producing an invention and the value it creates; and the consequences of the highly skewed distribution of inventions values. Kuznets also considered the benefits and drawbacks of patent statistics, and included a plea—to which the current volume is certainly responsive—to go beyond merely counting patents, and utilize the rich and detailed information about the inventive process itself that is revealed in patent documents.

A clear antecedent of the present volume can be seen in Jacob Schmookler's 1966 book, *Invention and Economic Growth*, as well as the posthumous volume of Schmookler's work published in 1972. Schmookler methodically went through (non-computerized) patent records to compile hundreds of time series of patent totals by industry, going back over a century. He also gave careful attention to the methodological issues arising from the use of these data, particularly the difficulty of identifying patents with particular industries based on their technological classification by the patent office. Using

---

3. Richard R. Nelson's Introduction to the 1962 volume contains an interesting account of the developments in the 1950s that led up to the conference.

these data, Schmookler provided strong evidence for the role of market forces in shaping the rate and direction of inventive activity. More important in the long run, he demonstrated that patent statistics, though perhaps cumbersome to accumulate and subject to issues of interpretation, provide a unique source of systematic information about the inventive process. In this volume we carry on Schmookler's work, both by publishing updated and expanded patent statistics for other researchers to use, and by analyzing in detail the methodological and interpretational issues that arise in the use of patent statistics.

In the late 1970s, Zvi Griliches took advantage of the computerization of the USPTO, as well as the availability of other micro-data in computerized form (such as Compustat), to launch a major new research initiative on the innovation process, that relied on the merger and joint use of these distinct data sources. His students and colleagues at the NBER, led by Bronwyn Hall, compiled a large firm-level panel dataset that combined patent totals with R&D and other financial information from firms' 10-K financial reports (Bound et al. 1984; Hall et al. 1988). Armed with the first plentiful crop from this research program, Griliches organized a conference on R&D, Patents and Productivity in the fall of 1981, and published the proceedings in a volume that echoed the 1962 Nelson's volume mentioned above (Griliches 1984). Over the ensuing decade, a large amount of research was done based on the NBER R&D panel dataset and its descendants, and established many of what we now think of as "stylized facts" about R&D and patents at the firm level:[4]

• In the cross-section, patents are roughly proportional to R&D, with the ratio varying by industry and being higher for small firms (Bound et al. 1984).

• For particular firms over time (the "within" panel dimension), patents are correlated with R&D, typically with decreasing returns to R&D, with the strongest relationship being simultaneous and contemporaneous between R&D and patent applications (Hall, Griliches, and Hausman 1986).

• In multivariate models including R&D, patents and performance measures (e.g. productivity growth, profitability, market value), most

---

4. We do not discuss here the even larger literature derived from these data relating to R&D and productivity, but not necessarily to patents; see for example Griliches, 1994.

of the information is in the correlation between R&D and performance. Patent counts are more weakly correlated with performance, and often do not have incremental explanatory power once R&D is included (Pakes 1985; Cockburn and Griliches 1988; Griliches, Hall, and Pakes 1991).

• Detailed information on the technological composition of firms' patents can be used to locate firms' research programs in "technology space;" variations across this space in technological opportunity and "spillovers" of R&D have measurable effects on research performance (Jaffe 1986).

In addition to this econometric work, the late 1970s and early 1980s saw important conceptual developments in modeling the research process and the role of patents in that process. Griliches (1979) and Griliches and Pakes (1984) extended and refined the concept of the "knowledge production function," a stochastic relationship in which current R&D investment, the firm's existing stock of knowledge, and knowledge from other sources combine to produce new knowledge. Patent applications can be viewed as a noisy indicator of the success of this stochastic knowledge production process, with the "propensity to patent"—the ratio of patents to the unobservable knowledge production—possibly varying over time and institutions. Griliches (1979) also suggested that the possibility of excess social returns in research should be explicitly modeled in relationship to flows of knowledge between and among different economic agents.

At about the same time, Schankerman and Pakes (1985, 1986) took another original track, using information on fees paid for the renewal of patents in European countries. These data allowed them to estimate the distribution of (private) patent values, as induced by the frequencies of renewal and the magnitude of the renewal fees at every stage. This line of research provided firm empirical evidence on the extent of heterogeneity in patent values, and also a great deal of stimuli for further research using novel aspects of patent data (Pakes and Simpson 1989).

The current volume is a direct outgrowth of and response to this research trajectory. First, we develop the use of patent citations to trace flows of technological knowledge from one inventor to another, thereby implementing Griliches' original suggestion. Second, we use the number and character of citations ultimately received by a given patent to characterize the technological and economic impact of a given invention. In so doing, we provide an empirically meaningful way of examining the issue of the magnitude of inventions raised by Kuznets. This approach also provides a way to deal with the apparently low "information content" of patent counts found in much of the 1980s econometric work: weighting patents by the number of citations that they later receive produces a much more meaningful measure of inventive output than simple patent counts. Finally, we continue with the tradition of Schmookler and Griliches by providing extensive analysis of how the process that generates the data affects their interpretation, and putting forward econometric techniques for dealing with some of these issues.

3   Overview of the Volume

The volume is organized in four major parts (following this introduction): Part I lays out the conceptual and methodological foundations that underlie the subsequent work. Part II focuses on the use of citations data to explore the geography of knowledge spillovers. Part III contains applications and analysis of particular institutions (e.g., universities), countries and policies. Finally, part IV returns to the patent data themselves, and will be of particular interest to readers planning to use the data in future research: it describes the data in detail, and offers tools to deal with some thorny issues of interpretation that are created by the way the patent and citations data are generated and collected. It also discusses a survey of inventors that sheds light on the meaning of citations.

The three chapters in part I, written in the late 1980s and early 1990s,[5] start with the premise that a patent citation constitutes a (probably noisy) signal of a technological relationship between the citing and cited inventions. Based on this premise, we formulate hypotheses about how the cumulative process of technological development ought to manifest itself in the citations data. Chapter 2 is both chronologically and conceptually the "first" paper in the book. Stemming from Trajtenberg's 1983 Ph.D. thesis, it constitutes the first systematic use (of which we are aware) of patent citation data, using information on patent citations related to a particular line of inventions (CT scanners) collected from paper patent records. It showed

---

5. Chapter 3, published in journal form in 1997, originally appeared as Trajtenberg, Jaffe, and Henderson 1992.

that the citation-weighted patent count received by CT patented inventions is highly correlated with the social surplus generated by these innovations. Thus, the frequency of subsequent citations turned out to be indicative of the "importance" of the underlying innovations, as measured by the ensuing welfare gains computed on the basis of a discrete choice demand model.

At a basic level, the "success" of this initial empirical exercise spawned the research trajectory reflected in this book, but it also anticipated many of the difficulties and limitations of citations data. First, one had to confront the truncation problem: patents receive citations from subsequent ones over a long period of time (up to several decades), and therefore at any given point in time, when the data are collected, we observe only a fraction of the citations that they will eventually receive. Clearly, older patents would have received a higher fraction of the total number of eventual citations, whereas for more recent patents the truncation problem is more acute. Chapter 2 deals with this issue in a straightforward way, foreshadowing the more systematic statistical approaches that we developed later.

Chapter 2 also illustrates both the value and the difficulty of "external" versus "internal" validation of patent-based measures.[6] By internal validation we mean attempts to substantiate the hypothesized role of patent and citations-based measures as indicators of technological impact by examining patterns and relationships wholly within the patent data themselves. By contrast, external validation substantiates the meaning of the patent-related data by correlating patent-based measures with independent technological or economic indicators whose meaning is more self-evident (e.g., the market value of firms). Construction of the estimates of social surplus associated with innovations in CT scanners (an example of such an independent indicator suitable for external validation) was in itself a major data and econometric task, even though it applied only to one specific case. Application of this method to anything like a comprehensive analysis of industrial innovation would be extremely difficult if not altogether impossible. Nonetheless, the fact that citations were found to be related to a well grounded, independent measure

6. Chapter 12 provides "validation" of a wholly different sort, by asking to what extent citation patterns are consistent with inventors' subjective assessments of spillovers and technological impact.

of importance made the results compelling in a way that is much harder to achieve using just internal validation methods.

Intrigued by the findings in the CT scanners case study, and interested in exploring the use of citations as indicators of knowledge spillovers, we constructed in the early 1990s, together with Rebecca Henderson, a dataset that consisted of all patents granted to universities in 1975 and 1980, and a matched sample of corporate patents.[7] Chapter 3 develops a series of novel citation-based measures, and explores how informative they are of the varied nature of inventions. It is based on the maintained hypothesis that university patents are, on average, likely to be more basic or fundamental in a technological sense than corporate patents, because universities engage in more basic research. And indeed, we found that citation-based measures related to the "basicness" of inventions exhibit higher scores for university patents than for corporate patents. Note that this tests the *joint* hypotheses that (i) citations are a proxy for technological impact, and (ii) university inventions have greater technological impact. Thus, positive findings in this kind of tests may be seen as providing both validation of citations as a proxy for the underlying phenomena, and information on the substantive questions of interest.

A number of themes emerged in this paper that have turned out to be of enduring significance. Thus for example, even if citations are indicative of importance, they do not themselves have any natural "calibration." That is, there is no way to say a priori whether 2 or 10 or 20 citations is "a lot." This is particularly true in the face of truncation, which causes more recent patents to have fewer citations. For this reason, all of our work uses "reference" or "control" groups, in which citation-based measures for a given institution, region or country are compared to the same measures calculated for some appropriate comparison group. Because patent and citation practices vary across technological areas and time, and because of the truncation problem, construction of these control groups must give careful attention to these dimensions of the data. Used first in chapter 3, this "matched sample" approach was refined and extended in several subsequent papers. Chapter 13 provides a systematic analysis of different ways to "benchmark" citation-based measures.

---

7. This dataset of a few thousand patents was purchased "retail" from a commercial data service. It forms the basis of chapters 3, 5, and 8. The apparent fruitfulness of these data convinced us to undertake the NSF-funded data construction effort encompassing the complete USPTO database.

Chapter 3 introduced for the first time a number of the "constructed" measures of the technological character and significance of innovations that have been applied in later work and which are contained in the attached CD. "Generality" is defined as a measure of the extent to which the citations received by a patent are widely dispersed across technology classes. Holding constant the number of citations, we suggest that higher dispersion of those citations across technologies indicates a wider technological impact, and hence potentially higher social returns. "Originality" is the analogous statistic calculated on the basis of citations made, rather than citations received. It is predicated on the notion that "original" research tends to be synthetic, drawing on previous research from a number of different fields. This chapter also introduced the measurement of rates of "self-citation" (that is, the proportion of citations made by the same assignee as the one owing the cited patent) and conjectured that these rates may reflect the degree of appropriation of potential spillovers from a given invention by the organization that owns it.[8]

Chapter 4 was conceived after Ricardo Caballero served as a discussant of a version of chapter 5 that was presented at an NBER conference in the spring of 1992.[9] It places the concept of knowledge spillovers, proxied by patent citations, within the context of an explicit general equilibrium model of knowledge-driven endogenous growth. It represents one of only a few attempts to link the endogenous growth literature to microeconomic empirical foundations. In so doing, it introduces several methodological innovations that are developed further in subsequent chapters. These include a "citations function" that models the citations generation process as the combined effects of gradual diffusion and of gradual obsolescence. The former causes citation rates to rise as time elapses after an invention, whereas gradual obsolescence causes citation rates to fall as time elapses. It also explores how multiple observations on citing and cited patent cohorts, across time and in different technological fields, can be used to identify empirically the extent to which observed patent rates and citation rates are affected by variations in the propensity to patent and the propensity to make patent citations.

8. Another measure developed there was the extent of reliance on science versus technology, as measured by the ratio of citations to the scientific literature ("non-patent citations") to all patent and non-patent citations appearing on the patent.
9. We thank Olivier Blanchard for brokering the Caballero/Jaffe research collaboration, which made an important contribution to the overall research trajectory.

The second part of this volume focuses on the use of citations data to explore the geography of knowledge spillovers. Prior to this, there had been extensive theoretical analysis of the implications of knowledge spillovers for economic growth, but little was done to give empirical content to this concept. A general skepticism about the difficulty of measuring spillovers is reflected in Paul Krugman's influential book on economic geography: "Knowledge flows ... are invisible; they leave no paper trail by which they may be measured and tracked, and there is nothing to prevent the theorist from assuming anything about them that she likes" (Krugman 1991, p. 53). Our work has shown that patent citations do constitute indeed a "paper trail" of knowledge spillovers, though one that is incomplete and mixed in with a fair amount of noise. Still, the large volume and wide coverage of patent citations data make them extremely useful for studying the geography of innovation. Chapter 5 was the first paper to demonstrate statistically significant geographic localization of knowledge spillovers as captured by patent citations. Specifically, we found that citing patents were more likely to come from the same metropolitan area, the same state and the same country as the cited patents, relative to a "control" sample of patents that were carefully matched for similarity in time and technological focus to the citing patents. Moreover, we found that localization tends to "fade" over time, that is, as time elapses the geographic differences in citation rates decreases. This finding corresponded well with intuition, and hence gave further credence to the results: whatever initial advantage geographic proximity may offer in terms of knowledge transmission and as stimuli for further knowledge creation, the very "ethereal" nature of knowledge dictates that such advantage should diminish with time. Other dimensions of "proximity" across inventions— technological, institutional, etc.—also appeared to matter. Thus, this paper helped established the notion that knowledge spillovers could after all be traced empirically across geographic and other dimensions, and that the junction between geography and time does matter.

Chapters 6 and 7 examine in more detail the patterns of geographic localization by using much richer data in the context of the citations-function estimation method developed in chapter 4.[10] We were thus

---

10. Chapter 6 was based still on partial data that limited the amount of parameter flexibility that could be implemented. Chapter 7 is based on the complete data through 1994, allowing examination of more countries and a richer econometric specification in which more parameter variation is allowed.

able to quantify quite precisely differences in spillover flows across countries, and to uncover interesting idiosyncrasies, such as the tendency of Japanese inventors to draw from more recent innovations compared to inventors in other countries. Above all, these papers demonstrate the research potential of this kind of approach for the study of the complex web of knowledge spillovers as they flow across locations, technologies, and time.

Part III deploys patent data to the analysis of the innovative performance of major research institutions (such as universities and national labs), and of particular countries (Israel). In so doing it expands the scope of patents as a research tool both to issues that have clear policy implications, and to units of analysis other than traditional firms and sectors. Chapter 8 examines the changes in the patenting of universities that occurred after the passage of the Bayh-Dole Act in 1980, which was explicitly intended to foster commercialization of university-derived inventions. The rate of patenting by universities was rising even before the passage of the act, but exploded in the 1980s and 1990s. However, using our citations-based measures of importance and generality, we find that the average significance of university inventions actually declined after the early 1980s. Thus, while promoting the *quantity* of technology transfer from universities, the change in policy regime brought about by Bayh-Dole apparently did not improve its *quality*.

Chapter 9 examines patenting by NASA and the rest of the U.S. government. Patents per dollar of federal research expenditure fell from the mid-1960s until the late 1980s. After 1980, federal agencies, with the exception of NASA, reversed this trend and increased their rate of patenting relative to the amount of research performed. Unlike universities, there is no evidence that changes in the ratio of patents to government R&D have been associated with changes in average importance, as measured by patent citations. This paper also contains a qualitative comparison of citation-based indicators of importance and knowledge flows with the inventor's perceptions regarding the underlying inventions, which served as a pilot study for the broader survey of inventors reported in chapter 12. Extending this line of inquiry, chapter 10 looks in detail at the patents and broader commercialization efforts of the "National Laboratories," the relatively large research facilities under the U.S. Department of Energy. As with universities, a number of policy changes in the 1980s and 1990s have sought to encourage commercialization of

technology from the National Labs. We find that these efforts
have had some success: patenting rates have risen with no apparent
decline in patent quality. Moreover, labs that maintained their technological focus, and those managed by universities, seem to have
had the most success.

Chapter 11 uses the patent data and citation measures to evaluate innovation in Israel. Israel ranks high in terms of patents per
capita, compared to most of the G7, the Asian Tigers' and a group of
countries with similar GDP per capita. Israeli patents are also of high
quality in terms of citations received (and getting better over time).
Moreover, Israeli inventors patent a great deal in the emerging fields
of computers and communications and in biotechnology. On the
other hand, Israel ranks low in terms of the percentage of patented
innovations that are assigned to local corporations, casting doubt
on the ability of the country to fully reap the benefits from those
innovations.

The final part of this volume returns to the patent data themselves,
and hence it will be particularly useful to readers interested in using
these data in future research. Chapter 12 reports on the results of a
survey of inventors/patentees, designed to elucidate the extent to
which our underlying assumptions about the patent and citation
processes conform with the participants' perceptions. Thus, this survey is another form of "validation" of the citations data as a proxy
for knowledge flows and technological impact. We surveyed both
inventors whose patents were cited, and patentees whose patents
made the citations. We find that citing inventors report significant
communication with cited inventors (statistically more than with a
control sample of inventors), some of it in ways that suggest that a
"spillover" took place. However, there is also a large amount of noise
in the citations data: about half of all citations do not correspond to
any perceived communication, or to a perceptible technological relationship between the two inventions. We also found a significant
correlation between the number of citations a patent received and
its importance (both economic and technological) as perceived by the
inventor.

Chapter 13 provides the basic roadmap to the data, and constitutes
a users' guide for the use of the data in research. It describes the patent process and the legal meaning of patent citations. It illustrates
basic statistics and trends in the data across technologies and countries and over time. Most important, it considers the econometric

implications of the process that generates patent citations. In particular, it explores biases and interpretational issues that arise from (i) variations in the propensity to patent over time; (ii) truncation of the patent series because we observe only patents granted before some cutoff date; and (iii) truncation in the citations series because we observe citations for only a portion of the "life" of an invention, with the duration of that portion varying across patent cohorts. It discusses possible econometric solutions to these problems, the identifying assumptions required, and pending problems that arise in implementing these solutions. This chapter is a "must read" for anyone contemplating doing analysis of their own with the data.

4 Linking Out: Market Value and Patent Citations

As already mentioned, a great deal of the work presented in this volume relies exclusively on data contained within the patent records themselves. However, many of the data items in patents offer exciting opportunities for linking them out with external data, which can greatly enrich the analysis. Thus, for example, the location of inventors or of assignees can be linked with geo-economic characteristics of their SMSAs, states, or countries; patent classes can be linked to industrial sectors; non-patent citations can be linked to scientific sources; application or grant dates can be linked to any relevant economic time series, etc. One of the potentially most fruitful linkages is through the identity of the assignee: after all, patents are meant to ensure some degree of appropriability to the owner of the patent rights, and hence at least the private value of the patented innovations should somehow be revealed in the performance of the assignees; likewise, the impact of spillovers as traced by citations should also manifest itself in that context.

The big stumbling block was matching the assignee names as they appear on the patent records (currently over 175,000 of them), to any external list of corporations: those names are not entirely standardized, companies take patents under a variety of different names (including subsidiaries), and there are just plenty of errors in spelling. Responding to this formidable challenge, Bronwyn Hall undertook to match the assignee names with the company names in the Compustat database of financial reporting data, and to further consolidate them following their mergers and acquisitions history. The result is a matched set of almost 5,000 publicly traded firms, that allows one to link between the majority of patents (about 2/3 of all patents assigned to U.S. inventors up to the early 1990s) and the corporations that own them.[11]

The first use of this invaluable resource was a recent project that we have done with Bronwyn Hall, on the relationship between patents, patents citations and the stock market valuation of firms (Hall, Jaffe, and Trajtenberg 2001). Previous work along those lines have found that patent counts add little to market value after R&D is included in a Tobin-q type equation. Here however we find a significant relationship between *citation-weighted patent stocks*, and the market value of firms. The market premium associated with citations appears to be due mostly to the high valuation of the upper tail of cited patents, as opposed to a smoother increase in value as citation intensity increases. After controlling for R&D and the unweighted stock of patents, there is no difference in value between firms whose patents have no citations, and those firms whose patent portfolio has approximately the median number of citations per patent. There is, however, a significant increase in value associated with having above-median citation intensity, and a substantial value premium associated with having a citation intensity in the upper quartile of the distribution. This confirms the finding in the CT scanners study reported in chapter 2, namely that value increases with citation intensity, apparently at an increasing rate. It is also consistent with the conventional wisdom about the innovation process more generally, that a large fraction of the value of the stream of innovations is associated with a small number of very important innovations.

This paper also extends our understanding of the relationship between citations and value by examining the differential impact of self-citations (i.e., citations from patents assigned to the same firm). On average, self-citations are associated with about *twice as much* market value as citations from others. This confirms the conjecture of chapter 3 that self-citations, because they represent subsequent building on the invention by the original firm, are indicative of the firm's capturing a larger share of the overall social value of the invention. Thus, the evidence shows that both social and private values are increasing in the citations intensity, apparently with increasing returns, and that a high rate of self-citation is indicative of a larger fraction of social returns accruing to the innovating firm.

---

11. The match file is included in the attached CD; see also chapter 13.

5 What's Next? Thoughts on the Future Research Agenda

Much of the work in this volume was meant to develop the infra-structure in terms of data, concepts, and method to allow the massive use of patents and citations in run-of-the mill economic research, to "validate" the novel measures used, and to demonstrate the viability of the whole approach. In so doing we responded to the aforementioned challenge posed by Kuznets (1962), and, we hope, made a few strides forward along the path initiated by Schmookler and followed by Griliches' NBER program. This is then just "the end of the beginning," to paraphrase Churchill's prophetic dictum: We have barely scratched the surface in terms of what could be done with these data and approach, in order to further elucidate the economics of technical change. Indeed, we have still opened only a small "window" into the mostly impenetrable "black box" of technological change, which has grown enormously in importance as the wonders of innovation engulf more and more of the economy. Here we offer a few additional thoughts on what we hope will be a vibrant research agenda.

The interactions among research spillovers, firms' efforts to appropriate the returns to their inventions, and observed citations within and across firms, constitute a fruitful area for further study. Our work so far has been entirely non-strategic, taking citation patterns as exogenous evidence of spillovers and/or cumulative innovation that is internal to the firm. The next step would be to marry the citations data to a model of innovation and competition, in which firms and their competitors choose levels of R&D, of effort in learning about the work of others, and of follow-up development when initial innovations appear promising. The existence of detailed data on inventions and citations, and the link between these and detailed data on firms, potentially offers an unusual opportunity for empirical testing of a rich strategic model.

Stock market valuation is, of course, only one dimension of value or importance. Harhoff et al. (1999) have confirmed the relationship between patent citations and "value" using survey-based measures of the value of specific important inventions. Recent work by Jenny Lanjouw and Mark Schankerman (1999) explores the information content of patent citations relative to other indicators also derived from patent data, and examines the relationship of these measures to other economic variables. They construct composite measures of patent "quality" based on the number of citations received, the number of citations made by the patent, the number of claims in the patent, and the number of countries in which patent protection is sought ("family size"). They show that this measure is related to the likelihood of patent renewal and patent litigation, and to measures of the economic significance of a patent to its owner. Finally, they show that the quality-adjusted rate of patenting by firms exhibits a more stable relationship to firm's R&D expenditure than simple patent counts.

There is clearly room for further work on the meaning of and relationships among these different indicators of quality, importance, and value. An important issue is the inter-relationships among the technological significance of an invention, the spillovers that it generates for future inventors, and the value of the invention to its owner. It remains to be seen whether the different measures of patent quality can shed light on these issues (beyond the self-citation effect mentioned above). One aspect of this is variations is patent "size," in the sense of different uses or applications for a single idea, as distinct from the intrinsic significance of the idea.

We have shown that citations exhibit an interesting geographic pattern: initial localization that fades over time. But there is much more that could be done to further explore these patterns. How important are "border" effects (continents, countries, metropolitan areas) as distinct from physical distance? Does language matter systematically? How about historical, social and cultural connections? For example, recent work by Hu and Jaffe (2001) shows that Korea is "closer" (in terms of frequency of patent citations) to Japan than to the United States, and Korea is much closer to Japan than Taiwan is to Japan. These relationships appear to be consistent with patterns of institutional and historical connections in these pairs of economies. As shown in Chapter 7, the large size and great detail of the patent dataset makes exploration of these kinds of questions feasible even for relatively small countries.

In addition to further empirical explorations, much could be gained by refining the modeling of the underlying processes. In principle, spillovers from an innovating unit A (e.g., inventor, firm, country) to another unit B benefit the latter by facilitating invention in B. This means that the rate of innovation and hence of patenting in B, as well as the citations made by B, are endogenous to the spillover process itself. Our work to date has ignored this, taking the flow of citations *to* A as telling us something about the importance of innovations in A, but not being themselves generated or stimulated *by* A. Modeling of this process would allow us to start thinking about connecting the empirical analysis of citations once again to the overall rate of productivity improvement and economic growth. The model in chapter 4 links R&D, innovation, citations and growth over time at an aggregate level within a single country. It would be very interesting to extend this approach to endogenous growth with spillovers among industries and countries.

Another idea in chapter 4 that has not been pursued is endogenous obsolescence. A patent that is highly cited is presumed "important," but it would also seem that the accumulation over time of many patents building on a given invention would eventually make it *less* valuable, at least in the private sense. In principle, it should be possible to implement a dynamic model of the process that might be able to shed light on the rate of private obsolescence of knowledge, and how that varies across different technologies or industries, as well as over time.

Finally, despite the potentially rich detail in the classification of patents by technology-based patent class, we have looked only in limited ways at spillovers across technologies. Just as with geography, there is significant localization, in the sense that citations are more likely to patents in the same class than in other classes. But does this fade over time? Are there particular classes that have unusually large spillovers, in the sense of greatly impacting "distant" technological areas as much as closely related ones? In principle, analysis of this kind offers the potential to test for and explore the significance of "general purpose technologies" (Bresnahan and Trajtenberg 1995).

It has been a major theme of the National Bureau of Economic Research since its inception that good economic research depends on the generation of appropriate and reliable economic data. It is generally agreed that the twenty-first century economy is one in which knowledge—particularly the technological knowledge that forms the foundation for industrial innovation—is an extremely important economic asset. The inherently abstract nature of knowledge makes this a significant measurement challenge. We believe that patents and patent citation data offer tremendous potential for giving empirical content to the role of knowledge in the modern economy. We hope that by constructing the NBER Patent Citations Data File, demonstrating some of the uses to which it can be put, and making it available to other researchers, we can provide a broader and deeper

measurement base on which research on the economics of technological change can prosper.

Appendix

United States Patent   **4,440,871**

Lok et al.   *Apr. 3, 1984*

Crystalline Silicoaluminophosphates

Abstract

A novel class of crystalline microporous silicoaluminophosphates
is synthesized by hydrothermal crystallization of silicoalumino-
phosphate gels containing a molecular structure-forming templating
agent. The class comprises a number of distinct species, each with a
unique crystal structure. The compositions exhibit properties somewhat analogous to zeolitic molecular sieves which render them useful
as adsorbent or catalysts in chemical reactions such as hydrocarbon
conversions.

Inventors: Lok, Brent M. (New City, NY); Messina, Celeste A.
             (Ossining, NY); Patton, Robert L. (Katonah, NY); Gajek,
             Richard T. (New Fairfield, CT); Cannan, Thomas R. (Val-
             ley Cottage, NY); Flanigen, Edith M. (White Plains, NY).

Assignee: Union Carbide Corporation (Danbury, CT).

Filed: Jul. 26, 1982

Intl. Cl.: B01J 27/14

[Some of the] Current U.S. Cl.: 502/214; 208/114; 208/136; 208/
138; 208/213; 208/254.H; 585/418; 585/467; 585/475; 585/481

Field of Search: 252/435, 437, 430, 455 R; 423/305; 501/80

[Some of the] References Cited

U.S. Patent Documents

4,158,621	Jun., 1979	Swift et al.	252/437 X
4,310,440	Jan., 1982	Wilson et al.	423/305 X
4,364,839	Dec., 1982	McDaniel	252/430

[Some of the] Foreign Patent Documents

984502   Feb., 1965   GB

Other References

"Phosphorus Substitution in Zeolite Frameworks," E. M. Flanigen et al. (1971), [Advances in Chemistry Series No. 101-ACS].

Primary Examiner: Wright, William G.

38 Claims, 3 Drawing Figures

References

Abramovitz, Moses (1956). "Resource and Output Trends in the United States Since 1870." *American Economic Review*, May 1956.

Bound, John, C. Cummins, Z. Griliches, B. Hall, and A. Jaffe (1984). "Who Does R&D and Who Patents?" In Griliches 1984.

Bresnahan, Timothy, and M. Trajtenberg, "General Purpose Technologies: 'Engines of Growth?'" (1995). *Journal of Econometrics, Annals of Econometrics* 65, no. 1: 83–108.

Cockburn, Iain, and Z. Griliches (1988). "Industry Effects and Appropriability Measures in the Stock market's Valuation of R&D and Patents." *American Economic Review* 78 (May): 419–423.

Griliches, Zvi, ed. (1984). *R&D, Patents and Productivity*. University of Chicago Press.

Griliches, Zvi (1990). "Patent Statistics as Economic Indicators." *Journal of Economic Literature* 28, no. 4: 1661–1707.

Griliches, Zvi (1994). "Productivity, R&D, and the Data Constraint." *American Economic Review* 84, no. 1: 1–23.

Griliches, Zvi, B. Hall, and A. Pakes (1991). "R&D, Patents and Market Value Revisited: Is There a Second (Technological Opportunity) Factor?" *Economics of Innovation and New Technology* 1: 183–202.

Hall, Bronwyn, C. Cummins, E. Laderman, and J. Mundy (1988). "The R&D Master File Documentation." NBER Technical Working Paper, no. 72.

Hall, Bronwyn, Z. Griliches, and J. Hausman (1986). "Patents and R&D: Is There a Lag?" *International Economic Review* 27, no. 2: 265–283.

Hall, Bronwyn, A. Jaffe, and M. Trajtenberg (2001). "Market Value and Patent Citations: A First Look." University of California, Berkeley, Department of Economics, Working Paper, no. E01-304.

Harhoff, Dietmar, F. Narin, F. M. Scherer, and K. Vopel (1999). "Citation Frequency and the Value of Patented Inventions." *Review of Economics and Statistics* 81, no. 3: 511–515.

Hu, Albert G., and A. Jaffe (2001). "Patent Citations and Knowledge Flow: Korea and Taiwan." NBER WP, no. 8528.

Jaffe, Adam (1986). "Technological Opportunity and Spillovers of R&D: Evidence from Firms' Patents, Profits and market Value." *American Economic Review* 76: 984–1001.

Krugman, Paul (1991). *Geography and Trade*. MIT Press.

Kuznets, Simon (1962). "Inventive Activity: Problems of Definition and Measurement." In Nelson 1962.

Lanjouw, Jean O., and M. Schankerman (1999). "The Quality of Ideas: Measuring Innovation with Multiple Indicators." NBER WP no. 7345.

Nelson, Richard R., ed. (1962). *The Rate and Direction of Inventive Activity: Economic and Social Factors*. Princeton University Press.

Pakes, Ariel (1985). "On Patents, R&D and the Stock Market Rate of Return. *Journal of Political Economy* 93: 390–409.

Pakes, Ariel, and M. Simpson (1989). "Patent Renewal Data." *Brookings Papers on Economic Activity (Micro)*, 331–410.

Schankerman, Mark, and A. Pakes (1985). "The Rate of Obsolescence and the Distribution of Patent Values: Some Evidence from European Patent Renewals." *Revue Economique* 36: 917–941.

Schankerman, Mark, and A. Pakes (1986). "Estimates of the Value of Patent Rights in European Countries During the Post-1950 Period." *Economic Journal* 96: 1052–1076.

Schmookler, Jacob (1966). *Invention and Economic Growth*. Harvard University Press.

Schmookler, Jacob (1972). *Patents, Invention, and Economic Change: Data and Selected Essays*. Edited by Zvi Griliches and Leonid Hurwicz. Harvard University Press.

Solow, Robert M. (1957). "Technical Change and the Aggregate Production Function." *Review of Economics and Statistics*, August 1957.

Trajtenberg, Manuel, A. Jaffe, and R. Henderson (1992). "Ivory Tower versus Corporate Lab: An Empirical Study of Basic Research and Appropriability." NBER WP, no. 4146.

I

Conceptual and Methodological Foundations

2

A Penny for Your Quotes: Patent Citations and the Value of Innovations

Manuel Trajtenberg

1 Introduction

The study of technological change has been hampered all along by the scarcity of appropriate data and, in particular, by the lack of good indicators of innovation having a wide coverage. Patents would seem to be the one important exception, since they are the only manifestation of inventive activity covering virtually every field of innovation in most developed countries and over long periods of time. Yet, their use in economic research has not lived up to expectations, primarily because patents exhibit an enormous variance in their "importance" or "value," and hence, simple patent counts cannot be very informative of innovative "output" (which is usually what we are after).

The goal here is to readdress this problem by examining the usefulness of patent indicators in the context of a particular innovation, Computed Tomography scanners, one of the most important advances in medical technology of recent times. The central hypothesis is that patent citations (i.e., references to patents appearing in the patent documents themselves), long presumed to be indicative of something like technological importance, may be informative of the economic value of innovations as well. Indeed, patent counts weighted by a citations-based index are found to be highly correlated (over time) with independent measures of the social gains from innovations in Computed Tomography. On the other hand, as in the previous literature, simple patent counts are found to be indicative only of the input side, as reflected in R&D outlays. Beyond

I am grateful to Tim Bresnahan, Zvi Griliches, an anonymous referee, and to participants in the productivity workshop of the NBER Summer Institute for helpful comments on an earlier draft.

establishing their role as indicators, the findings suggest that citations may reflect a sort of causal relationship between citing and
cited patents, which is consistent with the view of innovation as a
continuous and incremental process, punctuated by occasional
breakthroughs.

The article is organized as follows. Section 2 lays out the basis for
the use of patent citations. Section 3 offers a first view of the patent
data in Computed Tomography, and Section 4 briefly describes the
measures of the value of innovations in this field borrowed from a
previous study (Trajtenberg, 1989). The tests of the main hypotheses
are conducted in Section 5, and Section 6 offers some closing thoughts.
Finally, in view of the fact that the number of citations per patent
decreases drastically over time, I present in the Appendix a statistical procedure to test for "age versus importance" and for truncation
effects.

2 Using Patent Counts and Patent Citations

It has long been thought that the detailed information contained
in the patent documents may have a bearing on the importance of
the innovations disclosed in them and that it may therefore be possible to construct patent indicators that could serve as proxies for the
value of innovations.[1] Up to now, though, virtually the only patent
measures used in economic research have been simple patent counts
(henceforth SPC), that is, the number of patents assigned over a certain period of time to firms, industries, countries, *etc.*

The body of evidence that has accumulated since Schmookler
(1966) indicates fairly clearly that SPC are closely associated with the
input side of the innovative process, primarily with contemporaneous
R&D expenditures in the cross-sectional dimension (Griliches, 1984).
On the other hand, the few attempts to relate those counts to value
indicators (e.g., the market value of innovating firms) have been
largely unsuccessful. (See, for example, Griliches *et al.*, 1988.) As suggested above, those findings are hardly surprising, considering that
patents vary enormously in their technological and economic significance. Thus, the mere counting of patents at any level of aggregation

---

1. By value I mean the social benefits generated by the innovation in the form of
the additional consumer surplus and the profits stemming from the innovation. The
"value," "output," and "magnitude" of innovations are taken to mean exactly the same
thing. (For a detailed discussion of those concepts, see Trajtenberg (1990).)

cannot possibly render good value indicators: simple patent counts assign a value of one to all patents by construction, whereas their true values exhibit a very large variance. Furthermore, there is substantial evidence to the effect that the distribution of patent values is highly skewed toward the low end, with a long and thin tail into the high-value side. As Scherer (1965) notes, those Pareto-like distributions might not have finite moments and, in particular, they might not have a finite variance; clearly, that would make the use of patent counts as proxies even more problematic. It is important to emphasize that those problems are inherent to the patent system as such,[2] and therefore definite solutions can hardly be expected.

An idea that has often been suggested is to use patent *citations* as an index of the importance or value of patents,[3] i.e., to count the number of times that each patent has been cited in subsequent patents and use the number to compute weighted patent counts. (I am referring to the citations appearing on the front page of patents under *References Cited*.) The potential significance of patent citations can be inferred from the following quotation:

During the examination process, the examiner searches the pertinent portion of the "classified" patent file. His purpose is to identify any prior disclosures of technology ... which might anticipate the claimed invention and preclude the issuance of a patent; which might be similar to the claimed invention and limit the scope of patent protection ...; or which, generally, reveal the state of the technology to which the invention is directed.... If such documents are found they are made known to the inventor and are "cited" in any patent which matures from the application.... Thus, the number of times a patent document is cited may be a measure of its technological significance. (Office of Technology Assessment and Forecast, 1976, p. 167)

Moreover, there is a legal dimension to patent citations, since they represent a limitation on the scope of the property rights established by a patent's claims, which carry weight in court. Equally important, the process of arriving at the final list of references, which involves the applicant and his attorney as well as the examiner, apparently does generate the right incentives to have all relevant patents cited, and only those. (See Campbell and Nieves (1979).) The presumption

2. This is so because the importance of a patent—however defined—can hardly be assessed *ex ante* and because it is not the task of patent examiners to make sure that the patents granted are of comparable worth.
3. This idea draws from the extensive use of citations from and to scientific publications in the context of bibliometric studies. (See, for example, Price (1963).)

that citation counts are potentially informative of something like the technological importance of patents is thus well grounded.

The question is whether citations counts may also be indicative of the (*ex post*) value of the innovations disclosed in the cited patents.[4] This can only be answered empirically, but one can advance some further arguments that would strengthen the prior. Most patents cited are referenced in patents issued within the same narrowly defined field of innovation as the cited patents ("within citation"). The very existence of those later patents attests to the fact that the cited patents opened the way to a technologically successful line of innovation. Moreover, it presumably attests also to economic success (at least in expected value terms), since those subsequent patents are the result of costly innovational efforts undertaken mostly by profit-seeking agents. Given that citations to a patent are counted for a period of a few years following its issuance, there should be enough time for the uncertainty regarding the economic value of the innovation to resolve itself. Thus, if citations keep coming, it must be that the innovation originating in the cited patent had indeed proven to be valuable.

Whatever their merits, patent citations have rarely been used in economic research[5], probably because it used to be quite difficult to obtain the necessary data (i.e., the frequency of citations for each patent studied). Today, however, this is easily done with the aid of computerized search techniques, such as those offered by DIALOG or BRS. More important, the significance of a citations-based index can be ascertained only by relating it to independent measures of the value of innovations; given the scarcity of such measures, no firm conclusions could have possibly been drawn from citations-based statistical findings.[6] It is here that the advantage of having estimates

---

4. This clearly need not be the same as technological importance: the latter could be thought of as having to do only with the supply side of innovations, whereas value obviously reflects a market equilibrium.

5. An exception is Lieberman (1987). Other studies using patent citations in a related way (i.e., seeking to approximate something like importance) but not quite in the realm of economics proper include Carpenter *et al.* (1981), Ellis *et al.* (1978), and Narin and Wolf (1983).

6. A series of articles in the press proclaimed some time ago that "... Japanese Outpace Americans in Innovation," on the basis of findings showing that Japanese patents have been cited more often than U.S. patents. (See *New York Times*, (March 7, 1988) and *Time*, (March 21, 1988); the study cited was conducted by Computer Horizons, Inc. for the National Science Foundation.) While that may be so, the mere finding of a higher frequency of citations does not and cannot prove anything by itself.

of the social gains from innovation in Computed Tomography scanners from a previous study proved to be crucial. A further advantage is that both the patent counts and the value measures used to validate them refer in this case precisely to the same stretch of innovative activity, i.e., to advances in a carefully circumscribed product class and time period. Thus, the usual problems that arise when trying to match information belonging to disparate units (as often happens in this context) are altogether absent here.

Granted the use of citations, the next issue is how to go about constructing a sensible weighting scheme. A straightforward possibility is to weight each patent i by the actual number of citations that it subsequently received, denoted by C_i. Thus, if I were to compute an index of weighted patent counts (WPC) for, say, a given product class in a given year, t, I would have,

$$WPC_t = \sum_{i=1}^{n_t}(1 + C_i),\qquad(1)$$

where n_t is the number of patents issued during year t in that product class. This linear weighting scheme then assigns a value of one to all citations and all patents. Lacking more information on the citation process, this is a natural starting point but certainly not the only possibility; in fact, in Section 5, I compute a nonlinear index that allows for the existence of "returns to scale" in the informational content of citations.

3 Patents in Computed Tomography: A First Look

Computed Tomography (CT) is a sophisticated diagnostic technology that produces cross-sectional images of the interior of the body, allowing the visualization of a wide range of organs with great accuracy. It has been hailed as one of the most remarkable medical innovations of recent times, comparable to the invention of radiography. Originally developed at the British firm EMI in the early seventies, CT soon attracted some twenty other firms worldwide, and the fierce competition that ensued brought about a breathtaking pace of technical advance. The diffusion of the new systems also proceeded very quickly: first introduced in the U.S. in 1973, by 1985 almost 60% of hospitals (community hospitals with more than 100 beds) had at least one system installed. The pace of innovation subsided in the late seventies as the technology matured and ceded its dominant place to new developments, particularly to Magnetic Resonance Imaging.

Searching in the PATDATA database (available through BRS), I located and retrieved all U.S. patents granted in Computed Tomography from the very start of the field in 1971[7] up to the end of 1986, totalling 456 patents.[8] I am quite certain that this is indeed the complete set and that it includes patents in CT only.[9] Clearly, having a clean set of patents, and hence clean patent-based indicators, is crucial in order to assess the usefulness of those indicators; otherwise, it would be impossible to tell whether the results are spurious (due to errors of measurement) or reflect real phenomena.

As is by now standard practice, patents are dated according to their application, rather than granting, date. Examining the distribution of lags between these two dates, I concluded that the patent data comprise virtually all patents applied for up to the end of 1982, 96% of the patents applied for in 1983, and smaller percentages of those applied for in later years. Thus, the analysis will be confined to the period of 1972–1982, although the citations appearing in the 1983–1986 patents will be taken into account as well.

Citation counts can be done in two ways: counting all citations or just those appearing in the set of patents belonging to the same field. In the "within referencing" case, the citation counts will be associated with the value of the innovations in the specific technological field to which they belong. On the other hand, an all-inclusive count will presumably capture the value "spilled-over" to other areas as well. Given that the measures of innovation to be used in conjunction with the patent data refer to the gains from advances in CT as

---

7. In this case, it was easy to identify the very first patent: the origin of Computed Tomography is unequivocally associated with its invention by G. Hounsfield, as described in his U.S. patent #3778614, applied for in December 1971. Since there were no patents in CT in 1972, I shall treat this first patent as if it had been applied for in January 1972, rather than in December 1971, in order to avoid an unnecessary discontinuity in the data points.

8. See Trajtenberg (1990) for a detailed discussion of the long-standing classification problem (i.e., how to match patents to economic categories) and for the advantages of using computerized search techniques in order to tackle it.

9. The computerized search actually produced 501 patents, but 45 of them were eliminated after a careful examination of their abstracts; thus, I am certain that all the patents included do belong to CT. Furthermore, I am confident that the set includes all the relevant patents, since I was able to cross-check with other sources, including listings of patents from the manufacturers of CT scanners.

Table 1
Patents in computed tomography: counts and citations by year

	Patents		Citations		
				Percentage of patents with	
Year	Simple counts (SPC)	Weighted by citations (WPC)	Average no. per patent	0	5+
1972	1	73	72.0	0.0	100.0
1973	3	50	15.7	0.0	100.0
1974	21	199	8.5	4.8	76.2
1975	48	242	4.0	12.5	47.9
1976	66	235	2.6	21.2	22.7
1977	115	260	1.3	45.2	11.3
1978	71	126	0.8	54.9	4.2
1979	59	88	0.5	66.1	0.0
1980	26	33[a]	0.3	84.6	0.0
1981	15	18[a]	0.2	86.7	0.0
1982	12	13[a]	0.1	91.7	0.0
1983[b]	13	14	—	—	—
1984[b]	6	6	—	—	—
All	456	1357	2.1[c]	45.1[c]	16.2[c]

a. These figures are slightly biased downwards. (See the Appendix).
b. These are partial figures.
c. These are averages.

such, with no attempt to account for spillovers, I shall use the within referencing count.[10]

The first two columns of Table 1, graphically displayed in Figure 1, show the basic patent data to be used throughout. Note the smooth, cycle-like path followed by the yearly count of patents: it rises quite fast after 1973, peaks in 1977, and then declines steadily, carrying forward a thin tail. Notice also that the weighting scheme strongly influences the shape of the distribution, shifting it back toward the earlier period. In fact, the difference in the means of the two distributions is seventeen months; that is, the weighting scheme centers the action in mid-1976 rather than in late 1977. Given the very fast pace at which the CT technology evolved and that the period is just

10. In this case, it would not have mattered much which count was used: in a sample of 30 patents in CT, the correlation between the two counts was found to be .99. Similarly, Campbell and Nieves (1979) report a correlation of .73 between what they called "in-set" and total citations for some 800 patents in the field of catalytic converters.

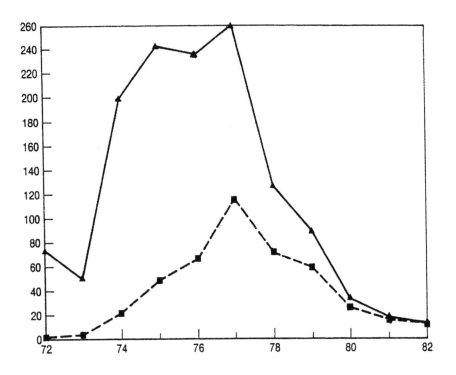

■ Simple patent count (Source: Table 1, Column 1).

▲ Count weighted by citations (Source: Table 1, Column 2).

Figure 1
Patents in CT: simple counts, and counts weighted by citations

eleven years long, a difference of one and one-half years in the means is certainly very significant. Clearly, this shift is due to the fact that earlier patents were cited more frequently than later ones: as Table 1 shows, the average number of citations per patent went down from 72 to less than one, and the percentage of patents with no citations increased from zero to 92%.

The question is whether the observed citation frequencies are to be regarded as real phenomema, presumably reflecting something like the importance of patents, or just as statistical artifacts, induced by the mere passage of time. Two concerns arise in this context. First, it could be that older patents are cited more often simply because they have had more opportunities to be cited, since they precede a larger set of patents that could cite them. Second, given that CT is an ongoing technology (albeit already mature), it is quite certain that additional patents have been issued since the time of the search and that more will be granted in the future. Thus, the data set is necessarily truncated, which might bias downward the citation counts of recent patents.

These are serious *a priori* objections that may arise whenever one tries to attach any meaning to citations data, and therefore deserve careful scrutiny.[11] The Appendix analyzes them in detail and shows that neither age nor truncation could possibly account for the observed distribution of citation counts. The issue of age is tackled by constructing a hypothetical "iso-important" distribution of citations and testing it against the observed distribution with the aid of a χ^2-test: the null hypothesis that older patents received more citations just because of the passage of time is rejected by a wide margin. As for the effect of truncation, the magnitude of the biases is estimated by extrapolating from the observed distribution of citation lags and application-granting lags. The main finding is that a bias does exist, but the absolute expected number of missing citations to recent patents is very small and hence could not possibly affect the results of the statistical analysis based on citation counts.

4   Estimates of the Value of Innovations in Computed Tomography

As stated earlier, I intend to relate patent counts weighted by citations to independent measures of innovation in CT taken from an earlier study (Trajtenberg, 1989). The basic idea behind those measures is as follows. Consider a technologically dynamic product class as it evolves over time, and assume that the different brands in it can be described in terms of a small number of attributes. Product innovation can then be thought of in terms of changes in the set of available products, both in that new brands appear and that the qualities of existing products improve. Applying discrete choice models to data on sales per brand and on their attributes and prices, one can estimate the parameters of the demand functions and, under some restrictions, of the underlying utility function. The social value of the

---

11. The issue of age versus importance (closely related to Price's "immediacy factor") has commanded a great deal of attention in the scientometric literature. However, to the best of my knowledge, it has not yet been addressed with rigorous statistical tests. (See, for example, Line (1970) and Campbell and Nieves (1979).)

innovations occurring between two periods can then be calculated as the benefits of having the latest choice set rather than the previous one in terms of the ensuing increments in consumer and producer surplus. That is, given an estimated social surplus function, $W(\cdot)$, and the sets of products offered in two successive periods, S_t and S_{t-1}, the value of innovation would be measured by $\Delta W_t = W(S_t) - W(S_{t-1})$.

The model used to estimate the function $W(\cdot)$ was the multinomial logit model, rendering the well-known choice probabilities $\pi_j = \exp\phi(z_{jt}, p_{jt}) / \sum_i^m \exp[\phi(z_{it}, p_{it})]$, where z is the vector of attributes, p is price, m is the number of alternatives in the choice set, and $\phi(\cdot)$ is the branch of the indirect utility function related to the product class in question. Integrating those probabilistic demand functions, one obtains measures of consumer surplus of the form[12]

$$W_t = \ln\left\{\sum_i^{m_t} \exp[\phi(z_{it}, p_{it})]\right\}\Big/ \lambda_t, \tag{2}$$

where λ stands for the marginal utility of income. The differences ΔW_t are then computed from (2) for every pair of adjacent years. Noting that ΔW_t refers to the gains accruing to the representative consumer, I also computed the total gains associated with the innovations at t, using

$$TW_t = \Delta W_t \left[n_t + K\left(\sum_{\tau=0}^{t} \Delta W_\tau\right) \int_{t+1}^{\infty} f(\tau)e^{-r(\tau-t-1)}\, d\tau\right] \equiv \Delta W_t(n_t + n_f), \tag{3}$$

where n_t is the number of consumers at t, $K(\cdot)$ is the ceiling of the diffusion curve (that shifts up as a consequence of successive innovations), $f(\cdot)$ is the diffusion path, and r is the interest rate. Thus, TW multiplies ΔW_t by the current and future number of consumers that

---

12. In the present case, ΔW was confined to changes in consumer surplus, since the net aggregate profits of CT manufactures were actually nil over the period studied. This may raise questions as to the rationale of the expected link between ΔW and patent indices, since, from the point of view of the incentives to innovate (and hence, to patent), what counts are the benefits appropriated by the firms, not consumer surplus. This is true *ex ante*; that is, firms innovate because they expect to be able to appropriate a great deal of the social surplus, but competition may significantly reduce (*ex post*) that portion. (Recall that competition in the CT market was indeed very intense during the period studied.) In that case one would still expect to find a significant correlation between total surplus and, say, WPC, even if the former is made just of consumer surplus.

Table 2
Measures of innovation and other data on computed tomography scanners

Year	ΔW	TW	R&D	Number of firms	Number of new brands	Number of new adopters
1973	2.99	638	20.6[a]	3	1	16
1974	8.71	6926	22.6	8	1	74
1975	1.51	1503	59.7	12	4	216
1976	4.78	5959	96.1	13	11	317
1977	0.94	997	79.7	14	14	328
1978	0.12	79	64.3	11	6	211
1979	0.14	73	56.1	9	5	209
1980	0.07	30	46.4	8	2	177
1981	0.18	79	37.9	8	3	101
1982	0.20	87	37.9	8	8	—

Source: Trajtenberg (1989).
The figures for ΔW, TW, and R&D are in millions of constant 1982 dollars.
a. This figure refers to total R&D expenditures from 1968 through 1973.

benefit from the innovations at t, the latter being assessed on the basis of the observed diffusion process.

For the earlier study, I gathered a comprehensive data set on CT scanners, including the prices and attributes of all scanners marketed in the U.S. since the inception of CT in 1973 up to 1982, and details of all sales to U.S. hospitals (over 2,000 observations). Applying the methodology just sketched to these data, I obtained yearly estimates of ΔW_t and of TW_t, as shown in Table 2 along with other data on CT. Note that ΔW_t and TW_t are very large at first and then decline sharply, carrying forward a thin tail. Thus, the bulk of gains from innovation were generated during the earlier years of the technology even though the action in terms of R&D and entry peaks later on.

5 Patents as Indicators of Innovation: The Statistical Evidence

The question to be addressed here is, then, To what extent can patent-based indices (denoted by P) serve as indicators of the value of innovations as measured by ΔW (or TW).[13] By indicators I formally mean predictors, and hence, the statistical criterion to be used

---

13. Recalling that ΔW refers to the incremental gains, whereas TW stands for total gains, it is not clear *a priori* which of them is more relevant in the present context.

is the mean-squared prediction error: $MSE = E(\Delta W - P)^2$. Assuming that the bivariate distribution $f(\Delta W, P)$ is such that the regression function of ΔW on P is linear (e.g., a bivariate normal), then the MSE of the (best) linear predictor is just $\sigma^2_{\Delta W}(1 - \rho^2)$, where ρ^2 is the correlation coefficient between ΔW and P. (See Lindgren (1976).) Thus, in probing the adequacy of alternative patent indicators, I used the correlation coefficient as the sole criterion.[14] The hypotheses tested are (note that they refer to a given technological field, or product class, as it evolves over time) as follows:

Hypothesis 1 Patent counts weighted by citations (WPC) are good indicators of the value of innovations as measured by ΔW or TW, but simple counts (SPC) are not.

Hypothesis 2 Simple patent counts are good indicators of the inputs to the innovative process as measured by R&D expenditures.

In order to examine them, I considered two alternative patent counts: one including all patents in CT and another based on patents granted just to CT manufacturers. (The latter accounted for 66% of all patents and 80% of all citations.) Since ΔW and TW were computed on the basis of the CT scanners actually marketed in the U.S., we would expect those measures to be more highly correlated with the patents granted just to firms in CT.[15] I also considered various lags between patent counts and the measures ΔW and TW. At issue here is the expected time interval between the application date of a patent and the appearance in the market of the innovation disclosed in that patent.[16] Since the interest of inventors is to file for a patent as early as possible, the actual timing must be effectively constrained by the stringency of the applications requirements set by the Patent Office. Those requirements are significantly more severe in the U.S. than in Europe; in fact, 56% of all patents in CT were applied for

---

14. Less formally, since the maintained hypothesis is that the measures $\{\Delta W, TW\}$ accurately capture the value of innovations, the only remaining question is whether patents (which could be at best just an indirect manifestation of the same) closely follow the path of those variables over time. More pragmatically, with the small number of observations available, it would have been very hard to estimate anything but simple correlations.

15. That would not be so only if the appropriability of the patents issued to the other assignees had been extremely low, i.e., only if CT manufacturers benefitted from the innovations done by other inventors as much as they did from their own.

16. For a detailed discussion of this issue, see Trajtenberg (1990).

in various European countries (primarily the U.K. and Germany) before being filed in the U.S., with an average lag between the two applications of thirteen months. Thus, we would expect the lag between patent counts and ΔW to be quite short if patents are dated according to the application date in the U.S. (as done here), and over a year longer than that (on average) if the application date abroad is taken into consideration.

The data used in testing the hypotheses consist of yearly observations on ΔW, TW, and patent counts, covering the period of 1973–1982. (See Tables 1 and 2.) As mentioned above, this is when the bulk of the innovative action in CT took place; in fact, the pace of advancement had already subsided in the late seventies, and the technology barely changed during the eighties. Thus, the fact that the period examined here is only a decade long does not impair the validity of the statistical analysis performed: the history of innovation in CT is short, and hence there are few observations; this is, however, essentially the whole history.

Testing the First Hypothesis

Table 3 presents the correlations between patent counts and $\{\Delta W, TW\}$, with the former variables lagged between zero and six months.[17] The first and most important finding is that WPC_t is, in effect, correlated with the value measures of innovation, whereas SPC_t clearly is not, in all the cases considered. Thus, the evidence provides ample support for the first hypothesis. Second, the correlations increase substantially as I narrow the scope of the (weighted) counts to the patents granted to firms in CT. This implies, as suggested, that the appropriability of patents awarded to other assignees was not nil. Third, the correlations peak when the patent counts are lagged just one quarter, declining monotonically as the lag increases.[18] Superimposing the mean foreign-U.S. application lag of

---

17. Even though the figures are annual, the lag could be varied by monthly increments, since the patent data are virtually continuous over time. Note also that since the ΔW series begins in 1973, I just added the 1972 (first) patent to the patent count of 1973; that is, the ΔW figure for 1973 refers to the first CT scanner marketed, and hence, it obviously corresponds to the initial patents in the field, including the very first.

18. Recall, however, from footnote 17 that the 1972 patent was simply added to the 1973 patents in computing the correlations. Thus, the first lag was actually longer (about one year long), and the overall lag would increase from three to four months if one averages that first lag with the rest.

Table 3
Correlations[a] of simple and weighted patent counts with ΔW, TW

Lags	All patents		Patents to firms in CT	
	ΔW	TW	ΔW	TW
(a) With weighted counts				
Contemporary	0.509	0.587	0.616	0.626
	(0.13)	(0.07)	(0.06)	(0.05)
3 months	0.513	0.635	**0.685**	**0.755**
	(0.13)	(0.05)	(0.03)	(0.01)
4 months	0.480	0.600	0.677	0.744
	(0.16)	(0.07)	(0.03)	(0.01)
6 months	0.317	0.466	0.495	0.605
	(0.37)	(0.17)	(0.15)	(0.006)
(b) With simple counts				
Contemporary	−0.162	0.032	−0.087	0.093
	(0.65)	(0.93)	(0.81)	(0.80)
3 months	−0.198	0.006	−0.076	0.131
	(0.58)	(0.99)	(0.83)	(0.72)
6 months	−0.283	−0.090	−0.175	0.027
	(0.43)	(0.81)	(0.63)	(0.94)

a. Pearson correlation coefficients.
Significance levels for H_0: corr $= 0$ are given in parentheses.

thirteen months mentioned earlier, one obtains an overall lead time of sixteen months. This is consistent with the intense technological rivalry that characterized the market for CT scanners in the seventies.

Returning to the basic finding of a high correlation between WPC_t and ΔW_t, I can now (re)interpret the distribution of citation counts across patents as an implied distribution of the value of innovations. As shown in Table 4, the observed distribution fits well the received wisdom on this matter (see, for example, Pakes and Schankerman (1984) and Pakes (1986)): it is very skewed, with almost half the patents never cited (and hence, of little *ex post* value) and a lucky few being worth a great deal.[19] Thus, contrary to the often-voiced view that patent data cannot possibly capture important innovations, the

19. Campbell and Nieves (1979) present the distribution of citations for all U.S. patents issued from 1971 to 1978, and Narin (1983) does the same for 13,264 chemical and allied product patents issued in 1975. Both distributions look remarkably similar to the one for CT scanners. Unfortunately, the citation values in Campbell and Nieves (1979) only go up to 13+, and therefore, I cannot be sure whether the distribution for CT is typical in its upper tail.

Table 4
Distribution of patents according to number of citations

Number of citations	Number of patents	Percentage of patents	Cumulative percentage
0	215	47.1	47.1
1	78	17.1	64.3
2	54	11.8	76.1
3	35	7.7	83.8
4	21	4.6	88.4
5	10	2.2	90.6
6	15	3.3	93.9
7	8	1.8	95.6
8	3	0.7	96.3
9	3	0.7	96.9
10	2	0.4	97.4
12	1	0.2	97.6
13	2	0.4	98.0
14	1	0.2	98.2
16	1	0.2	98.5
17	2	0.4	98.9
19	1	0.2	99.1
20	1	0.2	99.3
21	1	0.2	99.6
25	1	0.2	99.8
72	1	0.2	100.0

results here show that citation counts can span well the whole range of innovations.[20]

Nonlinearities in Citations

In constructing the weighting index, I have implicitly assumed so far that a citation is worth as much as a patent, i.e., that the weights are linear in the number of citations. However, there may be something akin to increasing or decreasing returns to the informational content of citations, in which case the weighting scheme would be nonlinear. Consider the more general specification

---

20. According to Scherer (1965), "... patent statistics are likely to measure run-of-the-mill industrial inventive output much more accurately than they reflect the occasional strategic inventions which open up new markets and new technologies." Of course, Scherer was quite right at the time, given the kind of data available then.

$$WPC_t(\alpha) = \sum_{i=1}^{n_t}(C_i^\alpha + 1) = n_t + \sum_{i=1}^{n_t} C_i^\alpha, \qquad \alpha > 0.$$

Notice that the nonlinearity is assumed to occur in the citations to each patent, rather than in some patent aggregate (e.g., in the yearly counts), since the results would otherwise be highly sensitive to the chosen aggregation scheme, which is rather arbitrary. The problem now is to find α_1^* and α_2^* such that[21]

$$\alpha_1^* = \operatorname*{argmax}_{\alpha} \ \operatorname{corr}[WPC_t(\alpha), \Delta W_t]$$

and

$$\alpha_2^* = \operatorname*{argmax}_{\alpha} \ \operatorname{corr}[WPC_t(\alpha), TW_t].$$

As can be seen in Table 5, the maxima occur when $\alpha_1^* = 1.3$ and $\alpha_2^* = 1.1$; that is, the weighting scheme is in fact convex in the number of citations per patent. (Note, however, that the relationship between WPC_t and ΔW_t is still linear.) This finding means that the marginal informational content of WPC_t increases with the number of citations, strengthening the potential role of WPC_t as an indicator of the value of innovations. Furthermore, it implies that the variance in the value of patents is larger and that the distribution of those values is more skewed than what could be inferred from the simple count of citations.

Notice that the results that $\alpha_i > 1$, $i = 1, 2$, are robust (that is, they occur also when there is no lag and when all patents, rather than patents to firms in CT, are used), and that α_1^* and α_2^* are global maxima. Note also that $\alpha_1^* > \alpha_2^*$; that is, the nonlinearity is stronger when patent counts are related to ΔW rather than to TW. Recall that ΔW is a measure of the gains to the representative consumer, whereas TW multiplies ΔW by the number of consumers that benefit from the innovation at present and in the future. Thus, the fact that $\alpha_1^* > \alpha_2^*$ and that $\operatorname{corr}[WPC(\alpha_1^*), \Delta W] > \operatorname{corr}[WPC(\alpha_2^*), TW]$, can be taken to mean that citations are more informative of the value of innovations *per se*, rather than of the size of the market for the products embedding those innovations. This is reassuring, since we expect that the factors related to the technology itself (rather than to market size) will be dominant in the citing process.

---

21. Notice that it is not possible to estimate those exponents by, say, running a regression in the logs, since the nonlinearity refers to the citations to each patent.

Table 5
Correlations[a] of WPC with ΔW and TW: searching for nonlinearities

Exponent α	Patents to firms in computed tomography				All patents Lagged three months	
	Contemporary		Lagged three months			
	ΔW	TW	ΔW	TW	ΔW	TW
0.80	0.455	0.543	0.512	0.653	0.329	0.503
	(0.19)	(0.10)	(0.13)	(0.04)	(0.35)	(0.14)
0.90	0.538	0.590	0.601	0.711	0.419	0.570
	(0.11)	(0.07)	(0.07)	(0.02)	(0.23)	(0.09)
1.00	0.616	0.626	0.685	0.755	0.513	0.635
	(0.06)	(0.05)	(0.03)	(0.01)	(0.13)	(0.05)
1.10	0.680	**0.642**	0.754	**0.777**	0.605	0.687
	(0.03)	(0.05)	(0.01)	(0.008)	(0.06)	(0.03)
1.20	0.721	0.635	0.798	0.770	0.684	0.719
	(0.02)	(0.05)	(0.006)	(0.009)	(0.03)	(0.02)
1.30	**0.738**	0.607	**0.813**	0.736	0.738	**0.720**
	(0.01)	(0.06)	(0.004)	(0.02)	(0.02)	(0.02)
1.40	0.730	0.560	0.800	0.677	**0.760**	0.689
	(0.02)	(0.09)	(0.006)	(0.03)	(0.01)	(0.03)
1.50	0.703	0.501	0.766	0.606	0.751	0.634
	(0.02)	(0.14)	(0.01)	(0.06)	(0.01)	(0.05)
1.60	0.663	0.436	0.718	0.527	0.719	0.562
	(0.04)	(0.21)	(0.02)	(0.11)	(0.02)	(0.09)

a. Pearson correlation coefficients.
Significance levels for H_0: corr = 0 are given in parentheses.

The Second Hypothesis

The relationship between patents and R&D has been intensively scrutinized in past research,[22] and the results appear to be quite uniform, centering around the following stylized facts: (a) there is a strong statistical association between patents and R&D expenditures; (b) this relationship appears to be mostly contemporaneous; and (c) R&D explains a great deal of the cross-sectional variance in patenting but not much of the variation over time. The second hypothesis also postulates a close association between patents and expenditures on R&D, but within a given field over time rather than across firms or industries. From Table 6 we see first that there is indeed a high correlation between SPC_t and $R\&D_t$ and a much weaker one

22. Many of the articles in Griliches (1984) have to do with this issue; extensive references to previous works can also be found there.

Table 6
Correlations[a] between patent counts and R&D

	All patents		Patents to firms in computed tomography	
Lags	SPC_t	WPC_t	SPC_t	WPC_t
None	0.869	0.609	0.843	0.525
	(0.0002)	(0.05)	(0.001)	(0.097)
Three months	0.919	0.591	0.912	0.495
	(0.0001)	(0.04)	(0.0001)	(0.102)
Four months	0.924	0.582	0.914	0.491
	(0.0001)	(0.05)	(0.0001)	(0.105)
Five months	0.933	0.577	0.918	0.483
	(0.0001)	(0.05)	(0.0001)	(0.112)
Six months	0.921	0.543	0.903	0.450
	(0.0001)	(0.07)	(0.0001)	(0.142)
One year	0.831	0.248	0.794	0.152
	(0.0008)	(0.44)	(0.002)	(0.638)

a. Pearson correlation coefficients.
Significance levels for H_0: corr = 0 are given in parentheses.

between $R\&D_t$ and WPC_t; the second hypothesis is therefore amply confirmed. Second, the degree of association peaks when $R\&D_t$ is lagged just five months, supporting previous findings of short gestation lags. Third, the correlations are slightly higher for counts of all patents than for patents to firms in CT, suggesting some degree of spillovers from the R&D done by CT manufacturers to other assignees.

It is also worth reporting the following correlations, which indicate that SPC_t tends to move together, not just with R&D, but also with other manifestations of the innovative action taking place in a given field over time. (All are contemporaneous; the data are taken from Table 2.)

corr(SPC_t, Number of Firms in the CT Market) = .858
(.0007)

corr(SPC_t, Number of New Scanners Introduced in the Market)
= .813
(.002)

corr(SPC_t, Number of New Adopters of CT) = .913.
(.0002)

The first two correlations reflect the fact that competition in the CT market was driven primarily by rivalry in innovation, whereas the third has to do with the interaction between innovation and diffusion.

6   The Usefulness and Meaning of Patent Data: Concluding Remarks

The findings presented above suggest that patent citations may be indicative of the value of innovations and, if so, that they may hold the key to unlock the wealth of information contained in patent data. In order to understand the various roles that patent-based indicators may thus come to play, it may be helpful to use a familiar analogy, namely, to think of patents as working papers in economics and, accordingly, of economic departments as firms, of fields in economics as industries, and so forth. Working papers are "produced" roughly in proportion to the number of faculty, as patents are with respect to R&D. The fact is that it does not take much to get a patent once the firm has an established R&D facility going, as it does not take much to write a working paper. Still, a larger number of patents presumably indicates that much research efforts have been invested by the R&D staff, as more papers would suggest that the faculty is "trying harder." Thus, a simple patent count could be regarded as a more refined input measure (vis-à-vis R&D), in the sense that it incorporates part of the differences in effort and nets out the influence of luck in the first round of the innovative process. Of course, as with patents, a mere count of working papers written does not say much about the value of the scientific contributions made; for that, one would need information on whether and where they get published, the number of citations that they receive over time, etc. Clearly, those indicators would be to working papers what patent citations are to patents.

Beyond establishing the role of citations as indicators in a purely statistical sense, the results of this article can also be seen as lending support to a particular view of the innovative process, in which context citations are associated with real phenomena rather than just being a useful data contrivance. This view sees innovation as a continuous time process that has a predominantly incremental nature, punctuated by occasional breakthroughs that bring forth subsequent innovative efforts and direct them into novel channels.[23] Congruent with such a view, a patent would be regarded as important if it opened the way to a successful line of further innovations; the patents coming in its wake would naturally cite it, and hence, those citations could be taken as first-hand evidence of the path-breaking nature of the original patent. A particular case is when the important patent(s) refers to a new product (as, say, the first few patents by Hounsfield in CT): truly novel ideas are almost by definition crude and lacking at first but get better over time as a result of further research efforts. These efforts would generate down-the-line patents aimed at refining and improving the original innovation and, again, these patents would be most likely to cite the basic one. The key point is that in this context, citing patents would bear a sort of causal relationship to the cited patent, with citations being the overt manifestation (instituted as common practice by the Patent Office) of such a link.

Once their meaning has been well established, the use of patent data may offer additional advantages in itself and over alternative data sources. First, patent data can be easily obtained all the way to the very beginning of a product class, whereas the gathering of conventional industry data usually starts only when a sector is well established. Thus, patent counts and citations may play an important role in studying the very emergence of new products, which seems to be the period when most of the important innovations occur. Second, patent data are richer, finer, and have a wider coverage than say, R&D expenditures, and are practically continuous in time.

All of my conclusions have been expressed in a qualified manner, since they are based upon the findings from a single case study. It is important to emphasize, however, that the sort of validation of the citation-based patent index attempted here could hardly have been done in a wider context simply because the measures of the value of innovations that would be required for that purpose are nowhere to be found. (If such measures were widely available, we would hardly need the more imperfect patent indicators.) I hope that future re-

---

23. This view stands in opposition to the innovative process being conceived of as a sequence of discrete, well-compartmentalized, and sizeable events that occur essentially in a random fashion from the point of view of technology itself. Such a view presupposes a one-to-one correspondence between each of those singular innovations and patents, leading to an interpretation of patent importance and of patent citations quite different from the one held here.

search along similar lines will bring in more supportive evidence and further demonstrate the attractiveness of the proposed indicators.

Appendix

A statistical analysis of truncation and age effects follows.

Testing Age versus Importance

The starting point for the test is the specification of a hypothetical citation process under which all patents are of equal importance, and hence the only differentiating factor is age. The distribution of citations thus generated could then be compared with the actual one, and the maintained hypothesis that all patents are equally important could be tested with the aid of a Pearson semiparametric χ^2-test. (See DeGroot (1975).) As a first step, patents are ordered according to their application date and indexed with $i = 1, \ldots, N$ ($N = 456$). (Thus, i indicates the cumulative number of patents in CT applied for up to patent i.) Denoting the probability that patent i will be cited in patent j by p_{ij} (for $i < j$) and the number of references to previous patents in CT appearing in patent j by r_j, I define the patents $1 \le i < j$ to be iso-important if

$$p_{ij} = \frac{r_j}{j-1} = p_j, \qquad j = 1, \ldots, N \tag{A1}$$

Thus, equal importance is taken to mean that all patents applied for up to a certain point in time have the same probability of being cited by a subsequent patent. In other words, (A1) means that the citations appearing in patent j are the result of r_j random drawings (without replacement) from a pool containing the $j - 1$ patents that preceeded it.[24] Noting that (A1) also implies time independence (that is, for any $i < j < k$, p_{ik} is independent of p_{ij}), the expected number of citations of patent i can be computed simply as $C_i^e \equiv E(C_i) = \sum_{j=i+1}^{N} p_j$. Obviously, $C_i^e > C_j^e$ for any $i < j$; that is, older patents will get more

---

24. Clearly, this is not the only possible definition of iso-importance. Notice, however, that by defining p_{ij} to be independent of the distance $(j - i)$, I implicitly favor the earlier patents, thus increasing the power of the test. That is, any plausible departure from (A1) would have the probabilities decrease with $(j - i)$, making the distribution of expected citations more uniform, and hence, making it easier to reject the null hypothesis.

citations on average than recent ones, just by virtue of their age. Notice also that p_j has to decrease eventually with j,[25] thus reinforcing the pure age effect. That is, not only do later patents miss the earlier p_j's, but those probabilities tend to be the large ones, a fact that further reduces the expected number of citations of recent patents vis-a-vis older ones.

In order to perform the χ^2-test, the data were aggregated by months, since it would be unreasonable to attach any significance (in the sense of differences in C_i^e) to the precise day of application. Indexing by τ and t the number of months elapsed since January 1972, the observed number of citations is $C_t^O = \sum_{i=1}^{n_t} C_i$, where n_t is the number of patents in month t. Similarly, redefining (A1) in monthly terms gives

$$p_\tau = \sum_{i=1}^{n_\tau} r_i \Big/ \sum_{j=1}^{\tau-1} n_j, \tag{A2}$$

and so, $C_t^e = n_t \sum_{\tau=t+1}^{T} p_\tau$. Turning now to the test,[26]

$$\chi^2 = \sum_{t=1}^{156} \frac{(C_t^e - C_t^O)^2}{C_t^e} = 1025 \gg 147 = \chi^2(110), \quad \text{where} \quad \alpha = .01.$$

Thus, the hypothesis that the observed distribution of citations is due solely to age is strongly rejected. As is to be expected, the largest discrepancies between actual and expected values occur at the very beginning of the period. In particular, the values for the first patent are $C_1^O = 72$, $C_1^e = 5.96$, and hence, $(C_1^e - C_1^O)^2/C_1^e = 731$, which amounts to .75 of the computed χ^2-statistic. Since this first patent can be regarded in many ways as an exception, the test was redone after deleting it; again, the null hypothesis is rejected by a wide margin.

Assessing the Truncation Bias

The other potential problem in this context is that the (unavoidable) truncation of the data might induce a bias in the citation counts; the

---

25. This must be true unless r_j increases indefinitely over time, which is highly unlikely; in the case of CT, r_j was quite stable over the whole period.

26. The summation is done in principle over 156 months, covering the thirteen years from 1972 to 1984. However, patents were actually applied for only in 111 months out of the 156, and hence, there are just 110 degrees of freedom (d). When d exceeds 100 (as it does here), the critical χ^2 value is to be computed as follows (see Harnett (1975)): $\chi^2 = 1/2(z_\alpha + \sqrt{2d-1})^2$, where z is the standardized normal deviate (for $\alpha = .01$, $z_\alpha = 2.3263$).

Table A1
Expected biases

Year of cited patents	v_t	Number of citations		
		Actual	Missing (rounded)	Fraction missing
Up to 75	1.000	491	0	0.00
76	0.998	169	0	0.00
77	0.990	145	1	0.01
78	0.969	55	2	0.04
79	0.930	29	2	0.07
80	0.861	7	1	0.14
81	0.732	3	1	0.33
82	0.527	1	1	1.00

extent of such bias, in turn, will depend upon the behavior of citation lags and the rate of new patent arrivals after the date of search. Citation lags refer to the length of time elapsed between the dates of the citing patents and of the cited patent: the shorter they are, the less severe the problem will be.[27] Denote the frequency distribution of citation lags by f_τ; for example, if year t patents are to receive (on average) C_t citations per patent, f_τ stands for the percentage of those citations to be received after τ years. (Thus, $\sum_{\tau=t}^{\infty} f_\tau = 1$.) Likewise, define $c_{t\tau} = f_\tau C_t$ and $g_{t\tau} = c_{t\tau}/n_\tau$, where n_τ is the total number of patents in year τ. Now, suppose that because of truncation, one can actually obtain only a fraction, h_τ, of them; then, assuming that $g_{t\tau}$ is invariant with respect to h_τ (i.e., that citations of year t patents are randomly distributed among the n_τ patents), the observed average number of citations to year t patents will be $c_{t\tau}^O = g_{t\tau} h_\tau n_\tau = h_\tau f_\tau C_t$. Thus, given the sequences $\{h_\tau, f_\tau\}$, one can compute for each year the fraction $v_t = \sum_{\tau=t}^{\infty} h_\tau f_\tau$, where v_t stands for the percentage of citations that patents in year t can be expected to receive out of the total that they would have received had it not been for the truncation of the data. Using the granting-application lags to obtain h_τ and the citation lags for f_τ, the expected biases are easily computed and presented in Table A1.

Thus, we do miss a few citations because of the truncation of the data; moreover, there is, as expected, a truncation bias in the sense

---

27. In the present case, these lags are relatively short (the mean lag is three years), suggesting that the truncation problem is not too severe on that account. For a detailed discussion, see Trajtenberg (1990).

that we have a smaller fraction of the true number of citations of later patents than of earlier ones. However, the absolute expected number of missing citations is very small, and hence, it is clear that the truncation problem cannot possibly affect the conclusions of this article. (This holds true even if the bias had been for some reason underestimated by, say, a factor of two.)

References

Campbell, R. S. and Nieves, A. L. *Technology Indicators Based on Patent Data: The Case of Catalytic Converters—Phase I Report: Design and Demonstration*. Battelle, Pacific Northwest Laboratories, 1979.

Carpenter, M. P., Narin, F., and Wolf, P. "Citation Rates to Technologically Important Patents." *World Patent Information*, Vol. 3 (1981), pp. 160–163.

DeGroot, M. H. *Probability and Statistics*. Reading, Mass.: Addison-Wesley, 1975.

Ellis, P., Hepburn, G., and Oppenheim, C. "Studies on Patent Citation Networks." *Journal of Documentation*, Vol. 34 (1978), pp. 12–20.

Griliches, Z., ed., *R&D, Patents, and Productivity*. Chicago: University of Chicago Press, 1984.

———, Hall, B. H., and Pakes, A. "R&D, Patents and Market Value Revisited: Is There a Second (Technological Opportunity) Factor?" Working Paper No. 2624, National Bureau of Economic Research, 1988.

Harnett, D. L. *Introduction to Statistical Methods*. 2nd ed. Reading, Mass.: Addison-Wesley, 1975.

Lieberman, M. B. "Patents, Learning-by-Doing, and Market Structure in the Chemical Processing Industries." *International Journal of Industrial Organization*, Vol. 5 (1987), pp. 257–276.

Lindgren, B. W. *Statistical Theory*. New York: MacMillan, 1976.

Line, M. B. "The Half-Life of Periodical Literature: Apparent and Real Obsolescence." *Journal of Documentation*, Vol. 26 (1970), pp. 46–52.

Narin, F. "Patent Citation Analysis as an Analytical Tool in Marketing Research." CHI Research/Computer Horizons, Inc., 1983.

Narin, F. and Wolf, P. "Technological Performance Assessments Based on Patents and Patent Citations." CHI Research/Computer Horizons, Inc., 1983.

Office of Technology Assessment and Forecast, U.S. Department of Commerce, Patent, and Trademark Office. *Sixth Report*. Washington D.C.: U.S. Government Printing Office, 1976.

Pakes, A. "Patents as Options: Some Estimates of the Value of Holding European Patent Stocks." *Econometrica*, Vol. 55 (1986), pp. 755–784.

——— and Schankerman, M. "The Rate of Obsolescence of Patents, Research Gestation Lags, and the Private Rate of Return to Research Resources." In Z. Griliches, ed., *R&D, Patents, and Productivity*. Chicago: University of Chicago Press, 1984.

Price, D. J. de Solla. *Little Science, Big Science*. New Haven: Yale University Press, 1963.

Scherer, F. "Using Linked Patent and R&D Data to Measure Interindustry Technology Flows." In Z. Griliches, ed., *R&D, Patents, and Productivity*. Chicago: University of Chicago Press, 1984.

———. "Firm Size, Market Structure, Opportunity, and the Output of Patented Innovations." *American Economic Review*, Vol. 55 (1965), pp. 1097–1123.

Schmookler, J. *Invention and Economic Growth*. Cambridge, Mass.: Harvard University Press, 1966.

Trajtenberg, M. *Economic Analysis of Product Innovation—The Case of CT Scanners*. Cambridge, Mass.: Harvard University Press, 1990.

———. "The Welfare Analysis of Product Innovations, with an Application to Computed Tomography Scanners." *Journal of Political Economy*, Vol. 97 (1989), pp. 444–479.

3 University versus Corporate Patents: A Window on the Basicness of Invention

Manuel Trajtenberg, Rebecca Henderson, and Adam B. Jaffe

1 Introduction

Progress in many areas of economics is often limited by the lack of empirical counterparts to the theoretical constructs that we believe to be important. This problem is particularly severe in the economics of technical change, where it is difficult to find good indicators even for such fundamental notions as the rate of invention or the value of innovations. Many widely used measures, such as simple patent counts or counts of expert identified innovations, are severely limited in that they cannot account for the enormous heterogeneity of research projects and outcomes that characterizes the R&D process.

Two sources of heterogeneity that occupy a prominent place in the economics of technical change are "basicness" and "appropriability." Basicness refers to fundamental features of innovations such as originality, closeness to science, breadth, etc., that impinge on the incentives to engage in R&D and on the choice of research projects. Appropriability refers to the ability of inventors to reap the benefits from their own innovations. A great deal of our theoretical understanding of the innovation process rests on these two notions, and on conjectures about the links between them. Thus, although appropriability problems plague all forms of investment in R&D, they are thought to be more severe as we move from applied to more basic research (Arrow, 1962). This view underlies a widespread division of labor whereby public institutions such as universities perform most of the basic research, and private firms do the bulk of the development.

We gratefully acknowledge support from the National Science Foundation through grant SES91-10516, and from the Ameritech Foundation via the Ameritech Fellows program of the Center for Regional Economic Issues at Case-Western Reserve University.

We focus in this paper on the construction of a set of measures that we believe capture key aspects of basicness and of appropriability. These measures are grounded in a view of technical change as a cumulative process, whereby each innovation builds on the body of knowledge that preceded it, and forms in turn a foundation for subsequent advances. We compute the measures using detailed information contained in patents, relying heavily on *citations* to other patents, since these citations provide good evidence of the links between an innovation and its technological "antecedents" and "descendants." We use matched samples of university and corporate patents to exploit our prior belief that university research is more basic than corporate research, and rely on the contrast between them in order to test the hypothesis that these measures are legitimate proxies for the fundamental attributes of innovations that we are after. In so doing we also explore the characteristics of university research and of university patented innovations, and examine the methodological underpinnings of the notion of "indicator" (or proxy variable).

The statistical analysis of these data lends ample support to the hypothesis that most of our measures indeed reflect aspects of basicness and appropriability. In particular, we find that measures of the overall importance of innovations, of generality of research outcomes, and of reliance on scientific sources discriminate well between more and less basic innovations. Additional evidence from a handful of fundamental innovations lends further support to these statistical results. Likewise, a measure of the proportion of follow-up technical developments performed by the organization responsible for the original innovation seems to capture aspects of appropriability. Since patent data cover the great majority of recorded inventions and have become available recently in easily-accessible computerized form, we believe that these measures hold the potential for becoming a standardized tool of wide applicability for research in the economics of technical change.

Section 2 explains in more detail the nature of the patent data used in this study. The measures themselves are motivated and described in section 3. In section 4 we lay out the methodological basis for testing the hypothesis that our measures capture aspects of basicness and appropriability. We discuss in section 5 the research design and data characteristics, and expand on the nature of university research. The statistical analysis and empirical results are in section 6. The last section contains concluding comments and suggestions for future research.

2 The Use of Patent Data

The measures of basicness and appropriability that we put forward rely exclusively on information contained in patents. We are thus tapping one of the richest sources of data on inventions (over 5 million patents have been granted so far by the US), and certainly the one with the widest coverage. We intend to exploit detailed information that appears on individual patents, and not just patent counts as has been common practice in much of the research in this area.[1]

A patent is a temporary monopoly awarded to inventors for the commercial use of a newly invented device. For a patent to be granted, the innovation must be non-trivial, meaning that it would not appear obvious to a skilled practitioner of the relevant technology, and it must be useful, meaning that it has potential commercial value. If a patent is granted, an extensive public document is created. The front page of a patent contains detailed information about the invention, the inventor, the assignee, and the technological antecedents of the invention, all of which can be accessed in computerized form. An item of particular importance for our purposes is the citations to previous patents. We believe that important aspects of basicness and of appropriability are embodied in the relationship between the innovation and its technological antecedents and descendants, and that patent citations, made and received, provide an effective means for identifying and tracing these relationships.

Patent citations serve an important legal function, since they delimit the scope of the property rights awarded by the patent. Thus, if patent 2 cites patent 1, it implies that patent 1 represents a piece of previously existing knowledge upon which patent 2 builds, and over which 2 cannot have a claim. The applicant has a legal duty to disclose any knowledge of the prior art, but the decision regarding which patents to cite ultimately rests with the patent examiner, who is supposed to be an expert in the area and hence to be able to identify

---

1. The use of patent counts as indicators of innovation has had varying degrees of success (see e.g. Griliches, 1984 and 1990; Jaffe, 1986). Related work has shown that patent citations contain information about the value of patents and the links among them (Carpenter et al, 1981; Carpenter and Narin, 1983; Trajtenberg, 1990a and 1990b; Jaffe, Trajtenberg and Henderson, 1993).

relevant prior art that the applicant misses or conceals.[2] The framework for the examiner's search of previous innovations is the patent classification system, which currently consists of over 100,000 patent subclasses, aggregated into about 400 3-digit patent classes. The combination of citation data, detailed technological classification, and information about each inventor provides a unique mechanism for placing research and research results in their broader technological and economic context.

These data have, however, two important limitations: first, the range of *patentable* innovations constitutes just a sub-set of all research outcomes, and second, patenting is a *strategic* decision and hence not all *patentable* innovations are actually *patented*. As to the first limitation, consider Figure 1a where we depict the "basicness" of research outcomes, ranging from the most applied on the left to the most basic on the right. Clearly, neither end of the continuum is patentable: Maxwell's equations could not be patented since they do not constitute a device (ideas cannot be patented); on the other hand, a marginally better mousetrap is not patentable either, because the innovation has to be non-trivial. Thus, our measures would not capture purely scientific advances devoid of immediate applicability, as well as run-of-the-mill technological improvements that are too trite to pass for discrete, codifiable innovations.

The second limitation is rooted in the fact that it may be optimal for inventors *not* to apply for patents even though their innovations would satisfy the criteria for patentability. For example, until 1980 universities could not collect royalties for the use of patents derived from federally funded research. This limitation greatly reduced the incentive to patent results from such research, which constitutes about 90% of all university research. Firms, on the other hand, may elect not to patent and rely instead on secrecy to protect their property rights (there is a large variance across industries in the reliance on patents versus secrecy: see Levin et al, 1987). Thus, patentability requirements and incentives to refrain from patenting limit the scope of measures built on patent data. It is widely believed that these

---

2. Because of the role of the examiner and the legal significance of patent citations, there is reason to believe that patent citations are less likely to be contaminated by extraneous motives in the decision of what to cite than other bibliographic data such as citations in the scientific literature (Van Raan, 1988; Weingart *et al*, 1988). Moreover, bibliometric data are of limited value in tracing the *economic* impact of scientific results, since they are not linked to economic agents or decisions.

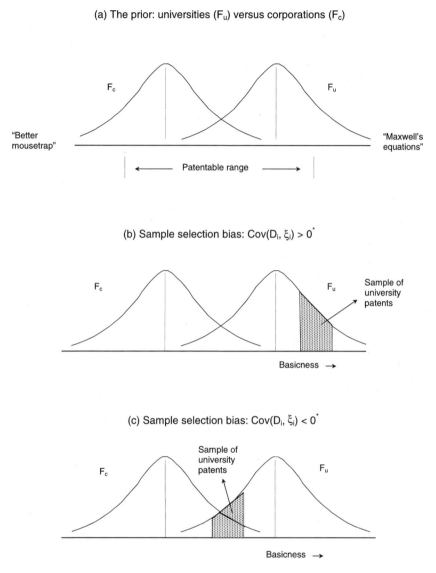

Figure 1
The distribution of basicness: universities vs. corporations. *$D_i = 1$ for universities, $D_i = 0$ for corporations.

limitations are not too severe, but that remains an open empirical issue.

3 Definition of the Measures

In searching for measurable aspects of basicness, we draw from the views of basic research expressed in the scientific and technological literature. Two parallel notions of basicness are found in this literature: one refers to the nature of research itself (that is, to the process leading to inventions), the other to the nature of research outcomes (Kuznets, 1962, made a similar distinction). Thus, research is regarded as basic if it focuses on scientific rather than on technological questions; if it seeks to elucidate general laws rather than solving particular technical problems; and if it addresses old puzzles with original methods (e.g. Kuhn, 1962; Rosenberg, 1982).[3] Research *outcomes* are held as basic if they have a major impact upon a given field, or a diffused but significant impact across a broad range of fields; if they are fundamental to much later work, and are often referred to and relied upon by scientists in the same or other fields (e.g. Watson and Crick's discovery of DNA).

We construct, accordingly, two sets of measures. "Backwardlooking" measures (B/measures for short) are derived from the relationship between a given patent and the body of knowledge that preceded it (i.e. its antecedents). "Forward-looking" measures (F/ measures for short) are derived from the relationship between a patent and subsequent technological developments that built upon it (i.e. its descendants). The presumption is that B/measures would be informative of the nature of research, whereas F/measures would be informative of the subsequent impact of research outcomes.

We use the patent citations made by each patent to identify its antecedents, and the subsequent patents that cite it to identify its descendants. For each of these patents we have information on their technological and temporal location (i.e. their patent class and date of application), the number of citations that they received, and the identity of the assignees. We can thus compute the number, technological diversity, and ownership pattern of patents corresponding to

---

3. Thus for example, the research activities of the team headed by William Shockley at the Bell Labs that led to the discovery of the transistor can be seen as basic in this sense (Nelson, 1962).

the antecedents and descendants of any patent, and the "distance" in time and technology space between these patents and the originating patent.[4] We can then use this information to construct measures of closeness to science, originality, subsequent impact, generality, etc. For the definition and computation of the measures we use the following notation (see figure 2):[5]

NCITING: number of patents citing the originating patent ("o-patent").

NCITED: number of patents cited by the o-patent.

NPCITES: number of non-patent sources cited by the o-patent.

NCLASS: 3-digit original patent class.

CATCODE: 2-digit technological class (built by aggregating NCLASS).

FIELD: 1-digit classification by main technological fields.

LAG: difference in years between the application date of a citing or cited patent, and the application date of the o-patent.

Index i corresponds to the patent under consideration, the originating or o-patent, $i + 1$ to citing patents, and $i - 1$ to cited patents. All measures but one (SCIENCE) will be defined and computed in equivalent ways backwards and forward; however, their precise meaning and interpretation varies in some cases across the forward/backward (F/B) divide. Table A provides an overview of the forward looking measures (the B-measures are defined analogously):

3.1   Forward-Looking Measures

The first, and probably the key aspect of the relationship between a patent and its descendants is what we call the overall "importance" of a patent, denoted IMPORTF (the F for forward). This measure is designed to capture the technological impact of an invention as reflected in the number and importance of its descendants, and hence corresponds to the most intuitively appealing notion of basic innovations. In the words of Kuznets (1962),

---

4. Patent information can also be used to characterize the distance in geographic space between an inventor and her descendants or antecedents. See Jaffe, Henderson and Trajtenberg, 1993.

5. CATCODE is taken from Jaffe (1986). The technological areas in FIELD are, 1: Drugs and Medical; 2: Chemical (except Drugs); 3: Electronics, Optics and Nuclear; 4: Mechanical Arts; 5: Other.

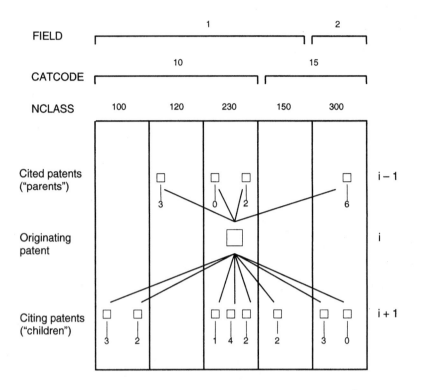

$IMPORTF_i = 8 + 0.5 \cdot 17 = 16.5$

$IMPORTB_i = 4 + 0.5 \cdot 11 = 9.5$

$GENERAL = 1 - \left[\left(\frac{2}{8}\right)^2 + \left(\frac{3}{8}\right)^2 + \left(\frac{1}{8}\right)^2 + \left(\frac{2}{8}\right)^2 \right] = \frac{23}{32}$

$ORIGINAL = 1 - \left[\left(\frac{1}{4}\right)^2 + \left(\frac{2}{4}\right)^2 + \left(\frac{1}{4}\right)^2 \right] = \frac{5}{8}$

$TECHF = \left[3 \cdot 0 + 2 \cdot \frac{1}{3} + 1 \cdot \frac{2}{3} + 2 \cdot 1 \right] \Big/ 8 = \frac{5}{12}$

$TECHB = \left[2 \cdot 0 + 1 \cdot \frac{1}{3} + 1 \cdot 1 \right] \Big/ 4 = \frac{1}{3}$

Figure 2
Computing the measures of basicness: an illustration

Table A
Forward-looking measures

1. Basicness measures		
1.1 IMPORTF	number of citing patents, including second generation cites	$\text{IMPORTF}_i = \text{NCITING}_i$ $+ \lambda \sum_{j=1}^{\text{nciting}_i} \text{NCITING}_{i+1,j}$
1.2 GENERAL	Herfindahl index on technological classes of citing patents	$\text{GENERAL}_i = 1 - \sum_{k=1}^{N_i} \left(\dfrac{\text{NCITING}_{ik}}{\text{NCITING}_i} \right)^2$
2. Distance measures		
2.1 TECHF	distance in technology space	$\text{TECHF}_i = \sum_{j=1}^{\text{nciting}_i} \dfrac{\text{TECH}_j}{\text{NCITING}_i}$
2.2 TIMEF	average citation lag	$\text{TIMEF}_i = \sum_{j=1}^{\text{nciting}_i} \dfrac{\text{LAG}_j}{\text{NCITING}_i}$
3. Appropriability		
3.1 PSELF	number of self-citations	

Some inventions, representing as they do a breakthrough in a major field, have a wide technical potential in the sense that they *provide a base for numerous subsequent technical changes* [our emphasis] ... the first steam engine, which initiated a whole series of major technical changes and applications ... is vastly different from the invention of the safety match or the pocket lighter. This wide range is for our purposes the major characteristic relevant to the problem of measurement. (p. 26)

Thinking of citations to a patent as coming from follow-up advances that at least in part build upon or stem from the originating patent, we would like IMPORTF to reflect both the number of subsequent citations, and *their* respective importance. Thus we define (see figure 2),[6]

$$\text{IMPORTF}_i = \text{NCITING}_i + \lambda \sum_{j=1}^{\text{NCITING}_i} \text{NCITING}_{i+1,j}$$

where $0 < \lambda < 1$ is an arbitrary "discount factor" that is meant to down-weight the "second-generation" descendants of a patent

---

6. Notice that the unavoidable truncation of the citation data at the point in time when the data are collected (T) means that IMPORTF is a lower bound, and should be taken to mean the "importance" of patent *i* as revealed—or realized—up to T.

relative to the first-generation citing patents. We introduce discounting to alleviate the thorny problem of attribution: suppose that patent A is cited just by patent B, but the latter is cited by many patents. Without discounting, IMPORTF for patent A will be larger than for patent B, but intuition says that patent B is the one that had the largest *direct* impact. In all calculations reported here we have set $\lambda = 0.5$, but none of the results appear to depend upon this choice (we experimented with values of λ in the 0.25–0.75 range). We present in the appendix the two patents with the highest values of IMPORTF in our sample: the first discloses an important innovation in the manufacturing of semiconductor devices, the second in fiber optics sensors and transducers (two cutting-edge technologies). We show for each the titles of a sample of citing patents, thus illustrating the notion that these subsequent patents constitute follow-up developments that build upon the originating patent.

The second measure of F/basicness is "generality" (GENERAL), that is, the extent to which the follow-up technical advances are spread across different technological fields, rather than being concentrated in just a few of them.[7] We compute GENERAL on the basis of the Herfindahl index of concentration, whereby the number of citations in each 3-digit patent class (NCLASS) plays the same role as the sales of each firm in the traditional industrial organization context, that is,

$$\text{GENERAL}_i = 1 - \sum_{k=1}^{N_i} \left(\frac{\text{NCITING}_{ik}}{\text{NCITING}_i} \right)^2$$

where k is the index of patent classes, and N_i the number of different classes to which the citing patents belong. Notice that $0 \leq$ GENERAL ≤ 1, and that higher values represent *less* concentration and hence more generality.

IMPORTF and GENERAL presumably capture important determinants of the *social* returns to innovations: those with many descendants, or with descendants that span a wide range of technical fields, are likely to have high social returns. For example, Trajtenberg (1990a) found that the social value of innovations in Computed Tomography (CT) Scanners is highly correlated with a citations-weighted count of

---

7. Thus for example, if a patent in solid-state physics is cited by later patents in chemistry, in superconductivity and in medical instrumentation, we would regard it as more general, and hence more basic, than a similar patent that received the same number of citations but all or most of them belong to the same field.

patents in that field (see also section 6.3). On the other hand, high marks of IMPORTF and GENERAL do not necessarily imply high *private* returns, the key intervening variable being of course appropriability. Thus, innovations with high IMPORTF may yield low returns if the follow-up innovations are done by other firms, whereas low-IMPORTF innovations can be highly profitable if they land in a market niche well-protected from competition. High generality may well interfere with appropriation and hence reduce private returns, particularly for small firms, who may find it difficult to assemble the complementary assets necessary to exploit a highly diverse set of market opportunities (Nelson, 1959).

We also compute measures of "distance" in time and technology space between the innovation and its antecedents, and between the innovation and its offsprings. The presumption is that remoteness in time and technology may be related to aspects of basicness and/ or to the conditions of appropriability. The F/looking time distance measure is defined simply as the average forward LAG, that is,

$$\text{TIMEF}_i = \sum_{j=1}^{\text{nciting}_i} \frac{\text{LAG}_j}{\text{NCITING}_i}$$

The F/distance in technology space is computed as follows: if the citing patent is in the same 3-digit class (NCLASS) as the originating patent, then the distance between them, TECH, is set to zero; if they are in the same 2-digit class (CATCODE) but not in the same 3-digit class, then TECH = 0.33; if they are in the same 1-digit class (FIELD) and not in the same 2- or 3-digit class, then TECH = 0.66; if they are even in different 1-digit classes then TECH = 1. The average distance for o-patent i is then,[8]

$$\text{TECHF}_i = \sum_{j=1}^{\text{nciting}_i} \frac{\text{TECH}_j}{\text{NCITING}_i}$$

We hypothesize that TIMEF will be related to basicness if the technical difficulties encountered in the R&D process are commensurable

---

8. Notice that TECHF is related to GENERAL, but it is by no means the same: a patent whose descendants are in a number of different classes, all of which are close in technology space to the originating class, would have a high value of GENERAL but a low value of TECHF. Conversely, a patent that spawns a single rich line of subsequent development would have a low value of GENERAL, but could have a high value of TECHF if those developments are in a field far away from the originating patent.

with the degree of basicness: in that case more basic innovations would take longer to generate offspring. As to TECHF, if basicness implies a higher probability of serendipitous discoveries, and if these tend to occur in remote technological areas, then it is plausible that the *incidence* of far-removed follow-ups would be higher the more basic a patent is. We also hypothesize that the distance measures may be related to the difficulty of appropriating the returns from innovations: the more technically dissimilar are the subsequent developments of an invention, and the more time that passes before they come to be, the more likely it is that other firms will overcome any advantages held by the original inventor and thereby take away a larger share of the economic returns (a similar reasoning applies to the equivalent B/measures, TIMEB and TECHB).

Our final F/looking measure relates to the ownership structure of the innovation's descendants. We propose a measure, PSELFF, that is defined simply as the percentage of citing patents issued to the same assignee as that of the originating patent. The rationale for this measure is that these subsequent patents are likely to reflect follow-up developments of the original invention, and that these developments are the conduit that leads to the appropriation of returns. Thus, the higher the proportion of these later developments that take place "in-house" the larger would be the fraction of the benefits captured by the original inventor.

3.2 Backward-Looking Measures

Turning now to the B/measures (that is, to the basicness of *research*), we define the equivalent to IMPORTF as,

$$\text{IMPORTB}_i = \text{NCITED}_i + \lambda \sum_{j=1}^{\text{ncited}_i} \text{NCITING}_{i-1,j}$$

Thus, IMPORTB will be large if the o-patent cites many previous patents, and these cited patents are "important" in the usual sense that they in turn were highly cited (as with IMPORTF we use $\lambda = 0.5$). In other words, IMPORTB reflects the extent to which a given o-patent stands on a wide base of previous innovations that are in themselves important. Our presumption is that more basic patents would have *fewer* and/or *less* important predecessors and therefore lower values of IMPORTB.

The equivalent B/measure for GENERAL, which we label ORIGINAL, is defined as,

$$\text{ORIGINAL}_i = 1 - \sum_{k=1}^{N_i} \left(\frac{\text{NCITED}_{ik}}{\text{NCITED}_i} \right)^2$$

Thus the larger is ORIGINAL the broader are the technological roots of the underlying research. Our notion is that synthesis of divergent ideas is characteristic of research that is highly original and hence basic in that sense. Finally, we define a measure of scientific base which lacks a F/counterpart,

$$\text{SCIENCE}_i = \frac{\text{NPCITES}_i}{\text{NPCITES}_i + \text{NCITED}_i}$$

that is, SCIENCE measures the predominance of scientific sources as proxied by NPCITES, over technological ones (embedded in NCITED). The non-patent references, which appear on the front page of patents under the heading "Other Publications", may include articles in scientific journals, books, abstracts, proceedings, etc. That is, they constitute prior scientific knowledge or ideas to which the patent is related. Our conjecture is that more basic research would tend to draw relatively more from scientific sources than from technology, and hence would be associated with higher values of SCIENCE.

The B/distance measures, TIMEB and TECHB, are defined in an analogous way to the F/distance measures, except that we substitute NCITED for NCITING in the corresponding formula. Their interpretation is straightforward: larger values of TIMEB indicate that the o-patent draws from older sources, large values of TECHB that the innovation has roots in remote technological fields. We define also an equivalent B/measure to PSELFF, PSELFB, which measures the extent to which the o-patent represents appropriation of benefits to its antecedents.

4 The Proposed Measures as Indicators of Basicness: A Statistical Test

The measures put forward above are predicated on the assumption that they capture aspects of basicness and appropriability. The question is how to test this hypothesis relying for that purpose just on patent data, since it is extremely hard to find independent indicators of basicness that could help legitimize our measures (see, however, section 6.3). The test that we suggest here relies on the prior that university research is more basic than corporate research, and exploits the consequent contrast between university and corporate patents.

The attributes of innovation that we are trying to capture with our measures are inherently unobservable, as is education or ability in the context of labor economics, or permanent income in macro. In these latter cases, the starting point of the analysis is usually an equation of the form,

$$y = \beta x^* + \varepsilon, \tag{1}$$

where y is observed but x^* is not, and ε is an i.i.d. disturbance (for example, y could be the wage rate and x^* education). Given the existence of a proxy variable x (e.g. years of schooling) such that,

$$x = x^* + v \tag{2}$$

where v is an i.i.d. measurement error, the issue is then how to obtain a consistent estimate for β, since if x were just used *in lieu* of x^* the resulting estimate will be biased and inconsistent. We start here a step earlier and ask, how can one establish the connection between a candidate proxy and x^* given that by definition no direct data exist on x^*? In other words, how can we test the hypothesis that x is indeed a proxy for x^* as described in (2)?[9] *A priori* reasoning may suffice in some cases (as in years of schooling as proxy for education), but in areas far removed from common experience that may not be so, and the area of innovation and patenting is certainly of that sort. Moreover, since many of the solutions to the errors in variables problem call for the use of multiple indicators, it is important to be able to assess in advance whether or not the various candidate variables qualify indeed as proxies.[10]

---

9. It is interesting to note that this question is rarely asked in economics, but rather (2) is taken for granted, and the problem is confined to the consistent estimation of (1) given the presence of a measurement error.

10. Obviously, estimating a regression of y on x will not do, since if (2) holds then the estimate of β will be biased towards zero. Moreover, y and x may exhibit some spurious correlation even if x and x^* are uncorrelated, or the model in (1) might be misspecified in the sense that $cor(x, x^*) = 0$ but x belongs in the model in its own right.

We propose to tackle the issue by resorting to additional information that takes the form of the following *prior*:[11] suppose we knew that there are two groups in the population from which x^* is drawn, S_1 and S_2, such that,

$$E(x^* \mid x^* \in S_1) > E(x^* \mid x^* \in S_2) \tag{3}$$

Consider the following hypothetical regression,

$$x_i^* = \alpha_0 + \alpha_1 D_i + \xi_i \tag{4}$$

where $D_i = 1$ if the ith observation belongs to S_1, and $D_i = 0$ otherwise. Clearly, if (3) is true then $\alpha_1 > 0$. Now take a candidate variable x; if it is indeed a proxy for x^* then,

$$x_i = \delta_0 + \delta_1 x_i^* + v_i, \quad \delta_1 > 0 \tag{5}$$

How do we know that (5) holds? Estimate the following equation,

$$x_i = \zeta_0 + \zeta_1 D_i + w_i \tag{6}$$

and test $H_0: \zeta_1 > 0$. If $\delta_1 > 0$ then it must be that H_0 holds, since $\zeta_1 = \alpha_1 \delta_1$ and we know from (4) that $\alpha_1 > 0$. In words, given the presumed differences in the unobservable between the two groups in the population, a finding that x is on average larger for one of the groups (i.e. $\zeta_1 > 0$) implies that x is a proxy of x^* in the sense of (5). This is so provided that $\hat{\zeta}_1$ is unbiased, which in turn requires that $\text{Cov}(D_i, w_i) = 0$. Noticing that $w_i = \delta_1 \xi_i + v_i$, this latter condition implies that the measurement error is not systematically higher for one of the groups, meaning that $\text{Cov}(D_i, v_i) = 0$, and that there is no sample selection bias, i.e. that $\text{Cov}(D_i, \xi_i) = 0$.

4.1 Applying the Test: Selectivity Biases?

The much larger fraction of R&D devoted by universities to basic research (see below) suggests that university patents are more basic than corporate patents. The presumption is thus that university patents correspond to S_1 in (3) above, and corporate patents to S_2. Thus, testing for the statistical significance of differences in the means of

---

11. We use here "prior" and "maintained hypothesis" interchangeably: the point is that we bring in a statement (such as eq. 3), presumably well-grounded on external information, that we regard as factually true. All subsequent steps rely on this being so, and hence all down-the-line inferences should be regarded as conditional on the prior being true.

the measures between universities and corporations (which is the same as testing for H_0: $\zeta_1 > 0$ in eq. 6) amounts to testing whether or not the measures are in fact indicators of the fundamental attributes of innovations that we are after.

The question is whether one can safely assume that $\text{Cov}(D_i, w_i) = 0$, and hence that $\hat{\zeta}_1$ is unbiased. It is hard to think of circumstances whereby $\text{Cov}(D_i, v_i) = 0$ would not hold, that is, that the measurement error of say, GENERAL as defined in section 3 (as a proxy for true "generality" of innovations) would be systematically larger for university patents; hence we disregard this possibility. On the other hand, selectivity biases of various types may cause $\text{Cov}(D_i, \xi_i) \neq 0$. Suppose for example that university patents were drawn from the upper half of the distribution of research outcomes, as shown in figure 1.b: that amounts to $\text{Cov}(D_i, \xi_i) > 0$, causing an upward bias in $\hat{\zeta}_1$, and hence invalidating the suggested test. Conversely, if university patents were drawn from the lower half the distribution as in figure 1.c, the resulting downward bias in $\hat{\zeta}_1$ would make it tougher to accept H_0: $\zeta_1 > 0$, but a finding to that effect would certainly be statistically valid.

Notice that in order for $\text{Cov}(D_i, \xi_i) > 0$, those research outcomes that are patented by universities would have to be on average more basic than the university average. This is very unlikely, considering that about $2/3$ of university research is defined as basic, and hence is not oriented towards innovations with practical potential. Patents do have to have such potential, and hence it is much more likely that they reflect research outcomes that are, if anything, *less* basic than the university average. The other fact to keep in mind in this context is that, as shown in section 5, university patents do reflect roughly the distribution of research over broad fields, and hence in that sense at least there is no presumption of selectivity bias. In sum, there is good reason to believe that $\text{Cov}(D_i, \xi_i) \leq 0$, and hence that the proposed test is statistically sound.

5   Research Design and Data Characteristics

5.1   Sample Design and Data Gathering

The choice of our sample of patents was dictated primarily by the requirements of the test outlined above. In addition, we needed to cover sufficiently long sequences of innovations so as to be able to compute measures that rely on backward and forward linkages, and to control for technological areas, since citation practices may vary systematically across them. Thus, we took as our core sample *all* university patents applied for in 1975 (319 patents) and in 1980 (482 patents), which gave us substantial time horizons backwards and forward.[12] We identified and gathered data on each of the (earlier) patents cited by these originating patents, and on each of the (subsequent) patents citing them, thus forming a complete set which encompasses three successive generations of related inventions.[13] We also obtained the number of citations made and received by each of the cited and citing patents, which gave us some information about the "grandparents" and the "grandchildren" as well (see figure 3). Empirical work rarely examines such long stretches of the innovational stream.

We then identified two samples of corporate patents in parallel to the university patents. The first was drawn from the universe of patents granted to the top 200 R&D-performing U.S. firms in 1986, as reported in 10-K reports and coded by the Compustat data service. We expect that at least some of these firms perform appreciable basic research. The other corporate sample was drawn from the universe of patents assigned to all other U.S. corporations, which perform by definition less R&D, and presumably devote a significantly smaller share of their R&D budget to basic research.

In order to control for technological field, each of these samples was drawn to match the university patent cohorts by patent class, application year and grant date. That is, for each originating university patent, we selected a corporate patent from each universe that had the same application year and the same (3-digit) patent class as the university patent, and was granted as close in time as possible. This design allows us to compare averages of our measures across institutional groups, without worrying that the estimates might differ

---

12. In principle there should always be enough of a backwards horizon, but in practice the availability of data declines dramatically as we go back in time, to the point that for the 1975 cohort, for example, a great deal of the data of the **cited** patents are missing, and that created serious problems in computing the measures. There is reason to believe though that this limitation will soon vanish, as more and more patent data become computerized and available as such.

13. The data on citing patents extend only up to 1989, primarily because we had to rely on "third parties" to obtain the data, and that meant long delays. Again, availability is constantly improving, so that in future research one should be able to obtain much more recent data.

1975 Cohort

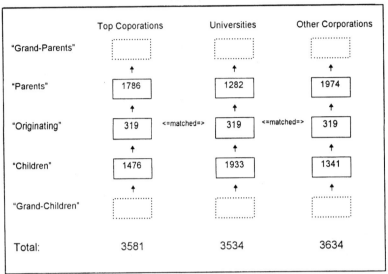

1980 Cohort

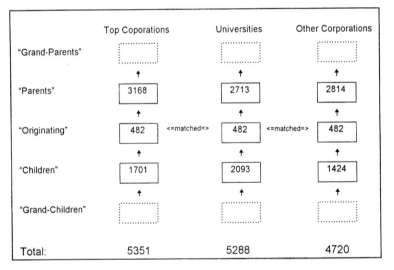

Figure 3
Sample design. Total number of patents for 1975: 10,749; for 1980: 15,359; grand total: 26,108

just because universities and corporations exhibit different distributions of patents across fields. We then collected data on the predecessors and successors of these corporate patents, exactly as we had for the set of university patents. As figure 3 makes clear, this sampling scheme lead to "explosive" data requirements: starting from just 319 university patents applied for in 1975 and 482 in 1980, we ended up collecting data on over 26,000 patents.

5.2   Characteristics of University Research and Patents[14]

Since the core sample is of university patents, it is important to describe the salient features of university R&D and university patents. The R&D performed by academic institutions in the US amounted to 17.2 billion dollars in 1991, which constituted 11.4% of total R&D expenditures in the US for that year (in 1970 the share was of 8.9%, and it has been rising steadily since). However, the role of universities in pushing the frontiers of science and technology go far beyond their share of total R&D, because of the nature of the research done at academic institutions: about 65% of it is defined as *basic* research, 30% as applied research, and just 5% as development (NSF, 1992). Thus, basic research performed at universities accounts for almost 50% of all basic research in the US, whereas academic R&D labeled as development accounts for less than 1% of all development.

Given the nature of academic research, it is no surprise that most of the research outcomes from universities (at least those that are observable and quantifiable) take the form of publications in scientific journals, and only a few end up as patents.[15] The incentives of universities to take patents were further dampened in the past by a law that precluded them from charging royalties for patents stemming from federally funded research (which accounts for the bulk of academic research). The lifting of this legal restriction in 1980, and the proliferation of collaborative ventures between industry and academic institutions in recent years (biotechnology is a prime example), brought about a steady increase in the absolute and relative

---

14. For a detailed account of university patenting over time see Henderson, Jaffe and Trajtenberg (1996).

15. In addition to the fact that most of the university research is "basic" and hence largely non-patentable, the incentives that university researchers face (in terms of promotion, prestige, etc.) encourage primarily publication in the scientific literature, and not patent applications.

number of university patents. Still, university patents account for a very small fraction of all patents granted in the US (1.2% in 1990, or 2.4% of all patents of US *origin* that same year).

Not surprisingly, university patents do not constitute a representative sample of the universe of US patents: during the years examined here they were concentrated in a relatively small number of fields, and their distribution differed greatly from that of all US patents. On the other hand, the technological mix of university patents do seem to reflect the distribution of academic R&D expenditures over broad scientific fields: at least 25–30% of university patents belong to patent classes related to the Biological and Medical Sciences, which commanded 45% of all academic R&D in 1980, and about 12% of patents belong to the Physical Sciences, to which universities allocated 11% of their R&D budget (not including engineering).

University patents are highly concentrated in the hands of relatively few academic institutions: of the 75 universities that were issued patents in 1975, half received just one patent, and the top ten received over 50% (similar figures apply for 1980). There seems to be also a positive link between the size of the university R&D budget and the number of patents received: 5 of the top 10 universities with the most patents in both 1975 and 1980 belong also to the top ten in terms of R&D expenditures in 1989.

6   Statistical Analysis and Results

6.1   A First Look at the Measures

Tables 1 and 2 present descriptive statistics of the measures and Pearson correlations between them, and figures 4 and 5 depict the empirical distributions of some of them. Notice first the striking similarity in the shape of the distributions of IMPORTF and IMPORTB, and likewise for GENERAL and ORIGINAL; as it turns out, this is true for *all* equivalent F/B measures, which is an interesting finding that deserves further scrutiny (see section 6.4).

As figure 4 shows, the distribution of IMPORTF is extremely skewed (for 1980 the mean is 12.6 and the median just 5.5). If we interpret IMPORTF as an indicator of the value of patents, the observed skewness would fit nicely with previous findings regarding the distribution of such values (e.g. Pakes 1986, Trajtenberg 1990): most patents turn out to be of very little value (i.e. to have few if any

Table 1
Descriptive statistics*

| (i) Basicness measures | | | | | |
Variable	N	Mean	Std Dev	Minimum	Maximum
IMPORTF (1975)	948	12.58	23.21	0	380.50
(1980)	1446	6.96	14.68	0	250.50
GENERAL	806	0.32	0.29	0	0.88
	1127	0.27	0.27	0	0.85
IMPORTB	763	21.34	22.10	0	204.50
	1340	27.76	33.33	0	393.50
ORIGINAL	719	0.22	0.27	0	0.82
	1261	0.27	0.27	0	0.88
SCIENCE	945	0.14	0.25	0	1.00
	1446	0.20	0.30	0	1.00

| (ii) Distance measures | | | | | |
Variable	N	Mean	Std Dev	Minimum	Maximum
TECHF	791	0.32	0.30	0	1.00
	1124	0.32	0.31	0	1.00
TIMEF	811	7.26	2.49	0	13.00
	1126	4.38	1.55	0	9.00
TECHB	708	0.31	0.34	0	1.00
	1261	0.30	0.31	0	1.00
TIMEB	909	7.66	3.95	0	17.00
	1367	9.17	4.85	0	22.00

| (iii) Appropriability measures | | | | | |
Variable	N	Mean	Std Dev	Minimum	Maximum
PSELFF	783	0.11	0.24	0	1.00
	1061	0.16	0.29	0	1.00
PSELFB	719	0.14	0.30	0	1.00
	1342	0.13	0.25	0	1.00

*The top line of each variable corresponds to the 1975 sample, the bottom one to the 1980 sample.

Table 2
Correlations between measures—1980 sample*

(i) Correlations between forward measures

	IMPORTF	GENERAL	TECHF	TIMEF	PSELFF
IMPORTF	1.0				
	0.0				
GENERAL	0.238	1.0			
	0.0001	0.0			
TECHF	0.003	**0.372**	1.0		
	0.927	0.0001	0.0		
TIMEF	−0.051	0.019	0.006	1.0	
	0.089	0.524	0.845	0.0	
PSELFF	−0.019	−0.074	−0.035	**−0.161**	1.0
	0.520	0.015	0.259	0.0001	0.0

(ii) Correlations across F/B measures

	IMPORTF	GENERAL	TECHF	TIMEF	PSELFF
IMPORTB	0.255	0.115	−0.047	0.046	0.014
	0.0001	0.0002	0.129	0.132	0.646
ORIGINAL	0.055	**0.246**	0.203	−0.011	0.006
	0.051	0.0001	0.0001	0.721	0.852
TECHB	−0.020	0.187	**0.387**	−0.027	0.051
	0.475	0.0001	0.0001	0.381	0.114
TIMEB	−0.167	−0.114	0.005	0.090	−0.012
	0.0001	0.0002	0.878	0.003	0.692
PSELFB	−0.057	−0.050	−0.013	−0.046	**0.211**
	0.037	0.103	0.657	0.130	0.0001
SCIENCE	−0.005	0.052	0.038	−0.029	0.017
	0.838	0.082	0.204	0.333	0.569

*Pearson correlation coefficients; significance probabilities right under.

descendants), and only a handful make it bit. IMPORTB is similarly skewed, which would mean that most patents come from "humble origins", and few have important technological predecessors. Thus important innovations appear to be in very short supply as one looks either up or down the innovational stream.

The distributions of GENERAL and of ORIGINAL are much closer to being bell-shaped, except for the large mass at zero (figure 5). Sixty percent of the patents with GENERAL = 0 had just one citing patent, which means that GENERAL could only be zero; an additional 25% of these patents had NCITING = 2, which are very likely to render GENERAL = 0. Still, the mass at zero is not an artifact: patents that

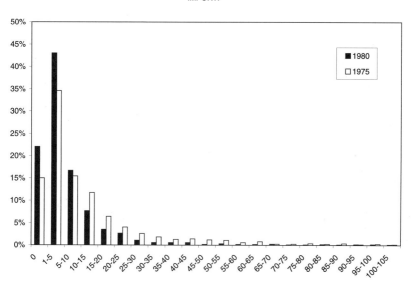

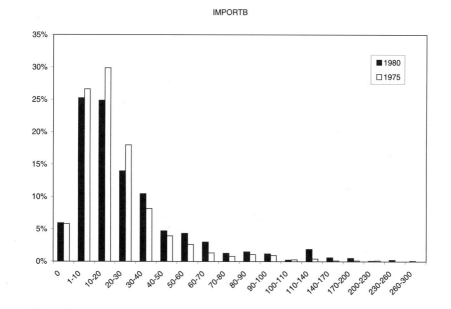

Figure 4
Frequency distribution of basicness measures. Truncated values of IMPORTF > 105 and truncated values of IMPORTB > 300 do not appear.

GENERAL

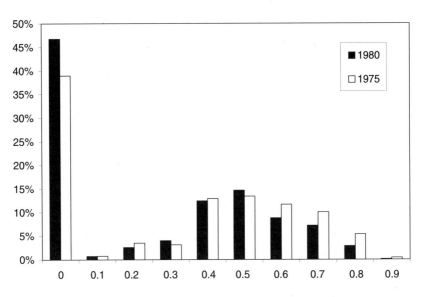

ORIGINAL

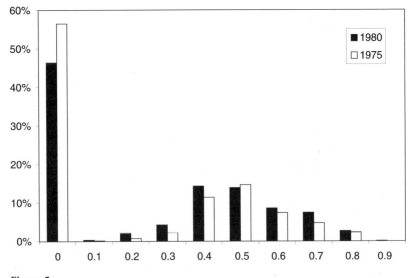

Figure 5
Frequency distribution of basicness measures

"fathered" just one or two further technological developments can claim indeed little generality.[16]

Turning to the correlations between F/measures and between B/measures, notice in table 2(i) that the various measures do capture different aspects of the underlying phenomena (the results for the 1975 sample are very similar and hence we show just those for 1980): none of the correlations exceeds 0.5, most are much smaller. The variables that exhibit the largest pairwise correlations are GENERAL and TECHF (and, in parallel, ORIGINAL and TECHB), which makes sense since both refer to the positioning of patents in technology space. Another pair exhibiting a high correlation is IMPORTF and GENERAL, and likewise IMPORTB and ORIGINAL.

Notice also the large negative correlation between PSELFF and TIMEF, implying that spillovers tend to occur in-house faster than externally. Thus the same R&D organization may be able to recognize earlier the potential for further developments of a given innovation, it may have already in place the requisite competencies needed to develop the successor innovations, etc. For the converse reasons outsiders would take longer in benefiting from spillovers originating in labs other than their own.

6.2   Universities vs. Corporations: Comparing the Means

Table 3 presents the sample means of the proposed measures for university and corporate patents, and t-tests for the significance of the differences between them. To recall, our prior is that research, and research outcomes from universities are more basic than those from corporations, and therefore if our measures do capture aspects of basicness university patents should rank higher than corporate patents along those dimensions.

The results for IMPORTF strongly support this hypothesis: university patents received significantly more first- and second-generation citations, and the difference seems to increase over time (see the results for 1975 vis-à-vis 1980). The figures for GENERAL indicate that

---

16. For ORIGINAL $= 0$ the percentage of patents with NCITED $= 1$ or NCITED $= 2$ was just 39% (25% for 1975), thus it would seem that the finding of a large mass at zero is more telling for ORIGINAL than for GENERAL. The only qualification is that there are many missing backwards data, and thus many of the patents for which NCITED $= 1$ or 2 might have received a value of zero for ORIGINAL (rather than missing) if the data had been available.

Table 3
Comparison of means: universities vs. corporations[a]

(i) Basicness measures

Variable	Universities	Corporations
IMPORTF (1980)	8.80	6.04***
(1975)	16.76	10.49***
TIMEF	0.31	0.25***
	0.34	0.31[b]
IMPORTB	26.83	28.22
	16.31	23.75***
ORIGINAL	0.28	0.27
	0.20	0.24[#]
SCIENCE	0.28	0.16***
	0.20	0.10***

(ii) Distance measures

Variable	Universities	Corporations
TECHF	0.35	0.30***
	0.32	0.31
TECHB	0.33	0.29**
	0.30	0.32[#]
TIMEF	4.44	4.34
	6.48	7.69[#]
TIMEB	9.08	9.22[#]
	7.50	7.73[#]

(iii) Appropriability measures

Variable	Universities	Corporations
PSELFF	0.09	0.19***
	0.07	0.13***
PSELFB	0.06	0.16***
	0.14	0.14

a. The top row of each variable corresponds to 1980, the bottom to 1975.

b. The difference is significant for a "truncated" sample—see text.

, * Differences from the mean of university patents statistically significant at the .05 and .01 level, respectively.

Figures for which the differences from universities have the "wrong" sign (i.e. contrary to the prior).

the follow-up innovations from universities spread indeed more widely over different technological areas, but the 1975 results suggest that these differences tend to narrow down over time. In fact, we recomputed GENERAL for the 1975 cohort truncating the citation data in 1984 so as to replicate the time span of the 1980 sample, and the results are almost identical to those for 1980. Thus the offsprings from corporate patents tend to be more technologically concentrated in the short term, but eventually these spillovers become more diffused, narrowing the gap between them and university patents. This fits the common wisdom regarding the way spillovers work, and goes in tandem with the finding in our companion paper (Jaffe et al, 1993) of diminishing geographic localization of spillovers over time.

As conjectured, IMPORTB shows that corporate innovations rely on more numerous and more "important" predecessors than universities (the differences though are significant for 1975 but not for 1980). Thus university research appears to be located nearer the origins of innovational paths, supporting the notion that this may be an aspect of basicness. ORIGINAL does not live up to expectations: there is a slight difference for 1980 but it lacks statistical significance, and for 1975 the difference even has the "wrong" sign. The measure SCIENCE does support the hypothesis, and strongly so: university patents do rely relatively more on non-patent (i.e. scientific) sources than corporate patents (recall that this cannot be a "field effect," since the samples are matched by technology field).[17]

The results for the distance measures are weak and inconclusive: the measure of technological distance is significantly different in 1980 but not in 1975, whereas in most cases the results for TIME (F and B) run contrary to the prior, that is, the follow-up innovations of corporations appear to take *longer* than those of universities. In sharp contrast to them, the appropriability measures do perform very well: PSELF (F and B) is much larger for corporations than for universities, suggesting that these measures may indeed be indicative of the extent to which inventors succeed in reaping the benefits of their own research.

---

17. It is possible though that this result reflects to some extent differences in citation *practices* between university and corporate researchers, and not just genuine differences in the *nature* of their research (i.e. more "scientific"). However, the fact that there are symbiotic linkages between universities and corporations in fields such as biotechnology (where most of the NPCITES occur) would suggest that citation practices are actually similar; unfortunately our data cannot discriminate between these effects.

In sum, with the exception of ORIGINAL, and with some reservation regarding the time span of GENERAL, the contrast between universities and corporations suggest that our basicness measures qualify as legitimate proxies for some fundamental features of innovations. On the other hand, the conceptual ambiguity of the distance measures surfaces also in the empirical results: there is some evidence that the offsprings from university innovations may be more remote in technology space, but certainly not in time. In general F/measures perform somewhat better than B/measures, and the 1980 sample shows crisper results than 1975.

A subsidiary hypothesis was that the basicness measures would exhibit higher values for patents of top corporations (i.e. the 200 corporations with the largest R&D outlays) than for those of other corporations. Presumably the larger corporations can afford to invest more in basic research, since they may be able to appropriate a larger fraction of the benefits. The evidence does not support this conjecture: with the notable exception of PSELF (which turned out to be significantly larger for top corporations), and to a lesser extent IMPORTF, the differences between top and other corporations were not statistically significant.

However, it is quite likely that the lack of contrast between them stems simply from the particular sample chosen, which is by no means representative of corporate research, but rather replicates exactly the composition of university patents. Thus, it may well be that in those particular fields there is little difference between small and large R&D performers, but that those differences do exist in the population of corporate innovations at large. In fact, a large proportion of our sample is in biotechnology, and we know that in this field small firms, both by themselves and in cooperation with universities, are particularly innovative. That may also explain the fact that we observe a significantly *lower* value of IMPORTB for the smaller corporations, which would imply that they engage in more original and creative research.

6.3 Additional Evidence

One of the limitations of the forgoing analysis is that it is entirely internal to patent data. As said above, though, it is extremely hard to obtain enough independent data on the basic features of innovations,

Table B
Patents selected

Innovation	Patent number	Inventors	Assignee	App. year	Grant year
Recombinant DNA	4,237,224	S. N. Cohen and H. W. Boyer	Stanford University	1979	1980
CT scanner	3,778,614	G. Hounsfield	EMI Ltd (UK)	1971	1973
Cardiac pacemakers	3,833,005	Wingrove	Medtronics, Inc.	1971	1974
Fiber optics	3,659,915	R. Maurer et al	Corning Glass Works (US)	1970	1972
	3,711,262	D. B. Keck et al	Corning Glass Works (US)	1970	1973
	3,737,293	R. Maurer	Corning Glass Works (US)	1972	1973
Ruby laser	3,353,115	T. Maiman	Hughes Aircraft Co. (US)	1965	1967

that would allow us to perform direct statistical tests of the proposed measures. Short of that, we present here a few bits of additional evidence that may help illustrate the meaning of the proposed measures, and perhaps also provide further support to their validity as indicators of basicness.

We searched for a small number of innovations that fulfill the following conditions: (i) that would be universally recognized as "basic"; (ii) that are embedded in one, or in a small number of easily identified patent(s); and (iii) that are sufficiently recent so that the citations data would be fairly complete (since the computerized patent citations data starts only in 1975).[18] We relied for that purpose primarily on Berry (1993), and on various publications of the Patent Office (such as OTAF, 1977). We retrieved for the handful of patents thus selected the corresponding citations data, and computed the main F-measures.[19] The patents selected were those in table B.

---

18. There probably are a large number of patents that conform to these criteria, but it would take a major research effort to identify them, and to make sure that there is indeed consensus about their being "basic" (for example by interviewing experts in the field). The patents selected here are not meant to be a "representative sample" (since it is not clear what the universe is), but just illustrative cases.
19. We could not obtain data on the *cited* patents, and hence could not compute B-measures.

Table C
The values of IMPORTF and GENERAL for the selected patents

	Citations		IMPORTF		GENERAL
Mean 1975 sample		(5)		(13)	0.32
Recombinant DNA	130	(107)	545	(273)	0.26
CT scanner	98	(95)	485	(380)	0.70
Cardiac pacemakers	35	(29)	166	(118)	0.17
Fiber optics	15	(13)	88	(60)	0.76
	32	(28)	199	(149)	0.59
	16	(16)	132	(114)	0.48
Ruby laser	6	(4)	21	(14)	0.67

The Cohen-Boyer patent is universally acknowledged as one of the fundamental innovations that paved the way for the emergence of biotechnology; CT (Computed Tomography) scanners revolutionized diagnostic medicine; cardiac pacemakers constituted a major improvement in the long-term treatment of cardiovascular disorders; the work by Maurer, Keck and their team at Corning Glass Works laid the foundations for the practical implementation of fibre optics; T. Maiman was the first to implement a ruby laser, which was a milestone in the development of lasers. This latter patent though was granted in 1967, and hence it does not fulfill the third condition stated above. Nevertheless, we present it here to illustrate the limitations of the data in the time dimension.

We computed for these patents the measures IMPORTF and GENERAL in two ways: (1) using all the citations data available at present (i.e. up to 1994), and (2) truncating the citations data in 1990, in order to make it comparable to the measures for the sample of university and corporate patents used in the analysis above; the latter are shown in parenthesis in the table C.

Except for the ruby laser, all these patents had a value of IMPORTF *5 to 10 times* higher than the mean for the 1975 sample of patents used in the previous analysis (using citations up to 1990). The fact that these innovations, which are surely "basic" by external criteria, show extremely high values of IMPORTF, can thus be seen as providing additional qualitative (or "anecdotal") support to the notion that this measure may indeed capture aspects of basicness. As to the ruby laser, it is remarkable that it received a value of IMPORTF similar to the average for the 1975 sample, even though it was awarded 10 years earlier.[20] This suggests that this patent had indeed a strong impact, of which we can observe only the end tail.

The results for GENERAL are very much in line with expectations: for the CT scanner, fiber optics and the ruby laser, its value is much higher than the average for the sample. Indeed, the impact of those innovations was very broad in scope, reaching a wide range of technological fields. For the pacemaker the value of GENERAL was much lower than the average, implying that the spillovers from it were strictly "local." The low value for the rDNA patent means that, although this was an extremely important innovation, its impact was confined to Biotechnology, and did not spill over to other fields, at least not as those are identified by 3-digit patent classes in the current patent classification system.

6.4   The Links Between F- and B-Measures

We turn now to a preliminary examination of the linkages between backward and forward measures, that may throw light on issues related to the R&D process. In particular, we would like to examine whether or not the nature of the research efforts (as captured by the B-measures) affect the features of the resulting innovations. As a first step, we present in table 2(ii) the correlations across the F/B divide. Notice that the largest correlations occur along the main diagonal, that is, between equivalent F/B measures.[21] Thus it would seem that "importance breeds importance," originality breeds generality, coming from far away in technology space leads far away as well, etc. In that sense, then, the (*ex post*) characteristics of patented innovations appear to be related to the attributes of the research that lead to them.

Probing further into these links, we run regressions of the two F/ measures of basicness, IMPORTF and GENERAL, on the B/measures, dummies for technological fields, and dummies for corporations (see table 4). The purpose was to estimate a sort of production function whereby the attributes of the patented innovations play the role of "outputs" and the features of the underlying research the role of

---

20. We know from further work done on patent citations that the vast majority of citations are received during the first 5–10 years after a patent is issued.

21. The one exception is TIMEB which shows a higher correlation with IMPORTF (and slightly higher with GENERAL) than with TIMEF; notice also that SCIENCE does not have an equivalent F/measure.

Table 4
Regressions of IMPORTF and GENERAL on B/variables*

	IMPORTF		GENERAL	
	1975	1980	1975	1980
Constant	19.7	8.2	0.3	0.2
	(5.7)	(5.1)	(6.8)	(5.9)
IMPORTB	0.3	0.1	0.0005	0.0005
	(6.7)	(8.8)	(0.9)	(1.9)
ORIGINAL	−4.0	−2.2	0.11	0.18
	(−1.0)	(−1.2)	(2.3)	(4.8)
TECHB	7.0	−0.04	0.17	0.11
	(2.3)	(−0.02)	(4.7)	(3.4)
TIMEB	−0.3	−0.4	−0.005	−0.005
	(−0.8)	(−3.9)	(−1.4)	(−2.2)
SCIENCE	−6.1	1.6	−0.04	0.14
	(−1.0)	(0.8)	(−0.5)	(3.7)
TC	−8.7	−3.1	−0.03	−0.05
	(−3.8)	(−3.0)	(−1.3)	(−2.4)
OC	−13.0	−3.0	−0.05	−0.05
	(−5.6)	(−2.9)	(−1.8)	(−2.3)
R^2	0.12	0.10	0.09	0.11
No. obs.	707	1259	612	1002

*t-values in parentheses. All regressions include 4 dummies for technological "fields."

"inputs," and to see whether the differences between universities and corporations remain there after controlling for the characteristics of research and technological fields.

In line with the findings of table 2(ii), the most significant coefficient in the regression of IMPORTF is its equivalent B/measure, IMPORTB, and likewise ORIGINAL is the most significant in the regression of GENERAL. Notice however that more basic innovations should be associated with *smaller* values of IMPORTB, and hence if basicness leads to basicness we would have expected a *negative* sign on the coefficient of IMPORTB. The positive and highly significant coefficient that we obtained instead may be interpreted as follows: very basic research (in the sense of small values of IMPORTB) is likely to exhibit a large variance in terms of its outcomes—some may do well, others may fail badly (i.e. high and low values of IMPORTF). On the other hand, once a research avenue has proven its worth (i.e. high values of IMPORTB), further significant innovations along those lines are very likely to come, showing up in high IMPORTF. If this effect dominates, we will find indeed a positive association between IMPORTF and IMPORTB.

The results for GENERAL suggest that more original research, as well as research that draws from far removed technological areas (high TECHB), lead to innovations of wider technological applicability. More reliance on scientific sources also enhances the generality of the outcomes (this finding does not hold for the 1975 sample). The negative signs on TIMEB in both regressions imply that more important and more general innovations stem from more *recent* (or *up to date*) research sources. It is also clear that there does remain an "institutional effect" after controlling for the type of research, meaning that even if universities and corporations were to engage in research having similar characteristics, universities would still produce on average more basic innovations.

7 Conclusions and Suggestions for Further Research

This chapter is a fresh attempt to quantify various aspects of basicness and appropriability of innovations with the aid of detailed patent data, particularly patent citations. Relying on the prior that universities perform more basic research than corporations, we find that the forward-looking measures of importance and generality do seem to capture aspects of the basicness of *innovations*; similarly, the reliance on scientific versus technological sources, and (to a less extent) the closeness to the origins of innovational paths, appear to reflect aspects of the basicness of *research*. On the other hand our measure of originality does not seem to be able to discriminate between more and less basic research.

The fraction of citations coming from patents awarded to the same inventor was found to be much higher for corporations than for universities, supporting the notion that PSELF may indeed be indicative of actual appropriability. The measures of technological distance appear to be related to basicness but the evidence is not clear-cut, whereas distance in time does not fit our conjectures. In all, then, the F/measures of basicness and the indicators of actual appropriability passed the test by ample margins, the measures of B/basicness did somewhat less well, and most distance measures failed. We also find interesting similarities and high correlations between equivalent F and B measures, suggesting that there may be strong "family effects" in successive generations of patents. Further work along these lines would seek to identify and characterize different "technological trajectories," and relate them to conventional economic data.

Having provided initial support for our measures, we plan in future work to use them on a wide scale in tandem with other economic data, and see whether or not they make a difference. An immediate target would be to redo studies that have used simple patent counts as indicators of innovation, usually with disappointing results. In particular, we would like to re-examine the series of studies by Griliches and associates at the NBER (Griliches, 1981; Pakes, 1985; Cockburn and Griliches, 1988), which sought to identify the impact of R&D and of patent counts on the market value of Compustat firms. We hypothesize that if we were to use composite indicators based on our measures instead of simple patent counts, the impact on stock market value would be much more noticeable.

In particular, we expect that IMPORTF would have a very significant effect, and that it will improve even further when adjusting it with PSELFF, since what should influence the worth of the invention is just the appropriable rents, not the total. Likewise, we expect that GENERAL would reduce the value of patents of small firms, but not of highly diversified corporations. Another hypothesis is that the B/ measures of basicness would be more closely related to R&D expenditures than to indicators of performance such as market value. This type of research may pave the way for the wide-scale use of the proposed measures as key variables in empirical studies of innovation.

Appendix

Examples of Patents with High IMPORTF

(i) Patent 4,059,461; Issued: 12/10/1975; Assignee: MIT

IMPORTF $= 380$; NCITING $= 64$

Title: Method for improving the crystallinity of semiconductor films by laser beam scanning and the products thereof.

Titles of sample of citing patents

1. Process for producing coarse-grain crystalline/mono-crystalline metal and alloy films

2. Method of making Schottky barrier diode by selective beam-crystallized polycrystalline/amorphous layer

3. Semiconductor embedded layer technology including permeable base transistor, fabrication method

4. Polycrystalline semiconductor processing

5. Method for manufacturing a semiconductor device having regions of different thermal conductivity

6. Metal surface modification

7. Process for manufacturing a semiconductor device having a non-porous passivation layer

8. Method of fabricating display with semiconductor circuits on monolithic structure and flat panel display produced thereby

9. Method of fabricating semiconductor devices using laser annealing

(ii)   Patent 4,071,753, Issued: 31/03/1975; Assignee: GTE Laboratories Inc.

IMPORTF $= 212.5$; NCITING $= 53$

Title: Transducer for converting acoustic energy directly into optical energy [using optical fibers].

Titles of sample of citing patents

1. Fiber optic magnetic sensors

2. Acoustic to optical pulse code modulating transducer

3. Method and sensor device for measuring a physical parameter utilizing an oscillatory, light modulation element

4. Alarm device with a condition sensor element

5. Fiber optic accelerometer

6. Fiber optics transducers for sensing parameter magnitude

7. Fiber optic hydrophone transducers

8. Coupled waveguide acousto-optic hydrophone

9. Fiber optics transducers for sensing parameter magnitude

References

Arrow, K. J., "Economic Welfare and the Allocation of Resources for Inventions," in R. Nelson (ed.) *The Rate and Direction of Inventive Activity*, Princeton University Press, 1962.

Berry, Clifton F., Jr., *Inventing the Future*. Washington: Brassey's Inc., 1993.

Caballero, R., and Jaffe, A., "How High are the Giants' Shoulders: An Empirical Assessment of Knowledge Spillovers and Creative Destruction in a Model of Economic Growth." In O. Blanchard and S. Fisher, eds., *NBER Macroeconomic Annual*, Vol. 8, M. I. T. Press, 1993.

Carpenter, M. P., Narin, F., and Wolf, P., "Citation Rates to Technologically Important Patents." *World Patent Information*, Vol. 3. No. 4., 1981.

Carpenter, M., and F. Narin, "Validation Study: Patent Citations as Indicators of Science and Foreign Dependence," *World Patent Information*, Vol. 5, No. 3, pp. 180–185, 1983.

Cockburn, I., and Z. Griliches, "Industry Effects and Appropriability Measures in the Stock Market's Valuation of R&D and Patents." *American Economic Review, Papers and Proceedings*, 1988 (78), pp. 419–423.

Griliches, Z., "Market Value, R&D and Patents." *Economic Letters* (1981) (7), pp. 183–187.

Griliches, Z. (ed.), *R&D, Patents and Productivity*. University of Chicago Press, 1984.

Griliches, Z., "Productivity, R&D and Basic Research at the Firm Level in the 1970's." *American Economic Review*, 1986.

Griliches, Z., "Patent Statistics as Economic Indicators: a Survey," *Journal of Economic Literature*, 1990, 28, pp. 1661–1707.

Henderson, R., Jaffe, A., and Trajtenberg, M., "Universities as a Source of Commercial Technology: A Detailed Analysis of University Patenting 1965–1988," in David, P. and E. Steinmueller (eds.), *A Productive Tension: University-Industry Research Collaboration in the Era of Knowledge-Based Economic Growth*. Stanford University Press, forthcoming 1996.

Jaffe, A., "Technological Opportunity and Spillovers of R&D: Evidence from Firms' Patents, Profits and Market Value," *American Economic Review*, 1986, 76(5), pp. 984–1001.

Jaffe, A., Trajtenberg, M., and Henderson, R., "Geographic Localization of Knowledge Spillovers, as Evidence by Patent Citations." *Quarterly Journal of Economics*, 1993, 108(3), pp. 577–598.

Kuhn, Thomas, *The Structure of Scientific Revolutions*. Chicago: University of Chicago Press, 1962.

Kuznets, S., "Inventive Activity: Problems of Definition and Measurement," in R. Nelson (ed.), *The Rate and Direction of Inventive Activity*, Princeton, NJ: Princeton University Press, 1962.

Levin, R., A. Klevorick, R. R. Nelson, and S. G. Winter, "Appropriating the Returns from Industrial Research and Development," *Brookings Papers on Economic Activity*, 1987, 3, 783–820.

National Science Foundation, *Science and Technology Data Book*, Washington, D.C.: NSF 1992.

Nelson, R., "The Simple Economics of Basic Scientific Research," *Journal of Political Economy*, 1959.

Nelson, R., "The link between science and invention: the case of the transistor," in R. Nelson (ed.), *The Rate and Direction of Inventive Activity*. Princeton University Press, 1962.

Office of Technology Assessment and Forecast (OTAF), U.S. Department of Commerce, Patent and Trademark Office, *Seventh Report*. Washington D.C.: U.S. Government Printing Office, 1977.

Pakes, Ariel, "On Patents, R&D, and the Stock Market Rate of Return." *Journal of Political Economy*, 1985, 93(2), pp. 390–409.

Pakes, Ariel, "Patents as Options: Some Estimates of the Value of Holding European Patent Stocks." *Econometrica*, 1986, 54(4), pp. 755–784.

Rosenberg, N., *Inside the Black Box: Technology and Economics*. Cambridge, England: Cambridge University Press, 1982.

Trajtenberg, M., "A Penny for Your Quotes: Patent Citations and the Value of Innovations," *Rand Journal of Economics*, 1990a, 21(1), pp. 172–187.

Trajtenberg, M., *Economic Analysis of Product Innovation: The Case of CT Scanners*. Cambridge, MA: Harvard University Press, 1990b.

Van Raan (ed.), *Handbook of Quantitative Studies of Science and Technology*, Amsterdam: North Holland, 1988.

Weingart, P., R. Sehringer, and M. Winterhager, "Bibliometric Indicators for Assessing Strengths and Weaknesses of West German Science." Ch. 13 in Van Raan (ed.), *Handbook of Quantitative Studies of Science and Technology*. Amsterdam: North Holland, 1988.

4

**How High Are the Giants'
Shoulders: An Empirical
Assessment of Knowledge
Spillovers and Creative
Destruction in a Model of
Economic Growth**

Ricardo J. Caballero and
Adam B. Jaffe

1 Introduction and Summary

There has been a rapid growth in recent years in the theoretical literature on industrial research as an engine of economic growth.[1] At a gross level, two key concepts are at the heart of the growth process in this literature. First, profit-seeking firms try to achieve market power by producing a better good than their competitors. Over time, new goods displace old ones, earn profits for some period of time, and are then displaced in turn. This process of "creative destruction" generates the incentive for and limits the private value of industrial innovation:

... The fundamental impulse that sets and keeps the capitalist engine in motion comes from the new consumers' goods, the new methods of production or transportation, the new markets, the new forms of industrial organization that capitalist enterprises creates ... [examples] ... [these examples] illustrate the same process of industrial mutation that incessantly revolutionizes the economic structure *from within*, incessantly destroying the old one, incessantly creating a new one. This process of Creative Destruction is the essential fact about capitalism.... (Joseph Schumpeter, 1942)

This paper was prepared for the NBER Macroeconomic Annual Meeting, March 14, 1993. We thank Philippe Aghion, Roland Benabou, Andrew Bernard, Olivier Blanchard, Zvi Griliches, Charles Jones, Paul Joskow, Boyan Jovanovic, Sam Kortum, Michael Kremer, Ariel Pakes, Michael Piore, Manuel Trajtenberg, and seminar participants at MIT, NYU, Georgetown, the Productivity group at the NBER, and the NBER Macroeconomic Annual 1993 meeting for their comments. Caballero thanks the National Science and Sloan Foundations for financial support; Jaffe thanks the National Science Foundation. Sam Kortum graciously shared his data on U.S. priority patents. We are particularly indebted to Manuel Trajtenberg, who created the patent citation data extract used in Section 3.2, and did so under extreme time pressure. We thank Olivier Blanchard for instigating our collaboration.

1. See Grossman and Helpman (1991a) and the references therein, in particular, Romer (1990), Grossman and Helpman (1991b), Aghion and Howitt (1992), Segerstrom (1991).

Thus, Schumpeter recognized that innovation was the engine of growth, and that innovation is endogenously generated by competing profit-seeking firms. The second key feature of models of this process is that public-good aspects of knowledge create economywide increasing returns. In the process of creating new goods, inventors rely and build on the insights embodied in previous ideas; they achieve their success at least partly by "standing upon the shoulders of giants."[2] The public stock of knowledge that accumulates from the spillovers of previous inventions is thus a fundamental input in the technology to generate new ideas. This is clearly reflected in Schmookler's (1966) description of the inventor's problem:

... the joint determinants of inventions are (a) the wants which inventions satisfy, and (b) the intellectual ingredients of which they are made. The inventor's problem arises in a world of work and play, rest and action, frustration and satisfaction, health and sickness, and so on.... [I]n order to analyze the problem, to imagine possible solutions to it, to estimate their relative cost and difficulty, and to reduce one or more to practice, the inventor must use the science and technology bequeathed by the past....

The rich theoretical development of the growth literature can thus be seen as combining the insights of Schumpeter and Schmookler and embedding them in a general equilibrium framework. This modeling advance has not, however, been accompanied by the development of a parallel empirical literature.[3] While there has been significant empirical work on different aspects of the microeconomics of technological change, there has been relatively little attempt to integrate individual micro empirical results into an overall framework for understanding growth. Our aim in this paper is to create a framework for incorporating the microeconomics of creative destruction and knowledge spillovers into a model of growth, and to do so in such a way that we can begin to measure them and untangle the forces that determine their intensity and impact on growth.

We develop a model in the spirit of Grossman and Helpman (1992) and Aghion and Howitt (1992) that gives a simple relationship for the effect of new products on the value of existing ones. At any given time, the economy consists of a continuum of monopolistically com-

---

2. "If I have seen further (than you and Descartes) it is by standing upon the shoulders of Giants." Sir Isaac Newton, letter to Robert Hook, February 5, 1675. Newton's aphorism was popularized by Robert K. Merton, *On the Shoulders of Giants*, New York (1965).
3. A notable exception is Kortum (1993).

petitive goods indexed by their quality, $q \in (-\infty, N_t]$. The newest goods are always the best, i.e., the process of research advances the frontier by increasing N_t. Because of the quality ranking implicit in this process, constant marginal cost producers see their profits— relative to those of the (new) leader—decline over time. The rate of decline depends (positively) on the degree of substitutability between new and old goods and on the pace at which new goods are introduced. This captures the endogenous process of creative destruction described earlier and, after a few algebraic steps, yields intuitive equations relating the rate of growth in a firm's value relative to that of the industry to the firm's number of new ideas relative to the industry average. By relating the concept of new ideas to that of new patents, it is possible to use these equations to gauge the empirical magnitude of creative destruction.

In order to estimate these equations, we use market value and patents data on 567 large U.S. firms. The data are annual for the period 1965–1981, and the firms are assigned to 21 technological sectors. We estimate 21 sectoral panels and find that, on average (over time and sectors), creative destruction is about 4% per year. That is, in an average sector at an average year a firm that does not invent sees its value relative to that of the industry erode by about 4%. This number varies widely across sectors; drugs has the largest average creative destruction, with about 25% per year.[4] Because of both the endogenous variation in creative destruction and changes in estimated parameters, we also find a sharp decline in average (across sectors) creative destruction over our sample period, from a high of 7% per year in the mid-1960s to a low of 2% in the late 1970s.

Turning from Schumpeter to Schmookler, we focus on the technology by which new ideas are produced, using as inputs private research effort and the public stock of existing ideas. We focus particularly on this ideas-stock, the process by which it accumulates, and the way in which it conditions the production of new ideas.

It is well known that the standard form of the kind of "quality ladder" model that we are using embodies a strong form of research spillovers, because the same amount of resources are consumed

---

4. We argue that, at least in part, this dispersion is due to the difficulties in measuring ideas, because patents play different roles in protecting innovation in different sectors. In other industries other mechanisms of appropriations, such as secrecy, learning curve advantages, and marketing and product support efforts are more important than patents as means of securing rents (Levin et al., 1987).

producing the blueprint for product $q = N_t$ at time t as were consumed producing the blueprint for product $q = N_{t-dt}$ at time $t - dt$,
even though the former is strictly superior to the latter. To pursue
Newton's metaphor, today's inventors stand on the shoulders of
giants that keep getting taller and never get old and weak. In order
to move to a spillover formulation that can be implemented empirically, we specify how the height of the shoulders is endogenously
determined by the path of previous invention.

We postulate a simple linear technology at the firm level, mapping
research inputs into new ideas. This mapping changes over time as a
function of the stock of public knowledge. That is, the productivity
of private inputs in research varies as a function of aggregate knowledge, which is outside the control of any individual firm. We proceed
to specify in some detail the process by which previous knowledge
accumulates and feeds into the generation of new ideas. We postulate that it takes time for additional knowledge to diffuse sufficiently
to be of use to other inventors; this tends to limit the usefulness of
very recent knowledge in generating new knowledge. On the other
hand, old knowledge eventually is made obsolete by the emergence
of newer, superior knowledge. We call this phenomenon "knowledge" or "technological" obsolescence, and distinguish it from the
obsolescence in value represented by creative destruction. That is,
new ideas have two distinct effects on the current stock of ideas. They
make the products represented by those ideas less valuable (creative
destruction or value obsolescence), and they make the knowledge
represented by those ideas less relevant in the production of new
knowledge (knowledge or technological obsolescence). The strength
of knowledge spillovers, and hence the growth of the economy, will
depend on the parameters of the processes of knowledge diffusion
and knowledge obsolescence.

At any point in time, we define the stock of knowledge available
to the production of new ideas as the sum of the contribution of all
previous ideas. These contributions are the product of the number of
ideas in each cohort and the usefulness of the average idea in that
cohort to current inventions. We describe the usefulness of an idea
generated at time s for the production of new knowledge at time t
$(t \geq s)$ in terms of a *citation function*. In order to capture knowledge
obsolescence, this function declines with the distance between t and
s in ideas-space—i.e., with the number of inventions that occur between the recipient and source cohorts. In order to capture gradual

knowledge diffusion, the usefulness of old ideas increases with the calendar time between these two cohorts. We also allow for a source-cohort specific multiplicative constant that indexes the potency of the spillovers emanating from the average idea in the given cohort.

In order to estimate the citation function, we use a 1 in 100 random sample of all patents granted in the United States from 1975 to 1992, and track all their citations to previous patents back to 1900. We assume that patents are proportional to ideas and that citations are proportional to ideas used, and we estimate time-varying proportionality factors for each along with the model parameters. Our sample contains 12,592 patents and over 80,000 citations.

Several interesting findings emerge from estimating the citation function and from constructing the stock of public knowledge implied by this function. First, we find that ideas diffuse quite rapidly, with a mean lag between one and two years, which is consistent with previous estimates by Mansfield (1985) derived from survey results. Second, as postulated, knowledge obsolescence is clearly an endogenous function of the number of new ideas, rather than an exogenous function of time. The sum of squared residuals falls by about 30% when straight time depreciation is replaced by endogenous obsolescence linked to the number of new ideas. Third, the average annual rate of knowledge or technological obsolescence over the century is about 7%, but both its secular and high-frequency (endogenous) changes are quite large. It rises from about 3% at the beginning of the century to about 10–12% in 1990, with a noticeable plateau during the 1970s. Fourth, the average size of patents (measured in terms of the average number of new ideas embodied in each of these) increased over the century until the 1960s or 1970s and has declined since then. A patent in 1990 seems to contain about three times more ideas than a patent in 1900, but about 10% less than a patent in 1970. Fifth, the potency of the spillovers emanating from each cohort seems to have declined dramatically over the century: Controlling for obsolescence, we estimate that the average idea at the beginning of the century generated about five times the level of spillovers as the average recent idea. Finally, as a result of this decline in spillover potency, we estimate that the effective (or marginal) public knowledge stock declined by about 30% from 1960 to 1990, suggesting that private research productivity should have fallen by that amount.

This last result is subject to a number of caveats relating to assumptions about the exact nature of the relationship between spillovers and citations. Its implications are, however, remarkably consonant with the data on the observed productivity of inputs in research. The observed decline in the productivity of private research, as measured by patent production, has been a subject of much research.[5] The ratio of patents to research inputs has declined steadily since the 1950s, almost regardless of the way research-input is measured (e.g., R&D expenditures, number of scientists and engineers engaged in research.)[6] It is certainly interesting, if not surprising, that our independent measure of research productivity, which is based on knowledge flows as measured by citations, has about the same trend as directly measured productivity. Put differently, the fit of the aggregate innovation function—i.e., the function that relates aggregate (private) research inputs to total innovations—improves markedly once we include our measure of the public stock of knowledge on the right-hand side.

In the last step of the empirical section, we relate aggregate consumption growth to the rate of new idea creation. In effect, this amounts to finding the normalization constant that allows us to estimate the overall average size of a patent—a parameter that is not identified from the citation estimation alone. With this, we have empirical estimates of all of the important model parameters. Combining these estimates with a free-entry condition in the research sector and a labor market equilibrium condition, we close the model and calibrate it to fit the average rate of growth of the United States during the postwar period. The model can then be used to perform several positive and normative experiments. Although we are uncomfortable making too much of results that depend on a long sequence of assumptions and approximations, we note that the model's behavior (1) is quite consistent with the aggregate productivity slowdown in the 1970s, (2) is also consistent with the stock market boom of the 1980s (because the estimated decline in the productivity of research implies an increase in the value of existing ideas), and (3) suggests that the optimal subsidy to private R&D expenditures is around 30%.

We do not view these specific results (which are perhaps better categorized as provocative conjectures) as the main contribution of the paper. Rather, we have shown that it is possible to construct an overall modeling framework into which the key microeconomic

---

5. See Griliches (1989 and 1990), Kortum (1993), and Evenson (1991).

6. See Kortum (1993). Schmookler (1966) suggests that patents per research effort has been declining throughout the century.

pieces of the processes of industrial innovation and growth can be fit, and empirical estimates of the model parameters do allow the model to mimic the economy's gross growth behavior.

The next pages describe the details behind this summary. We begin in Section 2 with the complete presentation of the model itself. Section 3 presents the empirical methodology and results; for reasons explained therein it is organized in a different order than this summary and the model presentation, beginning with the citation function and ending with the creative destruction equation. Section 4 calibrates the model and studies the impact of different policy and structural changes on growth and research incentives. Section 5 concludes the paper with a discussion of the overall significance of the results and suggestions for future work.

2 The Model

2.1 Goods Markets

There is a representative agent endowed with a stock of ideas, $\bar{L}$ units of labor, which have no direct utility value; an instantaneous utility function that is logarithmic in an aggregate consumption index, C_t; and a discount factor, ρ. Using aggregate consumption as numeraire and letting r_t represent the real interest rate, we obtain the standard condition on the growth rate of consumption, $\hat{C}_t$:

$$\hat{C}_t = r_t - \rho. \tag{1}$$

At any point in time, the aggregate consumption index is a composite of the quality weighted output of a continuum of monopolistic competitors, which produce goods indexed by their quality: $x_t(q)$ for $q \in (-\infty, N_t]$. Quality rises monotonically over time, so newer goods are better:[7]

$$C_t \equiv \left[\int_{-\infty}^{N_t} \{x_t(q)e^q\}^\alpha \, dq \right]^{1/\alpha} \quad 0 \leq \alpha \leq 1. \tag{2}$$

Given aggregate consumption and the prices of each of the components of it, $p_t(q)$, consumers choose $x_t(q)$ so as to minimize the cost

---

7. It is important to realize that the quality ladder aspect is in *addition* to the monopolistically competitive structure of the market. Stokey's (1992) elegant and general representation of preferences includes a discrete state space version of ours.

of that level of aggregate consumption:

$$\int_{-\infty}^{N_t} p_t(q) x_t(q) \, dq.$$

The first-order condition for this problem yields the system of demands for goods of different qualities:

$$x_t(q) = p_t(q)^{(-1/1-\alpha)} e^{(\alpha/1-\alpha)q} C_t. \tag{3}$$

At each point in time, producers take these demand functions, as well as factor (labor) prices, w_t, as given. For simplicity, let the production technology be linear and assume that process innovations have no distributive impact:[8]

$$x_t(q) = \eta_t L_t^p(q), \tag{4}$$

where $L_t^p(q)$ is labor allocated to production of $x_t(q)$ and η_t is labor productivity in the final goods sector at time t. More generally, this may be taken as the reduced form of a constant returns to scale technology including other factors of production. In the latter case the rental price of other factors would combine to add a multiplicative constant to the reduced form production function.

The linearity of technology, together with the common level of productivity and elasticities of demand faced by the infinitesimal producers of the different qualities, determines that at any given point in time all prices are identical and obey a standard markup rule:[9]

$$p_t(q) = \frac{1}{\alpha} \frac{w_t}{\eta_t}.$$

Replacing this expression in Equation (3) and the results of it in Equation (2), determines the consumption wage:

$$w_t = \alpha \eta_t \left(\frac{1-\alpha}{\alpha}\right)^{(1-\alpha/\alpha)} e^{N_t}.$$

Thus, the price can also be expressed in terms of labor's productivity in the goods sector, η_t, and the quality level of the leading good, N_t:

---

8. That is, these innovations affect the technologies of goods of all qualities similarly.
9. Because of their lower quality, older goods will have smaller market shares, but because of the assumed desire for variety they never disappear completely (except in the limiting case $\alpha = 1$).

$$p_t(q) = \left(\frac{1-\alpha}{\alpha}\right)^{(1-\alpha/\alpha)} e^{N_t}.$$

Profits accruing to a producer of a good of quality q can now be easily determined from the equilibrium values of $x_t(q)$, $p_t(q)$, and w_t:[10]

$$\pi_t(q) = \alpha C_t e^{(-\alpha/1-\alpha)(N_t-q)}.$$

It is interesting to notice that profits do not fall with increases in α for all levels of q. This is due to a *scope* effect. As goods become more substitutable, the profits generated by having a new—the best—good increase in spite of the reduced markup because the new product has a larger potential market. The other side of this is that goods become obsolete much faster (for a given rate of entry) because many newer goods can substitute them away: Simply put, a stronger creative destruction environment—indexed by α—is better for those that are creating and worse for those that have created in the past.

2.2 Valuation, Innovation, and Labor Market

The fundamental value of a new market created at time t is:

$$v_t = \int_t^\infty \pi_\tau(N_t) e^{-\int_t^\tau r_s\,ds}\,d\tau.$$

Dividing both sides by aggregate consumption, letting $V_t \equiv v_t/C_t$, differentiating this ratio with respect to time, and recalling Equation (1), yields a differential equation characterizing the dynamic behavior of the value of an innovation in terms of units of consumption:

$$\dot{V}_t = \left(\rho + \frac{\alpha}{1-\alpha}\dot{N}_t\right)V_t - \frac{\pi_t(N_t)}{C_t}.$$

Replacing the expression for profits in this equation yields:

$$\dot{V}_t = \left(\rho + \frac{\alpha}{1-\alpha}\dot{N}_t\right)V_t - \alpha, \tag{5}$$

---

10. Note that if the number of varieties is "small," as is the case in the standard variety model without quality ranking where $q \in [0, N_t]$, profits would be $\pi_t(q) = \alpha C_t e^{(-\alpha/1-\alpha)(N_t-q)}/(1 - e^{(-\alpha/1-\alpha)/N_t})$. The ranking aspect of quality introduces a "discounting-like" component to the aggregators so we can work immediately with an "infinite-variety" model. This eliminates a host of short-run dynamics issues that are standard in variety models. Also see Stokey (1992).

which is to be compared with the change in the value (in terms of units of consumption) of the idea that has just been left behind the frontier, V_t^0:

$$\dot{V}_t^0 = \rho V_t - \alpha. \tag{6}$$

Comparing Equations (5) and (6) shows that the "obsolescence" rate faced by owners of blueprints is $(\alpha/1 - \alpha)\dot{N}_t$, which we call the rate of creative destruction. It is proportional to the rate of advancement of the knowledge frontier. It also depends on consumers' demand for variety; as α approaches unity, the market share of the newest product approaches unity, so we truly have a "gale" of creative destruction. One focus of our empirical work will be to provide estimates of this term for different industries and periods. We return to this later.

The other side of the value of an innovation is the cost of generating it. As is standard in the literature, we postulate a simple linear research technology at the *firm* level. A firm that invests L_{it}^r units of effort in the time interval dt generates $\theta_t L_{it}^r\, dt$ new blueprints.[11] These blueprints are worth $\theta_t L_{it}^r V_t C_t\, dt$ to the inventing firm; thus, free entry guarantees that:

$$w_t \geq \theta_t V_t C_t,$$

with equality if there is positive innovation.

Aggregating over all innovators yields the demand for labor by the research sector:[12]

$$L_t^r = \frac{\dot{N}_t}{\theta_t}.$$

Similarly, we can obtain the demand for labor by goods producers, L_t^p:

$$L_t^p = \int_{-\infty}^{N_t} \frac{x_t(q)}{\eta_t}\, dq = \frac{\alpha C_t}{w_t}.$$

---

11. θ_t is assumed to be deterministic at the aggregate (sectoral) level; we will model it later as a function of past knowledge accumulation in the sector. We will assume that θ_t is independent of current and previous actions by i, so the value of any particular firm is just the goods market value of its blueprints. In other words, firms do not have private stocks of past knowledge. We discuss this issue further in Section 3.2.

12. Note that θ_t may depend on aggregate quantities, including L_t^r, although in the latter case the notation is less useful.

Full employment equilibrium in the labor market is then obtained by letting:

$$L_t^p + L_t^r = \bar{L}. \tag{7}$$

2.3   Spillovers, Knowledge Diffusion, and Knowledge Obsolescence

The innovation function described in words above corresponds to the demand for labor in the research sector, rearranged:

$$\dot{N}_t = \theta_t L_t^r. \tag{8}$$

This equation hides in θ_t most of what is of interest to economists. It is the average productivity of research in generating new blueprints; it may contain standard *aggregate* factors of production (e.g., capital and labor)[13] as well as spillovers from past knowledge production. We will focus on the latter but discuss briefly the former in the empirical section.

With few exceptions, the standard endogenous growth model treats θ_t as an arbitrary given constant. Such a specification conveys a strong form of intertemporal spillover, where the quality of new goods builds one for one on the top of the quality of the previous generation of goods. Labor productivity in research—i.e., θ_t—is independent of the level or pace at which ideas emerge, and is disconnected from the spillover process itself.

In this section we explicitly model several aspects of the process of diffusion of information that should influence θ_t. In particular, we consider three types of factors. First, there is the concept of endogenous obsolescence. Very old ideas are unlikely to contain much independent information that is useful for generating new ideas. Unlike the traditional notion of "depreciation," the obsolescence of old ideas ought to be connected to the distance between ideas in the state rather than the time dimension. That is, it is not the passage of time that makes old ideas less useful, it is the accumulation of new ideas. Second, inventors take time in seeing others' inventions, which suggests that there are diffusion lags. Unlike obsolescence, we treat the diffusion of knowledge as a function of time rather than

---

13. With either positive or negative coefficients, thus, with increasing or decreasing aggregate returns to scale in the research technology.

accumulated inventions.[14] Third, the spillover intensity between cohorts of ideas may vary independent of the effect of obsolescence of old ideas.

We capture these factors of the transmission mechanism by means of a "citations" function, $a(t,s)$ for $t \geq s$. We assume that this function depends on the probability of seeing or knowing about an idea $(t-s)$ years old; and the usefulness of old ideas in generating new ones. We take the probability of seeing an idea $(t-s)$ years old to be $(1 - e^{-\gamma(t-s)})$. As $\gamma \to \infty$, diffusion becomes instantaneous; $\gamma = 0$ means that all old blueprints are unavailable, so each inventor starts from scratch. In order to capture the first and last factors mentioned earlier, we assume an index of usefulness of the form $\delta e^{-\beta(N_t - N_s)}$. The term in the exponential reflects the notion that the usefulness of old ideas in the generation of new ideas depends on how far the technology has moved since the old idea. The parameter δ could capture two distinct effects. It could represent the "potency" of the spillovers emanating from each cohort of ideas. It could also represent an "absorption" parameter, measuring the intensity of use of old ideas by new ideas. The former interpretation implies that δ might vary over s; the latter interpretation suggests the possibility of variation over t. In principle, one could imagine interaction effects, i.e., variations over (s, t) pairs. In the empirical section, we focus on variation in δ over s, i.e., variations in the potency of the spillovers emanating from different cohorts of old knowledge. There are a combination of conceptual and practical reasons for this, as will be discussed later. For now we simply treat δ as a constant, because this simplifies the explanation of the basic elements of the process of knowledge accumulation.

The citations function is the product of the usefulness of old ideas and the probability of having seen them:[15]

$$a(t,s) = \delta e^{-\beta(N_t - N_s)}(1 - e^{-\gamma(t-s)}) \qquad t \geq s, \tag{9}$$

with $\gamma \geq 0$, $\beta \geq 0$, and $0 \leq \delta \leq 1$.

---

14. Some state dependency of knowledge diffusion is likely, but it seems plausible that time would be the primary factor.

15. We have saved on notation by working with a single-sector model, but it would be straightforward (from a modeling perspective) to add multiple sectors, with differing rates of obsolescence and diffusion within and across sectors. Empirical implementation of the multisector version would not be trivial. We will comment further on this in Section 5 later.

We let θ_t be the sum over all the potentially "citable" cohorts of ideas:[16]

$$\theta_t \equiv \int_{-\infty}^{N_t} a(t, s(q)) \, dq = \int_{-\infty}^{t} a(t, s) \dot{N}_s \, ds,$$

which can be written as:

$$\theta_t = \frac{\delta}{\beta} - \delta e^{-(\beta N_t + \gamma t)} \int_{-\infty}^{N_t} e^{\beta q + \gamma s(q)} \, dq. \tag{10}$$

This specification of the productivity of research effort, θ_t, has several interesting features. First, as the speed of diffusion goes to infinity, θ_t converges to a constant:

$$\lim_{\gamma \to \infty} \theta_t = \frac{\delta}{\beta}. \tag{11}$$

The insensitivity of the research productivity parameter to the rate of invention in this limiting case is the result of two offsetting factors. The increased obsolescence of the existing knowledge stock that is inherent in an economy moving (inventing) at a faster pace is exactly offset by the increased rate at which new knowledge is added to that stock. This is illustrated in Figure 1. There, we depict two economies—A and B—starting with the same level of knowledge (normalized to 0), but in A inventions occur at twice the rate of B (for reasons other than parameters of the innovation function). An inventor standing at t_1 in A has a larger number of inventions behind her, but the more rapid rate of invention means that a larger fraction of that stock is now obsolete. Equation (11) says that these forces exactly cancel each other when information diffusion is instantaneous, so that the marginal productivity of research in the two economies would be the same.[17] Put differently, with instantaneous diffusion the right "clock" for spillovers is determined by the number of inventions: If the pace at which these occur increases, so does the speed of the economic clock, bringing about offsetting obsolescence, which leaves the amount of spillover unchanged at the margin.

---

16. It is easy to add other standard ingredients to θ_t, including, e.g., decreasing returns to current labor in research. See, e.g., Kortum (1993), Stokey (1992), Jones (1992). We also comment on this possibility in Section 3.3 below.

17. That is, a given amount of research labor would generate the same $\dot{N}$ in the two economies.

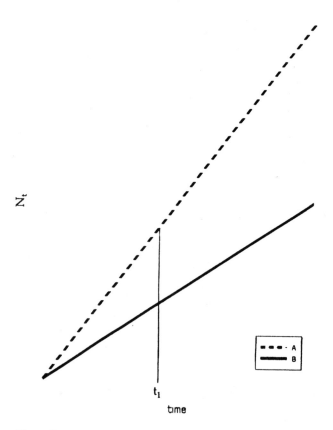

Figure 1
Two economies with different invention rates

Second, for given $\{\dot{N}_s\}_{s \leq t}$, θ_t is proportional to δ, which is the fraction of total knowledge that is of potential use for new inventions. Also, if diffusion is instantaneous, θ_t is inversely proportional to the rate at which new ideas outdate old ones, β. Thus, putting aside diffusion lags, the strength of spillovers depends directly on the exogenous usefulness of old knowledge, δ, and inversely on the rate at which it is made obsolete, β.

The third important feature of our formulation for θ_t is that lags in the diffusion of information—i.e., γ finite—change the relation between the pace of inventions and the productivity of labor in research by introducing a form of dynamic decreasing returns. If we return to Figure 1, if γ is finite it is no longer true that the marginal productivity of labor in research at t_1 is the same in economies A and B. Because of diffusion lags, an increase in the rate of innovation does not add to the stock of knowledge fast enough to offset the higher rate of obsolescence. The fraction of the stock of knowledge observed by inventors in an economy where the rate of inventions is relatively high is limited by the fact that a large amount of inventions have occurred only recently, when things are difficult to observe. In other words, in this case there is a second and exogenous clock that anchors the economy.[18] Thus, the productivity of research θ_t decreases with the rate of invention.

The next step in presenting the model is to describe the dynamic equilibrium behavior of the model. We postpone this until after estimating the key parameters of the model, for then the examples used to characterize equilibrium can be made more meaningful.

3 Empirical Analysis

3.1 Overview

The previous section presented a general equilibrium model of the processes of knowledge accumulation, research, innovation, product market competition, and economic growth. To estimate the parameters of the model and to test its predictions against economic experience requires finding measurable empirical constructs that correspond to the elements of the model. In this section, we plunge in and make attempts to estimate each of the important blocks of the model. We do not attempt to estimate the overall system of equations implied by the model as a whole, because the theoretical and empirical compromises that are necessary to find empirical counterparts to the model constructs cannot really be applied consistently across the different parts of the model. For example, the model has a highly stylized notion of "firms" who own no assets other than blueprints. The creative destruction Equation (5) describes the time path of the value of blueprints or ideas. To estimate this equation,

---

18. Although the model makes a stark distinction between lags (which occur by the "time clock") and obsolescence (which occurs by the "invention clock"), the effects discussed here will occur as long as the speed of diffusion is less responsive to changes in the rate of innovation than is technological obsolescence.

we will use data on real firms.[19] To do this, we will derive the model's implications for the value of a firm, conceived as a collection of blueprints. This will involve assumptions that we believe are reasonable, but we do not go back and work out the overall implications of these assumptions for the model as a whole. Similarly, confronting the data will require us to allow for lags between invention and patent applications, patent applications and patent grants, invention and new product introduction, etc. We try to allow for these lags in reasonable ways, but we do not formally incorporate them into the overall model. To say it differently, we recognize that the loose correspondence between the model and the data prevents us from interpreting the model too literally.

In the following subsections we will discuss measurement issues in some detail. Overall, we will use patents as corresponding to ideas, implying the number of patents in a period, country, sector, etc. can be taken as proportional—sometime with lags—to the corresponding N. We treat firms as agglomerations of ideas, represented by their patent holdings; we take their market value as representing the value of their idea portfolio. We use counts of Research Scientists and Engineers to represent research labor, although we explore the use of R&D expenditures as well. Finally, we use consumption expenditure from the National Income Accounts to measure total expenditure.

We present the empirical results in approximately the reverse order from the model development. We begin with the construction of θ_t, the productivity of labor in research. To do this, we use a random sample of all U.S. patents granted since 1975, and the complete history of previous patents cited by our sample patents. We take a citation as evidence that the earlier knowledge was used in the later invention, suggesting that the frequency of citation can be used to measure $a(t, s)$ in Equation (9). Because we observe many (t, s) pairs, we can estimate the parameters δ and γ of Equation (9), while at the same time estimating a (time-varying) proportionality factor between patents and βN. From this estimation, we construct an estimate of θ_t (up to additive and multiplicative factors).

---

19. The closest thing to an empirical analogue of the value of an idea is the work of Schankerman and Pakes (1986), Pakes (1986), and Pakes and Simpson (1989) on the value of patents. As these authors emphasize, however, they are estimating the value of patent protection, i.e., the *difference* between the value of the idea if it is patented and its value if it is not. Pakes (1985) estimates the stock market response to the "news" represented by a new patent. Thus, his estimates of the value of a patent exclude the portion that was predictable based on past patents and R&D.

Next, we move to the innovation function, Equation (8). Using the constructed θ_t from the citation distributions, we estimate the relationship between patents and corporate research at the aggregate level in the United States. We show that by converting patents to $\dot{N}$ using the parameter estimates from the first step, including θ_t, and normalizing the research measures in the way implied by the model, we can improve the fit between patents and research, and shed light on the puzzle noted by many researchers of the falling patent/R&D ratio in the last several decades (Griliches, 1989; Kortum, 1993). In Section 3.4, we look at the aggregate U.S. relationship between $\dot{N}$ and the growth rate of consumption, and compare it to the prediction of Equation (21). We find that the low-frequency movements in consumption follow a pattern very similar to those in $\dot{N}$, although displaced in time by a few years. We conjecture that this is consistent with the model if there is a lag (not in the model) between the act of invention and the product market introduction of new goods. Finally, we return to the value side of the model. We estimate a version of Equation (5), the "creative destruction" equation, using data on firms assigned to technological sectors. We construct estimates of the rates of endogenous obsolescence or creative destruction for these sectors during the decade of the 1970s.

3.2 Knowledge Diffusion, Technological Obsolescence, and Patent Citations

As discussed in Section 2.3, the limiting form of the model has a strong form of spillovers in which the incremental innovation always comes at the same cost, regardless of how far knowledge has advanced. More realistically, inventors can build on the existing stock of knowledge, but there are limits on its usefulness in creating the next idea. Equation (10) captures the more general case in which the research productivity parameter θ_t depends on the stock of existing ideas, with each existing idea weighted by the probability that it is useful in generating new knowledge at time t. These probabilities are, in turn, dependent on the likelihood that the previous idea is known to a current inventor, and the likelihood that it is useful.

To implement this approach, we use patents as an indicator of the creation of new ideas, and the "citations" (also called references) that patents make to previous patents as an indicator of "existing ideas used in the creation of new ideas." There is a vast literature on the virtues and vices of patent data, which addresses such issues as the large number of inventions that are never patented; variations in the "propensity to patent" of different institutions, different industries and over time; and the large variability in the "size" or importance of individual patents.[20] For our purposes, we will simply assume that $\dot{N}_t$ is proportional to the rate of patenting at time t, with the proportionality factor treated as a (time-varying) parameter to be estimated.

When a patent is granted, the patent document identifies a list of references or citations, which are previous patents upon which the current patent builds.[21] The citations serve the legal function of identifying previous patents that delimit the property right conveyed by the patent. Because citations indicate that a current invention builds on an older one, we will use the total number of citations *from* patents issued in year t *to* patents issued in year s as an indicator of the use of knowledge of vintage s in the production of new ideas at time t. Of course, not all citations represent spillovers; it is possible, e.g., that the inventor was not even aware of the earlier work at the time the invention was made.[22] As with variations in the number of new ideas represented by the average patent, we will deal with variations

---

20. For a recent survey, see Griliches (1990).

21. References are also made to nonpatent materials such as scientific articles; we are not using this information. For an application that does, see Trajtenberg, Henderson, and Jaffe (1992).

22. The final decision as to what citations must appear belongs with the patent examiner, but it is the result of an interactive process involving the inventor, the inventor's attorneys, and the examiner. All of these parties can identify potential citations by searching the relevant "prior art." Until the late 1970s, this was done by hand, using as a guide the Patent Office classification of the patent. Today, all parties have access to on-line text-search capabilities. The incentives faced by each of these parties are complicated. First, the applicant bears a legal obligation to disclose any prior art of which she has knowledge; the primary sanction for nonperformance appears to be the danger of losing the good will of the examiner (who also makes the decisions as to whether the patent will issue, what claims will be permitted, and so forth). Second, the applicant would, in a sense, prefer fewer citations, because citations may limit the scope of the property right. On the other hand, omission of important references can be grounds for invalidation of the patent, giving the applicant an incentive to make sure that citations appear. For the examiner, identifying citations not provided by the applicant is time-consuming. It appears that it is just as common for applicants and their attorneys to press for the inclusion of additional references as it is for them to resist inclusion of references (personal communication, Ms. Jane Myers, U.S. Patent Office). For more discussion on the interpretation of citations as evidence of knowledge flows, see Trajtenberg, Henderson, and Jaffe (1992), and Jaffe, Trajtenberg, and Henderson (1993).

in the relationship between citations and spillovers by allowing a (time-varying) proportionality factor between "ideas used" and citations, and estimating this factor as a parameter. Not surprisingly, the need to allow for this "slippage" between citations and spillovers will limit to some extent the conclusions that we can draw; we return to this issue later.

Thus, the empirical strategy of this subsection is to collect citation frequencies between patent cohorts, and use these to estimate $a(t, s)$ for many t and s. We then estimate econometrically a version of Equation (9), obtaining estimates of the parameters δ and γ, the "potency" of old ideas, and the diffusion rate of knowledge, as well as the proportionality factors that map patents into ideas and citations into "ideas used." Producing these estimates allows us to do two things. First, we can use our estimates of the proportionality factor between patents and ideas to construct a time series for $\dot{N}_t$ from the patent series. Second, we use the estimates of the parameters from the citation function, combined with the $\dot{N}_t$ series, to construct θ_t, the predicted contribution of old knowledge to the production of new ideas.

Our data consist of a 1 in 100 random sample of all patents in the United States granted between the beginning of 1975 and the fall of 1992.[23] Simple statistics on these data are shown in Table 1. They consist of 12,592 patents containing 81,777 citations. The sample varies (because of variations in the overall grant rate) from a low of 443 patents in 1979 to a high of 935 in 1991. We have valid citations going as far back as 1871.[24] Thus, we have observations over "t" from

---

23. Inventors from every country in the world take out patents in the United States. Of course, other countries also grant patents. We will use the phrase "patents in the United States" to refer to patents issued by the U.S. patent office, regardless of the nationality of the inventor or other considerations. In this subsection, we utilize a sample of all such patents. In the next subsection, we will use the phrase "U.S. patents" to mean patents (in the United States) that derive from research in the United States.

24. The citations are identified by patent number in a commercial database produced by Micropatent, Inc. Patent numbers can be used to assign grant years for the patents, because numbers are used sequentially; the patent number of the first patent issued each year back to 1836 is published in the *Historical Statistics of the U.S.* The Micropatent data contain a small but significant number (about .3%) of five-digit cited patents, which if correct would be patents issued before 1871. On inspection of the actual patent documents, we determined that many of these are, in fact, not patent numbers at all but "reissue" numbers. Thus, without manual inspection there is no way to know if any of these five-digit citations are actually valid early patents. Thus, we have simply dropped them from the dataset summarized in Table 1. Citations with six-digit or greater patent numbers appear to all be valid. Because patent number 100,000 was issued in 1870, we treat all citations 1871 or later as valid.

Table 1
Patent statistics by citing cohort

Citing year	Number of sample patents	Total sample citations	Average Citations made per patent	Average lag in years	Median lag in years	Modal lag in years	Average lag in patents	Median lag in patents
1975	694	3,493	5.03	15.30	9	2	838,442	631,512
1976	689	3,352	4.87	14.67	8	2	820,938	569,471
1977	650	3,322	5.11	15.21	8	2	857,036	580,613
1978	651	3,385	5.20	14.93	8	3	846,948	578,342
1979	443	2,391	5.40	15.65	9	3	891,220	644,482
1980	648	3,690	5.69	15.67	9	4	883,639	624,897
1981	650	4,044	6.22	16.12	9	3	908,679	611,175
1982	571	3,716	6.51	16.22	10	4	927,214	677,083
1983	550	3,520	6.40	15.99	10	5	914,550	658,850
1984	662	4,058	6.13	15.39	10	3	887,513	641,609
1985	706	4,733	6.70	16.10	10	3	924,547	632,644
1986	700	4,801	6.86	16.31	11	2	952,094	704,355
1987	821	5,665	6.90	16.39	11	2	970,055	703,255
1988	766	5,487	7.16	15.77	10	3	958,933	650,782
1989	932	7,130	7.65	16.43	11	2	1,003,940	728,840
1990	928	7,458	8.04	15.35	10	3	986,169	713,108
1991	935	7,017	7.50	16.39	10	3	1,056,534	737,182
1992	596	4,515	7.58	16.46	10	3	1,082,150	761,274
All yrs.	12,592	81,777						

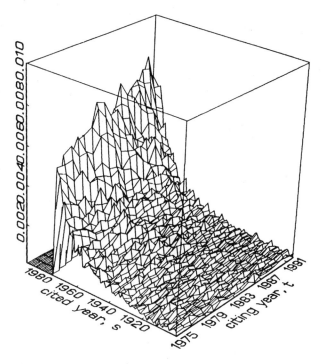

Figure 2a
$a^*[t,s]^*1,000$

1975 to 1992 and "s" from 1871 to 1992. As can be seen from Table 1, the distributions over $(t-s)$ have extremely long tails. The mean lag in years is about 16 years; the median is about 10, and the mode is about 3.

We want to use these citation frequencies to estimate $a(t,s)$. Let $C_{t,s}$ be the observed citations in the sample from patents in year t to patents in year s.[25] Let S_t be the number of sample patents in year t, and P_s be the number of total patents in the United States in year s. Define

$$a^*(t,s) \equiv \frac{C_{t,s}}{S_t P_s}.$$

Thus, $a^*(t,s)$ is an estimate of the probability that a patent in year t cites a patent in year s. Figure 2a shows the distribution of $a^*(t,s)$

25. Patents are dated here by the time of grant. We will discuss timing issues further later.

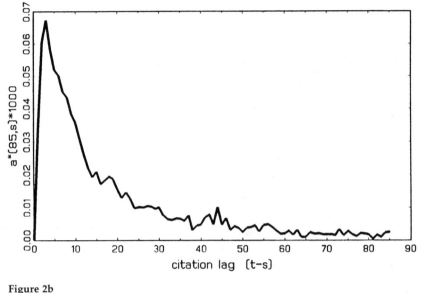

Figure 2b
$a^*[85,s]^*1,000$

over s from 1900 for each t. We restrict ourselves to the distributions since 1900; before that date the citation frequencies are often zero or one, and hence are very noisy estimates of the true frequency.[26] Figure 2b shows the function $a^*(t,s)$ for an arbitrary year (1985). The distributions shown in Figure 2a have the expected "double exponential" shape. Moreover, the increasing part is quite short, suggesting that speed of diffusion is fast. We return to this below.

To go from $a^*(t,s)$ to $a(t,s)$, we must be explicit about the relationships between (1) citations and "used ideas" and (2) patents and $\dot{N}$. We assume that citations are proportional to "used ideas" with a proportionality factor ϕ_t. That is, the patent office and its examiners have a set of rules and practices that determine what patents actually get cited. These do not affect the actual use of old knowledge in the generation of new, but they do affect the number of citations. Further, these practices can change over time. We also assume that $\beta\dot{N}$ is

---

26. We could, of course, estimate the variance of $a^*(t,s)$ and weight accordingly, but these estimations take very long to run as is. We decided that any additional information present in the noisy early years was not worth the increase in computational time necessary to include them.

proportional to patents, with proportionality factor ψ_t.[27] We can think of ψ/β as the "average size" of a patent.[28] Many interpretations can be given to this "size" and its variation over time. One can think of each patent as encompassing a set of distinct ideas. Alternatively, because not all ideas are patented, one can think of ψ/β as the reciprocal of the probability that any given idea is patented. Because we care about ψ only to the extent it lets us use patents for $\dot{N}$, we will consider these different interpretations only to the extent that they help us think about the plausibility of the estimates. Using $C_{t,s}/\phi_t$ for "ideas used" and $(\psi/\beta)P$ for $\dot{N}$, we can write an expression for $a(t,s)$ in terms of observables and parameters:

$$a(t,s) = \frac{C_{t,s}}{(\phi_t/\beta^2)\psi_t S_t \psi_s P_s} = (\beta^2/\phi_t)\psi_t^{-1}\psi_s^{-1}a^*(t,s). \tag{12}$$

Because ϕ_t is purely a measurement parameter, we will absorb $1/\beta^2$ into it and simply write ϕ_t from now on. This gets us almost to the point of being able to rewrite Equation (9) (the expression for the probability than an idea will be used as a function of elapsed time and elapsed N) in term of observables. The only additional step is to note that $(N_t - N_s)$—the number of ideas between s and t—is, under our assumptions, just the number of patents granted between s and t, weighted by the appropriate ψ_s/β. Equation (9) can be rewritten:

$$a^*(t,s) = \phi_t \psi_t \psi_s \delta_s \exp\left(-\beta \sum_{x=s}^{t} \frac{\psi_x}{\beta} P_x \right)(1 - e^{-\gamma(t-s)}), \qquad t \geq s. \tag{13}$$

Equation (13) is the key empirical construct of the paper. Because of the multiplicity of parameters and unfamiliarity of this sort of data, it requires several comments before we proceed to the results. First, because of the need to estimate the proportionality factor between patents and $\dot{N}$, we cannot estimate β from the citation data. That is, we can use Equation (13) to recover from the citation data the *relative* size of patents in different cohorts in terms of ideas, but we cannot estimate the overall average size without bringing in additional information.[29] (We will use the relationship between $\dot{N}$ and growth for this purpose.) Second, because we have multiple

---

27. We choose this parameterization to emphasize that the parameter β is not identified by the patent equation. We will identify it using the growth equation below.
28. The inverse of the "propensity to patent" (Griliches, 1990).
29. Equivalently, we can estimate $\beta\dot{N}$ but not $\dot{N}$.

observations over both s and t, the parameters in this equation are all identified in principle, up to a normalization that sets one δ_s.[30]

Third, although the parameters ϕ_t and δ_s appear symmetrically in Equation (13), we interpret them very differently. We treat ϕ_t—the proportionality factor between "ideas used" and citations—as a pure nuisance parameter, because the citations process holds no interest for us other than as a window on the spillover process. We need to allow ϕ to vary over t because citations per patent have been rising rapidly, and there are good reasons to believe that institutional changes are the reason. On the other hand, δ_s is a key model parameter; its variation over time captures changes in the potency of knowledge spillovers. As already mentioned, we find a significant fall in this potency over the century, and associate this fall with the observed reduced productivity of private research.

It is, of course, crucial for identification that we do not have parameters δ_t and ϕ_s, or δ_{st} and ϕ_{st}. That is, we do not allow the potency of spillovers to depend on the receiving cohort, we do not allow the proportionality factor between citations and "ideas used" to vary with the cited or "used" cohort, and we do not allow "interaction terms" in either. Each of these restrictions requires comment. By not allowing δ to vary over t or st, we are saying that new-invention cohorts do not vary in *their* ability to use the knowledge of the past, and that the potency of a given historic cohort in generating spillovers is a once-and-for-all attribute that does not vary over the succeeding cohorts. In other words, today's inventors may have available to them more or less knowledge than was available to yesterday's inventors, but there is nothing intrinsic about the nature of today's inventions or inventive process that makes previous knowledge more or less useful to today's inventors than yesterday's knowledge was to yesterday's inventors. Further, (holding obsolescence constant) the potency of, e.g., 1920 inventions for facilitating new inventions was the same in 1960 as it is today. In our model, in which quality is a unidimensional attribute so that the "nature" of inventions never really changes, these seem like natural restrictions. In a richer model, in which there were multiple quality dimensions, then one might imagine that the focus of invention today might be more or less similar to that of 1920 than the focus of invention was in 1960, suggesting that potency would

---

30. To see this, it is important to understand that ψ_s and ψ_t are not different parameters; for any given year we have the same "propensity to patent" whether we are looking at that year as a citing or cited year.

vary with t and/or st. Of course, to the extent that variations in citation practices make it necessary to allow for variations in ϕ_t, it is not clear how variations in δ across t could be identified.

The restriction on ϕ, although not empty, seems more innocuous. What we are saying is that the "propensity to cite" past patents does not vary over the different historic cohorts, and that patent office practices may change over time, and this may change the number of citations (holding spillovers constant), but that these changes do not affect past cohorts differentially. Both of these propositions seem to be consistent with our impressions of the examining process. The biggest changes have been computerization of the patent data base, allowing on-line text searches to facilitate identification of citations, changes in the procedures for bringing citations to the examiners' attention that have made it easier to include citations in the patent document, and a perceived increase in the enforcement of the legal obligation on inventors to disclose knowledge of prior art.[31]

A fourth observation of Equation (13) relates to the way the parameter ψ_t—number of ideas per patent over time—enters the equation. Because the flow of new ideas is not observed, any attempt to pin down variations in the propensity to patent requires having a second indicator (besides the rate of patenting) of the rate of knowledge generation.[32] In this case, our second indicator is the rate of decline in the citation of old knowledge. That is, if the patents during some historical period were unusually large, in the sense of incorporating many ideas in each patent, then they should have made previous knowledge obsolete to a greater extent than would be expected based on the number of patents. This will be reflected in the data in the form of a reduced number of citations to these previous periods. Of course, a period with larger than average patents would also receive more citations itself, and that is captured by the presence of ψ_s in front of the exponential.[33] Because of the presence of the δ and ϕ parameters, however, this effect probably contributes less to the estimation of the ψs than the exponential term.[34]

---

31. Personal communication, Jane Meyers, U.S. Patent Office.

32. See Pakes and Griliches (1984).

33. Similarly, if a period's patents are bigger than average, they will *make* more citations; this is captured by the presence of ψ_t out front.

34. If we estimated the model with a free and complete set of the parameters δ_s, there would be no contribution to the estimation of the time pattern of ψ from its presence out front. Because, however, we constrain the δ_s to follow particular functional forms, this is not the case.

Thus, the model has two distinct parameters that relate to the average "importance," broadly speaking, of patents of a given cohort.[35] The variation over time in the parameter ψ captures any differences in the number of new ideas embedded in the average patent. The variation over time in the parameter δ captures variations in the potency (in terms of spillover generation) of the ideas themselves.

Finally, we note that the diffusion of knowledge is assumed to occur at a rate that is measured in time rather than elapsed inventions. This seems natural. It is less obvious that the diffusion parameter γ need be constant over time, but we did not explore its variation.

We estimated variations of Equation (13) by nonlinear least squares on the set of observations consisting of (s, t) pairs with t varying between 1975 and 1992 and s varying between 1990 and t.[36] Although a model in which all of the δs and ψs are allowed to vary over all s and t is identified in principle, we did not attempt to estimate it. Rather, we followed a strategy of (1) always allowing a full set of multiplicative constants ϕ_t, to control for changes in citation practices, and (2) using a combination of dummies over longer time periods and polynomial functions of time to capture variations in both δ and ψ over time.

The results are presented in Table 2. The first column shows the simplest model one could imagine estimating, in which we ignore the "two clocks" and estimate both diffusion and depreciation off of the lag in years between s and t. Not surprisingly (having seen Fig. 1), this model fits the data reasonably well. We get an estimate for γ of about .8, and an estimate for the "obsolescence" rate of about .075 per year. As would be expected from the rising average citations made per patent shown in Table 1, the estimates of ϕ_t rise from 1975 to 1992. This is a result that is apparent in all specifications. Next, we substitute elapsed patents for time in the depreciation term, while still maintaining constancy over time in δ_s and ψ_s. To facilitate interpretation of the results, we use for the terms in the summation in Equation (13) the number of patents in each year divided by the

---

35. Note that the "size" of ideas themselves, in terms of the product quality improvement they allow, does not vary except in the specific way defined by the exponential form in which q enters the aggregate consumption good (Equation (2)).

36. Because the $a^*(t,s)$ are estimated and the frequencies differ greatly, the model is heteroskedastic. We did not deal with this problem explicitly, but dropping the early observations can be interpreted as limiting ourselves to that part of the data in which the heteroskedasticity is likely to be less. The standard errors reported are heteroskedasticity consistent, however.

Table 2
Citation function regression results

Parameter	1	2	3	4
γ	.816	.703	0.707	0.705
	(.019)	(.015)	(0.012)	(0.016)
ψ	.074	.062	a	a
	(.001)	(.001)		
ϕ_{1975}	1.000	1.000	1.000	1.000
	—	—	—	—
ϕ_{1992}	1.244	1.444	1.495	2.066
	(.028)	(.027)	(0.012)	(0.021)
MSE	0.184	0.130	0.124	0.122
2 (LLK − LLKpc)	—	537.6	70.6	15.0

Dependent variable: Sample citations from year t to year s/((Sample patents)$_t$ · (total patents)$_s$). Sample: t from 1975 to 1992; s from 1900 to t.
a. See Figure 2.
Estimates of $\phi_{1976} - \phi_{1991}$ are omitted to conserve space. (LLK − LLKpc): log-likelihood minus the log-likelihood of the previous column.

average (over the whole sample, 1900–1992) number of patents per year. This makes the parameter in front of the term $(N_t - N_s)$ the average annual obsolescence rate; it is therefore directly comparable to the time-obsolescence rate estimated in Column 1. Estimating obsolescence based on patents rather than time improves the fit markedly,[37] and also reduces the average obsolescence rate to just over 6% per year. Because the number of patents is greater in recent years, the observed prevalence of early citations is consistent with a lower average annual obsolescence rate than when the rate is held constant over time.

The third column of Table 2 "frees up" the parameter ψ to vary over both t and s, i.e., it allows for variations in the propensity to patent over time (while still keeping the spillover potency of ideas constant over time). Needless to say, there are many different ways to represent the movement in ψ_t. We explored a number of these, and they generally give similar overall results. The version reported in Column 3 of Table 2 models ψ_t with a single dummy for the years 1900–1919, a second dummy for 1920–1939, a third dummy for 1940–1959, and a cubic equation in the log of t for the period 1960–1992. This improves the fit further, and the parameter estimates are quite significant. The time path of ψ implied by these estimates can be seen

---

37. The sum of squared residuals is reduced by about 30%.

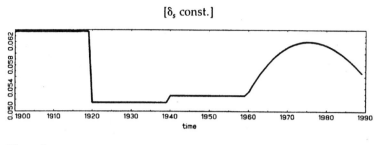

Figure 3a

ψ_t

in Figure 3a. Generally speaking, the path rises over the century, reaching a peak somewhere during the 1970s, and then begins to decline. Again, the patent counts have been divided by the average patents per year so that the magnitude of ψ can be interpreted as the annual rate of obsolescence created by an average year's worth of patents.[38]

Column 4 builds on Column 3 by freeing up δ_s. The parameterization of δ_s is parallel to that for ψ_s, with dummies for long periods early in the century and a cubic equation in t for the period 1960–1992. This yields a similar pattern for ψ_t to what we had before, except in the very beginning of the century. But δ_s moves significantly in the opposite direction, as shown in Figure 3b, falling significantly from the start of the century until about 1960, and then leveling off into a slower decline. As we will see later, the decline in δ_s shown in Figure 3b translates into a secular decline in the predicted productivity of research, θ_t. In other words, knowledge from successive patent cohorts over the century is being incorporated in current patents at rates that imply that the potency of later cohorts in facilitating new knowledge generation is markedly less than the potency of earlier cohorts. Because more recent cohorts get more weight (they are less obsolete) in current knowledge, the predicted effective spillover rate (and hence research productivity) falls over the century.[39]

---

38. The number of patents per year also changes over time, of course, causing the variation in the yearly rate of obsolescence to be much greater than the variation in ψ_t. See Figure 4.

39. One manifestation of this phenomenon is the presence of fat tails in the distribution of the $a^*(t,s)$'s. This is not enough, however: allowing for fat tails in estimation improves the fit but it leaves-to a large extent—unaffected the declining path of δ_s.

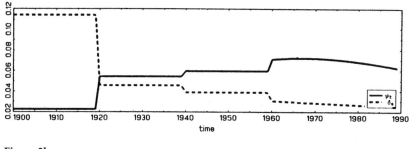

Figure 3b
ψ_t and δ_s

As noted earlier, the estimate of the diffusion parameter γ is not very sensitive to these specification issues. It is consistently about .7 to .8, suggesting an average lag until knowledge has diffused of between one and two years.

For obsolescence, it is not ψ_t that matters, but rather $\psi_t P_t$, which is equal to $\dot{N}' \equiv \beta \dot{N}$. Figure 4 shows different estimates of $\dot{N}'$, compared to the overall patent series itself. What the picture shows is that first, the variations in ψ over time are small relative to the movements in patents. Nonetheless, the "corrected" series does show a noticeably different pattern, particularly at the beginning of the century and from the end of World War II until the late 1970s. In this latter period, our estimate of $\dot{N}'$ increases almost 40% more than the patent series itself. After the early 1970s, ψ_t begins to decline, exacerbating the fall in the rate of patenting itself that occurs between 1970 and the early 1980s. Then patenting picks up again, and although ψ_t is still falling, $\dot{N}'$ picks up as well. It in the next subsection, we turn to a more detailed analysis of trends in $\dot{N}'$ versus trends in patents.

The last output of the citations analysis is the construction of the series θ_t, our estimate of the productivity of labor in research. From Equation (10), θ_t is the integral over all past ideas q of $a(t, s(q))$. We do not observe $a(t, s)$, but the estimated citation equation can be used to construct predicted values of $a(t, s)$, using the parameters γ, δ_s, and ψ_s and the data series P_t. This is easily done by replacing Equation (13) in (12).

Our estimate of θ_t (up to a constant) is then easily obtained from a discrete representation of the definition of θ_t:[40]

---

40. The fact that the summation starts from 0 rather than minus infinity is empirically irrelevant because the first t we study is sufficiently large (60) so the value of the excluded $a(t, s)\dot{N}$, is negligible.

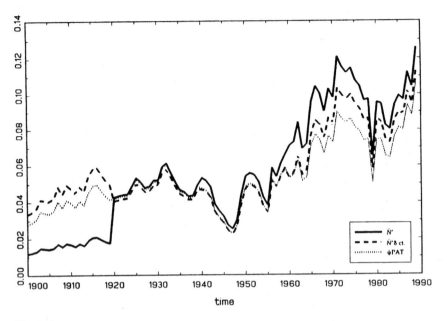

Figure 4
Technological obsolescence

$$\theta_t \approx \sum_{s=0}^{t} a(t,s)\psi_s P_s.$$

In the formulation described previously, in which ϕ_t enters the relationship between $a(t,s)$ and $a^*(t,s)$ but does not affect $a(t,s)$ itself, the parameters ϕ_t do not enter into the construction of $a(t,s)$ or θ_t. We also explore a variation in which we interpret the parameters ϕ_t as representing something real about the use of knowledge rather than a citation artifact. This will change the estimated path of θ_t after 1975.

Two potential estimates of θ_t from the citation function are plotted in Figure 5. The solid line corresponds to Column 4 of Table 2, in which δ_s is allowed to vary over time. It shows a dramatic fall in the predicted productivity of research labor, very rapid from the 1950s to the early 1970s, and then somewhat slower than that. The heavy dashed line in Figure 5 corresponds to Column 2 of Table 2, i.e., it holds δ_s constant over time. It shows a much flatter pattern of research productivity. In the next subsection, we will relate the estimated θ_t to the observed productivity of research in the United States. For now,

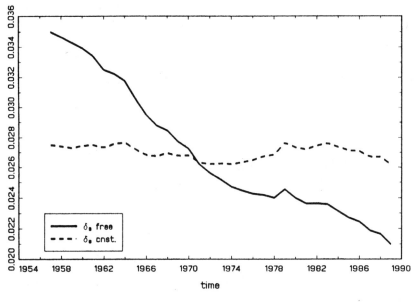

Figure 5
The stock of public knowledge (θ)

it is important to emphasize that this time series is not generated from data on the productivity of research. Rather, it is the model's *prediction* about the path of research productivity, based on the pattern of old knowledge used, as represented by citations, in the production of new knowledge. What is driving the trend is the path of δ_s. In a nutshell, the citations data show that recent cohorts of patents are less cited than older ones (controlling for obsolescence), suggesting that they are less potent in generating spillovers. Because obsolescence makes recent patents more important in the overall stock, the current stock is less potent overall than the stock that was available to previous inventors. With shorter shoulders to stand on, current inventors have to spend more on telescopes in order to see as far as their predecessors did.

Note that the estimated decline in θ_t is conditional on our assumption that the parameter ϕ_t captures only citation behavior and not any change in the actual use of old knowledge. If, on the other hand, one believed that the increase in the raw citation rate that can be seen in the data is a real (exogenous) increase in the use of old knowledge, then we would expect this increase to feed through into rising research productivity. It seems likely, a priori, that the large increase in citation intensities reflects primarily a change in citation practices. In addition, as we will show later, actual research productivity shows no evidence of increasing after 1975 as would be predicted if θ_t were rising steeply.

3.3 The Innovation Production Function

Equation (8) describes the production of innovations as a function of the research labor force L_t^r and a research productivity function or parameter θ_t. In the previous subsection we have developed a method for constructing an estimate of θ_t based on the "use," as evidenced by citations, of older knowledge. In this subsection we will incorporate this estimate into estimates of the innovation function itself.[41] We estimate the innovation function on aggregate time series for patents and two measures of research inputs—R&D spending and research scientists and engineers—for the period 1957–1989. If the data and model are interpreted literally, Equation (8) leaves large serially correlated disturbances unexplained. One possibility is to correct for serial correlation, leaving this dynamic pattern in the disturbance unexplained. Another possibility is to modify the theory so innovations are a direct function of current and lagged research. Doing the latter modifies our model only slightly if the lagged research that matters is the aggregate one, while it makes the theory more cumbersome if lagged research is private. From the point of view of estimation in this section, however, this distinction does not matter. Moreover, this common specification is indistinguishable from a third explanation where the serially correlated disturbance is attributed to the timing of research, innovation, and patenting. We explain and adopt the latter, but it should be clear that we have no strong position on the relative importance of these sources of serial correlation.

We will treat the fundamental innovation equation (8) as holding with respect to unobserved new ideas. These ideas do not, however, lead instantaneously to patent applications. Rather, patent applications P_t are given by:

$$\psi_t P_t = \dot{N}_t^{'ob} = \frac{(1-\rho)\dot{N}_t'}{1-\rho L}.$$

41. We will also use the estimates of ψ_t from the previous subsection to convert patents to $\dot{N}'$. Given the large inflow of foreign patents, this is likely to underestimate the change in size of U.S. patents, for on average there will be more inventions in between subsequent U.S. patents.

Thus, as previously, we allow for a time-varying propensity to patent or proportionality constant between ideas and patents; we call this ψ_t, and we will use the estimates from the previous subsection to convert P_t to $\dot{N}_t^{ob}$. In addition, however, we allow for lags in the conversion of ideas into patent applications. We will estimate these lags, parameterized by ρ, from the innovation function itself. We take the actual productivity parameter, $\tilde{\theta}_t$, to depend on the θ_t estimated earlier and exogenous research productivity: $\tilde{\theta}_t = \eta_0 + \eta_1 \theta_t$. The parameters η_0 and η_1 will also be estimated from the innovation function.

Note that patents are not actually granted until some later date, usually within two to three years of application but occasionally much later. Because this second lag is variable and results from the vagaries of the patent office, we estimate the innovation function using patents by year of application.[42] This is in contrast to our construction of θ_t, and the knowledge diffusion analysis more generally, which used patents by grant year. This was predicated on the assumption that knowledge does not begin to spread until the patent is actually granted. This seems plausible, because patent applications are secret. Only when the patent is granted is the technical knowledge contained in it published. We should note, however, that we will look below at the response of firms' market value to (ultimately successful) patent applications. We are implicitly assuming that, at the time of application, the market knows that an idea has been generated, and responds to that knowledge, even though its technical content is still secret.

We estimate the innovation function using measures of U.S. research inputs, and a measure of U.S. patents. Again, this differs from the previous subsection where, though we are using "patents in the United States," we include patents granted in the United States to foreigners in N. This means that, in estimating the relationship between U.S. research and U.S. patents, we include in the spillover function θ_t all patents, not just U.S. patents. Thus, we are assuming that U.S. research produces U.S. inventions, but it draws upon (and is made obsolete by) worldwide inventions.

It is well known that the productivity of research, as measured by patent output, shows a long-term decline from the 1950s until the

---

42. This is the standard practice in the patent literature. See, e.g., Hausman, Hall, and Griliches (1984).

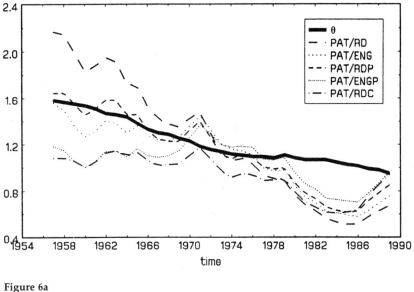

Figure 6a
Patents/research

mid-1980s (Griliches, 1989; Kortum, 1993). This is shown in Figure 6. Figure 6a shows the ratio of patents to several measures of research input; Figure 6b plots N', i.e., ψ_t times patents. The patent series is total "U.S. priority" patents,[43] by year of application. The research input measures include real nongovernment R&D expenditures and total research scientists and engineers, as well as each of these scaled by U.S. population,[44] and nominal R&D scaled by nominal expenditure. Explanations that have been put forward for the downward trend in patent productivity include (1) an exogenous fall in "technological opportunity," (2) aggregate decreasing returns to research, producing a fall in average productivity because research has risen significantly, and (3) a decline in the propensity to patent (Kortum, 1993).

Our estimates from the previous section shed significant light on these issues. First, as can be seen from Figure 6 (as well as Fig. 4), correcting for patent size using the estimated ψ_t does mitigate the fall in productivity up until 1970. Thereafter, unfortunately, the esti-

---

43. This means that the patent was applied for in the United States before being applied for anywhere else in the world.
44. Civilian population over the age of 16 (1991 Economic Report of the President).

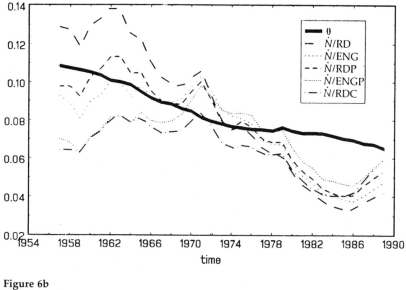

Figure 6b
$\dot{N}$/research

mated ψ_t begins to fall, aggravating the apparent fall in productivity. Our estimates for θ_t^* do, however, provide an explanation for much of the overall trend in patent productivity. This can be seen from Figure 6, in which the estimated θ_t is plotted along with the observed productivity. In both panels, it is clear that the overall downward movement in θ_t is quite consistent with the fall in research productivity, although it does not explain the high-frequency movements, including the precipitous drop in the late 1970s and the rapid rise in very recent years. In the terms of the previously offered explanations for the fall in patent productivity, our estimates suggest that "technological opportunity" has indeed fallen. In our model, this takes the form of decreased usefulness of the stock of existing knowledge in generating new ideas.[45] The previous section shows that this fall can

---

45. Note that the θ_t shown in Figure 6 is the one that results when we treat the increase in ϕ_t as an artifact of citation practices rather than a real phenomenon. On the one hand, the close correspondence of the resulting θ_t to measured productivity provides further support to our conjecture that the movements in ϕ_t are not "real." On the other hand, if this is wrong and the "abnormal" trend in citations corresponds to a true increase in spillovers, our measure of θ exacerbates rather than eliminates the patent/R&D ratio puzzle, at least until 1986.

Table 3
Innovation function results

Parameter	S-E 1	S-E/pop. 2	R&D 3	R&D/C 4	R&D/pop. 5
α_0	−0.012	−0.013	0.002	−0.009	−0.013
	(0.008)	(0.007)	(0.009)	(0.062)	(0.007)
ρ	0.953	0.934	0.887	0.912	0.934
	(0.069)	(0.062)	(0.076)	(0.074)	(0.062)
η_0	−0.380	0.002	−0.133	−0.042	0.028
	(0.134)	(0.056)	(0.133)	(0.052)	(0.056)
η_1	0.759	0.259	0.188	0.207	0.254
	(0.223)	(0.071)	(0.189)	(0.104)	(0.071)
LLK	180.0	182.4	176.6	177.9	178.6

Dependent variable: ψ_t weighted aggregate U.S. priority patents by year of application. Sample: 1958–1989.

be observed in the pattern of actual use of older knowledge, as evidenced by patent citations.

Figure 6 suggests that the estimated θ_t explains much of the observed trend in patent productivity. To push this a little further, we estimate the equation:[46]

$$\dot{N}_t^{/ob} = \alpha_0 + (1 - \rho)\tilde{\theta}_t R_t + \rho \dot{N}_{t-1}^{/ob},$$

with R_t a measure of research input and

$$\tilde{\theta}_t = \eta_0 + \eta_1 \theta_t.$$

The parameter estimates are presented in Table 3. The columns correspond to different measures of research input. In column 1, we use research scientists and engineers. The fit is quite good, and the estimates are all reasonable and statistically significant. As suggested earlier, θ_t is highly significant. The next column uses research scientists and engineers as a fraction of the population. The fit is approximately the same, and the role of θ_t is smaller but still positive and significant. In the next three columns, we report results of research input measured as real R&D expenditure, and R&D expenditure divided by consumption and population, respectively. Except for

---

46. We also estimated versions allowing for decreasing returns with respect to research input. The standard specification with decreasing returns but $\eta_1 = 0$ was uniformly and very significantly outperformed by the linear model with η_1 unrestricted. Adding decreasing returns to the model with η_1 unrestricted yielded unrealistically low and very imprecise estimates of the returns to scale parameter.

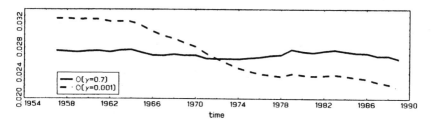

Figure 7a
θ for different γ with δ_s constant

unscaled R&D (where the signs are correct but the coefficients are not significant), the results are similar to those obtained with scientists and engineers.

Thus, the regression results confirm what can be seen in the pictures, that our estimated decline in θ_t, inferred from patent citations, "explains" much of the secular decline in measured patent productivity. In interpreting this, we must consider the factors determining the almost monotonic decline in θ_t through our sample period. First, there is the decline in δ_s, indicating a reduction in the usefulness of successive cohorts of ideas in generating spillovers to the creation of new ideas.[47] In principle, there is a second force potentially at work: θ_t is constructed using all patents, not just U.S. patents. The fraction of U.S. patents going to foreigners rose from about 11% in 1957 to about 44 percent in 1989. From the point of view of U.S. inventors, this increase in foreign patenting in the United States has the effect of speeding up the "$\dot{N}$ clock" without affecting the "time clock." New ideas are coming faster in the aggregate, making it harder for any inventor to take a step, and much of this new knowledge is too recent to have diffused and thereby spilled over to helping new invention.

Figure 7a shows that it is actually only the decline in δ_s that mattered. The solid line shows what θ_t would have looked like if δ_6 had been constant; it is itself quite constant. Figure 7b also shows why

---

47. The empirical regularity is that the citations to early patents are more frequent than would be expected based on the estimated rate of exponential obsolescence. We interpret this in terms of δ_s having been larger in the early years. Alternatively, one could say that the true obsolescence function is "slower" than exponential, i.e., the citation distributions have fatter tails than predicted by exponential obsolescence. Either way, the effect is similar; we would predict a decline in the effective spillover base as knowledge accumulates.

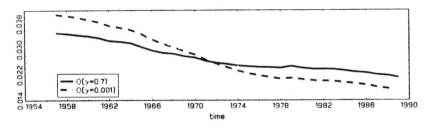

Figure 7b
θ for different γ with δ_s free

the increase in $\dot{N}'$ caused by foreign patenting did not matter: The rate of knowledge diffusion is fast enough so that the spillovers from this influx roughly balanced the increased obsolescence. This can be seen from the dashed line, which shows what θ_t would have looked like if γ were much smaller, i.e., .001. In that case, we would have had a marked decline in θ_t even if δ_s had been constant. The bottom panel reproduces these two cases for the actual (declining) path of δ_s. It shows that, if γ had been smaller, there would have been an additional downward effort on productivity from the influx of foreign patenting. But, given the actual γ, this effect is small; diffusion is close enough to instantaneous that we are, in effect, in the world described in Section 2.3 in which θ_t does not depend on $\dot{N}$.

3.4 $\dot{N}$ and Consumption Growth

As shown in Equation (21), the theoretical model predicts an extremely simple linear relationship between the growth rate of consumption and $\dot{N}$. Casual inspection of the data makes clear that such a relationship does not hold for annual data in the United States. The high-frequency movements in these series are not likely to be well explained by a growth model. Therefore, to explore whether we can find evidence of the predicted relationship, we smoothed both time series by using predicted values from a regression of the actual series on a fifth-order polynominal in the log of time. Figure 8a shows the resulting smoothed consumption growth rate and $\dot{N}$, using the same U.S. priority patent series, corrected by the estimated ψ_t from the citation data. The shapes are strikingly similar, especially considering that it is not clear that one can expect consumption, as actually

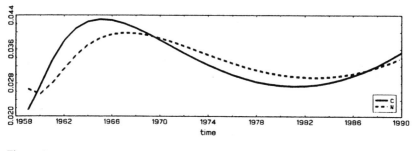

Figure 8a
Growth and innovation

measured in the National Income Accounts, to move as predicted by the model.[48]

Given the previous discussion, it is not clear how seriously one should take precise timing issues. For completeness, however, we mention that the $\dot{N}$ series appears to be displaced forward by one or two years up until the early 1980s. This suggests either that new ideas are incorporated in new products even before the date of patent application, or, perhaps more likely, that both series are moved by other shocks but exhibit different dynamic responses to these.

From Equations (2) and (4), it is possible to write:

$$\frac{C_t}{\eta_t} = \left[\int_{-\infty}^{N_t} \{L_t^p(q)e^q\}^\alpha \, dq \right]^{1/\alpha},$$

but because

$$\int_{-\infty}^{N_t} L_t^p(q) \, dq = \bar{L} - \frac{\dot{N}_t}{\theta_t},$$

and

$$L_t^p(q) = L_t^p(N_t)e^{(\alpha/1-\alpha)(q-N_t)},$$

we can express the rate of growth of consumption as:[49]

---

48. The essence of technological change in this model is the introduction of new goods. As has been emphasized by Griliches (1979) and others, the extent to which the statistics capture the increase in consumption that occurs when new goods are introduced varies greatly across industries. The authorities measure revenues, not output, and convert revenues to output using price deflators that generally ignore the quality improvement associated with new goods.

49. For this we use the approximation $\Delta \ln(1 - x) \approx -x$, for x small.

Table 4
Growth equation regression results

Parameter	1	2	3	4
λ_0	−0.0092	−0.0098	−0.0248	−0.0311
	(0.0044)	(0.0032)	(0.0132)	(0.0083)
λ_1	0.6121	0.5999	0.5162	0.5440
	(0.0629)	(0.0434)	(0.1872)	(0.1128)
ρ	—	0.9037	—	0.8993
	—	(0.042)	—	(0.0362)
R^2	—	—	—	—
LLK	5.752	7.237	4.697	6.315

Dependent variable: smoothed growth rate of U.S. consumption expenditure. Sample: 1958–1989.

$$\hat{C}_t \approx \hat{\eta}_t + \frac{1}{\beta}\dot{N}_t' - \Delta\left(\frac{\dot{N}_t'}{\beta\bar{L}\theta_t}\right).$$

We estimated the following empirical version of this equation:

$$\hat{C}_t = \lambda_0 + \lambda_1\dot{N}_t' - \lambda_2\Delta\left(\frac{\dot{N}_t'}{\theta_t}\right). \tag{14}$$

The coefficient λ_2 was never significant, so we omit the last term in the regressions reported below in Table 4. Columns 1 and 2 present results for the growth rate of consumption, with and without a serial correlation correction. Columns 3 and 4 present the same results using the growth rate of labor productivity instead of consumption as the dependent variable. All versions tell a similar story. The coefficient on $\dot{N}'$ is about .5 to .6 and significant.[50]

Figure 8b shows the (smoothed) growth rate of labor productivity (GNP over employment), and the "true" $\dot{N}$ that can be derived from $\dot{N}^{ob}$ using the estimated parameters from the innovation equation. Again, the movements are very closely related. Although we stress that the lag we have incorporated between the true and observed $\dot{N}$ is something of a black box, the model does seem to do a good job at predicting the longer-term movements in the productivity series.

---

50. All coefficients appear significant, but our transformation introduces large biases in the standard errors, so these should not be taken too seriously. Again, we only emphasize the coincidence in the general shape of the curves in Figure 8.

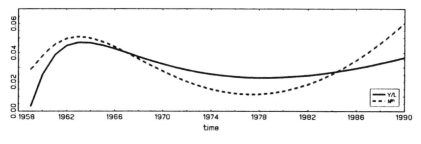

Figure 8b
Growth and innovation

3.5   *Creative Destruction*

All of the previous empirical subsections can be thought of as conditional on the path of research. In the model, the allocation of labor to research is determined by the value of new ideas, whose time path is given by Equation (5), the "creative destruction" equation. In this subsection, we present some empirical estimates of that equation.

As noted earlier, estimation of this equation requires confronting the notion of firms. It also requires identifying the concept of sectors, which have not been explicitly described in the models but whose dynamic properties can be easily understood by extension of the results from the single-sector model. We will treat firms as agglomerations of blueprints, although we will not seek to explain why any particular firm holds the particular portfolio of blueprints that it does.[51] We will assign firms to sectors, which will be defined as groups of firms whose research activities have historically focused on similar areas. With these assumptions, we can derive a version of the creative destruction equation that relates the deviations from the sector mean in firms' value growth rates to the deviations from the mean of the firms' N.

Let F_{its}, I_{ts} and I_{ts}^s represent the value of a firm i in sector s, the value of the entire sector, and the value of the firms in sector s that are included in the sample; all of them at time t and in terms of units of consumption. Letting $\Lambda_i(q)$ and $\omega_{ts}(q)$ be indicator functions, we have:

---

51. Although this definition of firms is consistent with the nonexcludability of knowledge implicit in the model, it is unlikely to hold true in reality. In other words, research know-how, organizational capital, and other forms of private knowledge must add value to a firm beyond the value of its patents.

$$F_{its} = \int_{-\infty}^{N_{ts}} \Lambda_t(q) V_t(q)\, dq,$$

$$I_{ts}^s = \int_{-\infty}^{N_{ts}} \omega_{ts}(q) V_t(q)\, dq,$$

$$I_{ts} = \int_{-\infty}^{N_{ts}} V_t(q)\, dq.$$

Differentiating these expressions with respect to time, using Equation (5), letting $\dot{N}_{its} \equiv \Lambda_i(N_{ts})\dot{N}_{ts}$, and assuming $\omega_{ts}(q) \approx \omega_{ts}$, we obtain our basic estimating equation:[52]

$$\hat{F}_{its} - \hat{I}_{ts}^s = \lambda_{ts} \frac{I_{ts}^s}{F_{its}} \left[\dot{N}_{it} - \frac{F_{its}}{I_{ts}^s} \dot{N}_{ts}^s \right], \tag{15}$$

where

$$\lambda_{ts} \equiv \frac{\alpha_s}{1 - \alpha_s} \frac{1}{\omega_{ts}}.$$

We estimate Equation (15) on an unbalanced panel of firms from the NBER R&D panel (Hall et al., 1988), which contains Compustat financial information and U.S. patent data. The assignment of these firms to technological sectors is described in Jaffe (1986). Briefly, the distribution of the firms' patents across patent classes for the period 1965–1972 was used in a multinomial clustering algorithm to identify groups of firms with "similar" patent class distributions. The 567 firms are assigned to a total of 21 sectors. Simple statistics for the sectors are presented in Table 5. In general the level of aggregation of the sectors is comparable to two- to three-digit SIC industries. The assignment is made, however, on the basis of areas of inventive activity rather than sales.

To estimate Equation (15), we need to parameterize the variation in the parameter λ_{st} over s and t. This parameter encompasses varia-

---

52. An alternative derivation of the same equation can be obtained by letting $\Lambda_t(N_{ts})$ be a random variable independent across i, so the best predictor of its realization is the share of the firm's value in the industry. Also, if one assumes that each sector is comprised of a large number of firms, the total number of new patents in the industry together with its change in value can be taken as known in advance (or at least uncertainty about these can be assumed to be negligible relative to the same concepts at the firm level).

tions in the CES parameter α, in the share of the sector represented by the firms in the sample, and also variations in the proportionality factor between patents and new ideas. We treat it as the product of a sector-specific constant and a cubic polynominal in t. We constrain λ to be positive by using an exponential time polynomial.[53] Although Equation (13) implies that the two terms in square brackets are constrained to have the same coefficient λ_{st}, we allow a free parameter on the sector patent total $\dot{N}_{ts}^s$. We also allow for year- and sector-specific intercepts, leading to the equation actually estimated:

$$\hat{F}_{its} - \hat{I}_{ts}^s = \alpha_{ts} + \lambda_t \lambda_s \left[\dot{N}_{it} \frac{I_{ts}^s}{F_{its}} - \mu \dot{N}_{ts}^s \right], \tag{16}$$

The results of estimating this equation on 8,457 observations are presented in Table 6. The coefficients λ_s are generally positive, although many are not significant.[54] The parameter μ, which should be unity if the proportionality (implied by the model) between value and patents holds, is about 1.4. This says that firm patents scaled by the ratio of firm to sector value averages less than sector patents. This is consistent with the general and intuitive finding that large firms have proportionally fewer patents than small firms.[55] The parameters P_1, P_2, and P_3 in the table are the coefficients of the cubic time polynomial for λ_t.

To interpret these results, we use the parameter estimates to calculate rates of creative destruction. The most straightforward way to do this is to multiply the estimated λ_{st} times the estimated μ times the number of patents in the sector in each year. Doing this yields estimates of the rate of creative destruction by sector by year. The average over the sample years of these numbers are presented in the last column of Table 5. They range from essentially zero for a number of sectors, including computers, to a high of 25% per year for drugs. The (unweighted) average across all sectors is about 3.5% per year. Some aspects of these results are quite consistent with previous findings. In particular, the very high rate of creative destruction for drugs is consistent with the general view that this is a very progressive sector *and* one in which patents are a very good measure of

---

53. If we do not constrain these estimates to be positive, we obtain negative estimates at the end of the sample, although these are insignificant. The overall fit was statistically unaffected by our nonnegativity constraint.
54. The time and sector intercepts are not generally significant.
55. See, e.g., Bound et al. (1984).

Table 5
Statistics for creative destruction, sample firms

Sector	Number of firms	Total observations	Average firm value	Average patents per firm	Average growth rate of value	Firm patents times sector/ firm value	Average sector value	Average sector patents	Average estimated rate of creative destruction
1	30	441	542.23	5.7642	0.04455	352.45	14735.46	167.02	0.0145
2	44	684	2351.03	67.0877	0.0743	3768.71	96900.08	2889.46	0.0318
3	16	226	4070.11	78.0487	0.03546	4622.25	57903.42	1141.43	0.0129
4	21	318	2652.53	45.1792	0.05299	1123.76	49921.29	907.29	0.2511
5	16	239	706.93	16.841	0.05748	337.34	9956.7	255.97	0.0304
6	20	303	8224.99	79.8119	0.05127	5477.57	146432.80	1544.65	0.0018
7	24	341	208.75	5.0469	0.07579	143.5	4158.79	112.46	0.0411
8	21	326	4530.83	58.7791	0.14140	3378.6	88065.11	1209.72	−0.0012
9	33	489	1286.94	54.1984	0.09234	2063.89	38265.89	1708.56	0.1313
10	27	418	1607.58	57.2847	0.12077	2159.74	39483.43	1508.15	0.0693
11	27	393	1147.94	34.916	0.02499	1349.37	27557.81	877.26	0.0246
12	34	511	1071.48	6.3053	0.03260	226.17	32952.44	205.77	0.0115
13	31	451	502.24	14.6386	0.08774	695.64	13135.86	418.41	0.0056
14	13	200	1726.71	15.34	0.08214	475.53	20197.74	195.03	0.0065
15	33	493	1333.17	16.7728	0.04794	872.42	39768.57	525.17	0.0105
16	23	342	547.36	9.462	0.07767	518.28	11241.32	207.74	0.0205
17	49	757	2145.09	41.749	0.06716	3995.33	99554.18	2018.69	0.0205

18	24	339	587.77	9.6962	0.04060	285.85	11881.87	208.21	0.0084
19	29	425	751.29	12.4965	0.05136	931.02	19417.10	346.84	0.0101
20	27	393	300.32	3.4122	0.10359	318.63	6767.87	85.57	0.0152
21	25	368	632.95	15.9484	0.05136	653.64	13540.95	375.9	0.0297
All sectors	567	8,457	1658.93	31.3948	0.06210	1712.52	43774.37	940.05	0.0355

Sectors: 1. Adhesives and coatings; 2. Chemicals; 3. Electrochemistry; 4. Drugs; 5. Cleaning and abrading; 6. Petroleum and refining; 7. Machinery (non-elec.); 8. Computers and data processing; 9. Electrical equipment; 10. Electronic communications; 11. Stone, clay, and glass; 12. Food; 13. Instruments; 14. Medical; 15. Primary metals; 16. Misc. consumer goods; 17. Automotive; 18. Paper and packaging; 19. Refrig. and heat exch.; 20. Static structures; 21. Farm and construction equipment.

Table 6
Creative destruction regression results

Parameter	Coefficient	Standard error
μ	1.383	.245
λ_1	.318	.185
λ_2	.037	.025
λ_3	.040	.019
λ_4	1.034	.297
λ_5	.425	.420
λ_6	.004	.009
λ_7	1.397	.767
λ_8	−.003	.030
λ_9	.283	.089
λ_{10}	.157	.046
λ_{11}	.098	.060
λ_{12}	.187	.238
λ_{13}	.045	.087
λ_{14}	.135	.178
λ_{15}	.072	.071
λ_{16}	.376	.177
λ_{17}	.038	.018
λ_{18}	.146	.271
λ_{19}	.108	.063
λ_{20}	.695	.249
λ_{21}	.316	.158
P_1	−.808	.206
P_2	.113	.034
P_3	−.0048	.0016
$R^2 = .0366$		
$MSE = .1612$		

Dependent variable: firm value growth rate minus sector value growth rate. Sample: 8,457 observations on 567 firms, 1966–1981.

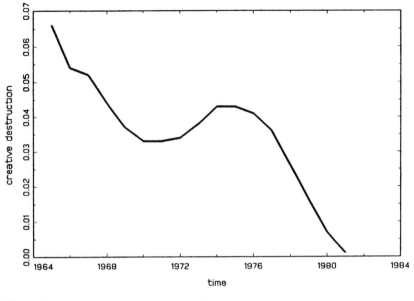

Figure 9
Creative destruction

technical advance (Mansfield, 1985; Levin et al., 1987). We also find relatively fast creative destruction as measured by patents in machinery, electrical equipment, and communications equipment. These are all sectors where patents are reasonably important. In contrast, our inability to find creative destruction in computers is probably related to the relative unimportance of patents in that sector (Bound et al., 1984; Levin et al., 1987), rather than a low rate of technological change.

We can also look at variations over time. Again, the most straightforward way to do this is to simply multiply the estimated λ_{st} and μ times the yearly sectoral patent total. If we do this, and average over sectors, we get the path shown in Figure 9. Beginning at a high of about 7% in 1965, creative destruction falls quickly into the range of 3–4%, and then falls close to zero at the end of the sample period in 1981. There is, however, reason not to take the time variation in total patents in these data too seriously. First, it is affected by the changing firm composition in the unbalanced panel. In addition, total patents in this sample fell precipitously in 1980 and 1981, because of the way the data set was created.[56] For these reasons, the very low rates at the end of the sample period should probably be ignored.

4 General Equilibrium, Calibration, and Implications of the Empirical Results

In the previous section we used the basic structure of the growth model presented in Section 2 to guide our search for empirical manifestations of creative destruction and knowledge spillovers. In this section we go back to the model itself and examine its properties, using the estimates obtained in the empirical section for the parameter values. The primary purpose of this section is simply to explore the static and dynamic behavior of the model using reasonable parameter values. We will also, however, go a little further and examine some strong positive and normative conjectures that arise from the behavior of the model when calibrated with the empirical parameter values.

In Section 2 we identified the following key parameters: ρ, α, δ, $\bar{L}$, γ, and β. Section 3 provides estimates of α, γ, and β, as well as of changes in δ (but not its level) and in α over time. Initially, we focus our attention on the average value of the parameters, and postpone the discussion of the impact of changes in parameters until later in this section. We set the discount rate, ρ, to 0.03,[57] and use average U.S. consumption growth together with the steady state of the model to calibrate δ and $\bar{L}$. In order to calibrate these parameters, we first need to go back to the model itself and characterize its equilibrium.

The dynamical system that emerges from the model described in Section 2 has a range of parameters for which innovation is unprofitable, so growth does not occur. We focus our analysis on cases where steady-state growth is strictly positive.

From the innovation function, labor market equilibrium and free-entry conditions, we obtain an expression for the rate of innovation as a function of the productivity of labor in research and of the value of the leading idea in units of consumption:

---

56. Recall that the data is patents by year of application. Because the data set was created in 1982, some ultimately successful applications from 1980 and 1981 had not yet been granted, leading to a systematic undercount in those years.

57. Quantitative conclusions are not affected by other "reasonable" assumptions about the discount rate, ρ.

$$\dot{N}_t = \theta_t \bar{L} - \frac{\alpha}{V_t}. \tag{17}$$

Replacing this in the valuation equation (5) yields the dynamic equation for V_t as a function of itself and θ_t:

$$\dot{V}_t = \left(\rho + \frac{\alpha}{1-\alpha}\theta_t\bar{L}\right)V_t - \frac{\alpha}{1-\alpha}. \tag{18}$$

Finally, the dynamic equation for labor productivity in research is obtained by differentiating Equation (10) with respect to time:

$$\dot{\theta}_t = \gamma\left(\frac{\delta}{\beta} - \theta_t\right) - \beta\theta_t\dot{N}_t,$$

which combined with Equation (17) yields:

$$\dot{\theta}_t = \gamma\left(\frac{\delta}{\beta} - \theta_t\right) - \beta\theta_t\left(\theta_t\bar{L} - \frac{\alpha}{V_t}\right). \tag{19}$$

Equations (18) and (19), together with initial conditions on θ and a transversality condition, form a self-contained dynamical system. After solving for the paths of θ_t and V_t from this system, the rate of innovation can be recovered from Equation (17).

Because we found large values of γ—i.e., a high speed of diffusion of ideas—in the previous section, it is convenient to first characterize the case where diffusion is infinitely fast; this is a good approximation, and it has the advantage of an extremely simple set of dynamic equations.

If there are no lags in the diffusion of knowledge, the system has no transitional dynamics.[58] As shown in Section 2, in this case $\theta_t = \delta/\beta$; which by Equation (18) and the transversality condition implies:

$$V = \frac{\alpha}{1-\alpha} \times \frac{1}{\rho + \frac{\alpha}{1-\alpha}\frac{\delta}{\beta}\bar{L}},$$

while the rate of innovation is:

$$\dot{N} = (1-\alpha)\left(\frac{\delta}{\beta}\bar{L} - \rho\right), \tag{20}$$

---

58. Obviously, anticipated changes will lead to non-steady state dynamics. The absence of transitional dynamics refers to the response of the system to a once-and-for-all unexpected change in a constant of the model.

and consumption growth is:

$$\hat{C}_t = \dot{N} + \hat{\eta}_t. \tag{21}$$

These expressions provide a simple setup to understand the main role of α, δ, β, and ρ in determining the equilibrium valuation of new ideas, knowledge spillovers, and the economy's rate of growth:[59]

$$\frac{\partial V}{\partial \alpha} = \frac{\rho V^2}{\alpha^2} > 0, \qquad \frac{\partial \dot{N}}{\partial \alpha} = -\frac{\dot{N}}{1 - \alpha} < 0, \qquad \frac{\partial}{\partial \alpha}\left(\frac{\alpha \dot{N}}{1 - \alpha}\right) = \frac{\dot{N}}{1 - \alpha} > 0, \tag{22a}$$

$$\frac{\partial V}{\partial \delta} = -\frac{\delta}{\beta}\frac{\partial V}{\partial \beta} = -\frac{\bar{L} V^2}{\beta} < 0, \qquad \frac{\partial \dot{N}}{\partial \delta} = -\frac{\delta}{\beta}\frac{\partial \dot{N}}{\partial \beta} = \frac{(1 - \alpha)\bar{L}}{\beta} > 0, \tag{22b}$$

$$\frac{\partial V}{\partial \rho} = -\frac{(1 - \alpha)V^2}{\alpha} < 0, \qquad \frac{\partial \dot{N}}{\partial \rho} = -(1 - \alpha) < 0. \tag{22c}$$

When the degree of substitutability among goods (α) rises, the value (per unit of consumption) of a new idea rises. This may seem surprising because an increase in α lowers the markup charged by firms. There are, however, three other effects that must be considered. First, as discussed in Section 2, the fall in the markup is outweighed by an increase in the size of the market faced by new ideas (the "scope effect"), so that the initial profit of the newest idea rises with α. Second, an increase in α raises creative destruction, which reduces expected future profits and, hence, the initial value of ideas. Third, it can be shown that from these effects alone, the ratio of the value to the wage would fall.[60] From the free-entry condition, this would be inconsistent with positive invention. Therefore, there must be an endogenous decline in creative destruction (fall in $\dot{N}$) in order to offset the fall in the value to wage ratio.[61]

The impact of an increase in the potency of spillovers (δ) as well as that of a reduction in the technological destructiveness of new ideas

---

59. One could also study the impact of $\bar{L}$, but we take this as a nuisance parameter. It is at best unclear which is the appropriate normalization.

60. An important mechanism behind the monotonic relation between growth and markups is that labor supply is completely inelastic. If this assumption is relaxed, then as the wage falls (i.e., markups rise), there would be a reduction in resources available and, under the appropriate functional assumptions, an eventual decline in equilibrium growth.

61. In the γ finite case, the endogenous decline in creative destruction would not completely offset the initial decline in the value to wage ratio.

(β) is shown in Equation (22b). They increase the pace of innovation, and through the impact of this on creative destruction, lower the equilibrium value of new ideas.[62] Finally, Equation (22c) shows that an increase in consumers' impatience, ρ, lowers both the value of new ideas and the rate of invention through standard discounting and savings mechanisms.

Although the intuition as well as the sign of the relations described earlier survive the introduction of a finite γ,[63] it is worth describing briefly the implications of frictions in the diffusion of ideas.

If γ is finite, the system exhibits transitional dynamics because "the clocks have to synchronize to the new pace." That is, if information diffuses slowly, "shocks" that lead to changes in $\dot{N}$ disrupt the balance between technological obsolescence and increases in the base of knowledge. Transitional dynamics occur while the new level of θ that restores this balance is reached. Before discussing dynamics, however, it is worth pausing to study the steady state and to calibrate the remaining parameters using average U.S. growth data.

The steady state can be found in closed form, although the equations are somewhat less informative than before:

$$\theta = \frac{\rho(1 - \alpha)\beta - \gamma + \sqrt{(\rho(1 - \alpha)\beta - \gamma)^2 + 4\delta\gamma\bar{L}(1 - \alpha)}}{2\beta(1 - \alpha)\bar{L}}, \tag{23a}$$

$$\dot{N} = \frac{\sqrt{(\rho(1 - \alpha)\beta - \gamma)^2 + 4\delta\gamma\bar{L}(1 - \alpha)} - \rho(1 - \alpha)\beta - \gamma}{2\beta}, \tag{23b}$$

and

$$V = \frac{\alpha}{1 - \alpha} \times \frac{1}{\rho + \dfrac{\alpha}{1 - \alpha}\theta\bar{L}}. \tag{23c}$$

It is apparent from these equations that using average growth data only (which we do here), it is neither possible nor relevant to separate $\bar{L}$ from δ; thus we set $\bar{L} = 1$. We can now recover all the

---

62. Alternatively, the fall in equilibrium value can be explained in terms of the increase in the productivity of research. This and the creative destruction interpretations of the decline in value are related in equilibrium by the free-entry condition.
63. This is particularly true for large values of γ, as is the one estimated in the empirical section.

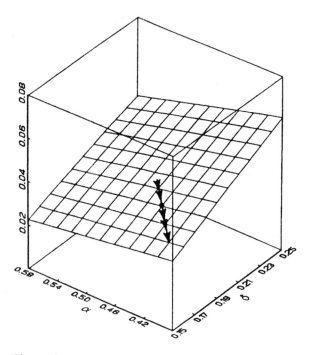

Figure 10a
$\dot{N}$

parameters of the model. We obtained $\gamma = 0.7$ directly from the citation function, and $\beta = 1.67$ is the inverse of the coefficient on the change in the number of ideas, as normalized in the citation function, in the growth equation. We recover α from the average of our creative destruction estimates, 0.035, which corresponds to $\alpha N/(1 - \alpha)$, and the average of $\dot{N}$, 0.042.[64] The estimate of α so obtained is 0.463. The last parameter, δ, is obtained from the steady-state equilibrium equation for $\dot{N}$ (Equation 23b) and is equal to 0.199.

Figure 10a plots the steady-growth rate for an economy with the same base parameters of the United States and a range of values of α, the index of creative destruction, and δ, the spillover potency index, that contain the U.S. values. Figure 10b does the same for the equilibrium value/consumption ratio. U.S. "average" equilibrium is depicted by a black dot in each figure.

---

64. For this we use that $\dot{N} = \dot{N}^{'ob}/\beta$, and $\dot{N}^{'ob} = 0.07$. Our sample for the estimate of creative destruction is 1965–1981, while we use the period 1960–1989 to compute the average change in ideas.

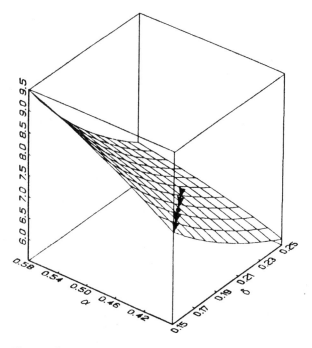

Figure 10b
V

One of our main empirical findings is that productivity of labor in research has declined sharply over the sample, and this seems to be mostly due to a decline in δ. According to Figure 10a, this ought to lower the equilibrium rate of innovation, $\dot{N}$, and raise the value of a new patent to consumption ratio, V. On the other hand, our empirical evidence on creative destruction suggests that α has decreased over time; this should raise $\dot{N}$ and V.

Splitting the sample into two periods, 1960–1974 and 1975–1989, associating the 1965–1974 and 1975–1981 averages of creative destruction to each of these periods, respectively,[65] we can calculate the model's predicted steady-state changes in $\dot{N}$ and V. We find that the effect of the decline in the power of spillovers dominates the effect of the decline in creative destruction on equilibrium growth, leading to a prediction that $\dot{N}$ should have fallen by about 50% from the first to the second periods. With respect to value, both of these effects go

---

65. Remember that the sample used to estimate the path of creative destruction goes from 1965 to 1981 only.

in the same direction, leading to a predicted increase of about 25% in the value to consumption ratio.

In reality, $\dot{N}$ (the patent series adjusted by our estimated ψ) fell about 15%. If we proxy the value to consumption ratio by the ratio of stock prices to nominal consumption, we find an actual rise in V of about 20%.[66] Thus, the qualitative predictions of the model are confirmed, although the actual magnitudes changed less than the model implies they should have.

We conclude this section by briefly addressing several issues that are tangential to our main concerns: (1) a description of the transitional dynamics of the model, (2) the long-run effect of changes in the speed of diffusion of ideas (γ) and in technological destructiveness (β), and (3) optimal R&D subsidy rates.

Figure 11 shows the phase diagram corresponding to a case with noninstantaneous diffusion. Point A corresponds to a steady-state equilibrium with the parameter configuration of the 1960–1974 period described earlier, while point B illustrates the steady state emerging from the 1975–1989 period. The thick line with arrows illustrates the saddle path of the new equilibrium. Because in reality the shift in parameters may have been slow, and the decline in δ seems to have compromised only newer cohorts, it seems unreasonable to assume that the actual dynamics can be characterized in terms of the new saddle path. Instead, a path like the one depicted by the thin line with arrows seems more likely.[67]

Figure 12 illustrates the long-run effect of changes in the speed of diffusion of ideas (γ) and in technological destructiveness (β), with the black dots representing the steady state of an economy with the parameter values we found for the United States. It shows that γ is large, in the sense that further increases in it do not increase equilibrium growth significantly. An increase in the destructiveness parameter β, by lowering the equilibrium productivity of labor in research, reduces equilibrium growth and raises the required value of a new idea.

---

66. There are several reasons to think that an index of aggregate stock prices is not a great proxy for the value of patents. In particular, the number of patents a firm has is likely to be an important component of the value of its stock and, for the experiments we discuss here, value and number of patents at the firm level are likely to be negatively correlated.

67. Note that the initial jump in θ is possible only if the initial change in δ involves the potency of older patents.

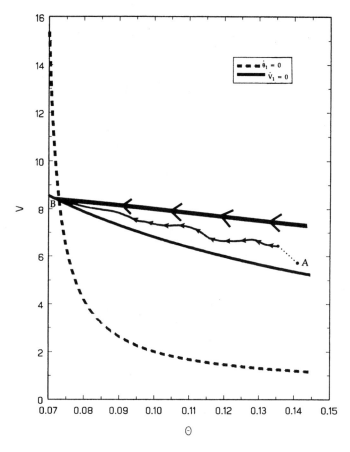

Figure 11
Phase diagram

Finally, we address the optimal subsidy issue, focusing on the case where $\gamma \to \infty$. We also assume that the subsidy to labor used in research is financed with a tax on labor used in production of consumption goods.

Setting $\bar{L} = \eta_t = 1$, and letting s be the subsidy rate (in terms of units of consumption), it can be shown that in equilibrium, $\dot{N}$ is:

$$\dot{N} = \left(\frac{1-\alpha}{1-s}\right)\left(\frac{\delta}{\beta} - \rho\frac{(\alpha-s)}{\alpha}\right), \tag{24}$$

which is clearly maximized as $s \to 1$. As always, however, there is a tradeoff between long-run growth and current consumption. Indeed:

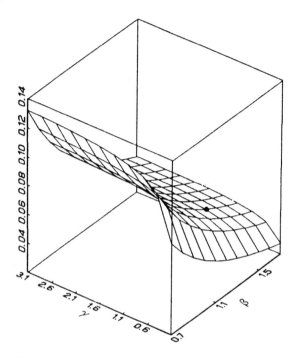

Figure 12a
$\dot{N}$

$$C_t = \left(\frac{1-\alpha}{\alpha}\right)^{1/\alpha}\frac{\beta}{\delta}\frac{(\alpha - s)}{(1-s)}\left(\rho + \frac{\alpha\delta}{\beta(1-\alpha)}\right)e^{N_t}, \tag{25}$$

which, for given N_t, is decreasing with respect to s, and reaches zero when $s = \alpha$. Because the utility function is logarithmic, the optimal subsidy rate must be less than α.

Because we have assumed that exogenous technological progress is negligible, we have that $\hat{C}_t = \dot{N}$, so we can write the present-value utility of the representative agent, U_0, as:

$$U_0 = \frac{1}{p}\left\{\ln C_0 + \frac{\dot{N}}{\rho}\right\}.$$

Maximizing this equation with respect to s, subject to Equations (24) and (25), yields the optimal subsidy rate, s^*:

$$s^* = \frac{\alpha^2(\delta/\beta - \rho)}{\rho + \alpha(\delta/\beta - 2\rho)}.$$

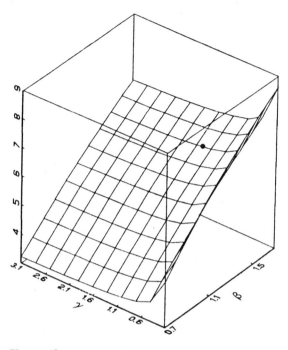

Figure 12b
V

Replacing the parameters calibrated in the previous subsection yields an optimal subsidy rate of 33% if $\rho = 0.03$. If one turns back to Equation (24), such subsidy rate almost doubles the rate of growth of an unsubsidized economy characterized by the parameters calibrated for the United States.[68]

5   Conclusion

We have constructed a model of economic growth through the creation of new goods, in which the phenomena of creative destruction and knowledge spillovers play prominent roles. The model has fairly simple and intuitive relationships between the existing public stock of knowledge and new ideas, between new ideas and growth, and

---

68. The optimal subsidy rate experiment raises the issue on whether our calibration exercise should be corrected to consider the fact that in the United States the subsidy rate is nonzero. We do not think that the precise numbers should be taken that literally.

between growth and the value of ideas or blueprints. The model produces endogenous growth for appropriate parameter values, and it highlights the importance of the speed of diffusion of existing knowledge and the endogenous rate of knowledge obsolescence.

We implemented the model empirically using patents as proxies for new ideas. First, we showed that it is possible to use patent citation information to put a fairly rich structure of knowledge diffusion and knowledge obsolescence onto the notion of research spillovers. We find that the rate of knowledge obsolescence rose from about 2 or 3% per year early in the century to about 10–12% per year at the end of the 1980s. Our results show that the process of knowledge diffusion is quite rapid, indeed, sufficiently rapid that the model performs essentially as if diffusion were instantaneous. In this context it is important to note that the lag we are measuring is between the grant date of the cited patent and the grant date of the citing patent. It seems plausible to view diffusion as beginning with the patent grant, because that is when the patent information is public. But the grant date of the citing patent is, of course, several months to a few years after its application date, and we take application date as being associated with invention. Thus, from the grant date of the cited patent to the application date of the citing patent would be even a shorter lag. Our results on the speed of diffusion seem to be broadly consistent with earlier work, particularly that of Mansfield (1985), who found that 70% of product innovations were known and understood by rivals within 12 months of the innovation, and only 17% took longer than 18 months.

This rapid diffusion rate prevented the large influx of foreign patenting in the United States in recent decades from lowering U.S. R&D productivity even further: With diffusion this rapid, the spillovers from the foreign knowledge creation approximately balance the increased rate of knowledge obsolescence that they also create.

This "good news" is overshadowed, however, by a measured reduction in the usefulness of existing public knowledge in generating new knowledge, as reflected in citation patterns. The estimated spillover potency (δ_s) fell by a factor of 5 over the century, with most of this occurring in the first few decades, and a fall of about 25% in the postwar period. When we translate this into the change in effective accumulated public knowledge, we predict a fall in the private productivity of research inputs of about 30% between the late 1950s and 1990.

We then move to the estimation of the innovation production function, the relationship between aggregate U.S. private research inputs and aggregate U.S. idea generation, as represented by U.S. patents. We confront the well-known "puzzle" of the large fall in the ratio of U.S. patents to U.S. research inputs in the postwar period. The citation function estimation could, potentially, explain this in two ways. If the size of patents was increasing fast enough, then the idea/research-input ratio may not be falling even if the patent/research-input ratio is. Second, if the effective stock of public knowledge is falling, then the reduced spillovers would explain the fall in the productivity of private research inputs. We find evidence of both effects, although the increase in patent size peaks in the early 1970s, so that our ideas/research-input ratio actually falls faster than the patent/research-input ratio after that. For the entire 1958–1990 period, we can explain the overall patent-productivity trend quite well, but we do not explain the accelerated decline in research productivity that occurred in the late 1970s, or the apparent reversal of the trend in the mid-1980s. One difficulty with understanding the very recent movements is that these patents have not had much time to be cited, so our estimates of both δ_s and ψ_s are very imprecise for the late 1980s. Given the large increases in the number of patents in this period, it will be interesting to see how these patents fare as time goes by.

As noted, we also found evidence that the "size" of patents has grown over the century, increasing by a factor of 3 from 1900 until 1940, and then by an additional 20% until it peaked in about 1970. This is consistent with previous conjectures about changes in the propensity to patent. The early rise, in particular, is probably traceable to changes in the legal treatment of patents and the "corporatization" of research (see Schmookler, 1966). It may also be that innovation has become more "systems" oriented as it has become increasingly science-based, so that each "invention" is actually a larger and larger package of component ideas. It is also interesting that we find the size of patents to be falling in recent years. There were two major institutional changes in the 1980s that might have been expected to affect the propensity to patent, in opposite directions. First, patent application fees were increased, and fees for patent renewal were instituted for the first time in the United States in 1981. These changes should have operated to increase the threshold for inventors to decide to make a patent application, reducing the propensity to patent. At approximately the same time, there has been a perceived increase in the strength of patent enforcement in the United States. This makes patents more valuable and should thereby increase the propensity to patent. Our results suggest that the latter effect may be empirically more important.[69]

Next we looked at the relationship between the rate of idea creation and consumption or productivity growth. We showed that, after removing high-frequency movements, the growth rates of either consumption or labor productivity display movements over the last several decades that correlate quite closely with the rate of invention that we measured. Thus, in our model, the productivity slowdown—the long fall in the smoothed growth rate of productivity from the mid-1960s—can be traced back to a fall in the rate of new product creation, which itself can be traced to a fall in research productivity connected to a decrease in the potency of old knowledge in generating new ideas.

The coincidence in timing of the fall in patenting in the 1970s and the slowdown in aggregate productivity has been noted by others. We have a story consistent with those facts, but we cannot push it too hard because so many of our assumptions about lags between observables and unobservables cannot be tested.

Our final empirical innovation is the measurement of rates of creative destruction, using data on patents and value at the firm and sectoral level. Unfortunately, these estimates can only be made for a shorter time period in the 1960s and 1970s, because the construction of patent totals for these firms in the 1980s has not been carried out. This exercise does give reasonable estimates for many sectors, varying between 0 for Petroleum Refining and 25% per year for Drugs, with a mean of about 3.5% per year. The estimated time path of the average rate of creative destruction is somewhat surprising, falling from a high of 7% in the mid-1960s towards zero by 1981. A challenge for future work will be to try to find alternative data series that would permit a richer analysis of rates of creative destruction by sector and over time.

We then took the empirical parameter estimates back to the model and showed that the observed decline in the productivity of research has implications for the innovation rate, the growth rate, and the

---

69. As can be seen from Figure 6, there has been a large increase in the patent/research ratio in the late 1980s. This would also suggest a possible rise in the propensity to patent (fall in the size of patents).

value of new ideas that are all roughly borne out. The model simulation also emphasizes the importance of the apparently rapid diffusion rate of knowledge. The fact that knowledge diffuses rapidly prevented what could otherwise have been an even greater productivity slowdown in the 1970s and early 1980s.

Stepping back from particular parameter estimates and the consistency of particular model blocks with observed trends, we have suggested an organizing framework for empirical research on the contribution of industrial innovation to aggregate growth. We believe that this framework offers many avenues for fruitful future work. Having demonstrated that the citation function works reasonably well, it would be interesting to go back to it and focus in more detail on issues of stochastic structure and identification. Further, to really understand the significance and interpretation of the observed decline in spillover potency, we need to look at the variations across sectors and geographic space in the size of patents, and in the diffusion and obsolescence rates. In principle, one could categorize citing patents by technological sector and by the national origin or U.S. state of origination. This would allow one to put a finer structure on our homogenous, public good called knowledge, examining, e.g., whether foreigners are slower to pick up knowledge in U.S. patents than are Americans. One could also, to some extent, examine whether knowledge seems to have a private component, by looking at whether the firm cites its own patents more often or more rapidly than it does patents owned by other firms.[70]

Consideration of cross-country citation patterns suggests that more thought needs to be given to how to think about the rate of invention, the rate of consumption growth, and the stock of public knowledge in an open economy. We have modeled U.S. consumption growth as depending on U.S. invention, U.S. invention as depending on U.S. research, but the "public" stock of knowledge available to U.S. researchers as being the worldwide stock. With respect to each of these, our assumption seems superior to the alternative polar extreme, but reality is probably somewhere between the extremes.

An interpretation of the decline in δ_s is that research is steadily becoming "narrower" and, hence, generates fewer spillovers because

---

70. There is evidence, e.g., that such "self-citations" are more prevalent for private firms than for universities, and that they come sooner in time than non-self-citations. See Trajtenberg, Henderson, and Jaffe (1992).

each new idea is relevant to a smaller and smaller set of technological concerns. Empirical testing of this notion would necessitate incorporating multiple dimensions of product quality into the model, so that there would be a notion of "technological distance" between different inventions.[71] This could perhaps be implemented empirically using the patent classification information,[72] although the classification information is not available in computerized form for patents before the late 1960s.

Finally, it would be interesting to look at the connections among the private value of particular inventions, the creative destruction they produce, and the knowledge spillovers they generate. To some extent, one would expect that important patents would be high on each of these scales, but ideas also probably vary in the magnitude of both of negative and positive externalities they generate.

References

Aghion, P., and P. Howitt (1992). A model of growth through creative destruction. *Econometrica* 60: 323–351.

Bound, J., et al. (1984). Who does R&D and who patents. In *R&D, patents and productivity*, Z. Griliches (ed.), Chicago: University of Chicago Press.

Cockburn, Iain, and Z. Griliches (1988). Industry effects and appropriability measures in the stock market's valuation of R&D and patents. *American Economic Review* 78: 420–423.

Cohen, W. M., and S. Klepper (1992). A reprise of size and R&D. Mimeo, November.

Evenson, R. (1991). Patent data by industry: Evidence for invention potential exhaustion? In *Technology and Productivity, the Challenge for Economic Policy*. Paris: OECD.

Gort, M., and S. Klepper (1982). Time paths in the diffusion of product innovations. *The Economic Journal* 92: 630–653.

Griliches, Zvi (1990). Patent statistics as economic indicators: A survey. *Journal of Economic Literature* 28, no. 4: 1661–1707.

Griliches, Zvi (1989). Patents: Recent trends and puzzles. *Brookings Papers on Economic Activity, Microeconomics* 291–330.

Griliches, Zvi, ed. (1984). *R&D, patents and productivity*. Chicago: University of Chicago Press.

Griliches, Z. (1979). Issues in assessing the contribution of R&D to productivity growth. *Bell Journal of Economics* 10(1): 92–116.

---

71. Ariel Pakes emphasizes this point in his discussion of this paper.
72. A version of this is presented in Trajtenberg, Henderson, and Jaffe (1992).

Grossman, Gene M., and Elhanan Helpman (1991a). *Innovation and Growth in the Global Economy*, Cambridge: The MIT Press.

Grossman, Gene M., and Elhanan Helpman (1991b). Quality ladders in the theory of growth. *Quarterly Journal of Economics* 106: 557–586.

Hall, B., et al. (1988). The R&D master file. NBER technical working paper No. 72.

Hall, B., Z. Griliches, and J. Hausman (1986). Patents and R&D: Is there a lag? *International Economic Review* 27: 265–283.

Hausman, J., B. Hall, and Z. Griliches (1984). Econometric models for count data with an application to the patents-R&D relationship. *Econometrica* 52: 909–938.

Jaffe, A. (1986). Technological opportunity and spillover of R&D: Evidence from firms' patents, profits, and market value. *American Economic Review* 76: 984–1001.

Jaffe, A., M. Trajtenberg, and R. Henderson (1993). Geographic localization of knowledge spillovers as evidenced by patent citations. *Quarterly Journal of Economics*, forthcoming (NBER working paper No. 3993).

Kortum, S. (1993). Equilibrium R&D and the decline in the patent-R&D ratio: U.S. evidence. *American Economic Review: Papers and Proceedings*, forthcoming.

Jones, C. (1992). R&D-based models of economic growth. MIT mimeo, November.

Levin, R., et al. (1987). Appropriating the returns from industrial research and development. *Brookings Papers on Economic Activity* 3: 784–829.

Mansfield, E. (1985). How rapidly does new industrial technology leak out? *The Journal of Industrial Economics* 34-2, December.

Mansfield, E., M. Schwartz, and S. Wagner (1981). Imitation costs and patents: An empirical study. *The Economic Journal* 91: 907–918.

Mansfield, E., et al. (1977). Social and private rates of return from industrial innovation. *Quarterly Journal of Economics* 91(2): 221–240.

Merton, R. K. (1965). On the Shoulders of Giants. New York.

Pakes, A. (1986). Patenting as options: Some estimates of the value of holding European patent stocks. *Econometrica* 54: 766–784.

Pakes, A. (1985). On patents, R&D and the stock market rate of return. *Journal of Political Economy* 95: 390–409.

Pakes, A., and Z. Griliches (1984). Patents and R&D at the firm level: A first look. In *R&D, patents and productivity*. Z. Griliches, ed. Chicago: University of Chicago Press.

Pakes, A., and M. Simpson (1989). Patent renewal data. *Brookings Papers on Economic Activity, Microeconomics*.

Romer, P. M. (1990). Endogenous technological change. *Journal of Political Economy* 98: S71–S102.

Segerstrom, Paul S. (1991). Innovation, imitation and economic growth. *Journal of Political Economy*.

Schankerman, M., and A. Pakes (1986). Estimates of the value of patent rights in European countries during the post-1950 period. *Economic Journal* 96: 1077–1083.

Schmookler, J. (1966). *Invention and Economic Growth*. Cambridge, MA: Harvard University Press.

Schumpeter, J. (1942). *Capitalism, Socialism and Democracy*. New York: Harper.

Stokey, N. L. (1992). R&D and economic growth. Mimeo, June.

Trajtenberg, M., R. Henderson, and A. Jaffe (1992). Ivory tower versus corporate lab: An empirical study of basic research and appropriability. NBER working paper No. 4146, August.

II

**The Geography of
Knowledge Spillovers**

5

Geographic Localization
of Knowledge Spillovers
as Evidenced by Patent
Citations

Adam B. Jaffe, Manuel
Trajtenberg, and Rebecca
Henderson

The last decade has seen the development of a significant body of empirical research on R&D spillovers.[1] Generally speaking, this research has shown that the productivity of firms or industries is related to their R&D spending, and also to the R&D spending of other firms or other industries. In parallel, economic growth theorists have focused new attention on the role of knowledge capital in aggregate economic growth, with a prominent modeling role for knowledge spillovers (e.g., Romer [1986, 1990] and Grossman and Helpman [1991]).

We know very little, however, about where spillovers go. Is there any advantage to nearby firms, or even firms in the same country, or do spillovers waft into the ether, available for anyone around the globe to grab? The presumption that U.S. international competitiveness is affected by what goes on at federal laboratories and U.S. universities, and the belief that universities and other research centers can stimulate regional economic growth[2] are predicated on the existence of a geographic component to the spillover mechanism. The existing spillover literature, however, is virtually silent on this point.[3]

We gratefully acknowledge support from the Ameritech Foundation, via the Ameritech Fellows program of the Center for Regional Economic Issues at Case Western Reserve University, and from the National Science Foundation through grant SES91-10516. We thank Neil Bania, Ricardo Caballero, Michael Fogarty, Zvi Griliches, Frank Lichtenberg, Francis Narin, seminar participants at NBER and Case Western Reserve University, and two anonymous referees for helpful comments. Any errors are the responsibility of the authors.
1. E.g., Jaffe [1986] and Bernstein and Nadiri [1988, 1989]. For a recent survey and evaluation of this literature, see Griliches [1991].
2. See, e.g., Minnesota Department of Trade and Economic Development [1988]; Dorfman [1988]; Feller [1989]; and Smilor, Kozmetsky, and Gibson [1988].
3. Jaffe [1989] provides evidence that corporate patenting at the state level depends on university research spending, after controlling for corporate R&D. Mansfield [1991] surveyed industrial R&D employees about university research from which they benefited. He found that they most often identified major research universities, but that there was some tendency to cite local universities even if they were not the best in their field.

In the growth literature it is typically assumed that knowledge spills over to other agents within the country, but not to other countries.[4] This implicit assumption begs the question of whether and to what extent knowledge externalities are localized. As emphasized recently by Krugman [1991], acknowledging the importance of spillovers and increasing returns requires renewed attention by economists to issues of economic geography. Krugman revives and explores the explanations given by Marshall [1920] as to why industries are concentrated in cities. Marshall identified three factors favoring geographic concentration of industries: (1) the pooling of demands for specialized labor; (2) the development of specialized intermediate goods industries; and (3) knowledge spillovers among the firms in an industry. Krugman believes that economists should focus on the first two of these, partially because he perceives that "[k]nowledge flows, by contrast, are invisible; they leave no paper trail by which they may be measured and tracked, and there is nothing to prevent the theorist from assuming anything about them that she likes" [Krugman, p. 53].

But knowledge flows do sometimes leave a paper trail, in the form of citations in patents. Because patents contain detailed geographic information about their inventors, we can examine where these trails actually lead. Subject to caveats discussed below relative to the relationship between citations and spillovers, this allows us to use citation patterns to test the extent of spillover localization. We examine citations received by patents assigned to universities, and also the citations received by a sample of domestic corporate patents. If knowledge spillovers are localized within countries, then citations of patents generated within the United States should come disproportionately from within the United States. To the extent that regional localization of spillovers is important, citations should come disproportionately from the same state or metropolitan area as the originating patent.[5]

---

4. The existence of this implicit assumption was noted by Glaeser, Kallal, Scheinkman, and Shleifer [1991]: "After all, intellectual breakthroughs must cross hallways and streets more easily than oceans and continents." Grossman and Helpman [1991] consider international knowledge spillovers explicitly.

5. Glaeser, Kallal, Scheinkman, and Shleifer [1991] characterize the "Marshall-Arrow-Romer" models as focusing on knowledge spillovers within the firms in a given industry. They examine the growth rate of industries in cities as a function of the concentration of industrial activity across cities, within-city industrial diversity, and within-city competition. They find that within-city diversity is positively associated

The most difficult problem confronted by the effort to test for spillover-localization is the difficulty of separating spillovers from correlations that may be due to a pre-existing pattern of geographic concentration of technologically related activities. That is, if a large fraction of citations to Stanford patents comes from the Silicon valley, we would like to attribute this to localization of spillovers. A slightly different interpretation is that a lot of Stanford patents relate to semiconductors, and a disproportionate fraction of the people interested in semiconductors happen to be in the Silicon valley, suggesting that we would observe localization of citations even if proximity offers no advantage in receiving spillovers. Of course, the ability to receive spillovers is probably one reason for this pre-existing concentration of activity. If it were the *only* possible reason, then, under the null hypothesis of no spillover localization we should still see no localization of citations. As discussed above, however, there are other sources of agglomeration effects that could explain the geographic concentration of technologically related activities without resort to localization of knowledge spillovers. For this reason, we construct "control" samples of patents that are not citations but have the same temporal and technological distribution as the citations. We then calculate the geographic matching frequencies between the citations and originating patents, and between the controls and originating patents. Our test of localization is whether the citation matching frequency is significantly greater than the control matching frequency. Since the "control" matching frequency is, itself, likely to be partly the result of spillover-localization, we believe this to be a conservative test for the existence of localization.

The first section of the chapter describes patents and patent citations, explains the construction of the control samples, and considers more carefully how citations might be used to infer spillovers. The second section presents the results of the tests of geographic localization. The following section examines whether the probability of geographic localization of any given citation can be explained by

---

with growth of industries in that city, while concentration of an industry within a city does not foster its growth. They interpret this contrast to mean that spillovers across industries are more important than spillovers within industries. As is discussed below, there is evidence from the R&D spillover literature to suggest that across-industry knowledge spillovers are, indeed, important. In this study, we do not consider the *industrial* identity of either generators or receivers of spillovers, though we do have some information on their *technological* similarity.

attributes of the originating or citing patents, or of relationships between them. A concluding section follows.

I Experimental Design

A Patents and Patent Citations[6]

A patent is a property right in the commercial use of a device.[7] For a patent to be granted, the invention must be nontrivial, meaning that it would not appear obvious to a skilled practitioner of the relevant technology, and it must be useful, meaning that it has potential commercial value. If a patent is granted,[8] a public document is created containing extensive information about the inventor, her employer, and the technological antecedents of the invention, all of which can be accessed in computerized form. Among this information are "references" or "citations." It is the patent examiner who determines what citations a patent must include. The citations serve the legal function of delimiting the scope of the property right conveyed by the patent. The granting of the patent is a legal statement that the idea embodied in the patent represents a novel and useful contribution over and above the previous state of knowledge, as represented by the citations. Thus, in principle, a citation of Patent X by Patent Y means that X represents a piece of previously existing knowledge upon which Y builds.

The examiner has several means of identifying potential citations. The applicant has a legal duty to disclose any knowledge of the prior art that she may have. In addition, the examiner is supposed to be an expert in the technological area and be able to identify relevant prior art that the applicant misses or conceals. The framework for the

---

6. All of the data we use relate to patents granted by the U.S. patent office. About 40 percent of U.S. patents are currently granted to foreigners. Other countries, of course, also grant patents, leading to some ambiguity in the meaning of phrases like "U.S. patent" and "foreign patent." We shall use the phrase "U.S. patent" to mean a patent granted by the U.S. patent office, regardless of the residence of the inventor. We shall use the phrase "domestic patent" to refer to a patent granted (by the U.S. patent office) to an inventor residing in the United States. We shall use the phrase "foreign patent" to refer to a patent granted by the U.S. patent office to non-U.S. residents.

7. Ideas are not patentable; nor are algorithms or computer programs, though a chip with a particular program coded into it might be. The definition of a device was recently broadened to include genetically engineered organisms.

8. There is no public record of unsuccessful patent applications.

search of the prior art is the patent classification system. Every patent is assigned to a nine-digit patent class (of which there are about 100,000) as well as an unlimited number of additional or "cross-referenced" classes. An examiner will typically begin the search of prior art using her knowledge of the relevant classes. For the purpose of identifying distinct technical areas, we utilize aggregations of subclasses to a three-digit level; at this level there are currently about 400 technical classes.[9]

For this study, we begin with two cohorts of "originating" patents, one consisting of 1975 patent applications and the other of 1980 applications. In each cohort we include all patents granted to U.S. universities and two samples of U.S. corporate patents[10] chosen to match the university patents by grant date and technological distribution. These sets of originating patents were chosen because we conjectured that the extent of geographic localization might differ depending on the nature of the originating institution. As discussed below, such differences turn out to be minor. The 1975 originating cohort contains about 950 patents that had received a total of about 4750 citations by the end of 1989. The 1980 originating cohort contains about 1450 that had received about 5200 citations by the same time.

B   Construction of "Control" Samples

The main idea of this paper is to compare the geographic location of the citations with the originating patent that they cite. But to make such a comparison meaningful, we have to consider how often we would expect them to match under some "null" hypothesis. That is, we need to compare the probability of a patent matching the originating patent by geographic area, *conditional* on its citing the originating patent, with the probability of a match *not conditioned on the existence of a citation link*. This noncitation-conditioned probability gives us a baseline or reference value against which to compare the

---

9. Examples of three-digit patent classes are "Batteries, Thermoelectric and Photoelectric"; "Distillation: Apparatus"; "Robots"; seventeen distinct classes of "Organic Compounds"; and the ever-popular "Whips and Whip Apparatus."

10. The "top corporate" sample consists of patents granted to the 200 top-R&D-performing firms in the United States, as reported in S.E.C. 10-k forms and compiled by Compustat. The "other corporate" sample contains patents assigned to U.S. corporations that are not universities and not in the "top corporate" sample.

proportions of citations that match. We call this baseline or reference probability the "control frequency."

Two considerations drove our choice for constructing the control frequency. First, the fraction of U.S. patents granted to foreigners has been climbing steadily during the period under study here. We do not want to conclude that citations are initially localized, but that this localization fades over time, simply because of this aggregate trend. Second, countries (and cities and states) differ in their areas of technological focus. Although such technological specialization is probably due, in part, to geographic localization of spillovers, we want to be conservative and test whether spillovers are localized *relative to what would be expected given the existing distribution of technological activity*.

To derive a control frequency that would be immune to contamination from either aggregate movements over time or localization based on the pre-existing concentration of technological activity, we went back to the patent data base and found a "control patent" to correspond to each of the citing patents. For each citing patent, we identified all patents in the *same patent class* with the *same application year* (excluding any other patents that cited the same originating patent). We then chose from that set a control patent whose grant date was as close as possible to that of the citing patent. This process yielded, for each set of citing patents, a corresponding control sample of equal size, whose distribution across time and technological areas is essentially identical to that of the citation data set. Each control patent is paired with a particular citing patent, allowing us to compare the geographic location of the control patent with that of the originating patent cited by its counterpart in the citing dataset. The frequency with which these control patents match geographically with the originating patent is an estimate of the frequency with which a randomly drawn patent that is not a citation, but has the same technological and temporal profile as the citation, matches geographically.

To put it slightly differently, when we calculate the frequency with which the citations match the geographic location of the cited patents, we are estimating the probability of geographic match for two patents, *conditional on there being a citation link and also conditional on the technological nature and timing of the citation*. When we calculate the frequency with which the "control" patents match geographically with the cited patents, we are estimating the probability of geographic match for two patents, *conditional only on the technological nature and timing of the citation.* If the citation match frequency is significantly higher, then that implies that citations are localized even after controlling for timing and technology.

C Issues Relating to the Use of Citations to Infer Spillovers

With the construction of the control samples, we believe that we have designed a very clean test of the extent to which patent citations are geographically localized. Before going on, we must address the validity of drawing inferences about knowledge spillovers from patent citations. For discussion purposes, we can classify the links that might exist between two inventions into one of three groups: spillovers accompanied by citations, citations that occur where there was no spillover, and spillovers that occur without generating a citation. Our experiment uses the first set, but clearly the other two are non-empty. The key question is whether and to what extent we expect that either of the latter two groups would be systematically more or less localized than the group we examine. Though there are a number of considerations, all difficult to quantify, we believe that on balance it is reasonable to draw inferences about spillovers from citations.

As a general consideration, it is important to keep in mind that any analogy between patent citations and academic article citations cannot be taken too far. Academics may cite a friend (or neighbor) just to be nice, since the price of doing so is infinitesimal, or even negative if a longer list of references is perceived as making the research look more thorough. An inventor who did the same in a patent application is, in effect, leaving money lying on the table: if those citations are included in the final patent the inventor has reduced the scope of her monopoly. Further, the patent examiner should not include such citations in the patent even if the inventor did put them there. Thus, it does not seem that "gratuitous" citations are a serious concern.

A deeper problem is created by "real" citations that are not spillovers. For example, suppose that a firm gets a patent on an invention and then contracts with another firm to make some part of it, or a machine necessary to make it, or any other aspect of the downstream development. It is possible that such a contractor might later get a patent on a related technology. To the extent that the flow of rents between these parties is governed by a complete contract, there could conceivably be no externality running from the original inventor to the contractor. If we now add to this hypothetical contract the assumption that such contracted development is relatively likely to be localized, we have the potential for the observed localization of citations to be greater than the true localization of knowledge spillovers.[11]

Although such "internalized spillovers" surely exist, it is likely that most citations that are not spillovers are of a different sort: citations (added by the examiner) to previous patents of which the citing inventor was unaware. Clearly, no spillover occurs in this case. Further, it seems likely that citations of this sort should not be any more geographically localized than the control patents. If many citations are in this category, it introduces "noise" into the citations as a measure of spillovers, and biases the results *away* from finding significant localization. Our a priori belief is that this category is much larger than the previous one, suggesting that spillovers are, on balance, probably more localized than citations, but readers with different beliefs should interpret our results accordingly.

Finally, there are an enormous number of spillovers with no citations, since only a small fraction of research output is ever patented. In particular, much of the results of very basic research cannot be patented. It is plausible that basic research generates the largest spillovers,[12] and also that basic research is communicated via mechanisms that are less likely to be localized, such as international journals. For this reason, it is probably appropriate to view our results as related to applied research, and to exercise care in extrapolating to the localization of spillovers from extremely basic research.

D   Geographic Assignment of Patents

The preceding discussion has presumed that the "location" of a patent is an unambiguous construct. The patent data contain the country of

---

11. As discussed below, we focus on tests of localization that exclude citing patents that are owned by the same organization as the originating patent, precisely because such "self-citations" do not represent an externality. Citations by other organizations that have an economic relationship with the original inventor could be viewed as similar to self-citations. There is, however, a significant difference: we expect that, in general, the contract between the two parties will be quite incomplete, making it more likely than not that the citing organization could capture some rents from the original invention and hence benefit from at least a partial spillover.

12. This question is analyzed in detail in Trajtenberg, Henderson, and Jaffe [1992].

residence of each inventor, and the city and state of residence of U.S. inventors.[13] Use of this information is complicated by the fact that patents can have multiple inventors who can live in different places. The following procedure was followed:

1. For U.S. *inventors*, city/state combinations were placed in counties using a commercially available city directory; each U.S. inventor was then assigned to an SMSA[14] based on state and county. For this purpose an additional "phantom" SMSA was created in each state, encompassing all counties in the state outside of defined SMSAs. Approximately 98 percent of inventors were successfully assigned to SMSAs.

2. Assignments of each *patent* to a country, a state, and an SMSA were then made based on pluralities of inventors. So, for example, a patent with one inventor living in Bethesda, MD, one in Alexandria, VA, and one in rural Virginia would be assigned VA for its state and Washington, DC, for its SMSA. Ties were assigned arbitrarily, except that ties between true SMSAs and phantom SMSAs were resolved for the true one and ties between United States and foreign were resolved in favor of foreign.[15]

II   Results on Extent of Localization

As a prelude to the geographic analysis, Table I and Figure I present some descriptive data about the citations and their relationship to

---

13. Published data on the geographic distribution of U.S. patents (including those cited in the popular press) are based on the location of the organization or individual to which the patent is "assigned" by the inventor (usually her employer). For analysis of localization, the location of the assignee is not a desirable datum. There is an ambiguity in such data relating to the way employees of multinational corporations make their assignments. An employee of "Honda" in the United States could assign her patent to "Honda U.S.A., Inc." or she could assign it to the parent company in Japan. In the former case, the patent office would call it a domestic patent, and in the latter case a foreign patent; similarly for IBM Switzerland.

14. These assignments were made based on the 1981 SMSA definitions. In areas where Consolidated Metropolitan Statistical Areas were defined in 1981, these were used; elsewhere Metropolitan Statistical Areas were used. Hence we use the generic term "SMSA."

15. At the country level, 98 percent of patents were assigned unanimously. At the state level, 90 percent were assigned unanimously; an additional 4 percent had more than half of inventors in a single state. At the SMSA level, 86 percent were assigned unanimously, and an additional 6 percent had a clear majority. Overall, 4.5 percent of patents were assigned to "phantom" SMSAs.

Table I
Descriptive statistics

Originating dataset	Percent receiving citations	Total no. of citations	Mean citations received	Average citation lag[a,b]	Percent self-citations[b]	Percent same patent class[b,c]
1975						
University	88.6	1933	6.12	6.53	5.6	54.3
Top corporate	84.2	1476	4.70	7.17	18.6	55.7
Other corporate	82.3	1341	4.22	7.82	9.1	57.5
1980						
University	79.9	2093	4.34	4.36	8.9	56.3
Top corporate	79.9	1701	3.54	4.41	24.6	58.3
Other corporate	74.1	1424	2.95	4.46	12.6	57.2

a. Application year of citing patent minus application year of originating patent.
b. For those patents receiving any citations.
c. Comparison is at the three-digit level (see text).

the originating patents. Table I shows that about 80–90 percent of the 1975 patents and 70–80 percent of the 1980 patents had received at least one citation by the end of 1989, with the higher proportion in each case applying to the university patents. Mean citations received (including zeros) were four–six for 1975 and three–four for 1980, again with the higher numbers corresponding to the university patents.[16] The average lag between the originating application year and the application year of the citing patent is 6.5 to 8 years for the 1975 cohort, and a little over 4 years for the 1980 cohort.

The inference that a citation indicates a possible knowledge spillover is much less clear in the case where the citing patent is owned by the same organization as the originating patent. For this reason, we distinguish what we call "self-citations." A self-citation is defined as a citing patent assigned by its inventors to the same party as the originating patent, which is, by construction, either a university or a domestic corporation. Not surprisingly, the self-citation rate differs for the different sources of originating patents, with universities having the lowest and top corporations the highest rates.[17] Finally,

---

16. Our companion paper [Trajtenberg, Henderson, and Jaffe, 1992] explores in detail the use of citation intensity and related measures for measuring the basicness and appropriability of inventions.
17. The apparent increase in self-citation rates between 1975 and 1980 is probably spurious; self-citations tend to come earlier than other citations. See Trajtenberg, Henderson, and Jaffe [1992] for more on this issue.

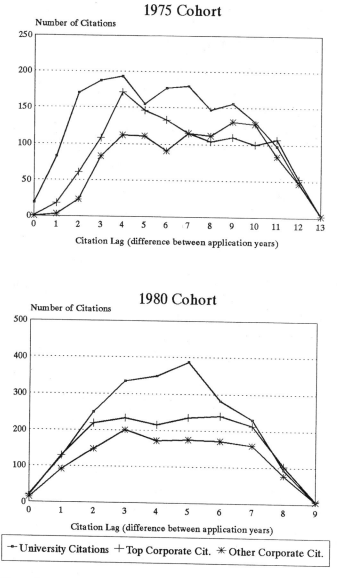

Figure I

Table I shows that 55 to 60 percent of citations have a primary patent class that is the same as the primary patent class of the originating patent, indicating that the originating and citing patents are *technologically* close to one another.

Figure I provides additional detail on the distribution of lags between originating and citing patents, again defined as the difference in application years. The figure shows that citations are few in the early years,[18] and reach a plateau after about three years. It is not possible to tell for sure from these data when (if ever) that plateau tails off; the apparent tail-off in both panels of the figure is due at least in part to the 1989 observational cutoff.[19] For 1975 the higher citation rate for university patents is particularly pronounced in the early years; this pattern is not apparent in the 1980 cohort.

Before getting to our formal test of localization, an examination of Table II is useful to get a sense for the extent of geographic concentration in these data. It shows the fraction of patents coming from abroad and from a selection of major U.S. SMSAs for several of the datasets. Not surprisingly, a measurable fraction of university patents comes from Madison, WI; this is not true for corporate patents. A measurable (though smaller) fraction of the *citations* of university patents comes from Madison, and this fraction is larger than that for the controls. Indeed, the controls for the university citations look generally "more like" corporate patents than do the citations, suggesting that localization may be present. Other qualitative evidence of localization is apparent in the table, including the high percentage of NY SMSA citations that come from the NY SMSA.

The basic test of localization is presented in Table III. For each geographic area and each originating dataset, it presents the proportion of citations that geographically matched the originating patent. These proportions are shown both with and without self-citations. The matching proportions for the control samples are then shown, as

---

18. Patents are typically granted one to three years after application; thus, a citation lag of zero or one implies that the citing patent may well have been applied for before the originating patent was actually granted. Pending applications are not public, so in this case the citation would almost surely have been identified by the examiner.

19. The dropoff in both panels corresponds approximately to application year 1987 (1975 + 12 and 1980 + 7). Typically, a significant fraction of applications have not been granted within two years, so when we looked in 1989 this fraction of 1987 applications were not yet granted.

Table II
SMSA distributions for some datasets

Location	1975 University originating	1975 Top corporate originating	Citations to 1975 university	Citations to 1975 top corporate	Controls for citations to 1975 university	All citations to patents from in NY SMSA
Foreign	—	—	31.8	31.4	35.8	31.2
Boston	15.0	3.1	7.5	4.6	5.1	4.0
Los Angeles/Anaheim	7.0	4.8	9.0	5.7	6.1	3.9
San Francisco/Oakland	5.1	1.4	3.8	3.7	6.1	3.5
Madison, WI	4.2	—	1.6	—	0.5	0.6
Philadelphia/Wilmington	4.2	9.3	5.4	8.2	4.5	9.1
Rural Iowa	3.8	—	1.6	0.6	0.2	—
San Jose	3.5	2.8	4.0	3.4	—	1.9
New York/NJ/CT	3.2	13.5	9.7	11.7	13.7	28.5
Salt Lake City	3.2	—	2.1	—	0.5	0.4
Detroit/Ann Arbor	2.6	2.4	2.6	1.7	1.7	1.2
Minneapolis/St. Paul	1.3	5.2	2.8	2.9	1.9	2.1
Chicago	1.9	4.2	3.9	5.7	5.6	4.2
Albany	0.6	3.1	1.9	2.1	1.3	0.8

All figures are percentages. SMSA percentages for citations and controls are relative to *domestic* total.

Table III
Geographic matching fractions

	1975 Originating cohort			1980 Originating cohort		
	University	Top corporate	Other corporate	University	Top corporate	Other corporate
Number of citations	1759	1235	1050	2046	1614	1210
Matching by country						
Overall citation matching percentage	68.3	68.7	71.7	71.4	74.6	73.0
Citations excluding self-cites	66.5	62.9	69.5	69.3	68.9	70.4
Controls	62.8	63.1	66.3	58.5	60.0	59.6
t-statistic	2.28	−0.1	1.61	7.24	5.31	5.59
Matching by state						
Overall citation matching percentage	10.4	18.9	15.4	16.3	27.3	18.4
Citations excluding self-cites	6.0	6.8	10.7	10.5	13.6	11.3
Controls	2.9	6.8	6.4	4.1	7.0	5.2
t-statistic	4.55	0.09	3.50	7.90	6.28	5.51
Matching by SMSA						
Overall citation matching percentage	8.6	16.9	13.3	12.6	21.9	14.3
Citations excluding self-cites	4.3	4.5	8.7	6.9	8.8	7.0
Controls	1.0	1.3	1.2	1.1	3.6	2.3
t-statistic	6.43	4.80	8.24	9.57	6.28	5.52

Number of citations is less than in Table I because of missing geographic data for some patents. The t-statistic tests equality of the citation proportion excluding self-cites and the control proportion. See text for details.

well as a *t*-statistic testing the equality of the control proportions and the citation proportions (excluding self-citations).[20]

We focus first on the 1975 results on the left of the table. Starting with the country match, we find that citations *including self-citations* are domestic about 6 or 7 percent more often than the controls. Excluding self-citations eliminates this difference for the top corporate citations and cuts it roughly in half for the others. The remaining difference between the citations excluding self-cites and the controls is only marginally significant statistically.

Looking at the 1975 results for states, we find that citations of university patents come from the same state about 10 percent of the time; this rises to 15 percent for other corporate and 19 percent for top corporate. Excluding self-citations, however, makes a big difference. The university and top corporate proportions are cut to 6–7 percent, and the other corporate to just over 10. For the university and other corporate cohorts, the matching frequencies excluding self-citations are significantly greater than the matching control proportions.

At the SMSA level, 9 to 17 percent of total citations are localized. This again drops significantly when self-citations are excluded, but 4.3 percent of university citations, 4.5 percent of top corporate citations, and 8.7 percent of other corporate citations are localized excluding self-cites. This compares with control matching proportions of about 1 percent, and these differences are highly significant.

The results for citations of 1980 patents (right side of Table III) are even stronger and more significant. For every dataset, for every geographic level, the citations are quantitatively and statistically significantly more localized than the controls. The general increase in the proportion of U.S. patents taken by foreigners is reflected in a decline of 3 to 6 percent in the control percentages matching by country. The citation matching percentages actually rise, however, particularly for top corporate citations. It is impossible to tell from this comparison

---

20. Let p_c be the probability that a citation comes from the same geographic unit as the originating patent; let p_o be the corresponding probability for a randomly drawn patent in the same patent class (control). We test $H_o : p_c = p_o$ versus $H_a : p_c > p_o$ using the test statistic:

$$t = \frac{\hat{p}_c - \hat{p}_o}{\sqrt{[\hat{p}_c(1 - \hat{p}_c) + \hat{p}_o(1 - \hat{p}_o)]/n}},$$

where $\hat{p}_c$ and $\hat{p}_o$ are the sample proportion estimates of p_c and p_o. This statistic tests for the difference between two independently drawn binomial proportions; it is distributed as t.

whether this represents a real change, or whether it is the result of the 1980 citations having shorter average citation lags. Since this gets to the issue of explaining which citations are localized, we postpone discussion until the next section.

Before moving on, the results on the extent of localization can be summarized as follows. For citations observed by 1989 of 1980 patents, there is a clear pattern of localization at the country, state, and SMSA levels. Citations are five to ten times as likely to come from the same SMSA as control patents; two to six times as likely excluding self-citations. They are three to four times as likely to come from the same state as the originating patent; roughly twice as likely excluding self-cites. Whereas about 60 percent of control patents are domestic, 70 to 75 percent of citations and 69 to 70 percent of citations excluding self-cites are domestic. Once self-cites are excluded, universities and firms have about the same domestic citation fraction; at the state and SMSA level there is weak evidence that university citations are less localized. For citations of 1975 patents, the same pattern, but weaker, emerges for citations of university and other corporate patents. For top corporate there is no evidence of localization at the state or country levels, though the SMSA fraction is significantly localized. Thus, we find significant evidence that citations are even more localized than one would expect based on the pre-existing concentration of technological activity, particularly in the early years after the originating patent.

III   Factors Affecting the Probability of Localization

The contrast between the 1975 and 1980 results suggests that localization of early citations is more likely than localization of later ones. This accords with intuition, since whatever advantages are created by geographic proximity for learning about the work of others should fade as the work is used and disseminated. Another hypothesis that is implicit in the previous discussion is that citations that represent research that is technologically similar to the originating research are more likely to be localized, because the individuals pursuing these related research lines may be localized. In addition, attributes of the originating invention or the institution that produced it may affect the probability that its spillovers are localized.

To explore these issues, we pooled the citations (excluding self-cites) to university and corporate patents for each cohort, and ran a probit estimation with geographic match/no match between the originating and citing patents as the dependent variable. As independent variables we included the log of the citation lag (set to zero for lags of zero), dummy variables for top corporate and other corporate originating patents, interactions of the lag and these dummies, and a dummy variable equal to unity if the citation has the same primary class as the originating patent. We also included a dummy variable that is unity if the *control* patent corresponding to this citation matches geographically with the originating patent, to control for the general increase over time in the fraction of U.S. patents granted to foreigners.

We also included two variables relating to the originating patent suggested by our work on basicness and appropriability of inventions [Trajtenberg, Henderson, and Jaffe, 1992]. The first, "generality," is one minus the Herfindahl index across patent classes of the citations received.[21] It attempts to capture the extent to which the technological "children" of an originating patent are diverse in terms of their own *technological* location. Thus, an originating patent with generality approaching one has citations that are very widely dispersed across patent classes; generality of zero corresponds to all citations in a single class. We argue elsewhere that generality is one aspect of the "basicness" of an invention. One might hypothesize that basic research results are less likely to be localized, because their spread is more likely to be through communication mechanisms (e.g., journals) that are not localized. The other variable characterizing the originating invention is the fraction of the originating patent's citations that were self-cites. We take a high proportion of self-cites as evidence of relatively successful efforts by the original inventor to appropriate the invention. We expect that the nonself-citations to such a patent are more likely to be confined to suppliers, customers, or other firms that the inventing firm has a relationship with, and may therefore tend to be localized.

Finally, the extent of localization depends fundamentally on the mechanisms by which information flows, and these mechanisms may

---

21. Let C_{ik} be the number of citations received by patent i from subsequent patents whose primary patent class is k, and let C_i be the total number of citations received by patent i. The measure of generality is then

$$G_i = 1 - \sum_k \left(\frac{C_{ik}}{C_i}\right)^2.$$

be different in different technical fields. For this reason, we also included dummy variables for broad technological fields.[22]

The results are presented in Table IV. Because of the presence of the interaction terms between the lag and the corporate dummies, the coefficient on the lag itself corresponds to the fading of localization of citations of university patents. There is evidence in the 1975 results of such fading. This effect is statistically significant at the state and SMSA levels; its quantitative significance is discussed further below. For the citations of corporate patents, the interaction terms measure the difference between their fading rates and those of university citations. These terms are generally not statistically significant. In only one case (other corporate, 1975) could we reject the hypothesis of equality of fading rates at traditional confidence levels. There is, however, weak evidence that the corporate citations do not fade as rapidly as those of university patents, at least at the state and SMSA levels. The coefficients on the corporate dummies themselves capture differences in the predicted probability of localization for citations with lags of zero or one year. These are all insignificant, and there is no clear pattern.

The matching-patent-class and generality variables do not work well. The effects are generally insignificant, and show no consistent pattern. The effect of the self-citation fraction, however, is strong and puzzling. At the state and local level, there is a very significant effect in the predicted direction: citations of patents with a high self-citation fraction are more likely to be localized. This is *not* just saying that self-citations are localized, since they are excluded; it is the other citations that are more localized. At the country level, at least in 1975, this effect is reversed and is significant. Taking all results together, it suggests that for patents with a lot of self-citations, the nonself-citations are more likely to be foreign, but those that are domestic are more likely to be in the same state and SMSA as the originating patent.

The 1980 results are disappointing. The coefficient on the time lag term switches sign, though it is generally insignificant. One possibility is that these citations span too short a time period to capture the lag effect well. To test this possibility, we reran the estimation in Table IV on the 1975 citations, excluding all that were granted after

22. (1) Drugs and Medical Technology; (2) Chemicals and Chemical Processes Excluding Drugs; (3) Electronics, Optics, and Nuclear Technologies; (4) Mechanical Arts; and (5) All Other.

Table IV
Geographic probit results

	Country match		State match		SMSA match	
	1975	1980	1975	1980	1975	1980
Dummy for control sample match	0.139 (0.045)	0.085 (0.041)	0.396 (0.124)	0.300 (0.102)	*	0.283 (0.172)
Log of citation lag	−0.078 (0.049)	0.094 (0.056)	−0.264 (0.073)	0.198 (0.079)	−0.123 (0.057)	0.037 (0.086)
Dummy for top corporate	−0.114 (0.168)	−0.010 (0.127)	−0.383 (0.249)	0.013 (0.177)	−0.234 (0.288)	−0.208 (0.200)
Dummy for other corporate	0.069 (0.209)	0.053 (0.134)	−0.214 (0.277)	−0.007 (0.189)	0.325 (0.291)	−0.042 (0.207)
Log-lag, top corp. dummy	0.046 (0.091)	−0.016 (0.086)	0.226 (0.138)	0.007 (0.115)	0.102 (0.156)	0.156 (0.131)
Log-lag, other corp. dummy	0.008 (0.108)	−0.026 (0.091)	0.307 (0.147)	0.036 (0.124)	0.037 (0.155)	0.039 (0.138)
Dummy for matching patent class	−0.085 (0.050)	0.069 (0.045)	−0.013 (0.073)	0.034 (0.058)	−0.057 (0.080)	−0.016 (0.068)
Generality of origin patent	0.092 (0.091)	0.177 (0.088)	0.026 (0.136)	−0.140 (0.111)	0.013 (0.150)	−0.298 (0.130)
Origin fraction self-citations	−0.813 (0.180)	0.162 (0.124)	0.815 (0.246)	0.883 (0.134)	1.174 (0.237)	0.828 (0.154)
No. of observations	3581	4217	3573	4215	3566	3972
No. of matches	2363	2925	256	490	197	298
Log likelihood	−2269	−2559	−894	−1459	−736	−1022

*The number of observations for which the control patent matched at the SMSA level was so small that this parameter could not be estimated.
Standard errors are in parentheses. All equations also included five technological field dummies.

1984. This analysis tells us what we would have believed about citations of 1975 patents if we had looked for them only as long as we have looked for the citations of the 1980 patents. The results (not reported here) looked "more like" the 1980 results than the original 1975 results did. In particular, the coefficient on the lag term was insignificant, and was positive at the SMSA level. Thus, it may be that the "perverse" results for the 1980 sample would go away if we had later citations to include.

A probit coefficient does not have an economically meaningful magnitude, because of the need to standardize the variance of the underlying error distribution. However, we can calculate what the

Table V
Predicted localization percentages over time (based on 1975 probit results for citations of university patents)

Lag	Predicted percentage for		
	same country	same state	same SMSA
0 or 1 year	67.1	9.7	4.8
5 years	65.5	6.5	4.0
10 years	64.6	5.3	3.7
25 years	63.5	4.0	3.3

coefficients imply about changes in the predicted probabilities. This is done in Table V, using the 1975 lag coefficient.[23] Table V was constructed by calculating the predicted localization probability using the results of Table IV, evaluating the citation lag at different values, and evaluating the other independent variables at the mean of the data. It shows that the estimates correspond to a reduction in the localization fraction after, for example, ten years, from 67.1 percent to 64.6 percent at the country level, 9.7 percent to 5.3 percent at the state level, and 4.8 percent to 3.7 percent at the SMSA level.

IV   Discussion and Conclusion

Despite the invisibility of knowledge spillovers, they do leave a paper trail in the form of citations. We find evidence that these trails, at least, are geographically localized. The results, particularly for the 1980 cohort, suggest that these effects are quite large and quite significant statistically. Because of our interest in true externalities, we have focused on citations excluding self-cites. For some purposes, however, this is probably overly conservative. From the point of view of the Regional Development Administrator, it may not matter whether the subsequent development that flows from an invention is performed by the inventing firm, as long as it is performed in her state or city. Our results are also conservative because we attribute none of the localization present in the control samples to spillovers, despite the likelihood that spillovers are, indeed, one of the major reasons for the pre-existing concentration of research activity.

---

23. As discussed above, this is the point estimate of the lag coefficient for citations of university patents. The point estimates are different for the corporate originating patents, but we have not performed separate calculations for each dataset.

We also find evidence that geographic localization fades over time. The 1980 citations, which have shorter average citation lags, are systematically more localized than the 1975 citations. By using a probit analysis, we produced estimates of the rate of fading. These estimates seem to suggest a rate of fading that is both smaller than one would expect, and smaller than would be necessary to explain the difference between the 1975 and 1980 overall matching fractions. One possibility is that the difficulty of measuring the rate of fading is due to the "contamination" of citations by the patent examiner. As noted in footnote 18, it is particularly likely that citations with very short lags were added by the examiner. If we believe that such citations are less likely to represent spillovers and less likely to be localized, then this would tend to bias toward zero our measure of the effect of time on localization.[24]

We find less evidence of the effect of technological area on the localization process. Citations in the same class are no more likely to be localized. Overall, there is not really any evidence in these data that the probability of coming from a given geographic location conditional on patent class is different from the unconditional probability. This may be due to the arbitrary use of the "primary" patent class, to the exclusion of the "cross-referenced" classes. There is no legal difference in significance between the primary and cross-referenced classes, and in many cases the examiners do not place any significance on which class is designated primary. In future work we hope to explore whether using the full range of information contained in the cross-referenced classes provides a better technological characterization of the patents.

In this context it is worth noting that part of what is going on is probably that knowledge spillovers are not confined to closely related regions of technology space. Approximately 40 percent of citations do not come from the same primary patent class; even at the level of the five broad "technological fields" listed in footnote 21, 12 to 25 percent of citations are across fields. This is consistent with Jaffe [1986], which found that a significant fraction of the total "flow" of spillovers affecting firms' own research productivity comes from firms outside of the receiving firm's immediate technological neighborhood.

---

24. Attempts to test for this possibility by including a dummy variable for age 0 or 1, as well as other explorations of possible nonlinearity in the match-lag relationship, were inconclusive.

We find surprisingly little evidence of differences in localization between the citations of university and corporate patents. The largest difference is that corporate patents are more often self-cited, and self-cites are more often localized. The probit results do not allow rejection of the hypothesis that the initial localization rates for nonself-citations are indistinguishable for the different groups. They do provide some weak evidence that this initial localization is more likely to fade for the university patents, at least at the state and local levels.

In order to provide a true foundation for public policy and economic theorizing, we would ultimately like to be able to say more about the mechanisms of knowledge transfer, and about something resembling social rates of return at different levels of geographic aggregation. The limitations of patent and citation data make it difficult to go much farther with such questions within this research approach. Ex post, the vast majority of patents are seen to generate negligible private (and probably social) returns. In future work we plan to identify a small number of patents that are extremely highly cited. It is likely that such patents are both technologically and economically important [Trajtenberg, 1990]. Case studies of such patents and their citations could prove highly informative about both the mechanisms of knowledge transfer, and the extent to which citations do indeed correspond to externalities in an economic sense.

References

Bernstein, J., and M. Nadiri, "Interindustry R&D Spillovers, Rates of Return, and Production in High-Tech Industries," *American Economic Review Papers and Proceedings*, LXXVIII (May 1988), 429–34.

Bernstein, J., and M. Nadiri, "Research and Development and Intra-industry Spillovers: An Empirical Application of Dynamic Duality," *Review of Economic Studies*, LVI (April 1989), 249–67.

Dorfman, N., "Route 128: The Development of a Regional High-Technology Economy," D. Lampe, ed., *The Massachusetts Miracle: High Technology and Economic Revitalization* (Cambridge, MA: MIT Press, 1988).

Feller, Irwin, "R&D Theories and State Advanced Technology Programs," Paper prepared for the American Association for the Advancement of Science Annual Meeting, January 1989.

Glaeser, Edward, H. D. Kallal, J. A. Scheinkman, and A. Shleifer, "Growth in Cities," NBER Working Paper No. 3787, July 1991.

Griliches, Z., "The Search for R&D Spillovers," NBER Working Paper No. 3768, July 1991.

Grossman, G., and E. Helpman, *Innovation and Growth in the Global Economy* (Cambridge, MA: M.I.T. Press, 1991).

Jaffe, Adam, "Technological Opportunity and Spillovers of R&D: Evidence from Firms' Patents, Profits and Market Value," *American Economic Review*, LXXVI (1986), 984–1001.

———, "Real Effects of Academic Research," *American Economic Review*, LXXIX (1989), 957–70.

Krugman, P., *Geography and Trade* (Cambridge: M.I.T. Press, 1991).

Mansfield, E., "Sources and Characteristics of Academic Research Underlying Industrial Innovations," mimeo, University of Pennsylvania, 1991.

Marshall, A., *Principles of Economics* (London: Macmillan, 1920).

Minnesota Department of Trade and Economic Development, Office of Science and Technology, *State Technology Programs in the United States*, 1988.

Romer, P., "Increasing Returns and Long-Run Growth," *Journal of Political Economy*, XCIV (1986), 1002–37.

———, "Endogenous Technological Change," *Journal of Political Economy*, XCVIII (1990), S71–S102.

Smilor, R., G. Kozmetsky, and D. Gibson, *Creating the Technopolis: Linking Technology, Commercialization and Economic Development* (Cambridge, MA: Ballinger Publishing Co., 1988).

Trajtenberg, M., "A Penny for Your Quotes: Patent Citations and the Value of Innovations," *Rand Journal of Economics*, XXI (1990), 172–87.

Trajtenberg, M., R. Henderson, and A. Jaffe: "Ivory Tower Versus Corporate Lab: An Empirical Study of Basicness and Appropriability," NBER Working Paper No. 4146, 1992.

6

Flows of Knowledge from Universities and Federal Laboratories: Modeling the Flow of Patent Citations over Time and across Institutional and Geographic Boundaries

Adam B. Jaffe and Manuel Trajtenberg

The rate at which knowledge diffuses outward from the institutional setting and geographic location in which it is created has important implications for the modeling of technological change and economic growth and for science and technology policy. Models of endogenous economic growth, such as Romer (1) or Grossman and Helpman (2), typically treat knowledge as completely diffused within an economy, but implicitly or explicitly assume that knowledge does not diffuse across economies. In the policy arena, ultimate economic benefits are increasingly seen as the primary policy motivation for public support of scientific research. Obviously, the economic benefits to the United States economy of domestic research depend on the fruits of that research being more easily or more quickly harvested by domestic firms than by foreign firms. Thus, for both modeling and policy-making purposes it is crucial to understand the institutional, geographic, and temporal dimensions of the spread of newly created knowledge.

In a previous paper Henderson *et al.* (3) we explored the extent to which citations by patents to previous patents are geographically localized, relative to a baseline likelihood of localization based on the predetermined pattern of technological activity. This chapter extends that work in several important dimensions. (i) We use a much larger number of patents over a much longer period of time. This allows us to explicitly introduce time, and hence diffusion, into the citation process. (ii) We enrich the institutional comparisons we can make by looking at three distinct sources of potentially cited patents: United States corporations, United States universities, and the United States government. (iii) The larger number of patents allows us to enrich the geographic portrait by examining separately the diffusion of knowledge from United States institutions to inventors in Canada, Europe, Japan, and the rest of the world. (iv) Our earlier work took the act of citation as exogenous, and simply measured how often that citation came from nearby. In this chapter we develop a modeling framework that allows the generation of citations from multiple distinct locations to be generated by a random process whose parameters we estimate.

The Data

We are in the process of collecting from commercial sources a complete data base on all United States patents[1] granted since 1963 (≈ 2.5 million patents), including data for each indicating the nature of the organization, if any, to which the patent property right was assigned; the names of the inventors and the organization, if any, to which the patent right was assigned; the residence of each inventor[2]; the dates of the patent application and the patent grant; and a detailed technological classification for the patent. The data on individual patents are complemented by a file indicating all of the citations made by United States patents since 1977 to previous United States patents (≈ 9 million citations). Using the citation information in conjunction with the detailed information about each patent itself, we have an extremely rich mine of information about individual inventive acts *and* the links among them as indicated by citations made by a given patent to a previous one.

We and others have discussed elsewhere at great length the advantages and disadvantages of using patents and patent citations to indicate inventions and knowledge links among inventions (3–5). Patent citations perform the legal function of delimiting the patent right by identifying previous patents whose technological scope is explicitly placed outside the bounds of the citing patent. Hence, the

---

1. By "United States patents," we mean in this context patents granted by the United States Patent Office. All of our research relies on United States patents in this sense. Currently, about one-half of United States patents are granted to foreigners. Hence, later in the paper, we will use the phrase United States patents to mean patents granted to residents of the United States, as opposed to those granted to foreigners.
2. The city and state are reported for United States inventors, the country for inventors outside the United States.

appearance of a citation indicates that the cited patent is, in some sense, a technological antecedent of the citing patent. Patent applicants bear a legal obligation to disclose any knowledge that they might have of relevant prior inventions, and the patent examiner may also add citations not identified by the applicant.

Our basic goal in this chapter is to explore the process by which citations to a given patent arrive over time, how this process is affected by characteristics of the cited patent, and how different potentially citing locations differ in the speed and extent to which they "pick up" existing knowledge, as evidenced by their acknowledgment of such existing knowledge through citation. Because of the policy context mentioned above, we are particularly interested in citations to university and government patents. We recognize that much of the research that goes on at both universities and government laboratories never results in patents, and presumably has impacts that cannot be traced via our patent citations-based research. We believe, however, that at least with respect to relatively near-term economic impacts, patents and their citations are at least a useful window into the otherwise "black box" of the spread of scientific and technical knowledge.

The analysis in this chapter is based on the citations made to three distinct sets of "potentially cited" patents. The first set is a 1-in-10 random sample of all patents granted between 1963 and 1990 and assigned to United States corporations (88,257 patents). The second set is the *universe* of all patents granted between 1965 and 1990 to United States universities, based on a set of assignees identified by the Patent Office as being universities or related entities such as teaching hospitals (10,761 patents).[3] The third set is the universe of patents granted between 1963 and 1990 to the United States government (38,254 patents). Based on comparisons with numbers published by the National Science Foundation, these patents are overwhelmingly coming from federal laboratories, and the bulk come from the large federal laboratories. The United States government set also includes, however, small numbers of patents from diverse parts of the federal government. We have identified all patents granted between 1977 and 1993, which cite any of the patents in these three sets

---

3. There are, presumably, university patents before 1965, but we do not have the ability to identify them as such.

Table 1
Simple statistics for patent subsamples

	United States corporations	United States universities	United States government
Range of cited patents	1963–1990	1965–1990	1963–1990
Range of citing patents	1977–1993	1977–1993	1977–1993
Total potentially cited patents	88,257 (1 in 10)	10,761 (Universe)	38,254 (Universe)
Total citations	321,326	48,806	109,729
Mean citations	3.6	4.5	2.9
Mean cited year	1973	1979	1973
Mean citing year	1986	1987	1986
Cited patents by field, %			
Drugs and medical	4.89	29.12	3.36
Chemicals excluding drugs	30.37	28.71	20.73
Electronics, optics, and nuclear	26.16	27.39	45.40
Mechanical	28.18	9.51	17.09
Other	10.39	5.28	13.42
Citations by region, %			
United States	70.6	71.8	70.8
Canada	1.6	1.7	1.7
European Economic Community	14.5	13.2	16.8
Japan	11.3	11.0	8.6
Rest of world	1.9	2.4	2.1

(479,861 citing patents). Thus we are using temporal, institutional, geographic, and technological information on over 600,000 patents over about 30 years.

Some simple statistics from these data are presented in Table 1. On average, university patents are more highly cited, despite the fact that more of them are recent.[4] Federal patents are *less* highly cited than corporate patents. But it is difficult to know how to interpret these averages, because many different effects all contribute to these means. First, the differences in timing are important because we know from other work that the overall rate of citation has been rising over time

---

4. In previous work (6), we showed that university patents applied for up until about 1982 were more highly cited than corporate patents, but that the difference has since disappeared.

(7), so more recent patents will tend to be more highly cited than older ones. Second, there are significant differences in the composition of the different groups by technical field. Most dramatically, university patents are much more highly concentrated in Drugs and Medical Technology and less concentrated in Mechanical Technology, than the other groups. Conversely, the federal patents are much more concentrated in Electronics, Optics, and Nuclear Technology than either of the other groups, with less focus on Chemicals. To the extent that citation practices vary across fields, differences in citation intensities by type of institution could be due to field effects. Finally, different potentially citing locations have different field focuses of their own, with Japan more likely to cite Electronics patents and less likely to cite Drug and Medical patents. The main contribution of this paper is the exploration of an empirical framework in which all of these different effects can be sorted out, at least in principle.

The Model

We seek a flexible descriptive model of the random processes underlying the generation of citations, which will allow us to estimate parameters of the diffusion process while controlling for variations over time and technological fields in the "propensity to cite." For this purpose we adapt the formulation of Caballero and Jaffe (7), in which the likelihood that any particular patent K granted in year T will cite some particular patent k granted in year t is assumed to be determined by the combination of an exponential process by which knowledge diffuses and a second exponential process by which knowledge becomes obsolete. That is:

$$p(k, K) = \alpha(k, K) \exp[-\beta_1(k, K)(T - t)][1 - \exp(-\beta_2(T - t))], \qquad [1]$$

where β_1 determines the rate of obsolescence and β_2 determines the rate of diffusion. We refer to the likelihood determined by Eq. 1 as the "citation frequency," and the citation frequency as a function of the citation lag $(T - t)$ as a citation function. The dependence of the parameters α and β_1 on k and K is meant to indicate that these could be functions of certain attributes of both the cited and citing patents. In this paper, we consider the following as attributes of the cited patent k that might affect its citation frequency: t, the grant year of

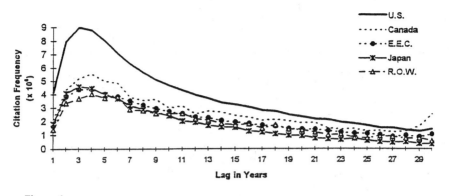

Figure 1
Plot of the average citation functions for each of five geographic regions (citation frequency as a function of time elapsed from each potentially cited patent)

the potentially cited patent; $i = 1..3$, the institutional nature of the assignee of the potentially cited patent (corporate, university, or government); and $g = 1..5$, the technological field of the potentially cited patent. As attributes of the potentially citing patent K that might affect the citation likelihood we consider: T, the grant year of the potentially citing patent, and $L = 1..5$, the location of the potentially citing patent.

To illustrate the plausibility of this formulation, we plot the average citation functions (citation frequency as a function of time elapsed from the potentially cited patent), for each of the five geographic regions in Fig. 1. This figure shows that citations display a pattern of gradual diffusion and ultimate obsolescence, with maximal citation frequency occurring after about 5 years. The contrasts across countries in these raw averages are striking: United States patents are much more likely to cite our three groups of United States patents than are any other locations, with an apparent ranking among other regions of Canada, Rest of World (R.O.W.), European Economic Community (E.E.C.), and then Japan. Although many of these contrasts will survive more careful scrutiny, it is important at this point to note that these comparisons do not control for time or technical field effects.

Additional insight into this parametrization of the diffusion process can be gained by determining the lag at which the citation function is maximized ("the modal lag"), and the maximum value of the citation frequency achieved. A little calculus shows that the modal lag is approximately equal to $1/\beta_1$; increases in β_1 shift the citation function to the left. The maximum value of the citation frequency is approximately determined by β_2/β_1; increases in β_2 holding β_1 constant increase the overall citation intensity.[5] Indeed, increases in β_2, holding β_1 constant, are very close to equivalent to increasing the citation frequency *proportionately* at every value of $(T - t)$. That is, variations in β_2 holding β_1 constant are not separately identified from variations in α. Hence, because the model is somewhat easier to estimate and interpret with variations in α. we do not allow variations in β_2.

Consider now a potentially cited patent with particular i, t, g attributes, e.g., a university patent in the Drug and Medical area granted in 1985. The expected number of citations that this patent will receive from a particular T, L combination (e.g., Japanese patents granted in 1993) is just the above likelihood, as a function of i, t, g, T, and L, times the *number* of patents in the particular T, L group that are thereby potential citing patents. Even aggregating in this way over T and L, this is still a very small expected value, and so it is not efficient to carry out estimation at the level of the individual potentially cited patent. Instead we aggregate across all patents in a particular i, t, g cell, counting all of the citations *received* by, e.g., university drug patents granted in 1985, *given by*, e.g., Japanese patents in 1993. The expected value of this total is just the expected value for any one potentially cited patent, times the number of potentially cited patents in the i, t, g cell. In symbols

$$E[c_{itgTL}] = (n_{TL})(n_{itg})\alpha_{itgTL} \exp[-(\beta_1)_{itgTL}(T - t)]$$
$$\times [1 - \exp(-\beta_2(T - t))] \qquad [2]$$

or

$$\frac{E[c_{itgTL}]}{(n_{TL})(n_{itg})} = \alpha_{itgTL} \exp[-(\beta_1)_{itgTL}(T - t)][1 - \exp(-\beta_2(T - t))], \qquad [3]$$

implying that the equation

---

5. The approximation involved is that $\log(1 + \beta_2/\beta_1) \approx \beta_2/\beta_1$. Our estimations all lead to β_2/β_1 on the order of 10^{-6}, and indeed the approximation holds to five significant figures for lags up to 30 years.

$$p_{itgTL} \equiv \frac{c_{itgTL}}{(n_{TL})(n_{itg})} = \alpha_{itgTL} \exp[-(\beta_1)_{itgTL}(T-t)]$$
$$\times [1 - \exp(-\beta_2(T-t))] + \varepsilon_{igtTL} \qquad [4]$$

can be estimated by non-linear least squares if the error ε_{igtTL} is well behaved. The data set consists of one observation for each feasible combination of values of i, t, g, T, and L. The corporate and federal data each contribute 9,275 observations (5 values of g times 5 values of L times 28 values of t times either 17 (for years before 1977) or $1993 - t$ (for years beginning in 1977) values of T.[6] Because the university patents start only in 1965, there are only 8,425 university cells, for a total number of observations of 26,975. Of these, about 25% have zero citations;[7] the mean number of citations is about 18 and the maximum is 737. The mean value of p_{itgTL} is 3.3×10^{-6}.

Model Specification and Interpretation

The first specification issue to consider is the difficulty of estimating effects associated with cited year, citing year, and lag. This is analogous to estimating "vintage," time and age effects in a wage model or a hedonic price model. If lag (our "age" effect) entered the model linearly, then it would be impossible to estimate all three effects. Given that lag enters our model non-linearly, all three effects are identified in principle. In practice, we found that we could not get the model to converge with the double-exponential lag function and separate α parameters for each cited year and each citing year. We were, however, able to estimate a model in which cited years are grouped into 5-year intervals. Hence, we assume that $\alpha(t)$ is constant over t for these intervals, but allow the intervals to differ from each other.

All of the estimation is carried out including a "base" value for β_1 and β_2, with all other effects estimated relative to a base value of unity.[8] The various different effects are included by entering multiplicative parameters, so that the estimating equation looks like:

---

6. We exclude cells for which $t = T$, where the model predicts that the number of citations is identically zero. In fact, the number of citations in such cells is almost always zero.

7. About two-thirds of the zero citation observations are for cells associated with either Canada or Rest of World.

8. As noted above, α is not separately identified from β_1 and β_2. Hence, we do not estimate a "base" value for the parameter α; it is implicitly unity.

$$p_{itgTL} = \alpha_i \alpha_{tp} \alpha_g \alpha_T \alpha_L \exp[-(\beta_1)\beta_{1i}\beta_{1g}\beta_{IL}(T-t)]$$

$$\times [1 - \exp(-\beta_2(T-t))] + \varepsilon_{igtTL}, \qquad\qquad [5]$$

where $i = c, u, f$ (cited institution type); $t = 1963$–1990 (cited year) $tp = 1 \ldots 6$ (5-year intervals for cited year, except the first interval is 1963–1965); $g = 1 \ldots 5$ (technological field of cited patent); $T = 1977 \ldots 1993$ (citing year); and $L = 1 \ldots 5$ (citing region). In this model, unlike the linear case, the null hypothesis of no effect corresponds to parameter values of unity rather than zero. For each effect, one group is omitted from estimation, i.e., its multiplicative parameter is constrained to unity. Thus, the parameter values are interpreted as relative to that base group.[9]

The estimate of any particular $\alpha(k)$, say $\alpha(g = \text{Drugs and Medical})$, is a proportionality factor measuring the extent to which the patents in the field "Drugs and Medical" are more or less likely to be cited over time vis à vis patents in the base category "All Other." Thus, an estimate of $\alpha(k = \text{Drugs}) = 1.4$ means that the likelihood that a patent in the field of Drugs and Medical will receive a citation is 40% higher than the likelihood of a patent in the base category, controlling of course for a wide range of factors. Notice that this is true across all lags; we can think of an α greater than unity as meaning that the citation function is shifted upward proportionately, relative to the base group. Hence the integral over time (i.e., the total number of citations per patent) will also be 40% larger.

We can think of the overall rate of citation intensity measured by variations in α to be composed of two parts. Citation intensity is the product of the "fertility" (7) or "importance" (4) of the underlying ideas in spawning future technological developments, and the average "size" of a patent, i.e., how much of the unobservable advance of knowledge is packaged in a typical patent. Within the formulation of this paper, it is not possible to decompose the α-effects into these two components.[10]

In the case of $\alpha(K)$, that is, when the multiplicative factor varies with attributes of the *citing* patents, variations in it should be inter-

---

9. The base group for each effect is: Cited time period (tp), 1963–1965; Cited field (g), "All Other"; Type of Cited Institution (i), Corporate; Citing year (T), 1977; Citing region (L), United States.
10. Caballero and Jaffe (7) attempt to identify the size of patents by allowing exponential obsolescence to be a function of accumulated patents rather than elapsed calendar time. We intend to explore this possibility in future work.

preted as differences in the "propensity to cite" (or in the probability of *making* a citation) of patents in a particular category vis à vis the base category of the citing patents. If, for example, $\alpha(K = \text{Europe})$ is 0.5, this means that the average patent granted to European inventors is one-half as likely as a patent granted to inventors residing in the United States to cite any given United States patent.

Variations in β_1 (again, by attributes of either the cited or the citing patents) imply differences in the rate of decay or "obsolescence" across categories of patents. Higher values of β_1 mean higher rates of decay, which pull the citations function downwards and leftward. In other words, the likelihood of citations would be lower everywhere for higher β_1 and would peak earlier on. Thus, a higher α means more citations at all lags; a lower β_1 means more citations at *later* lags.

When both $\alpha(k, K)$ and $\beta_1(k, K)$ vary, the citation function can shift upward at some lags while shifting downward at others. For example, if $\alpha(g = \text{Electronics}) = 2.00$, but $\beta_1(g = \text{Electronics}) = 1.29$, then patents in electronics have a very high likelihood of citations relative to the base category, but they also become obsolete faster. Because obsolescence is compounded over time, differences in β_1 eventually result in large differences in the citation frequency. If we compute the ratio of the likelihood of citations for patents in electronics relative to those in "all other" using these parameters, we find that 1 year after being granted patents in electronics are 89% more likely to be cited, but 12 years later the frequencies for the two groups are about the same, and at a lag of 20 years Electronics patents are actually 36% *less* likely to be cited than patents in the base category.

Results

Table 2 shows the results from the estimation of Eq. 5, using a weighted non-linear least-squares procedure. We weight each observation by $nn = (n_{\text{tgi}} {}^* n_{\text{TL}})^{**}0.5$, where n_{tgi} is the number of potentially cited patents and n_{TL} the number of potentially citing patents corresponding to a given cell. This weighting scheme should take care of possible heteroskedasticity, since the observations correspond essentially to "grouped data," that is, each observation is an average (in the corresponding cell), computed by dividing the number of citations by $(n_{\text{tgi}} {}^* n_{\text{TL}})$.

Table 2
Non-linear least-squares regression results

	Parameter	Asymptotic standard error	t-statistic for H_0 (parameter $= 1$)
Citing year effects (base $= 1977$)			
1978	1.115	0.03449	3.32
1979	1.223	0.03795	5.88
1980	1.308	0.03943	7.80
1981	1.400	0.04217	9.48
1982	1.511	0.04637	11.01
1983	1.523	0.04842	10.80
1984	1.606	0.05209	11.64
1985	1.682	0.05627	12.12
1986	1.753	0.06073	12.40
1987	1.891	0.06729	13.24
1988	1.904	0.07085	12.76
1989	2.045	0.07868	13.29
1990	1.933	0.07795	11.97
1991	1.905	0.07971	11.36
1992	1.994	0.08627	11.52
1993	1.956	0.08918	10.73
Cited year effects (base $= 1963$–1965)			
1966–1970	0.747	0.02871	-8.82
1971–1975	0.691	0.02820	-10.97
1976–1980	0.709	0.03375	-8.62
1981–1985	0.647	0.03647	-9.69
1986–1990	0.728	0.04752	-5.72
Technological field effects (base $=$ all other)			
Drugs and medical	1.409	0.01798	22.73
Chemicals excluding drugs	1.049	0.01331	3.65
Electronics, optics, and nuclear	1.360	0.01601	22.51
Mechanical	1.037	0.01370	2.69
Citing country effects (base $=$ United States)			
Canada	0.647	0.00938	-37.59
European Economic Community	0.506	0.00534	-92.49
Japan	0.442	0.00542	-102.99
Rest of world	0.506	0.00824	-59.93

Table 2 (continued)

	Parameter	Asymptotic standard error	t-statistic for H_0 (parameter $= 1$)
University/corporate differential by cited time period			
1965	1.191	0.12838	1.49
1966–1970	0.930	0.04148	−1.70
1971–1975	1.169	0.02419	7.00
1976–1980	1.216	0.01765	12.26
1981–1985	1.250	0.01718	14.55
1986–1990	1.062	0.01746	3.57
Federal government/corporate differential by cited time period			
1963–1965	0.720	0.04592	−6.11
1966–1970	0.739	0.02498	−10.45
1971–1975	0.744	0.01531	−16.71
1976–1980	0.759	0.01235	−19.51
1981–1985	0.754	0.01284	−19.15
1986–1990	0.709	0.01551	−18.78
$\beta 1^*$	0.213	0.00247	86.28
$\beta 2^*$	3.86E−06	1.97E−07	19.61

Total observations, 26,975; R-square $= 0.5161$.
$*$ t-statistic is for H_0, parameter $= 0$.

Time Effects

The first set of coefficients, those for the citing years (α_T), and for the cited period (α_{tp}), serve primarily as controls. The α_T show a steep upward trend, reaching a plateau in 1989. This reflects a well-known institutional phenomenon, namely, the increasing propensity to make citations at the patent office, due largely to the computerization of the patent file and of the operations of patent examiners. By contrast, the coefficients for the *cited* period decline steadily relative to the base (1963–1965 $= 1$), to 0.65 in 1981–1985, recovering somewhat in 1986–1990 to 0.73. This downward trend may be taken to reflect a decline in the "fertility" of corporate patents from the 1960s until the mid-1980s, with a mild recovery thereafter. The timing of such decline coincides, with a short lag, with the slowdown in productivity growth experienced throughout the industrialized world in the 1970s and early 1980s. This suggests a possible causal nexus between these two

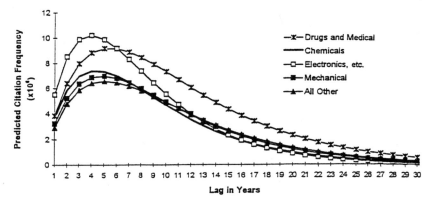

Figure 2
Plot of the predicted citation function for patents in Electronics, Optics, and Nuclear versus patents in the base field (All Other)

phenomena, but further work would be required to substantiate this conjecture.

Technological Fields

We allow both for variations in the multiplicative factor α_g and in the β_1 of each technological field of the cited patents. Thus, fields with α larger than one are likely to get more citations than the base field at any point in time. On the other hand, the rate of citations to patents in fields with larger β_1 decays faster than for others. For example, we see in Table 2 that α(Electronics, etc.) = 2.00, meaning that patents in this field get on average twice as many citations as those in the base field. However, β_1(Electronics, etc.) = 1.29 and hence the large initial "citation advantage" of this field fades rather quickly over time. This is clearly seen in Fig. 2, where we plot the predicted citation function for patents in Electronics, Optics, and Nuclear, *versus* patents in the base field ("All Other"). Patents in electronics are much more highly cited during the first few years after grant; however, due to their faster obsolescence, in later years they are actually less cited than those in the base group.

To grasp the meaning of these estimates, we present in Table 3 the ratio of the citation probability of each of the technological fields, to the citation probability of the base field, at different lags (1, 5, 10, 20, and 30 years after the grant date of the cited patent). Looking again

Table 3
Citation probability ratio by technological field

Technological field	β_1	Lag, yrs.				
		1	5	10	20	30
Drugs and medical	0.932	1.33	1.40	1.50	1.71	1.96
Chemical	1.158	1.27	1.12	0.96	0.70	0.51
Electronics, etc.	1.288	1.89	1.50	1.13	0.64	0.36
Mechanical	1.054	1.11	1.06	1.01	0.91	0.81
Other	1.000	1.00	1.00	1.00	1.00	1.00

at Electronics, we see that the ratio starts very high at 1.89, but after 12 years it is the same as the base field, after 20 years it declines to 0.64, and declines further to 0.36 after 30 years. This implies that this field is extremely dynamic, with a great deal of "action" in the form of follow-up developments taking place during the first few years after an innovation is patented, but also with a very high obsolescence rate. Thus, a decade later the wave of further advances subsides, and 30 years later citations have virtually ceased. Commonly held perceptions about the technological dynamism of this field are thus amply confirmed by these results, and given a precise quantitative expression.

For other fields the results are perhaps less striking but still interesting. Drugs and Medical begins at 133% of the base citation frequency, but due to the low obsolescence rate it actually grows over time (at a slow pace), so that 20 years later it stands at 170% relative to the base field. Again, this is shown graphically in Fig. 2 and numerically in Table 3. The conjecture here is that due to the long lead times in pharmaceutical research, including the process of getting approval from the Federal Drug Administration, follow-up developments are slow in coming. Thus, whereas in Electronics a given innovation has very little impact 10–20 years later because the field is evolving so fast, in pharmaceuticals a new drug may still prompt follow-up innovations much later, after its medical and commercial viability have been well established.

As to the Chemical field, we see that it starts off at 127% of the base field, but due to a high obsolescence rate the advantage fades over time (though not as fast as in Electronics), falling behind the base field in less than a decade. The Mechanical field is similar to the base field, slowly losing ground over time. Note that after 20 years

Table 4
Citation probability ratio by institution

Research institution	β_1	Lag, yrs.				
		1	5	10	20	30
Universities 1981–1985	0.978	1.23	1.25	1.28	1.34	1.40
Universities 1986–1990	0.978	1.08	1.10	1.12	1.18	1.23
Federal labs 1981–1985	0.932	0.69	0.73	0.78	0.90	1.03
Federal labs 1986–1990	0.932	0.67	0.70	0.75	0.86	0.99
Corporate	1.000	1.00	1.00	1.00	1.00	1.00

the ranking of fields changes dramatically compared with the ranking at the beginning, suggesting that allowing for variations in both α and β_1 is essential to understand the behavior of fields over time.

Institutional Type

To capture the various dimensions of institutional variations we interact the α of each institutional type with the cited period (except for corporate, which serves as the base), and allow also for differences across institutions in the rate of decay β_1. The results show that the estimates of β_1 for universities and for Government are less than 1, but only slightly so, and hence we limit the discussion to variations in α (see Table 4 for the effects of the variations in β_1.)

Ignoring 1965, we see that university patents became increasingly more "fertile" than corporate ones in the 1970s and early 1980s, but their relative citation intensity declined in the late 1980s. This confirms and extends similar results that we obtained in previous work (6). Government patents, on the other hand, are significantly less fertile than corporate patents, with a moderate upward trend over time (from 0.59 in 1963–1966 to 0.68 in 1981–1985), except for a decline in the last period. Their overall lower fertility level may be due to the fact that these laboratories had been traditionally quite isolated from mainstream commercial innovations and, thus, those innovations that they did choose to patent were in some sense marginal. By the same token, one might conjecture that the upward trend in the fertility ratio may be due to the increasing "openness" of federal laboratories, and their efforts to reach out and make their innovations more commercially oriented.

Table 5
Citation probability ratio by citing geographic area

Location	β_1	Lag, yrs.				
		1	5	10	20	30
Canada	0.914	0.58	0.62	0.67	0.80	0.95
Europe	0.899	0.44	0.48	0.53	0.65	0.79
Japan	1.002	0.44	0.44	0.44	0.44	0.44
Rest of world	0.900	0.44	0.48	0.53	0.64	0.78
United States	1.000	1.00	1.00	1.00	1.00	1.00

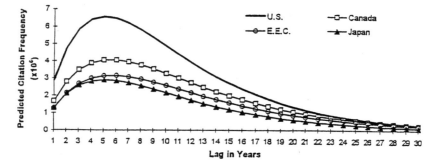

Figure 3
Frequency of citations to U.S. patents, from patents originating in the United States, the European Economic Community, Canada, and Japan. The localization effect fades over time.

Location

The regional multiplicative coefficients show very significant "localization" effects. That is, patents granted to United States inventors are much more likely to cite previous United States patents than are patents granted to inventors of other countries: α for the different foreign regions/countries is in the 0.43–0.57 range, as opposed to the (normalized) value of 1 for the United States. At the same time, though, all foreign countries except Japan have lower β_1 than the United States. Thus, the propensity to cite (i.e., to "absorb spillovers") for Canada and Europe increases over time relative to patents in the base category. This means that the localization effect fades over time. This can be seen clearly in Table 5 and in Fig. 3: the probability that a foreign inventor would cite a patent of a United States inventor is 42–56% lower than that of a United States resident inventor 1 year after grant, but 20 years later the difference has shrunk to 20–36%. The puzzling exception is Japan; the estimates imply that the "receptiveness" of Japanese inventors to United States inventions remains low, since β_1 (Japan) does not differ significantly from unity.

The "fading" effect in the geographic dimension corresponds to the intuitive notion that knowledge eventually diffuses evenly across geographic and other boundaries, and that any initial "local" advantage in that sense will eventually dissipate. Once again, these results offer a quantitative idea of the extent of the initial localization and the speed of fading. Notice also that starting a few years after grant, the differences across regions seem to depend upon a metric of geographic, and perhaps also cultural, proximity: at lag 10, for example, Canada is highest with a coefficient of 0.67, followed by Europe with 0.53, and Japan with 0.44.

Further Results

Finally, the overall estimate of $\beta_1 = 0.2$ means that the citation function reaches its maximum at about 5 years, which is consistent with the empirical citation distribution shown in Fig. 1. The R^2 of 0.52 is fairly high for models of this kind, suggesting that the postulated double exponential combined with the effects that we have identified fit the data reasonably well.

Conclusion

The computerization of patent citations data provides an exciting opportunity to examine the links among inventions and inventors, over time, space, technology, and institutions. The ability to look at very large numbers of patents and citations allows us to begin to interpret overall citation flows in ways that better reflect reality. This chapter represents an initial exploration of these data. Many variations that we have not explored are possible, but this initial foray provides some intriguing results. First, we confirm our earlier results on the geographic localization of citations, but now provide a much more compelling picture of the process of diffusion of citations around the world over time. Second, we find that federal government patents are cited significantly less than corporate patents, although they do have somewhat greater "staying power" over time. Third, we confirm our earlier findings regarding the importance or fertility of university patents. Interestingly, we do not find that university patents are, to any significant extent, more likely to be cited after long periods of time. Finally, we show that citation patterns across technological fields conform to prior beliefs about the pace of innovation and the significance of "gestation" lags in different areas, with Electronics, Optics, and Nuclear Technology showing very high early citation but rapid obsolescence, whereas Drugs and Medical Technology generate significant citations for a very long time.

The list of additional questions that could be examined with these data and this kind of model is even longer. (i) It would be interesting to examine if the geographic localization differs across the corporate, university, and federal cited samples. (ii) The interpretation that we give to the geographic results could be strengthened by examining patents granted in the United States to foreign corporations. Our interpretation suggests that the lower citation rate for foreign inventors should not hold for this group of cited patents. (iii) We could apply a similar model to geographic regions within the United States, although some experimentation will be necessary to determine how small such regions can be and still yield reasonably large numbers of citations in each cell while controlling for other effects. (iv) It would be useful to confirm the robustness of these results to finer technological distinctions, although our previous work with citations data lead us to believe that this will not make a big difference. (v) We would like to investigate the feasibility of modeling obsolescence as a function of accumulated patents. Caballero and Jaffe (7) implemented this approach, but in that analysis patents were not distinguished by location or technological field.

Acknowledgments

We acknowledge research support from National Science Foundation Grants SBR-9320973 and SBR-9413099.

References

1. Romer, P. M. (1990) *J. Pol. Econ.* 98, S71–S102.

2. Grossman, G. M. & Helpman, E. (1991) *Q. J. Econ.* 106, 557–586.

3. Jaffe, A. B., Henderson, R. & Trajtenberg, M. (1993) *Q. J. Econ.* 108, 577–598.

4. Trajtenberg, M., Henderson, R. & Jaffe, A. B. (1996) *University Versus Corporate Patents: A Window on the Basieness of Invention, Economics of Innovation and New Technology*, in press.

5. Griliches, Z. (1990) *J. Econ. Lit.* 28, 1661–1707.

6. Henderson, R., Jaffe, A. B. & Trajtenberg, M. (1996) in *A Productive Tension: University–Industry Research Collaboration in the Era of Knowledge-Based Economic Growth*, eds. David P. & Steinmueller, E. (Stanford Univ. Press, Stanford, CA).

7. Caballero, R. J. & Jaffe, A. B. (1993) in *NBER Macroeconomics Annual 1993*, eds. Blanchard, O. J. & Fischer, S. M. (MIT Press, Cambridge, MA), pp. 15–74.

7 International Knowledge Flows: Evidence from Patent Citations

Adam B. Jaffe and Manuel Trajtenberg

1 Introduction

The rate at which knowledge diffuses outward from the institutional setting and geographic location in which it is created has important implications for the modeling of technological change and economic growth, and for science and technology policy. Models of endogenous economic growth, such as Romer (1990) or Grossman and Helpman (1991), typically treat knowledge as completely diffused within an economy, but implicitly or explicitly assume that knowledge does not diffuse across economies. In the policy arena, ultimate economic benefits are increasingly seen as the primary policy motivation for public support of scientific research. Obviously, the economic benefits to the U.S. economy of domestic research depend on the fruits of that research being more easily or more quickly harvested by domestic firms than by foreign firms. Thus for both modeling and policy-making purposes it is crucial to understand the institutional, geographic and temporal dimensions of the spread of newly created knowledge.

There is an existing empirical literature on international technology flows. Much of this literature focuses on what might be described as "technology" diffusion rather than knowledge diffusion. For example, Teece (1977) discusses the difficulties that a multinational firm has in applying technology developed in one country to its operations overseas. Park (1995) and Coe and Helpman (1995) examine the impact on a country's productivity growth of the trade-weighted R&D of other countries. Generally, a positive effect is found, which can be interpreted as reduced-form evidence of knowledge spillovers across international boundaries. While the mechanism for such spillovers is not identified, it seems reasonable that many forms of communication and information transfer would be correlated with bilateral trade flows. In these analyses, however, it is difficult to distinguish the effect of "pure" knowledge flows from the effect of technology flows embodied in advanced capital goods sold from one country to another. This distinction is crucial. Knowledge is inherently nonrival in its use, and hence its creation and diffusion are likely to lead to spillovers and increasing returns; it is this nonrival property of knowledge that is at the theoretical heart of models that produce endogenous growth from research. But to the extent that the knowledge or technology flow is embodied in a purchased piece of equipment, it may not produce a spillover, or, if it does, the spillover may take the form of a pricing or pecuniary externality rather than a technological one (Griliches, 1979).

Knowledge spillovers are much harder to measure than technology transfer, precisely because they tend to be disembodied. In previous work (Jaffe and Trajtenberg, 1996; Jaffe, Henderson and Trajtenberg, 1993), we have looked at citations made by patents to previous patents as a "window" on the process of knowledge flow. Jaffe, Henderson and Trajtenberg, 1993, showed that patent citations do appear to be somewhat localized geographically, implying that a region or country does utilize knowledge created within it somewhat more readily than do more remote regions. In Jaffe and Trajtenberg, 1996, we went further, looking in detail at citations from other countries' patents to those of the U.S. We showed there that there is a clear time path to the diffusion of knowledge, in which domestic inventors' citation probabilities are particularly high in the early years after an invention is made.

While this previous work indicates the usefulness of patent citations for exploring knowledge flows, it also highlights the need for careful attention to the details of the patenting and citation processes. In particular, changes in citation practices, truncation biases, technology field effects, and the presence of large numbers of "self-citations" must all be taken into account in using citation data to examine knowledge flows.

We have three goals in this chapter. First, we demonstrate how an econometric model can be used to make citations a potentially useful measure of knowledge flows, by controlling for the effects of truncation, changes in citation patterns, and technology field effects. Second, we explore for the first time the citation patterns among all combinations of the G-5 countries, the U.S., Great Britain, France,

Germany and Japan. This gives a much richer picture of the geographic dimension of citation diffusion, by examining the extent and speed of diffusion of citations within and among all combinations of these countries. This permits us to estimate the extent and nature of "localization" of citations within each of these countries, to examine differences among the countries in their apparent absorption of foreign technology, and to identify some interesting pairwise interactions. Finally, we add the dimensions of "institutional localization" and "technological localization" to the modeling, and examine the interactions between localization in these dimensions and in geography.

2 Knowledge Flows and Patent Citations

Consider a researcher or inventor working on a given technological problem at a given time in a given geographic location and institutional setting. This inventor might find it easier, cheaper or faster to solve her technological problem by virtue of access to knowledge created earlier by other inventors and researchers. For linguistic color and convenience, call the invention that is facilitated by some earlier piece of research the "descendant" and the earlier work that contributed to it the "antecedent." The question we want to ask is: how is the probability that a given descendant will benefit from a specific antecedent affected by the time, geographic location, institutional setting and technological nature of each, and by the relationship between the two along each of these dimensions. In particular, we are interested in the extent of "localization" in geography, institutional setting and technology space, and how localization interacts with time. That is, is a descendant more likely to benefit from an antecedent that is nearby geographically, comes from within the same institution, and is technologically similar, and does this increased likelihood of benefiting from nearby antecedents vary with the length of time elapsed.

Our expectation is that knowledge follows a diffusion process through geographic, institutional and technological spaces. Thus, researchers that are "nearby" along each of these dimensions would be particularly likely to benefit disproportionately in the time period immediately after the antecedent innovation occurs. We expect, however, that this "localization effect" will tend to fade over time, so that eventually the probability of an antecedent benefiting a remote descendant may be no lower than the probability of benefiting one nearby.

Thus localization and the fading of localization are phenomena that derive from the *relationship between* two inventions or inventors. But these relational phenomena are intrinsically tied up with the attributes of the antecedent and descendant themselves. A particular inventor (or group of inventors) may just be good at picking up and implementing others' ideas quickly, and others may be good at disseminating or spreading the implications of their research, or may produce research which is systematically more "fruitful" in stimulating others. The probability that a particular group will benefit from some other group (and the changes over time of this probability) will therefore be determined jointly by the properties of each group, and the properties of the relationship between the groups.

In addition to diffusing outward over time, bits of knowledge also become obsolete. Thus, though the probability that a given inventor will know of a given antecedent increases as the time lag between them grows, the probability that the antecedent will actually be helpful declines, on average. The combination of diffusion and obsolescence processes may cause the probability of using a given antecedent to first rise and then fall with elapsed time.

Our maintained assumption is that patents are a proxy for "bits of knowledge" and patent citations are a proxy for a given bit of knowledge being useful in the development of a descendant bit. This permits us to use the probability of citation as a proxy for the probability of useful knowledge flow, and empirical citation frequencies as a measure of that probability. Of course, the frequency with which generation of knowledge bits leads to a patent (the "propensity to patent") varies over time and space, as does the frequency with which use of earlier knowledge produces a citation (the "propensity to cite"). These variations in the correspondence between the data and the underlying constructs of interest create problems of interpretation that must be dealt with via a combination of multiple measurements and identifying assumptions.

The nature of these issues can be seen in Figure 1, which plots empirical citation frequencies from other countries to the U.S., as a function of the time lag between the citing and cited patents. The citation frequency is calculated as the total number of citations divided by the product of the number of potentially citing and number

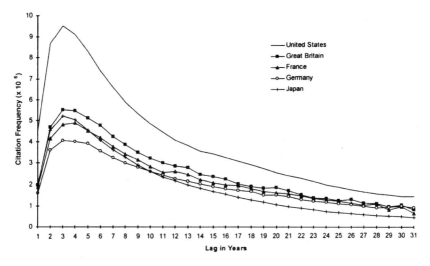

Figure 1
Raw citation frequencies to U.S.-invented patents, by citing country

of potentially cited patents. For example, Japanese inventors took out about 22 thousand patents in 1993. U.S. inventors took out about 36 thousand patents in 1969. A total of about 800 citations from 1993-Japanese patents were made to 1969-U.S. patents. Hence the estimated citation frequency for this combination is about 1×10^{-6} (800/ (22000*36000)). The citation frequencies plotted in Figure 1 are averages for all combinations with a given lag for which we have data, e.g., the calculated frequency at lag 30 derives from citations from 1993 to 1963 (our earliest data year) and 1994 (our last data year) to 1964. We interpret the citation frequency as an estimate of the probability that a randomly drawn patent in the citing group will cite a randomly drawn patent in the cited group.

Important features of these data are immediately visible in Figure 1. First, the citation frequency rises rapidly in the first few years after the cited patent, then peaks and declines slowly over time. A significant number of citations are still being received many years after initial grant. Second, a U.S.-invented patent is much more likely to be cited by a U.S.-invented patent than it is by a foreign-invented patent. Finally, even putting aside the domestic/foreign distinction, there are noticeable differences in the citation frequencies across citing countries. For example, the likelihood of a random U.K.-invented patent citing a U.S.-invented patent is about 40% higher than the like-lihood of a random German-invented patent citing a U.S.-invented patent.

Although all of these qualitative features illustrated in Figure 1 are in some sense "real," raw citation frequencies are afflicted by numerous theoretical and actual biases that make their interpreta-tion dangerous. First, the observation of citations is always subject to truncation bias. Since we can observe only the citations already granted, we can see citations at long lags only for citations *from* very recent cohorts *to* very old cohorts. The significance of the truncation problem is greatly exacerbated by the fact that the number of cita-tions *made* per patent has been rising significantly in the last two decades (Caballero and Jaffe, 1993). Thus the observations at long lags in Figure 1 all come from patents granted when relatively many cita-tions were made (e.g., citations from 1993 patents to 1963 patents), whereas the observations at short lags are mixtures of many different cited cohort/citing cohort combinations (e.g., for lag = 5 we have 1977 to 1972, 1987 to 1982, and so forth). We will see below that con-trolling for these interacting time effects yields predicted probabilities for long lags considerably lower than those shown in Figure 1.

In addition to artifacts of the citation process, the numbers in Fig-ure 1 contain effects operating along the institutional and technolog-ical dimensions that interact non-randomly with geography. Not surprisingly, the probability that an inventor will cite another inven-tor employed by the same firm is much higher than the probability of citing a random inventor employed elsewhere. And, inventors employed by the same firm are more likely to live in the same country than random inventors employed by different firms. Hence the higher citation frequency for U.S. to U.S. than for Japan to U.S. is partly due to a higher citation frequency within firms, combined with a geo-graphic localization of employees within firms. While for some pur-poses it might be appropriate to include this "firm self-citation" effect within what we call the geographic localization effect, for other pur-poses we may want to separate the two. Similarly, though ultimately less important empirically, an inventor is much more likely to cite previous patents that are in closely related technological fields to her own, and one might expect that inventors working in the same field are more likely to live in the same country. Again, we would like to be able to measure the geographic localization effect while controlling for technological localization effects. The econometric model that we develop below is meant to allow us to sort out and measure each of these different effects.

3   The Data

We are in the final stages of collecting from commercial sources a complete database on all U.S. patents[1] granted since 1963. It includes data for each patent indicating the nature of the organization, if any, to which the patent property right was assigned; the names of the inventors and the organization, if any, to which the patent right was assigned; the residence of each inventor;[2] the date of the patent application and the patent grant; a detailed technological classification for the patent; and miscellaneous other information. A file indicating all of the citations made by U.S. patents since 1977 to previous U.S. patents complements the data on individual patents. Using the citation information in conjunction with the detailed information about each patent itself, we have a rich mine of information about individual inventive acts and the links among them as indicated by citations made by a given patent to a previous one.

We have discussed elsewhere at great length the advantages and disadvantages of using patents and patent citations to indicate inventions and knowledge links among inventions (Jaffe, Henderson and Trajtenberg, 1993; Trajtenberg, Henderson and Jaffe, 1997; see also Griliches, 1990). Patent citations perform the legal function of delimiting the patent right by identifying previous patents whose technological scope is explicitly placed outside the bounds of the citing patent. Hence the appearance of a citation indicates that the cited patent is, in some sense, a technological antecedent of the citing patent. Patent applicants bear a legal obligation to disclose any knowledge that they might have of relevant prior inventions, and the patent examiner may also add citations not identified by the applicant. In related work, Jaffe, Fogarty and Banks (forthcoming) examined in detail the patents that did and did not contain citations to a specific set of important NASA patents. The conclusion was that, while citations contain much "noise" in the form of apparently spurious

---

1. By "U.S. patents," we mean in this context patents granted by the U.S. patent office. All of our research relies on U.S. patents in this sense. Currently about half of U.S. patents are granted to foreigners.
2. City and state for U.S. inventors, country for non-U.S. inventors.

implied connections, on the whole they do provide useful information about the generation of future technological impact of a given
invention.

The analysis in this paper is based on citations to patents granted
between 1963 and 1993. We examine a set of "potentially cited"
patents whose primary inventor resided in the U.S., Great Britain,
France, Germany or Japan, and which were assigned to corporations.
There are a total of about 1.5 million such patents. About 65% of
these are from the U.S. (i.e., their inventors reside in the U.S.), 17%
are from Japan, 10% from Germany, 5% from Great Britain, and 4%
from France. We then examine all citations made to these corporate
patents (whether or not the citing patent is itself corporate) from
patents granted in any of these five countries between 1977 and
1994. There are about 1.2 million "citing" patents, and they made a
total of about 5.0 million citations to the set of "potentially cited"
patents that we are considering.

Patenting in different countries differs in ways that affect observed
citation frequencies. Some indications of these differences are presented in Table 1, which summarizes the patent data, from both the
cited and citing perspectives, for the five different countries. We also
classify patents into five broad technological fields, based on the
main patent class assigned to the patent by the patent examiner.[3]
These fields are: Drugs and Medical Technology; Chemicals, excluding Drugs; Electronics, Optical and Nuclear Technology; Mechanical
Technology; and All Other. Table 1 gives some totals for patents and
citations for each of the five countries and five technology fields.
Overall, 6% of the cited patents are in Drugs and Medical, 28% in
Chemicals, 22% in Electronics, etc., 35% in Mechanical and 9% All
Other. There are, however, significant variations across the countries
in the field composition of their patents. In particular, Japan has a
larger share of electronic patents and Germany a larger share of
chemical patents than the U.S. Since citation intensities vary by field
within countries, raw differences between countries as in Figure 1
are a mixture of country effects, field effects, and field-country interaction effects. We discuss below how to sort out these effects.

Table 1 also shows that a significant fraction of citations from each
country are "self-citations." Self-citations are defined as those for
which the citing and cited patent are both assigned to the same cor-

---

3. There are about 400 of these patent classes.

Table 1
Patents and citations by country

	Potentially cited patents	Average citations per patent	Fraction of self-cites	Potentially citing patents
United States				
1969	36,406	2.74	0.07	
1993	36,512	0.31	0.31	53,235
average per year	31,135	3.50	0.29	42,494
Drugs and Medical	5%	4.54	0.22	
Chemical, exc. Drugs	29%	3.35	0.34	
Electronics, Optics and Nuclear	21%	3.84	0.26	
Mechanical	34%	3.32	0.30	
All Other	11%	3.30	0.25	
Great Britain				
1969	2713	1.98	0.02	
1993	1995	0.23	0.16	2294
average per year	2223	2.86	0.22	2471
Drugs and Medical	8%	3.10	0.22	
Chemical, exc. Drugs	29%	2.89	0.24	
Electronics, Optics and Nuclear	20%	3.17	0.17	
Mechanical	35%	2.66	0.23	
All Other	9%	2.64	0.18	
France				
1969	1341	2.04	0.01	
1993	2446	0.22	0.24	2908
average per year	1673	2.58	0.18	2457
Drugs and Medical	8%	2.40	0.19	
Chemical, exc. Drugs	28%	2.42	0.20	
Electronics, Optics and Nuclear	22%	2.84	0.14	
Mechanical	35%	2.63	0.18	
All Other	8%	2.40	0.16	
Germany				
1969	3785	2.15	0.06	
1993	6255	0.21	0.27	6891
average per year	4894	2.64	0.22	6603
Drugs and Medical	6%	2.72	0.20	
Chemical, exc. Drugs	34%	2.56	0.27	
Electronics, Optics and Nuclear	17%	2.73	0.18	
Mechanical	35%	2.71	0.20	
All Other	8%	2.42	0.19	

Table 1 (continued)

	Potentially cited patents	Average citations per patent	Fraction of self-cites	Potentially citing patents
Japan				
1969	1758	2.02	0.05	
1993	20,997	0.31	0.28	22,291
average per year	8040	3.44	0.19	13,780
Drugs and Medical	5%	2.80	0.18	
Chemical, exc. Drugs	23%	3.21	0.22	
Electronics, Optics and Nuclear	30%	3.72	0.19	
Mechanical	36%	3.54	0.18	
All Other	6%	2.82	0.19	
All				
1969	46,003	2.60	0.04	
1993	68,205	0.30	0.25	87,619
average per year	47,965	3.34	0.22	67,805
Drugs and Medical	6%	3.89	0.20	
Chemical, exc. Drugs	28%	3.18	0.25	
Electronics, Optics and Nuclear	22%	3.66	0.19	
Mechanical	35%	3.24	0.22	
All Other	9%	3.12	0.19	

porate organization.[4] Self-citations are more common in the U.S. than in other countries. It also turns out that self-citation come more quickly on average, and are more geographically localized. In order to get measures that more closely correspond to knowledge "spillovers," most of the analysis below is carried out excluding these self-citations.

Finally, the number of patents taken out in the U.S. has grown at dramatically different rates for different countries. In particular, while the number of U.S. invented patents in 1993 was essentially equal to the number in 1969, the number of Japanese-invented pa-

---

4. Identifying self-citations is complicated by the fact that patents may be assigned to corporate entities that are affiliates or subsidiaries of other entities. We are in the process of refining the corporate assignments of the patents in the database to take this into account, but the results in this paper are based on self-citation defined only in terms of patents assigned to the same corporate entity. This almost certainly understates the extent of self-citation.

tents increased by 1194% over that same period, and the number of Great Britain-invented patents declined by about 26%.[5] Thus when we compare overall citation frequencies for the different countries, we are looking at averages which are tilted towards different citing cohorts.

4 Modeling

A Patent-Pair Citation Frequencies

We seek to model the citation frequencies described in Section II above, the way in which these frequencies evolve over time, and how they are affected by characteristics of the citing and cited patent. One way to approach this would be with a probit-type model, in which each citation is an observation, and the regression dataset is created by combining the actual citations with a random sample of patent pairs that did not cite each other. One could then ask how the predicted probability that a patent pair will result in a citation is affected by various regressor variables.[6]

In this application, however, we observe approximately five million citations; if this were combined with an equal number of non-citing patent pairs, the regression dataset would have ten million observations. The number of unique combinations of values of potential regressor variables is, however, a small fraction of that. Put differently, if one were to run a probit with those ten million observations, very many of those observations would have identical values for any conceivable set of right-hand-side variables. In such a case, no information is lost by combining observations into "cells" characterized by the values of the regressor variables, and making the dependent variable the *fraction* of the patent pairs in the cell for which a citation occurred. In this way, we reduce the number of observations from more than five million (the exact value depending on the sampling from the non-citing pairs) into a dataset with about 50,000 observations, with little loss of relevant information.

Most of our potential regressors are categorical rather than continuous variables, such as cited country, citing country, technology

---

5. As a reminder, these numbers are for patents taken out in the U.S. and assigned to a corporation; U.S.-invented versus Japanese-invented is determined on the basis of the postal address of the primary inventor.
6. See Podolny and Shepard, 1997, for an application of this approach.

field, cited year and citing year. In addition to these effects, we wish to capture the evolution of citations over elapsed time as shown in Figure 1. For this purpose we adapt the formulation of Caballero and Jaffe (1993) and Jaffe and Trajtenberg (1996). The citation frequency (the likelihood that any particular patent K granted in year T will cite some particular patent k granted in year t) is assumed to be determined by the combination of an exponential process by which knowledge diffuses and a second exponential process by which knowledge becomes obsolete. That is:

$$p(k, K) = [1 + \gamma D(k, K)]\alpha(k, K) \exp[-\beta_1(k, K)(T - t)]$$
$$\times [1 - \exp(-\beta_2(T - t))] \tag{1}$$

where β_1 determines the rate of obsolescence and β_2 determines the rate of diffusion. The parameter α is a shift parameter that depends on the attributes of both the patent k and the patent K. $D(k, K)$ is a dummy variable, set equal to unity if the patent k is in the same patent class as the patent K, and zero otherwise. Thus, the parameter γ measures the overall increase in citation frequency associated with the two patents matching by patent class. The dependence of the parameters α and β_1 on k and K is meant to indicate that these could be functions of certain attributes of both the cited and citing patents. In this paper, we consider the following as attributes of the cited patent k that might affect its citation frequency:

· t, the grant year of the potentially cited patent,
· l, the "location" of the cited inventor (U.S., Great Britain, France, Germany or Japan),
· $g = 1 \ldots 5$, the technological field of the potentially cited patent.

As attributes of the potentially citing patent K that might affect the citation likelihood we consider:

· T, the grant year of the potentially citing patent, and
· $L = 1 \ldots 5$, the location of the potentially citing patent.

Additional insight into this parameterization of the diffusion process can be gained by computing the lag at which the citation function is maximized ("the modal lag"), and the modal probability of citation. A little calculus shows that the modal lag is approximately equal to $1/\beta_1$; increases in β_1 shift the citation function to the left.

The maximum value of the citation frequency is approximately determined by β_2/β_1. Increases in β_2 holding β_1 constant increase the overall citation intensity,[7] and are roughly equivalent to increasing the citation frequency *proportionately* at every value of $(T - t)$. That is, variations in β_2, holding β_1 constant are not separately identified from variations in α. Thus, since the model is somewhat easier to estimate and interpret with variations in α, we do not allow variations in β_2.

B Expected Citation Count for "Cells"

Consider a potentially cited patent with particular t, l, g attributes, e.g., a Japanese-invented patent in the Drug and Medical area granted in 1985. The expected number of citations that this patent will receive from a particular patent with a given T, L combination (e.g., a British patent granted in 1993 that happens to be in the same patent class) is just the above likelihood, as a function of l, t, g, T, L and $D(k, K)$. The expected number of citations *from all* patents with a given T, L combination is found by summing the frequency shown in Eq. 1 over all such patents. Similarly, the expected total number of citations *to all* patents with the particular l, t, g combination will be found by summing over all such patents. The only tricky part of this double summation is dealing with $D(k, K)$. We show in Appendix A that one can start from Eq. (1) and aggregate to derive a relationship for "cells" identified by l, t, g, T and L, where the dependent variable is the expected frequency of citation

$$p_{ltgTL} \equiv \frac{C_{ltgTL}}{(N_{TL})(N_{ltg})},$$

i.e., the ratio of the number of citations to the product of the number of potentially citing and potentially cited patents. In expectation, this frequency is a function of the characteristics of k and K, and the variable:

$$\text{PROX}_{ltgTL} = \sum_{s} f_{ltgs} f_{TLS}$$

---

7. The approximation involved is that $\log(1 + \beta_2/\beta_1) \approx \beta_2/\beta_1$. Our estimations all lead to β_2/β_1 on the order of 10^{-6}, and indeed the approximation holds to five significant figures.

Table 2
Statistics for regression variables

Label	Mean	Std dev	Minimum	Maximum
Number of citations	98	341	0	6326
Number of non-self-cite citations	78	270	0	5010
Potentially cited patents	1791	2928	16	14735
Potentially citing patents	14,164	16,141	1610	56,065
Cited grant year	1974.4	7.4	1963	1993
Citing grant year	1986.7	5.0	1977	1994
Citation frequency ($\times 10^6$)	3.85	5.34	0	123.24
Non-self-cite citation frequency ($\times 10^6$)	2.78	3.11	0	40.57
Technological proximity of cells	0.0075	0.0069	0.0008	0.0620
Lag in years	12.3	7.4	1	31
Regression weight (square root[ncited $\times$ nciting])	3391	3745	160	28742

where f_{ltgs} is the fraction of potentially cited patents in patent class s and f_{TLS} is the fraction of potentially citing patents in patent class s. PROX measures the extent to which the potentially citing and potentially cited patents overlap in their patent class distribution.[8] It is closely related to the technological proximity measure of firms used in Jaffe (1986). This brings us to the following equation:

$$p_{ltgTL} = \alpha_{ltgTL}[1 + \gamma \text{PROX}_{ltgTL}] \exp[-(\beta_1)_{ltgTL}(T - t)][1 - \exp(-\beta_2(T - t))]$$
$$+ \, \varepsilon_{lgtTL} \qquad\qquad\qquad (2)$$

which can be estimated by non-linear least squares if the error ε_{lgtTL} is well-behaved.

The data set consists of one observation for each feasible combination of values of l, t, g, T and L. Since t runs from 1963 to 1993 and T runs from (the greater of 1977 and $t + 1$) to 1994, the number of cells for each l, g, L combination is $14 \times 18 + (17 + 16 + 15 + 14 + 13 + \cdots + 1)$. There are 125 l, g, L combinations, so the total number of cells is 50,625. Simple statistics for this dataset are presented in Table 2. The average number of cited patents in a cell is about 1800;

---

8. Recall that there are about 400 such patent classes, so that even within the five broad technology fields, country-year pairs will vary in the extent of overlap in patent classes.

the minimum is 16 (French Drug and Medical patents in one particular year) and the maximum is almost 15,000 (U.S. Mechanical patents in one particular year). The number of citations varies from 0 to over 6000 with a mean of about 100; the mean of the citation frequency is about 4×10^{-6}.

C Econometric Issues and Interpretation

The first specification issue to consider is the difficulty of estimating effects associated with cited year, citing year and lag. This is analogous to estimating "vintage," time, and age effects in a wage or a hedonic price model. If lag (our "age" effect) entered the model linearly, then it would be impossible to estimate all three effects. Given that lag enters our model non-linearly, all three effects are, in principle, identified. In practice, however, we found that we could not get the model to converge with the double-exponential lag function and separate α parameters for each cited year and each citing year. We were, however, able to estimate a model in which cited years are grouped into five-year periods, indexed by p. Hence we assume that $\alpha(t)$ is constant over t within these periods, but allow the periods to differ from each other.

The estimation is carried out including "base" values for β_1 and β_2. Location, field, cited period and citing year effects are all estimated relative to a base value of unity.[9] The various different effects are included by entering multiplicative parameters, so that the estimating equation looks as follows:

$$p_{ltgTL} = [1 + \gamma \text{PROX}_{ltgTL}] \alpha_t \alpha_g \alpha_T \alpha_{lL}$$

$$\times \exp[-(\beta_1)\beta_{1g}\beta_{1lL}(T-t)][1 - \exp(-\beta_2(T-t))] + \varepsilon_{lgtTL} \qquad (3)$$

Thus we allow α to vary by cited period, cited field, citing year and all possible combinations of citing country and cited country. We allow β_1 to vary by cited field, and every possible combination of cited and citing countries. In this model, unlike the linear case, the null hypothesis of no effect corresponds to parameter values of unity rather than zero (except for γ, and the "base" values of β_1 and β_2). For each effect, one group is omitted from estimation, i.e., its multiplicative

---

9. As noted above, α is not separately identified from β_1 and β_2. Hence we do not estimate a "base" value for the parameter α; it is implicitly unity.

parameter is constrained to unity. Thus the parameter values are interpreted as relative to that base group.[10]

The estimate of any particular $\alpha(k)$, say $\alpha(g = \text{Chemical})$, is a proportionality factor measuring the extent to which the patents in the Chemical field are more or less likely to be cited over time vis-à-vis patents in the base category (Drugs). Thus, an estimate of $\alpha(g = \text{Chemical}) = 1.5$ means that the likelihood that a patent in the field of Chemicals will receive a citation is 50% higher than the likelihood of a patent in the base category, controlling for other factors. Notice that this is true across all lags; we can think of an α greater than unity as meaning that the citation function is shifted upward proportionately, relative to the base group. Hence the integral over time (i.e., the total number of citations per patent) will also be 50% larger. Similarly, if a $(l = \text{Japan}, L = \text{U.S.})$ is .72, this means that a Japanese patent is 28% less likely to get a citation from a random U.S. patent than is a random U.S. patent.

We can think of the overall citation intensity measured by variations in α as composed of two parts. Citation intensity is the product of the "fertility" (Caballero and Jaffe, 1993) or "importance" (Trajtenberg, Henderson and Jaffe, 1997) of the underlying ideas in spawning future technological developments, and the average "size" of a patent, i.e., how much of the unobservable advance of knowledge is packaged in a typical patent. Within the formulation of this paper, however, it is not possible to decompose the α-effects into these two components.[11]

In the case of $\alpha(K)$, that is, when the multiplicative factor varies with attributes of the citing patents, variations in it should be interpreted as differences in the probability of *making* a citation, all else equal, for patents in a particular category à vis the base category. If, for example, $\alpha(l = \text{U.S.}, L = \text{Japan})$ is 0.76, this means that the average patent granted to Japanese inventors is three-quarters as likely as a patent granted to inventors residing in the U.S. to cite any given U.S. patent. Note that, just as variations in α across cited patents are composed of both variations in fertility or importance and variations in "patent size," variations across citing patents can be caused by both

---

10. The base group for each effect is: Cited time period (p), 1963–65; Cited field (g), "Drugs and Medical"; Citing year (T), 1977; and Cited/Citing country (IL), U.S.-citing-U.S.

11. Caballero and Jaffe (1993) attempt to identify the size of patents by allowing exponential obsolescence to be a function of accumulated patents rather than elapsed calendar time. We intend to explore this possibility in future work.

variations in true "knowledge use" and variations in the "propensity to cite." Because there are institutional reasons why the propensity to cite may vary across countries, this has important consequences for interpreting the results. We return to this issue below.

Variations in β_1 (by attributes of either the cited or the citing patents) imply differences in the timing of citations across categories of patents. Higher values of β_1 mean higher rates of decay, which pull the citations function downwards and leftward. In other words, the likelihood of citations would be lower everywhere for higher β_1, and would peak earlier on. Thus a higher α means more citations at all lags; a lower β_1 means more citations at later lags.

When both α and β_1 vary, the citation function can shift upward at some lags while shifting downward at others. For example, if α for citations from Japan to Japan is 2.32 and the β_1 for Japan to Japan is 1.54, this implies that the likelihood of citation in early years is higher than the base group, but because of the higher β_1, this difference fades over time. Because obsolescence is compounded over time, differences in β_1 eventually result in large differences in the citation frequency.[12] If we compute the ratio of the likelihood of citations for Japan-to Japan relative to U.S.-to-U.S. using these parameters, we find that one year after being granted, Japan-to-Japan citations are about twice as likely as U.S.-to-U.S., but nine years down the road the frequencies for the two groups are about the same, and at a lag of 20 years Japan-to-Japan citations are actually about 70% *less* likely than for the base category.

A final interpretation issue relates to citations from patents assigned to the same firm as is the cited patent, so-called "self-citations." As discussed by Jaffe, Henderson and Trajtenberg (1993), self-citations cannot be regarded as evidence of spillovers. Hence if we are interested in geographic localization of spillovers, we want to exclude self-citations. On the other hand, self-citations are an important indicator of the cumulative nature of technology, and of firms' ability to appropriate the returns to their inventions.[13] Thus for some purposes,

---

12. Since increases in β_1 both reduce the peak frequency (β_2/β_1) and cause the function to decay from the peak faster, such increases reduce the cumulative citation frequency or integral over time non-linearly. The cumulative frequency is approximately $\alpha\beta_2/(\beta_1)^2$.

13. The extent of self-citation is an indicator of firms' successful appropriation. See Trajtenberg, Jaffe, and Henderson, 1997. Putnam (1997) finds that the number of self-citations is a good predictor of firms' decision to pay renewal fees for patents that would otherwise expire.

such as assessing the overall role of technology in regional economic development, localization of citations inclusive of self-citations is of interest. In order to focus on spillovers, we concentrate on the results exclusive of self-citations, but we comment briefly on the very high degree of localization of self-citations.

We estimate Eq. 3 by non-linear least squares. Since the left-hand variable is an empirical frequency, the model is heteroskedastic. To improve efficiency and get the right standard errors, we weight the observations by the reciprocal of the estimated variance,

$$\sqrt{(N_{ltg})(N_{LT})}.$$

In general, this weighting greatly improves the fit of the model, but does not alter the parameter estimates materially.

4   Results

Complete results from the estimation of Eq. 3 are presented in Appendix B. The model has 82 parameters (γ, base values of β_1 and β_2); 24 cited country/citing country interactions for α; 4 technology field effects for α; 6 cited time period effects for α; 17 citing year effects for α; 24 cited country/citing country effects for β_1; 4 technology field effects for β_1). Overall, the model fits the data reasonably well. Because of the large sample size, the estimated standard errors are quite small. The base value for β_1 is about .2, suggesting a modal lag of about five years, which is not surprising based on Figure 1. The estimate for the technology match parameter γ is 99, which means that a patent is about 100 times more likely to cite a patent in the same patent class as it is to cite a random patent in some other class. In reality, of course, some classes are "closer" to each other than others in technology space, but it is not surprising that, on average, patents in the same class are much more likely to cite each other than to cite patents in any of the other classes.[14]

Technology field effects are present in both the α's and the β_1's, but the β_1 effects are not large. The α's greater than 1 mean that all other fields receive more citations than Drug and Medical patents (the base group). The β_1's greater than 1 mean that other fields receive cita-

---

14. Podolny and Shepard (1997), looking only at patents within a group of classes related to semiconductor technology, found that citations from patents in the same class where about 15 times as likely.

tions somewhat faster than Drugs.[15] The cited time period and citing year effects are similar to what we have found before: the number of citations received rises in the 1970s and 1980s, and the number of citations made rises essentially throughout the whole period.

Table 3 presents the estimates of the α and β_1 parameters in several different ways. The top panel simply reproduces the α estimates presented in Appendix B, but arrays them in matrix form. The second panel presents the estimated values (with standard errors) in terms of $(1/\beta_1)$, which has years as units and is equal to the lag at which the citation frequency reaches its maximum value. The bottom panel presents estimated values (with standard errors) for $\alpha\beta_2/(\beta_1)^2$, which is the integral of the citation function from $t = 0$ to infinity. This is an estimate of the expected number of citations that a single patent will receive from a set of patents consisting of one random patent per year forever. Thus the middle panel of the table measures the "speed" of citation diffusion and the bottom panel measures the overall intensity of citation.[16]

Several features of these matrices are worth noting. Looking first at the α's, the diagonal elements strongly dominate both the rows and columns of the matrix. What this means is that there is a strong pattern of geographic localization, in the sense that the domestic citation function is shifted upward. This is true for all countries, and it is true whether one compares the domestic citations to citations *received from* other countries (across the rows) or citations *made to* other countries (down the columns). The other notable feature of the top panel of Table 3 is the symmetry of the matrix. For example, α for Germany citing U.S. and for U.S. citing Germany are the two lowest numbers in the matrix. Conversely, the two highest non-diagonal numbers in

15. The field differences found here for β_1 are smaller than we found in our previous paper (Jaffe and Trajtenberg, 1996). Since that paper looked only at citations to U.S. patents, this suggests that there is a greater variation in citation speed across fields in U.S. patents than in other countries' patents. In particular, we found that the citations to U.S. patents came much faster in electronics than in the other fields; this effect is present in the overall data but is not as big.

16. We also tested various restricted versions of this model to see if the parameter differences reported here are jointly significant. The following restricted versions of the model were all rejected, with p-values of .0001 or less in the appropriate chi-squared test, in favor of the reported model: country effects in the α's but not the β_1's; effects for each cited and citing country, plus a "domestic localization" effect common to all countries, but no cited country/citing country interaction effects; cited country/citing country interaction effects in the α's but only cited and citing country effects plus the localization effect in the β_1's.

Table 3
Regression coefficients in matrix form

Alphas

Cited	Citing				
	United States	Great Britain	France	Germany	Japan
United States	1.00	0.72	0.65	0.56	0.76
Great Britain	0.71	1.78	0.79	0.75	0.66
France	0.60	0.72	2.17	0.73	0.63
Germany	0.55	0.73	0.74	1.32	0.83
Japan	0.72	0.62	0.67	0.81	2.32

Modal lag

Cited	Citing				
	United States	Great Britain	France	Germany	Japan
United States	5.25	5.08	5.08	5.08	4.41
	(0.049)	(0.070)	(0.077)	(0.074)	(0.051)
Great Britain	5.39	4.24	4.63	4.68	4.46
	(0.073)	(0.049)	(0.103)	(0.092)	(0.088)
France	5.43	4.85	4.02	4.67	4.51
	(0.087)	(0.114)	(0.047)	(0.101)	(0.098)
Germany	5.42	4.56	4.58	4.23	4.14
	(0.079)	(0.093)	(0.096)	(0.051)	(0.062)
Japan	4.99	4.80	4.52	4.45	3.40
	(0.061)	(0.104)	(0.102)	(0.070)	(0.030)

Cumulative probability

Cited	Citing				
	United States	Great Britain	France	Germany	Japan
United States	1.49	1.01	0.91	0.78	0.80
	(0.109)	(0.075)	(0.068)	(0.058)	(0.059)
Great Britain	1.11	1.72	0.92	0.88	0.71
	(0.082)	(0.128)	(0.070)	(0.066)	(0.053)
France	0.95	0.91	1.89	0.85	0.70
	(0.071)	(0.070)	(0.141)	(0.065)	(0.053)
Germany	0.86	0.82	0.84	1.28	0.76
	(0.064)	(0.062)	(0.064)	(0.095)	(0.057)
Japan	0.97	0.77	0.74	0.87	1.45
	(0.071)	(0.059)	(0.056)	(0.065)	(0.108)

the α table are for Germany citing Japan and Japan citing Germany. Although these differences among the off-diagonal elements are not as large as the localization effect of domestic citation, it suggests that inter-country knowledge flows are typically bi-directional, with relatively large or small flows in one direction being associated with similar flows in the other direction.

Geographic localization is also evident in the β_1 parameters, presented in the middle panel of Table 3 in the form of the estimated modal lag. Here the diagonal elements are generally the *smallest* entry in each row and column, meaning modal citation lags are noticeably shorter for domestic citations, relative to citations to and from others. The only exception to this general pattern is the U.S. U.S. inventors are slightly faster to cite Japanese inventors than they are to cite U.S. inventors ($\beta_1 = 1.05$), and Japanese inventors are faster to cite U.S. inventors than are U.S. inventors ($\beta_1 = 1.19$).

There are also systematic variations across the countries that are superimposed on top of the general pattern of localization. While the modal lags for citations made by the U.S. range from 5 to 5.4 years (depending on the cited country), those for Japan range from 3.4 to 4.4. Indeed, it appears that the overall tendency of the U.S. to both generate and receive long-lagged citations is part of the reason why U.S.-to-U.S. citations do not come more quickly than those from and to others.

The fact that domestic citations generally involve both higher α and higher β_1 creates offsetting effects for the overall number of citations, since the higher β_1 means that citations fade faster and hence reduces the total holding α constant. The bottom panel of Table 3 combines these effects by presenting the overall cumulative probabilities. The estimates show that, in terms of total citations, the variations in α dominate the variations in β_1; the matrix is still strongly diagonal, indicating localization. These differences are quite significant statistically, although it should be noted that this calculation relies heavily on the assumed functional form as it integrates the citation function into the infinite future.

Also noticeable in the cumulative probabilities is that the U.S. tends to both make and receive more citations than other countries. Note, for example that the entry in the U.S. column contains the largest figure other than the diagonal in every row, and the U.S. row contains the largest figure other than the diagonal in every column except Germany. This result could be driven by differences between the U.S.

and other countries in the propensity to patent. If the U.S. has a low propensity to patent, then each patent granted represents (on average) a larger chunk of knowledge, which could result in more citations made and received per patent (Caballero and Jaffe, 1993). It is more likely, however, that the propensity of U.S. inventors to patent *in the U.S.* is greater than that of foreigners (Eaton and Kortum, 1996). That is, U.S. inventors are more likely to take out a U.S. patent on a trivial invention than are foreigners. All else equal, this should make the average citation rate to and from the U.S.-invented patents *lower* than the corresponding rates for foreign-invented patents. Since we find the opposite, this may be evidence confirming a view of the U.S. as the most open and interconnected economic and technological system.

There are also some interesting pairwise effects. The U.S. and Great Britain are "closer" to each other (in terms of overall probability of citation) than any other country pair, suggesting a possible effect of common language. Japan is closer to the U.S. than it is to any of the European countries. Britain and France are closer to each other than to Germany, but closer to Germany than to Japan. Note, however, that not all of these differences are statistically significant.

Figures 2 through 6 show the effects of these parameter differences graphically, and also present a useful pictorial comparison to the raw data presented in Figure 1. Each Figure presents the estimated citation functions for citations *to* one of the countries, with the different lines within each Figure corresponding to the different citing countries. Comparing Figure 2 to Figure 1 shows some of the effects of controlling for non-geographic effects. First, as suggested above, the "tails" in the estimated functions in Figure 2 are much thinner. Second, while geographic localization is clearly present in Figure 2, its magnitude is noticeably diminished, with the citation frequency for other countries at the modal lag being roughly 55–75% of U.S.-U.S. as compared to 40–60% in Figure 1. As discussed further below, this is primarily the effect of eliminating self-citations.

In terms of the effects seen numerically in Table 3, the Figures show the "speed" of Japan, as its line typically peaks early and then fades, and the "slowness" of the U.S., whose predicted frequency of citation is the highest after long lags in all of the pictures. The graphs also show that the differences among non-domestic citing countries are always smaller than the localization effect that separates domestic citations from foreign ones.

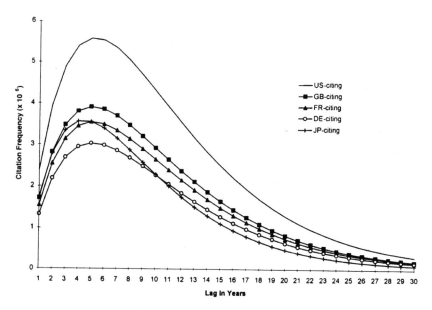

Figure 2
Estimated citation functions for citation to U.S. invented patents (excluding self-citation)

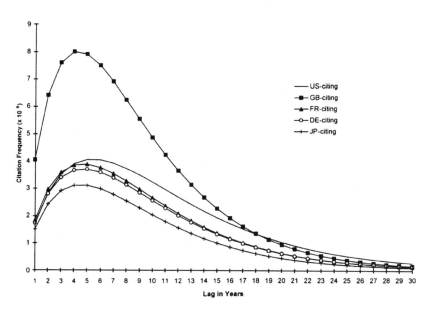

Figure 3
Estimated citation functions for citations to British-invented patents (excluding self-citations)

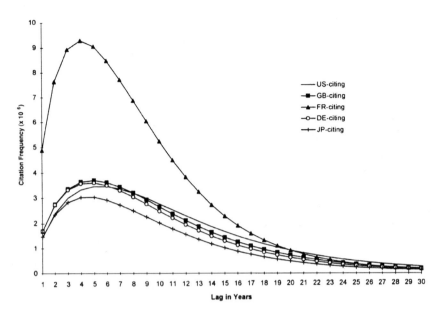

Figure 4
Estimated citation functions for citations to French-invented patents (excluding self-citations)

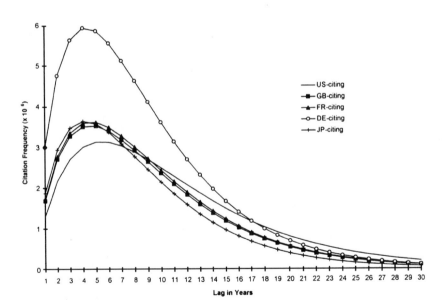

Figure 5
Estimated citation functions for citations to German-invented patents (excluding self-citations)

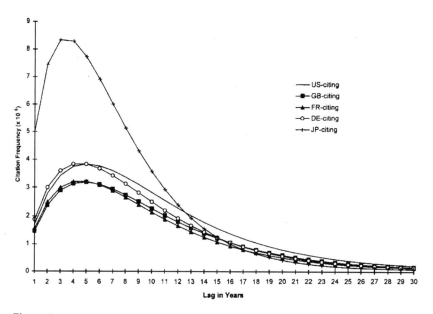

Figure 6
Estimated citation functions for citations to Japanese-invented patents (excluding self-citations)

Figures 2 to 6 generally show a pattern of "fading" of geographical localization. The combination of relatively high α and relatively high β_1 for domestic citations means that the initial domestic probability is much higher, but that it fades faster, so that other countries typically catch up eventually. This can be seen in the "crossing" of the domestic citation function with the others after 15 to 25 years. This phenomenon is also illustrated in Table 4, which gives the probability of citation from various countries *relative to* the domestic citation probability, for each cited country, in the first year and after 20 years. For every cited country except the U.S., the relative citation frequency of the other countries is greater after 20 years than in the first year. Indeed, for Japan, every other country cites its twenty-year-old patents with greater frequency than it does itself. This results from the combined effect of fading of localization and the fact that Japan is generally a high-β_1 (fast-fading) maker of citations. Conversely, the lack of fading of geographic localization in citations to the U.S. reflects the general tendency of the U.S. toward low β_1 (slow fading).

All of the results discussed so far derive from estimation of the "full" model of Eq. 3. For comparison to our earlier paper, as well as

Table 4
Fading of geographic localization over time

Relative citation rate for citations to U.S.

	Citing country				
Lag in years	United States	Great Britain	France	Germany	Japan
1	1.00	0.72	0.65	0.56	0.73
20	1.00	0.64	0.58	0.49	0.37

Relative citation rate for citations to Great Britain

	Citing country				
Lag in years	United States	Great Britain	France	Germany	Japan
1	0.42	1.00	0.45	0.43	0.37
20	1.10	1.00	0.67	0.65	0.47

Relative citation rate for citations to France

	Citing country				
Lag in years	United States	Great Britain	France	Germany	Japan
1	0.29	0.34	1.00	0.35	0.30
20	1.00	0.77	1.00	0.67	0.50

Relative citation rate for citations to Germany

	Citing country				
Lag in years	United States	Great Britain	France	Germany	Japan
1	0.44	0.56	0.57	1.00	0.62
20	1.16	0.77	0.81	1.00	0.56

Relative citation rate for citations to Japan

	Citing country				
Lag in years	United States	Great Britain	France	Germany	Japan
1	0.34	0.29	0.31	0.38	1.00
20	2.01	1.49	1.23	1.39	1.00

for the light it sheds on the interaction of different effects, it is useful to consider briefly how the results differ in less complete or different models. In particular, our earlier research did not exclude self-citations, and did not include the "technological proximity" effect. These effects are interesting in their own right, and may also be expected to interact in important ways with geographic localization. Table 5 summarizes the results with and without these non-geographic effects. Generally, excluding self-cites significantly reduces the apparent geographic localization, as well as reducing the extent to which that localization "fades". That is, the citation intensity from other countries, relative to the domestic citation rate, is lower in columns 1 and 2 than in columns 3 and 4 in the first year, but is higher in columns 1 and 2 than in columns 3 and 4 after 20 years. What this means is that self-cites are highly geographically localized (which should not be a surprise) and generally come at shorter lags (Trajtenberg, Henderson and Jaffe, 1997). Thus including them creates strong localization particularly in early years; excluding them dilutes localization; this weaker initial localization then also fades less.

Inclusion of the technological proximity parameter has an effect similar to the exclusion of self-cites, but much smaller. That is, except for citations to the U.S., column 3 shows slightly less localization than column 4 (and column 1 slightly less than column 2), whereas both columns 1 and 2 show dramatically less than either 3 or 4. What this suggests is that citations within the same patent class have a slight tendency to geographic localization, but, not surprisingly, much less so than citations within the same organization. Finally, there does not appear to be much interaction between the self-cite and technological proximity effects. The parameter γ is not much different in column 2 from in column 4. What this means is that self-citations exhibit approximately the same tendency toward concentration in the same patent class as non-self-citations.

5 Conclusions

In our view, the results in this paper demonstrate that there is much to be learned about international knowledge diffusion from patents and their citations. Despite the fact that we focus on patents granted by the U.S. patent office, rich patterns of interaction are revealed, including interesting findings about the diffusion of citations within

Table 5
Comparison of models

	No tech. proximity parameter, incl. self-cites	With tech. proximity parameter, incl. self-cites	No tech. proximity parameter, excl. self-cites	With tech. proximity parameter, excl. self-cites
R^2	0.779	0.813	0.746	0.765
Beta 1	0.205	0.208	0.191	0.190
Beta 2	5.258×10^{-6}	2.019×10^{-6}	7.309×10^{-7}	2.891×10^{-7}
Technological proximity parameter	n.a.	101.24	n.a.	99.49
Citations to U.S. (citation intensity relative to U.S.-U.S.)				
Year 1				
Great Britain	0.54	0.50	0.75	0.72
France	0.45	0.44	0.66	0.65
Germany	0.36	0.37	0.54	0.56
Japan	0.49	0.51	0.72	0.73
Year 20				
Great Britain	0.80	0.78	0.67	0.64
France	0.73	0.74	0.59	0.58
Germany	0.65	0.67	0.50	0.49
Japan	0.44	0.44	0.38	0.37
Citations to France (citation intensity relative to France-France)				
Year 1				
U.S.	0.09	0.11	0.26	0.29
Great Britain	0.14	0.12	0.36	0.34
Germany	0.11	0.12	0.31	0.35
Japan	0.09	0.11	0.26	0.30
Year 20				
U.S.	1.56	1.84	0.87	1.00
Great Britain	1.43	1.35	0.82	0.77
Germany	1.23	1.35	0.62	0.67
Japan	0.87	0.99	0.45	0.50
Citations to Japan (citation intensity relative to Japan-Japan)				
Year 1				
U.S.	0.16	0.20	0.27	0.34
Great Britain	0.15	0.17	0.26	0.29
France	0.15	0.17	0.25	0.31
Germany	0.18	0.21	0.30	0.38

Table 5 (continued)

	No tech. proximity parameter, incl. self-cites	With tech. proximity parameter, incl. self-cites	No tech. proximity parameter, excl. self-cites	With tech. proximity parameter, excl. self-cites
Year 20				
U.S.	2.12	2.75	1.61	2.01
Great Britain	1.70	2.05	1.27	1.49
France	1.43	1.76	1.03	1.23
Germany	1.62	2.00	1.16	1.39

and between countries other than the U.S. Some widely-held notions about differences in the inventive processes across countries were confirmed, such as the reliance of the Japanese on a relatively recent technological base. Others are less obvious, such as the strong symmetry between citing and cited intensities, and the greater proximity of Japan to the U.S. relative to Europe.

Overall, the results confirm our earlier findings that there is significant geographic localization of knowledge flows. We can now, however, tell a more complete story about the localization process, distinguishing the issue of speed from the issue of total intensity, and describing how citations diffuse over time to more distant locations. In future work, we intend to extend this in two directions. First, we will continue to look at more and finer geographic distinctions, including other countries and regions within the U.S. We conjecture, for example, that the West Coast of the U.S. is "closer" in technology space to the Pacific Rim, while the East Coast is closer to Europe, for both geographic and cultural reasons.

The second research avenue we are pursuing is to relate the knowledge flows implied by the citation patterns to the commercial impact of invention as measured by productivity improvements. If citations are a proxy for the pathways by which the cumulative impact of new technology is brought to bear, then they ought to play in a measurable intermediating role between the R&D series of various countries and the international productivity series. Thus our estimated citation flows can be used in place of trade flows to construct weighted stocks of foreign R&D to search for international R&D spillovers as in Park (1995) and Coe and Helpman (1995).

An issue that remains for further study is the extent to which the results may be tainted by systematic biases in the patent approval process that generates citations. Our maintained hypothesis is that the citation process itself does not differ depending on the domicile of the inventor. One possible bias is introduced by the fact that we are examining citations within the U.S. patent system. If a given invention is covered by patents issued in more than one country, then the obligation to cite this invention can be discharged by a citation to any of the members of the patent "family" around the world that cover the same invention in different countries. Further, U.S. inventions are often patented in the U.S. but not in Japan, while Japanese inventions patented in the U.S. are usually also patented in Japan. As a result, localization of citations to U.S. patents might be explained by a tendency of Japanese inventors to cite the Japanese patent covering prior art rather than the U.S. patent on the same invention, combined with the fact that such a patent will often be unavailable for U.S.-invented patents. This would not, however, explain why U.S. patents issued to Japanese inventors are *more* likely to cite other U.S. patents issued to Japanese inventors than they are to cite U.S. patents issued to *German* inventors; if anything, the bias introduced by patent families would suggest that our estimates of localization for citations to countries other than the U.S. are understated.

Our basic goal in this paper was to explore the process by which citations to a given patent arrive over time, how this process is affected by characteristics of the cited patent, and how different potentially citing locations differ in the speed and extent to which they "pick up" existing knowledge, as evidenced by their acknowledgment of such existing knowledge through citation. Recognizing that many inventions are never patented, that knowledge can flow from one inventor to another without being acknowledged by a citation, and that many citations probably do not reflect knowledge flow, we nonetheless view this process as a useful window into the otherwise "black box" of the spread of scientific and technical knowledge. The value of this view could obviously be enhanced, however, by a deeper understanding of the relationship between patent citations and knowledge flows. This will require more qualitative and institutional examination of inventions, patents and citations. A fruitful avenue is to build on the work of Jaffe, Fogarty and Banks by using inventors' detailed knowledge of the technological relationship between inventions to "test" the links implied by citations.

Patent citations offer a rich repository of information about the locus of technological activity, and the relationships among activities in different places. Systematic use of these data requires, however, careful attention to the need to control for time and technology field effects that otherwise have an impact on simple comparisons across countries or other units of observation. Fortunately, the patent data are sufficiently numerous that detailed controls can, in fact, be implemented. Though any model obviously imposes structure on the data, one can allow for complex patterns of interactions among effects. Indeed, readers of this paper have no doubt already thought of additional interactions that we could have estimated with our data but did not. We hope that, as these data become more widely available, other researchers will pursue questions that we have not considered.

Appendix A: Derivation of Expected Citation Frequency for a "Cell"

Let s index the patent classes represented by patents with the t, l, g attributes, and S index the patent classes represented in the set of patents with the T, L attributes. Let N_{tgls} represent the number of cited patents in a given class s, N_{TLS} the number of citing patents in a given class S, and $C_{tlgsTLS}$ be the total number of citations *from* class S in year T and country L *to* class s in year t, country l and field g. Starting from Eq. 1, the expected value of the citation count for a given "cell" is:

$$E[C_{tlgsTLS}] = (N_{TLS})(N_{ltgs})[1 + \gamma D(s, S)]\alpha_{ltgTL}$$
$$\times \exp[-(\beta_1)_{ltgTL}(T - t)][1 - \exp(-\beta_2(T - t))] \qquad (A1)$$

where $D(s, S)$ is now unity for $s = S$ and zero otherwise. We can now sum over all s and S to yield:

$$E[C_{tlgTL}] = \sum_s \sum_S (N_{TLS} N_{ltgs})[1 + \gamma D(s, S)]\alpha_{ltgTL}$$
$$\times \exp[-(\beta_1)_{ltgTL}(T - t)][1 - \exp(-\beta_2(T - t))]$$

or

$$E[C_{tlgTL}] = N_{TL} N_{tgl} \alpha_{ltgTL} \exp[-(\beta_1)_{ltgTL}(T - t)]$$
$$\times [1 - \exp(-\beta_2(T - t))] \sum_s \sum_S [1 + \gamma D(s, S) f_{TLS} f_{ltgs}]$$

where $f_{TLS} = (N_{TLS}/N_{TL})$ and analogously for f_{ltgs}. The double summation over s and S can be replaced by a single sum over s, because the only non-zero entries are where $D(s, S)$ is unity or $s = S$. Thus

$$\frac{E[c_{ltgTL}]}{(N_{TL})(N_{ltg})} = \alpha_{ltgTL} \exp[-(\beta_1)_{ltgTL}(T-t)]$$

$$\times [1 - \exp(-\beta_2(T-t))] \left[1 + \gamma \sum_s [f_{TLs}f_{ltgs}]\right] \qquad (A2)$$

Table B
Complete regression results

	Estimate	Asymptotic standard error	Asymptotic t-statistic
Parameter			
Technology Match (gamma)	99.489	2.903	34.3*
Beta1	0.190	0.002	107.5*
Beta2 ($\times 10^6$)	0.289	0.022	13.3*
Alphas			
U.S. citing U.S.	1.000	n.a.	n.a.
U.S. citing Great Britain	0.710	0.013	−22.6
U.S. citing France	0.600	0.013	−30.0
U.S. citing Germany	0.545	0.011	−42.7
U.S. citing Japan	0.720	0.011	−25.9
Great Britain citing U.S.	0.722	0.014	−19.9
Great Britain citing Great Britain	1.781	0.031	25.2
Great Britain citing France	0.717	0.026	−10.8
Great Britain citing Germany	0.729	0.023	−12.0
Great Britain citing Japan	0.623	0.020	−19.3
France citing U.S.	0.654	0.014	−24.3
France citing Great Britain	0.791	0.028	−7.6
France citing France	2.170	0.037	31.2
France citing Germany	0.744	0.024	−10.8
France citing Japan	0.671	0.022	−14.8
Germany citing U.S.	0.560	0.012	−38.1
Germany citing Great Britain	0.746	0.023	−11.3
Germany citing France	0.726	0.024	−11.3
Germany citing Germany	1.320	0.022	14.5
Germany citing Japan	0.813	0.018	−10.4
Japan citing U.S.	0.761	0.012	−20.4
Japan citing Great Britain	0.659	0.020	−16.9
Japan citing France	0.634	0.021	−17.1
Japan citing Germany	0.827	0.018	−9.4
Japan citing Japan	2.318	0.025	53.1

Table B (continued)

	Estimate	Asymptotic standard error	Asymptotic *t*-statistic
Beta1s			
U.S. citing U.S.	1.000	n.a.	n.a.
U.S. citing Great Britain	0.973	0.011	−2.4
U.S. citing France	0.967	0.014	−2.4
U.S. citing Germany	0.969	0.012	−2.5
U.S. citing Japan	1.052	0.010	5.0
Great Britain citing U.S.	1.033	0.012	2.6
Great Britain citing Great Britain	1.239	0.013	18.1
Great Britain citing France	1.083	0.025	3.3
Great Britain citing German	1.151	0.023	6.7
Great Britain citing Japan	1.094	0.023	4.1
France citing U.S.	1.033	0.014	2.3
France citing Great Britain	1.133	0.024	5.4
France citing France	1.306	0.014	22.0
France citing Germany	1.146	0.023	6.3
France citing Japan	1.163	0.025	6.4
Germany citing U.S.	1.033	0.013	2.5
Germany citing Great Britain	1.122	0.021	5.8
Germany citing France	1.125	0.023	5.4
Germany citing Germany	1.240	0.013	18.5
Germany citing Japan	1.180	0.017	10.6
Japan citing U.S.	1.190	0.011	17.1
Japan citing Great Britain	1.178	0.022	8.2
Japan citing France	1.164	0.024	6.8
Japan citing Germany	1.269	0.017	15.6
Japan citing Japan	1.543	0.010	54.3
Alphas			
Drugs & Medical	1.000	n.a.	n.a.
Chemical, excl. Drugs	1.529	0.022	23.9
Electronics, etc.	2.279	0.031	41.8
Mechanical	1.857	0.025	33.9
All Other	1.765	0.032	24.2

Table B (continued)

	Estimate	Asymptotic standard error	Asymptotic t-statistic
Beta1s			
Drugs & Medical	1.000	n.a.	n.a.
Chemical, excl. Drugs	1.018	0.008	2.3
Electronics, etc.	1.144	0.008	17.2
Mechanical	1.069	0.008	8.7
All Other	0.993	0.009	−0.8
Citing time period			
1963–65	1.000	n.a.	n.a.
1966–70	2.523	0.180	8.5
1971–75	4.048	0.288	10.6
1976–80	4.257	0.307	10.6
1981–85	3.936	0.289	10.1
1986–90	3.877	0.291	9.9
1991–93	3.276	0.253	9.0
Citing year			
1977	1.000	n.a.	n.a.
1978	1.100	0.015	6.5
1979	1.094	0.016	6.0
1980	1.136	0.016	8.5
1981	1.152	0.016	9.4
1982	1.166	0.017	9.8
1983	1.167	0.017	9.6
1984	1.176	0.018	9.8
1985	1.228	0.019	11.8
1986	1.253	0.020	12.4
1987	1.334	0.022	15.0
1988	1.349	0.024	14.8
1989	1.355	0.025	14.4
1990	1.292	0.025	11.9
1991	1.266	0.025	10.7
1992	1.289	0.026	11.0
1993	1.298	0.028	10.8
1994	1.361	0.030	12.1

50,625 observations. R^2 = .7648. Standard error of the regression = 7.55×10^{-5}. t-statistics are calculated for H_0: parameter = 1, except as noted.
*t-statistic is for H_0: parameter = 0.

Acknowledgment

We acknowledge with gratitude financial support from the National Science Foundation, Grant No. SBR-9320973 and No. SBR-9413099, and from the Israeli Science Foundation, Grant 874/96. We appreciate comments from seminar participants at Brandeis University, Harvard University, NBER Science and Technology Policy Research Group, NBER Productivity Summer Institute, and Northwestern University.

References

Caballero, Ricardo J. and Adam B. Jaffe (1993), "How High are the Giants' Shoulders: An Empirical Assessment of Knowledge Spillovers and Creative Destruction in a Model of Economic Growth," in Olivier J. Blanchard and Stanley Fischer, eds., *NBER Macroeconomics Annual 1993*, Cambridge. MA: MIT Press.

Coe, David and Elhanan Helpman (1995), "International R&D Spillovers," *European Economic Review*, vol. 39, 859–887.

Eaton, Jonathan and Samuel Kortum (1996), "Trade in Ideas: Patenting & Productivity in the OECD," *Journal of International Economics*, 40(3–4): 251–278.

Griliches, Zvi (1979), "Issues in Assessing the Contribution of R&D to Productivity Growth," *Bell Journal of Economics*, 10: 92–116.

Griliches, Zvi (1990), "Patent Statistics as Economic Indicators: A Survey," *Journal of Economic Literature*, 28(4): 1661–1707.

Grossman, Gene M. and Elhanan Helpman (1991), "Quality Ladders in the Theory of Growth," *Quarterly Journal of Economics*, 106: 557–586.

Jaffe, Adam B. (1986), "Technological Opportunity and Spillovers of R&D: Evidence from Firms' Patents, Profits and Market Value," *American Economic Review*, 76: 984–1001.

Jaffe, Adam B., Michael S. Fogarty and Bruce R. Banks (1998), "Evidence from Patents and Patent Citations on the Impact of NASA and Other Federal Labs on Commercial Innovation," *Journal of Industrial Economics* 96: 183–205.

Jaffe, Adam B., Rebecca Henderson and Manuel Trajtenberg (1993), "Geographic Localization of Knowledge Spillovers as Evidenced by Patent Citations," *Quarterly Journal of Economics*, 108: 577–598.

Jaffe, Adam B. and Manuel Trajtenberg (1996), "Flows of Knowledge from Universities and Federal Laboratories," *Proceedings of the National Academy of Sciences*, 93: 12671–12677, November 1996.

Krugman, Paul (1991), *Geography and Trade*, Cambridge, MA: MIT Press.

Park, Walter G., "International R&D Spillovers and OECD Economic Growth," *Economic Inquiry*, 33: 571–591, October 1995.

Podolny, Joel and Andrea Shepard (1997), "When Are Technological Spillovers Local?: Patent Citation Patterns in the Semiconductor Industry," mimeo.

Putnam, Jonathan (1997), "How Many Pennies for Your Quote? Estimating the Value of Patent Citations," mimeo.

Romer, Paul M. (1990), "Endogenous Technological Change," *Journal of Political Economy*, 98: S71–S102.

Teece, D. J. (1977), "Technology Transfer by Multinational Firms: The Resource Cost of Transferring Technological Know-How," *Economic Journal*, 87: 242–261.

Trajtenberg, Manuel, Rebecca Henderson and Adam B. Jaffe (1997), "University Versus Corporate Patents: A Window on the Basicness of Invention," *Economics of Innovation and New Technology*.

III

**Policy-Motivated
Evaluation of Institutions
and Countries**

8

Universities as a Source of Commercial Technology: A Detailed Analysis of University Patenting, 1965–1988

Rebecca Henderson, Adam B. Jaffe, and Manuel Trajtenberg

I Introduction

Recent work in both macroeconomic theory and technology policy has focused renewed attention on the role of spillovers in general and on university research in particular in driving economic growth (Caballero and Jaffe (1993) and Romer (1986, 1990)). Since universities are in principle dedicated to the widespread dissemination of the results of their research, university spillovers are likely to be disproportionately large and may thus be disproportionately important (Dasgupta and David (1987), Jaffe (1989), Merton (1973), Zucker et al. (1997), and National Academy of Sciences (1995)).

This focus on university research comes at a time when universities have been under increasing pressure to translate the results of their work into privately appropriable knowledge. In 1980 and 1984 major changes in federal law made it significantly easier for universities to retain the property rights to inventions deriving from federally funded research. At the same time increasing competition for federal resources has forced many universities to turn to alternative sources of funding. Many universities have established technology licensing offices and are actively pursuing industrial support.

At first glance these changes appear to have had a dramatic effect on the way in which university research is transferred to the private sector. University patenting has exploded. In 1965 just 96 U.S. patents were granted to 28 U.S. universities or related institutions. In 1992 almost 1500 patents were granted to over 150 U.S. universities or related institutions. This 15-fold increase in university patenting occurred over an interval in which total U.S. patenting increased less than 50%, and patents granted to U.S. inventors remained roughly constant. However, the extent to which this explosion should be taken as evidence of a large increase in the contribution of universities to commercial technology development depends on the extent to which it represents more commercially useful inventions versus the extent to which it represents simply increased filing of patent applications on marginal inventions.

This paper explores this issue in some detail, both as a phenomenon of interest in its own right and as a window into the changing role of universities as sources of technology for the private economy. A number of surveys and some detailed case study work have documented substantial shifts in the nature of the relationship between universities and the private sector (Blumenthal (1986), Cohen et al. (1994), David et al. (1992), and National Science Foundation (1982)). Here we focus on university patents, both because patents are a unique and highly visible method of "technology transfer" (Archibugi (1992), Basberg (1987), Boitani and Ciciotti (1990), Schwartz (1988), and Trajtenberg (1990a)), and because their accessibility allows for a more comprehensive analysis than is possible with either surveys or case study work.

We draw on a comprehensive database consisting of *all* patents assigned to universities or related institutions from 1965 until mid-1992, a 1% random sample of all U.S. patents granted over the same time period, and the complete set of all patents that cite either of these groups. We show that averaged over the whole time period, university patents are both more important and more general than the average patent, but that this difference has been declining over time, so that by the late 1980s we cannot find significant differences between the university patent universe and the random sample of all patents. We suggest that the observed increase in university patenting may reflect an increase in their "propensity to patent"—and possibly an associated increase in the rate of knowledge transfer to the private sector—rather than an increase in the output of "important" inventions.

The chapter is organized into five sections. The following section describes our data, and explains some of the institutional changes that appear to be driving the growth of university patenting. Section III demonstrates the difference between university and other patents in the citation-based measures of importance, and the decline of that difference in the 1980s. Section IV explores possible explanations for that decline. Section V provides concluding observations.

II   The Growth of University Patents

A   The Basic Numbers

This chapter is part of a larger research project that exploits the declining cost of access to large quantities of patent data. In prior work we have used patent data to show that spillovers are geographically localized (Jaffe et al. (1993)), that spillovers from university research are less likely to be geographically localized than privately funded research (Henderson et al. (1996)), and to explore the degree to which citation-based measures provide useful information about the scientific and economic impact of the idea captured in a patent (Trajtenberg et al. (1996)). Here we draw on these data to explore how the quantity and "quality" of university patents have changed over time, and to compare both to the overall universe of U.S. patents.[1]

We use four sets of patents: all university patents granted between 1965 and mid-1992 (12,804 patents); a 1% random sample of all U.S. patents[2] over the same period (19,535 patents); all patents after 1974 that cited the university patents (40,859 patents), and all patents after 1974 that cited the random sample patents (42,147 patents).[3] For these patents we know the year of application,[4] the identity of the institution to which it is assigned, and the "patent class," a detailed technological classification provided by the patent office.

Figure 1 illustrates the dramatic increase in patenting we have already described. The top panel compares the rate of university

---

1. In our earlier paper (Henderson et al. (1996)) we documented the existence of a decline in the "quality" of university patents. However, in that paper we were not able to control for problems such as truncation bias or shifts in citation patterns over time, and we were not able to explore the causes of the decline in any detail.

2. By "U.S. patents" we mean patents granted by the U.S. Patent Office. By the end of this period, about half of such patents were granted to non-U.S. residents. About 1% of the patents assigned to U.S. universities were taken out by individuals who gave the patent office non-U.S. addresses.

3. A detailed description of the data set is given in Henderson et al. (1995) or is available from the authors as a technical appendix.

4. We prefer to date patents by the year of application rather than the year of grant, because that is when the inventor identified the existence of a new invention, and there are variable lags involved between application and grant date. Because of these lags, however, totals by date of application are incomplete for years approaching the 1992 data cutoff date, since some patents applied for at the end of the period were almost certainly still under review at the time we collected our data. Thus we terminate our time-sensitive analyses in 1988.

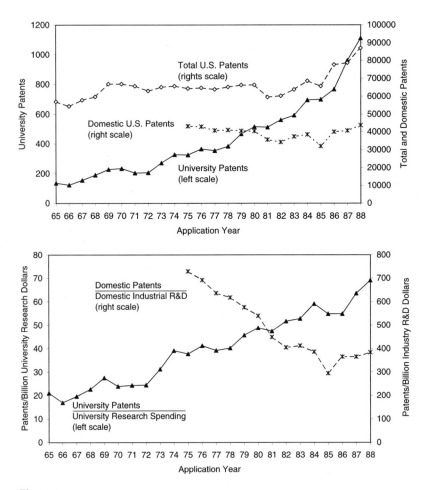

Figure 1
Increase in patenting

patenting to all U.S. patents and to domestic U.S. patents. The bottom panel shows university patenting relative to university research, and an analogous ratio for the U.S. industrial sector. University patenting has not only increased, it has increased more rapidly than overall patenting and much more rapidly than domestic patenting, which is essentially flat until the late 1980s. In addition, university patenting has increased more rapidly than university research spending, causing the ratio of university patents to R&D to more than triple over the period. In contrast the ratio of domestic patents to domestic R&D nearly halved over the same period. Thus universities' "propensity to

Table 1
Top 10 institutions for university patents, 1991

Institution	Patent count
Massachusetts Institute of Technology	100
University of California	91
University of Texas	82
Stanford University	56
Wisconsin Alumni Research Foundation	44
University of Florida	43
Iowa State University Research Foundation Inc.	39
California Institute of Technology	32
University of Minnesota	30
Johns Hopkins University	26

patent" has been rising significantly at the same time that the overall propensity to patent has been falling. Note that the increase in university patenting has been fairly continuous since the early 1970s. There is some evidence of an acceleration in the late 1980s, but this is a period in which both university research and overall patenting accelerate as well, making it difficult to assess its significance.

This increasing propensity to patent is also evident in a significant increase in the number of universities taking out patents. Whereas in 1965 about 30 universities obtained patents, in 1991 patents were granted to about 150 universities and related institutions. Nevertheless, university patenting remains highly concentrated, with the top 20 institutions receiving about 70% of the total, and MIT, the most prolifically patenting institution, alone receiving about 8%. The top 10 institutions and their total patent grants for 1991 are shown in table 1.

The increase in university patenting has not been uniform across the spectrum of technologies. The top panel of figure 2 shows the breakdown of university patents by field over time,[5] the bottom panel shows it for all patents.[6] The differences are dramatic, if not surprising. By the end of the 1980s, drug and medical patents

---

5. Full details of this classification by field are given in Jaffe (1986).
6. This and all subsequent analyses are based on our 1/100 random sample of all patents. Given the large number of such patents (over 500 per year), the composition by field of the sample is very likely to be close to the composition by field of the universe of all patents. Note that the random sample does *not* exclude university patents. Even at the end of the period, however, university patents are less than 2% of the total.

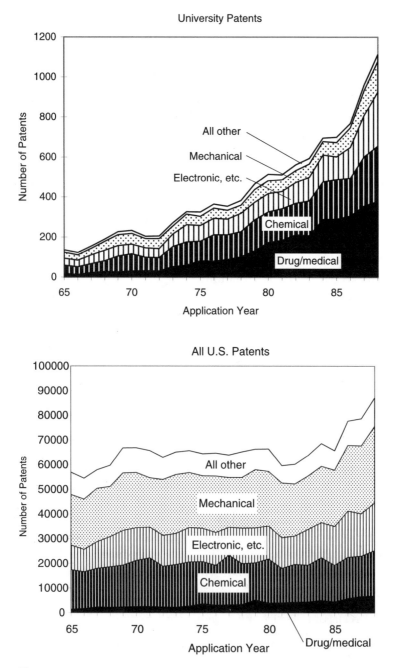

Figure 2
Patents by broad fields

comprised about 35% of the university total, up from less than 15% in 1965; chemical patents 25–30%; electronic and related patents 20–25%; mechanical patents 10–15%; and about 5% other. In contrast, overall patenting is 30–35% mechanical; 20–25% each for chemical and electronics, 10–15% other; and less than 10% drugs and medical. Thus universities are much more interested in drugs and medical technologies, and much less interested in mechanical technologies, than other inventors, and the difference has increased over time.

B   The Broader Context of Increased University Patenting

There are several possible explanations for this dramatic increase in patenting behavior. Changes in federal law affecting university patenting in 1980 and then again in 1984 made it significantly easier for universities to patent the results of federally funded research. Industry funding of university research has notably increased and at the same time there has been a substantial increase in organized university "technology transfer" or "licensing" offices. Since all three changes occurred roughly simultaneously, their different effects cannot be easily separated, but it seems plausible that all three have played an important role in increasing the number of university patents.

Federal Law Affecting University Patenting

Before 1980 the federal government had the right to claim all royalties or other income derived from patents resulting from federally funded research. Federally funded researchers could apply for patents, and could assign those patents to universities, but the exclusive property right associated with the invention remained with the government whether or not a patent was issued. The only way that a university could profit from federally derived patents was to seek a title rights waiver from the funding agency. Since approximately 70% of university research during this period was funded by the federal government, this was a major barrier to widespread university patenting.

   In 1980 Congress passed The Patent and Trademark Amendments of 1980 (Public Law 96-517), also known as the Bayh-Dole Act. The Bayh-Dole Act gave universities (and other nonprofit institutions, as well as small businesses) the right to retain the property rights to inventions deriving from federally funded research. The 1984 passage of Public Law 98-620 expanded the rights of universities further by removing certain restrictions contained in the Bayh-Dole Act regarding the kinds of inventions that universities could own, and the rights of universities to assign their property rights to other parties.

Thus since 1984 universities have had very broad rights to exploit inventions derived from their research, even if it is federally funded. They can charge royalties for the use of the patent, and they can assign the patent to a third party if they so desire. As a result, major research universities now typically have explicit policies requiring faculty and other researchers to assign patents deriving from on-campus research to the university, and specifying how any income deriving therefrom is to be divided among the institution, the researcher, and research centers or departments.

Increase in Organized University "Technology" Offices
Though it is obviously difficult to separate the chicken from the egg, since the passage of the Bayh-Dole Act there has been a dramatic increase in the scale and significance of the patenting and technology licensing function at universities. The Association of University Technology Administrators (AUTM) has recently begun conducting surveys of its members. The surveyed institutions[7] employed 767 full-time equivalent professional employees in technology transfer and licensing activities. In 1993 they received royalties totaling about $375 million on about 4016 licensing agreements; more than 4000 additional active agreements were not currently generating revenue.[8]

Increased Industry Funding of University Research
Another factor that may be related to the increase in university patenting is an increase in industry funding of university research from 2.6% in 1970 to 3.9% in 1980 and 7.1% in 1994.[9]

It is clearly impossible to assign the roles of "cause" and "effect" to these different trends. The increase in university patenting predates

---

7. Survey responses came from 112 U.S. institutions that were granted 1169 patents in Fiscal Year 1992, compared to our data, which indicate that about 1500 patents were granted to over 150 institutions. Thus survey totals are lower bounds on the actual numbers.

8. *The AUTM Licensing Survey, Fiscal Years 1991, 1992, and 1993.* AUTM categories included in the quoted totals are U.S. universities, U.S. hospitals, third-party management firms, and research institutes. Excluded are government and Canadian universities. The royalty total has been adjusted to eliminate double counting, which results from shared license agreements (personal communication, Ashley Stevens, AUTM).

9. With federal funding at 60 to 70% of the total, the remainder is funded by state and local governments and institutions' own funds.

Table 2
Correlation coefficients across key patent-related variables, 1993 data

	FTEs for licensing activities	Disclosures	Gross royalties	Industry support	Public support
Total U.S. patents field	0.88 (113)	0.91 (112)	0.71 (112)	0.69 (110)	0.82 (113)
FTEs		0.84 (112)	0.81 (112)	0.61 (110)	0.86 (113)
Disclosures			0.72 (112)	0.66 (109)	0.83 (112)
Royalties				0.53 (109)	0.71 (112)
Industry support					0.64 (110)

Source: *The AUTM Licensing Survey.*
Figures in parentheses are number of observations. The number of observations varies because not all universities participating in the survey provide comprehensive data.

the passage of the Bayh-Dole Act, but continued exponential growth probably could not have been sustained without removal of the cumbersome barriers to patents from federal research. The increase in universities' institutional commitment to patenting, in the form of new and expanded licensing offices, would likely not have occurred if the impetus toward more commercial research and the change in federal law had not occurred. But once created, these offices presumably facilitate the patent application process and thereby contribute to the increased patenting. Finally, increased industry funding is probably partially a response to universities' increased interest in applied research, but it, in turn, increases the resources for these activities and thereby also supports increased patenting.

Table 2 illustrates this close correlation quantitatively. For the 113 universities reporting comprehensive data to AUTM it presents correlations across patenting rates, employees in the licensing office, invention disclosures, gross royalties, and the level of industrial and publicly funded support. In these cross-sectional data patenting rates are less correlated with levels of industry funding than with levels of public funding, disclosure rates, or the size of the licensing office, suggesting that increased industry funding may be less important in driving patenting behavior than changes in the law and the expansion of technology licensing offices, but the high degree of serial correlation evident in the raw longitudinal data make it impossible to draw any firm conclusions as to the relative importance of these various factors.

III   Characterizing University Patenting

A   Citation-Based Measures of Importance and Generality

The flow of technology out of universities almost certainly contributes to technological innovation in the private sector (Jaffe (1989)), and there is a widespread belief that more effective transfer of technology from universities to the private sector would be beneficial to innovation and growth (U.S. GAO (1987) and National Academy of Sciences (1995)). In this light, to the extent that it signals an increase in the successful commercial application of university-derived technology, the rapid increase in university patenting would appear to be a highly desirable trend. However, patents vary tremendously in their importance, making it dangerous to draw conclusions about aggregate technology flows based on numbers of patents (Griliches (1990)). In this section we look more carefully at the university patents, to understand better what the patent data do and do not say about increases in the flow of technology out of universities.

In an earlier paper (Trajtenberg et al. (1996)) we used patent citation data to construct a variety of measures that we interpreted as capturing the importance or "basicness" of the invention covered by a patent. Implicit in this approach is a view of technology as an evolutionary process, in which the significance of any particular invention is evidenced, at least partly, by its role in stimulating and facilitating future inventions. We assume that at least some of such future inventions will reference or cite the original invention in their patents, thereby making the number and character of citations received a valid indicator of the technological importance of an invention (Trajtenberg (1990a) and Carpenter and Narin (1993)).[10]

---

10. Citations or references serve the legal function of delimiting the scope of patent protection by identifying technological predecessors of the patented invention. Thus if patent 2 cites patent 1, it implies that patent 1 represents a piece of previously existing knowledge upon which patent 2 builds, and over which patent 2 cannot have a claim. The applicant has a legal duty to disclose any knowledge of the prior art, but the decision as to which patents to cite ultimately rests with the patent examiner, who is supposed to be an expert in the area and hence to be able to identify relevant prior art that the applicant misses or conceals. Trajtenberg (1990a,b) showed that citation-weighted patents were a good proxy for the consumers' surplus generated by inventions. For more discussion of the value and limitations of citation data, see Trajtenberg et al. (1996).

We use two citation-based measures: *importance* and *generality*. We define importance as

$$Importance_i = Nciting_i + \lambda \sum_{j=1}^{Nciting_i} Nciting_{i+1,j}$$

where $0 < \lambda < 1$ is defined as an arbitrary discount factor, which in the previous paper we set to 0.5. In the absence of data about "second-generation" citations in the data set on which this paper relies, we here set λ equal to zero and measure importance simply by total citations received.

The second citation-based measure that we use is *generality*. We hypothesize that patents that cover more "basic" research will be cited by work in a broader range of fields, and define generality as

$$General_i = 1 - \sum_{k=1}^{N_i} \left(\frac{Nciting_{ik}}{Nciting_i} \right)^2$$

where k is the index of patent classes and N_i is the number of different classes to which the citing patents belong. Notice that $0 \leq General \leq 1$, and that higher values represent less concentration and hence more generality. In our previous paper we were able to show that both of these measures were reassuringly high for a number of patents that are known to have had a very significant impact on their field.

Citation-based measures of importance and generality are, to some extent, influenced by variations in citation practices across time and technological areas. They are also very influenced by the fact that when we count the citations of a patent issued in, for example, 1989, we are missing many more of the citations that it will ultimately receive than we are missing in our count of the citations of a patent issued in 1975. For these reasons, when comparing importance or generality it is necessary to control for both time and technological field effects.

B Comparing University and Random Sample Patents

As a first step in exploring the degree to which the increase in university patenting rates reflects an increasing transfer of knowledge to the private sector, we first explore the degree to which university patents are more important or more general than the random sample of patents and the degree to which this has changed over time.

Table 3
Comparison of university and random sample patents

	Importance 1965–1988 $n = 28{,}313$	Generality 1975–1988 $n = 14{,}775$
Random sample mean		
Drug/medical	4.00	0.258
Chemical	3.87	0.296
Electronics, etc.	4.23	0.288
Mechanical	3.77	0.265
All other	3.47	0.203
Overall university difference, controlling for field	0.918 (0.072)	0.0452 (0.0049)
University difference by field		
Drug/medical	0.311 (0.199)	−0.0168 (0.0135)
Chemical	0.416 (0.124)	0.0480 (0.0087)
Electronics, etc.	1.718 (0.141)	0.0582 (0.0094)
Mechanical	1.290 (0.153)	0.0740 (0.0107)
All other	0.396 (0.255)	0.0148 (0.0180)

Standard errors are in parentheses. Differences are estimated controlling for application-year effects.

Table 3 presents the results of regressions of our measures of importance and generality on a series of dummy variables for application years and technological areas, and dummy variables for whether or not the original patent was a university patent. These regressions are based on application years 1965–1988 for importance and 1975–1988 for generality.[11] Over the entire period, controlling for technological field effects and time effects, university patents received almost 25% more citations on average, and this difference is highly significant statistically. They were also about 15% more general, again a statistically significant difference. These overall averages conceal a

11. The generality measure cannot be calculated for the pre-1975 patents because we lack information on the citing patents before 1975, and we terminate the analysis in 1988 because a significant fraction of 1989 applications might be granted after mid-1992, when our data end. Also, those granted in 1990 and 1991 would have very little time to receive citations.

moderate amount of variation across fields. The difference between university and random sample patents is largest in electronics and mechanical patents, and smallest in the drug/medical area.

These results control for time effects, but they do not allow the university/random sample difference itself to vary over time. Results of regressions that allow each year cohort of patents to have its own university/random sample difference are shown in table 4 and again graphically in figure 3.[12] While the year-by-year differences are somewhat noisy, there is a clear overall trend: the university/random sample difference grew during the 1970s, reached a plateau during the period from about 1975 through about 1982, and fell significantly after that. The differences between the two groups are statistically significant between 1970 (1975 for generality) and about 1982 or 1983. After that the two groups are not statistically different from one another in either generality or importance.

C Robustness of the Apparent Decline

This decline in relative importance and generality appears to be robust to a number of factors, including truncation bias or possible shifts in citation patterns over time.[13] In the first place, they are robust to time-field interaction effects. If it were the case, for example, that drug patents have become increasingly less citation intensive over time, then university patents (which are increasingly concentrated in the drug/medical area) would appear to be increasingly less important in the sense of receiving fewer citations, because the regressions reported in table 4 control only for the *average* level of citations in drug-related patent classes. However, rerunning the regressions of table 4 *separately* for each of the five major fields yields results (not reported here) that suggest that the decline in the university advantage occurs across all fields and is thus not a result of any difference in composition by field across the two groups.

A second possibility is that the decline is an artifact of the truncation of the citation information in 1992. There are a number of rea-

---

12. To make sure that the university/random sample difference is not due to the different technological foci of the two samples, the regressions reported in table 4 replace the five technology field dummies used in table 2 with 364 separate dummies for patent office patent classes.

13. Details of the analyses summarized in this subsection are given in Henderson et al. (1995) or are available from the authors.

Table 4
Comparison of university and random sample patents over time

| | University/random sample mean difference | |
| | Importance (1) | Generality (2) |
Year		
1965	0.42 (0.29)	
1966	1.63[a] (0.52)	
1967	−0.15 (0.41)	
1968	0.10 (0.35)	
1969	0.06 (0.44)	
1970	0.82[b] (0.42)	
1971	1.35[a] (0.41)	
1972	1.48[a] (0.41)	
1973	1.84[a] (0.38)	
1974	1.08[a] (0.35)	
1975	2.54[a] (0.35)	0.053[a] (0.019)
1976	1.82[a] (0.34)	0.065[a] (0.019)
1977	1.31[a] (0.34)	0.048[a] (0.020)
1978	2.04[a] (0.34)	0.040[b] (0.019)
1979	1.13[a] (0.31)	0.052[a] (0.018)
1980	1.91[a] (0.31)	0.051[a] (0.017)
1981	1.68[a] (0.31)	0.080[a] (0.018)
1982	0.96[a] (0.31)	0.051[a] (0.018)
1983	0.97[a] (0.30)	0.028[c] (0.017)
1984	0.47[c] (0.28)	0.024 (0.017)

Table 4 (continued)

| Year | University/random sample mean difference | |
	Importance (1)	Generality (2)
1985	0.40	0.037[b]
	(0.28)	(0.017)
1986	0.06	0.013
	(0.27)	(0.017)
1987	−0.07	0.043[a]
	(0.25)	(0.017)
1988	−0.08	0.012
	(0.24)	(0.019)
Year dummies	Significant	Significant
Patent class controls	Significant	Significant

a. Significant at the 1% level.
b. Significant at the 5% level.
c. Significant at the 10% level.

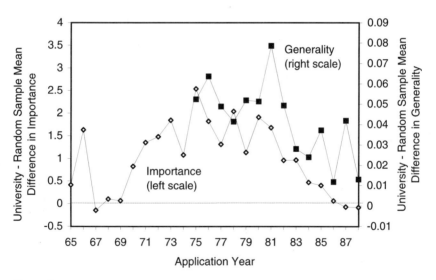

Figure 3
University random sample contrast over time

sons to suspect that such bias could be present. Suppose, first, that the pattern of the distribution of citations over time is identical for both university and random sample patents, but that in every year university patents receive proportionately more citations. Thus it might take several years for the cumulative difference between university and other patents to become significant, and the apparent disappearance of the difference between the two groups at the end of the observed period could simply reflect the fact that there has been insufficient time for the difference between the two groups to become apparent. However, a simple test of this idea—rerunning the regression in logs, thereby capturing the *proportionate* difference between the two groups rather than the absolute difference—produces results, (not reproduced here) that are broadly consistent with those reported above.[14] Thus the results probably cannot be explained by truncation of lag distributions, if the two distributions have the same shape.

A third, more subtle possible problem is that university patents may on average come later than those for private firms, so that the truncation has a more severe effect on them than on the random sample patents. However, a regression that estimates the difference between the average university and random sample patents in a given year, controlling for the predicted levels based on the years remaining to truncation and the average citation lag structure for each sample, gives very similar results to the simpler ones reported earlier, with the university/corporate difference declining sharply around 1981 or 1982 and becoming statistically insignificant shortly thereafter.

In summary, then, university patents in all fields were more important and more general than average in the 1970s. This advantage disappeared in all fields by the mid-1980s; and this disappearance does not appear to be an artifact of truncation or of the way in which citation patterns have changed over time.

IV   The Nature of the Decline

What, then may be causing this decline? One logically plausible candidate—the increasing importance of nonuniversity patents—can probably be easily dismissed, given that, as shown in figure 1, the

---

14. This requires eliminating from both groups those patents with zero citations. The overall difference in importance between the two groups is about 15%. This overall difference conceals variation, with a high of about 30% in the mid to late 1970s, falling to insignificance by 1984.

late 1980s were a time of increasing propensity to patent. The overall patent/R&D ratio, which had been falling for most of this century, began to rise slightly, probably in response to the creation of a special court of appeals for hearing patent cases, and the issuance of several decisions that have increased the perceived likelihood that patents will be enforced (Schwartz (1988)). We suspect that these changes have made patenting slightly more attractive, all other things equal, thus making it economic to patent ideas of lower expected quality and thereby *reducing* the overall importance of private sector patents.

Our results suggest instead that the decline in the relative importance and generality of university patents had two principal components. First the fact that an increasing fraction of university patents is coming from smaller institutions, which have always produced patents that were not as highly cited as those from the larger institutions, and second a general decline in average quality that encompasses even the best institutions triggered largely by a large increase in the number of patents that receive no citations at all.

Simple counts suggest that smaller institutions are indeed patenting more intensively. Since 1965 the fraction of patents going to the top four institutions has fallen from about 50% to about 25%. The Herfindahl index of concentration across institutions has also declined, from about 0.1 in 1965 to about 0.04 in 1988. These smaller institutions are indeed getting less important patents. Figure 4 shows the results of running regressions analogous to that underlying figure 3, but allowing the difference between university and random sample patents to differ not only over time but also according to the size of the institution. To control for size we grouped all institutions that got any patents over the period into three categories: (1) those institutions in the top decile in terms of the number of successful patent applications in 1988;[15] (2) those institutions that got fewer patents than the top decile but more than the bottom quartile in 1988; and (3) those institutions that were in the bottom quartile in terms of patent total in 1988 plus those that had no successful applications in 1988 but received at least one patent from some other year. The results are illustrated in figure 4. The results show that, except possibly for a few years in the second half of the 1970s, the bottom group of universities never produced patents that were statistically distinguishable

---

15. The distribution of patenting activities across universities is very stable over time, so that the choice of a particular year to divide the sample—in this case 1988—seems unlikely to introduce any particular bias into the results.

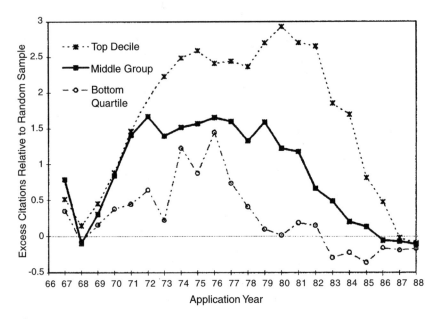

Figure 4
Citation intensity of university patents relative to random sample over time by patent ranking of institution in 1988. Top decile—top 10% of institutions in terms of patents in 1988; bottom quartile—bottom quartile in 1988 plus institutions that had no patents in 1988; middle group—everyone else.

from the random sample, whereas the 15 schools that comprise the top decile of institutions had patents that were even more superior to the random sample than those of other universities. Thus the fact that an increasing fraction of university patents is coming from smaller institutions does indeed seem to be partially responsible for the overall decline in the average importance of university patents. Notice that figure 4 also suggests, however, that even the very best institutions have seen a decline in the relative quality of their patents since about 1983.

The second major component of the decline in average quality appears to be the presence of an increasing number of "low quality" university patents as the institutional changes that we outlined above have substantially increased universities' propensity to patent. Figure 5 illustrates this trend dramatically. It shows the overall increase in patenting (the heavy middle line), juxtaposed with two contrasting components of that total.

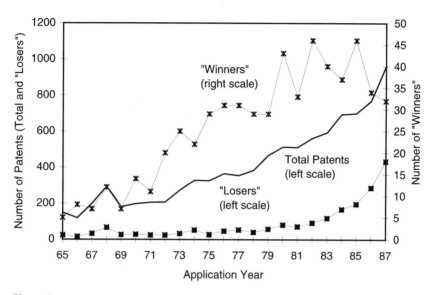

Figure 5
Total university patents, "winners," and "losers." Losers—patents with no citations by end of period; winners—patents with more citations than mean of top 10% of random sample patents from same year

The dashed line at the top is the number of high-importance patents, dubbed "winners" in the graph and plotted on the right-side axis. This is the number of patents that received more citations than the mean of the top 10% of random sample patents from the same year. This series increases *faster* than the overall total up until the early 1980s, implying that the proportion of very important patents was increasing over this period. From 1981 on, however, this series fluctuates up and down with no clear trend and despite the approximate doubling in the total number of patents after 1980, there is no increase in the number of very important patents.

The bottom line is the number of "losers"—the number of patents each year that received no citations. It is virtually flat until the early 1980s, showing that the roughly fivefold increase in overall patenting up until that time was not accompanied by much of an increase in the number of these low-importance patents. After about 1981, however, this number increases dramatically, until by 1987 nearly half of all university patents are receiving no citations. This increase appears to reflect a real change in the composition of university patents, and is quite robust to controls for both field and truncation bias.

V Conclusion

We have shown that the relative importance and generality of university patents has fallen at the same time as the sheer number of university patents has increased. This decrease appears to be largely the result of a very rapid increase in the number of "low-quality" patents being granted to universities.

What are the policy implications of this result? From a theoretical perspective, the Bayh-Dole Act and the increase in industry funding had two distinct effects on university incentives. Both the incentive to perform research that could be expected to produce important commercial inventions, and the incentive to patent and license whatever commercial inventions were produced increased. Clearly, the Bayh-Dole Act has been a success with respect to the second of these incentive effects. Both the rate of patenting and the extent of licensing have increased dramatically. In this context it is important to emphasize that even thought the body of uncited university patents that we have observed is probably less valuable *per patent* than previous university patents, these patents are not worthless in the aggregate. Some of these uncited patents are licensed and are commercially valuable. Before the Bayh-Dole Act they would probably not have been either patented or licensed, and the invention underlying them would have been unlikely to generate commercial benefits. Thus the increase in university patenting probably reflects an increased rate of technology transfer to the private sector, and this has probably increased the social rate of return to university research.

In contrast to the impact on the *transfer* of technology, our results suggest, however, that the Bayh-Dole Act and the other related changes in federal law and institutional capability have not had a significant impact on the underlying rate of *generation* of commercially important inventions at universities. Universities either did not significantly shift their research efforts toward areas likely to produce commercial inventions, or, if they did, they did so unsuccessfully. It is unclear, of course, whether it would be socially desirable if universities shifted their research efforts toward commercial objectives. It is likely that the bulk of the economic benefits of university research come from inventions in the private sector that build upon the scientific and engineering base created by university research, rather than from commercial inventions generated directly by universities. In other words, if commercial inventions are inherently only a secondary product of university research, then it makes sense for policy to seek to ensure that those inventions that do appear are transferred to the private sector, but not to hope to increase significantly the rate at which university research directly generates commercial inventions. This appears to be what has occurred.

From a methodological perspective, our results show that it is possible to use citations to improve the usefulness of patent statistics as economic indicators. The economic usefulness of these widely available data has been limited by their perceived noisiness. Even in the time-series dimension, where cohort effects and truncation bias make citation comparisons difficult, the use of a reference group and careful controls for technology field allowed us to produce fairly clear results regarding the changing nature of university patents. We believe that this technique can be readily applied to other data, thereby greatly increasing the signal-to-noise ratio in patent data.

References

Archibugi, D., "Patenting as an Indicator of Technological Innovation: A Review," *Science and Public Policy* 19 (1992), 357–368.

AUTM, *The AUTM Licensing Survey, Fiscal Years 1993, 1992, 1991* (Norwalk, CT: Association of University Technology Managers, 1994).

Basberg, B., "Patents and the Measurement of Technological Change: A Survey of Literature," *Research Policy* 16 (1987), 131–141.

Biumenthal, D., "Academic–Industry Relationships in the Life Sciences (Extent, Consequences, and Management)," *Journal of the American Medical Association* 268 (1986), 3344–3349.

Boitani, A., and E. Ciciotti, "Patents as Indicators of Innovative Performances at the Regional Level," in R. Cappellin and P. Nijkamp (eds.), *The Spatial Context of Technological Development* (Aldershot: Gower, 1990), 139–163.

Caballero, R., and A. Jaffe, "How High Are the Giants' Shoulders: An Empirical Assessment of Knowledge Spillovers and Creative Destruction in a Model of Economic Growth," in O. Blanchard and S. Fischer (eds.), *NBER Macroeconomics Annual*, vol. 8 (Cambridge, MA: MIT Press, 1993).

Carpenter, M., and F. Narin, "Citation Rates to Technologically Important Patents," *World Patent Information* 5 (1993), 180–185.

Cohen, Wesley, Richard Florida, and W. Richard Goe, "University–Industry Research Centers in the United States," Research Report, Center for Economic Development, Heinz School of Public Policy and Management, Carnegie-Melon University (1993).

Dasgupta, P., and P. David, "Information Disclosure and the Economics of Science and Technology," in G. Feiwel (ed.), *Arrow and the Ascent of Modern Economic Theory* (New York: NYU Press, 1987), chap. 16.

David, P. A., D. Mowery, and W. E. Steinmueller, "Analyzing the Economic Payoffs from Basic Research," *Economics of Innovation and New Technology* 2 (1992), 73–90.

Griliches, Z., "Patent Statistics as Economic Indicators: A Survey," *Journal of Economic Literature* 28 (1990), 1661–1707.

Henderson, Rebecca, Adam Jaffe, and Manuel Trajtenberg, "Universities as a Source of Commercial Technology: A Detailed Analysis of University Patenting 1965–1988," Working Paper 5068, NBER (Mar. 1995).

———— "The Bayh-Dole Act and Trends in University Patenting 1965–1988," in *Proceedings of the Conference on University Goals, Institutional Mechanisms and the "Industrial Transferability" of Research*, Stanford Center for Economic Policy Research (1996).

Jaffe, Adam, B., "Technological Opportunity and Spillovers of R&D: Evidence from Firrus Patents, Profits and Market Value," *American Economic Review* (Dec. 1986), 984–1001.

———— "Real Effects of Academic Research," *American Economic Review* 79 (1989), 957–970.

Jaffe, Adam, Manuel Trajtenberg, and Rebecca Henderson, "Geographic Localization of Knowledge Spillovers as Evidenced by Patent Citations," *Quarterly Journal of Economics* (1993).

Merton, D., in N. W. Starer (ed.), *The Sociology of Science: Theoretical and Empirical Investigation* (Chicago: University of Chicago Press, 1973).

National Academy of Sciences, *Allocating Federal Funds for Science and Technology* (Washington, DC: 1995) National Academy Press.

National Science Foundation, *University Industry Research Relationships: Myths, Realities and Potentials.* (Washington, DC: U.S. Government Printing Office, 1982).

Romer, Paul, "Increasing Returns and Long-Run Growth," *Journal of Political Economy* 94: 5 (1986), 1002–1037.

———— "Endogenous Technological Change," *Journal of Political Economy* 98: 5 (1990), S71–S101.

Schwartz, H. F., *Patent Law and Practice* (Washington, DC: Federal Judicial Center, 1988).

Trajtenberg, M., "A Penny for Your Quotes: Patent Citations and the Value of Innovations," *Rand Journal of Economics* 21: 1 (1990a), 172–187.

———— *Economic Analysis of Product Innovation: The Case of CT Scanners* (Cambridge, MA: Harvard University Press, 1990b).

Trajtenberg, M., R. Henderson, and A. Jaffe, "University versus Corporate Patents: A Window on the Basicness of Invention," *Economics of Innovation and New Technology* 5: 1 (1997), 19–50.

U.S. GAO "Patent Policy: Recent Changes in Federal Law Considered Beneficial," GAO/RCED-87-44, General Accounting Office, (1987).

Zucker, Lynn, Michael Darby, and Marilynn Brewer, "Intellectual Human Capital and the Birth of U.S. Biotechnology Enterprises," *American Economic Review* 87: 3 (June 1997).

9

Evidence from Patents
and Patent Citations on
the Impact of NASA and
Other Federal Labs on
Commercial Innovation

Adam B. Jaffe, Michael S.
Fogarty, and Bruce A. Banks

I Introduction

Federal research institutions comprise a significant component of the
US research infrastructure. The approximately 700 federal labs are
extremely heterogeneous, varying from the large "National" laboratories of the Department of Energy, such as Los Alamos and Oak
Ridge, to small, highly specialized facilities. They include "intramural" facilities that are owned and operated by the federal government, and also Federally Funded Research and Development Centers
("FFRDCs"), which are operated by a university, a private firm, or a
non-profit organization, but receive all or most of their funding from
the federal government. Examples of intramural labs include the
National Institutes of Health, the National Institute of Standards and
Technology (NIST) within the Department of Commerce, and the
research centers of the National Aeronautics and Space Administration (NASA). Examples of FFRDCs include the DOE National Labs
and the NASA-funded Jet Propulsion Laboratory operated by Cal
Tech. In 1995, approximately $25 billion of R&D was performed at
federal research institutions, which is about 14% of the aggregate
US research effort, and about 41% of federal spending on R&D. For

This project could not have been completed without generous contributions of time for
discussions by individuals at NASA and a number of private firms. We thank, without
implicating, Daniel J. Adams, Tim Gurin, Richard Hullihen, Sylvia Kraemer, Norman
Smith, Allan Vogele, and Warren W. Wolf. We also benefited from comments at the
NBER Productivity Lunch, and from the referees and editor of this Journal. We appreciate the able research assistance of Margaret Lister Fernando and Chu Chi-Leung.
We are grateful for financial support from the Alfred P. Sloan Foundation, via the
National Bureau of Economic Research Project on Industrial Technology and Productivity. Bruce A. Banks' participation in this research project was as an individual and
not an employee of NASA-Lewis.

comparison, universities—the other major locus of public research—performed about $22 billion of R&D, of which about $13 billion was funded by the federal government, only 21% of federal research expenditures [National Science Board, 1996].[1]

The last 15 years have seen increasing focus of US policy on improving the links between public science and commercial innovation. Beginning with the Stevenson-Wydler Technology Innovation Act and the Bayh-Dole Act in 1980, and continuing with the Federal Technology Transfer Act of 1986, the National Competitiveness Technology Transfer Act of 1989, and the Defense Conversion, Reinvestment, and Transition Assistance Act of 1992, Congress has implemented statutory changes explicitly designed to foster the transfer of technology from the public sector into the private sector. The biannual *Science and Engineering Indicators* now publishes a wealth of statistics documenting technology transfer activities at the labs. There have been several studies by the Congressional General Accounting Office of such activities.[2]

This gradual policy shift has coincided with increasing academic interest in the contribution of public research to commercial innovation, and to "spillovers" of R&D across institutional boundaries more generally. A number of authors have explored the use of patent citation information as a way of tracing the impact that one organization's or a group of organizations' inventions have on the broader economy.[3] In this chapter, we look at the patents of NASA and other federal laboratories through this lens. In addition, we take advantage of direct access to research records of one NASA research group to look qualitatively at the nature of interactions of federal scientists with commercial firms, and to examine the extent to which patent citations received by this group are indeed indicative of external technological impact.

---

1. It is important to note that the overall research budgets of intramural federal labs such as the National Institutes of Health or the NASA research centers include large dollar amounts that are distributed as research grants or contracts to other parties; the amount of research funding actually spent at the facility may be a small fraction of the total budget. The dollar figures cited in this paragraph come from compilations by the National Science Foundation of research expenditure by locus of the research, and hence include only the expenditures for research performed at the labs. Comparable numbers for individual agencies are not generally published.
2. Most recently, "National Laboratories: Are Their Activities Related to Commercial Product Development?" GAO/PEMD-95-2, November 1994.
3. See, e.g. Henderson, Trajtenberg and Jaffe (forthcoming), and Podolny and Shepard [1997].

II   Patents and Patent Citations

(i)   Background

There is a long history in economics of the use of patent data to understand the processes of invention and innovation [Schmookler, 1966; Griliches, 1984 and 1990; Jaffe, 1986]. A patent is a temporary monopoly awarded to inventors for the commercial use of an invention. For a patent to be granted, the invention must be non-trivial, meaning that it would not appear obvious to a skilled practitioner of the relevant technology, and it must be useful, meaning that it has potential *commercial* value. If a patent is granted, an extensive public document is created, containing detailed information about the invention, the inventor, the organization (if any) to which the inventor assigns the patent property right, and the technological antecedents of the invention. All of this information can be accessed in machine-readable form. As a result, there has been much recent interest in exploiting this more detailed information to understand the invention process.

In particular, the "references" or "citations" that appear in a patent identify earlier inventions whose claims are sufficiently close to the claims of the citing patent that the patent examiner deems it necessary to identify them. The citations that appear in a patent serve the important legal function of delimiting the property right granted by the patent, by identifying "prior art" that is not covered by the property right granted in the citing patent. Thus the citations contained within a patent convey information about the technological antecedents of the invention covered by the patent. Conversely, we can identify the subsequent patents that later make citations to a given patent, thereby learning something about the technological descendants of the cited invention.

Previous research has used information on citations made and received by patents to draw inferences about the process of technological accumulation [Caballero and Jaffe, 1993]; about the "basicness" or importance of particular inventions [Trajtenberg, Henderson and Jaffe, 1997]; about changing patterns of importance of university patents over recent decades [Henderson, Jaffe and Trajtenberg, forthcoming] and about the extent to which knowledge spillovers are geographically localized [Jaffe, Trajtenberg and Henderson, 1993]. Trajtenberg [1990a and 1990b] has shown that there is a correlation within a family of products between the number of citations received by the patent covering a particular model and the consumers' surplus generated by that model.

In this paper, we examine the patenting behavior of NASA and other federal agencies over the last several decades, and indicators of the average impact of these patents, based on citations they receive. Consistent with the statutory encouragement of technology transfer, we find some evidence of increased patenting activity by these agencies in the last decade. In previous work, Henderson, Trajtenberg and Jaffe found that an analogous increase in patenting by universities since the early 1980s has been accompanied by a significant decline in citation-based measures of the average impact of university patents. Interestingly, we do not find consistent evidence that the increase in federal patenting was associated with any decline in the average impact of the federal patents. Many questions remain, however, about the interpretation of the patent and citation series.

(ii) Details

The data are drawn from the universe of patents granted by the US patent office between 1963 and 1994, with information on the citations made to these patents for the period 1977–1994. The computerized patent office files only identify the "assignee" by name beginning in 1969, although the data back to 1963 are coded to distinguish patents on the basis of whether the patent was assigned to a corporation, the government, or unassigned. For this reason, we can only identify patents assigned to NASA beginning in 1969, but we can identify US government patents throughout the 1963–1994 period.

We construct three distinct sets of patents for analysis. The first consists of the 3782 patents assigned to NASA between 1969 and 1993[4] (the "NASA sample"). The second sample consists of the 37 939 patents assigned to the US government between 1963 and 1993, excluding those identified as belonging to NASA (the "other federal" sample). This sample includes patents from 1963–1968 assigned to NASA. For the period after 1969 when we are able to identify the specific department or agency to which the assignment was made, 67% are assigned to the armed services, 19% are assigned to the De-

---

4. We terminate the samples in 1993 because our citations data end in 1994, and patents granted in 1994 are unlikely to have been cited in that year.

partment of Energy, 6% are assigned to the Department of Agriculture, and 3% are assigned to Health and Human Services (which includes the National Institutes of Health).

The last sample consists of a 1 in 100 random sample of all patents granted to inventors residing in the US (the "random sample").[5] This sample contains 13 997 patents for the period 1963–1993. Thus pooling the NASA, other federal and random samples yields the basic dataset used in the analysis, which contains 55 710 patents.

For descriptive purposes, we will categorize patents into five broad fields: Drugs and Medical Technology; Chemicals and Chemical Processes Excluding Drugs; Electronic, Optical and Nuclear Technologies; Mechanical Technologies; and All Other. These fields are based primarily on the 3-digit patent class assigned by the patent examiner.[6]

III NASA and Other Federal Patents: Trends and Patterns

Figures 1A–1C show the trends in three patent series: NASA, other federal, and aggregate patenting over time, broken down by the five major technology fields cited above. Not surprisingly, the rate of NASA patenting at the end of the 1960s was much higher than in subsequent years. From a peak of almost 350 patents granted in 1971, patenting fell rapidly to a low of about 75 patents per year between 1979 and 1982. This increased to about 150 per year in the early 1980s, fell again in 1986, and has been rising since 1988, recently recovering to the level of 150 per year.

The interpretation of the NASA patent series over time is clouded by changing NASA policy with respect to patenting by NASA contractors. By law, NASA retains the property right to any invention developed by private firms using NASA research or procurement funds. Such firms can, however, seek a waiver of this right in order to patent commercially valuable inventions in their own name. If such a waiver is granted, then any patent that results will be assigned to the firm and will not show up as a NASA patent in our data. On the

---

5. This sample consists of patents granted to corporations, to individual inventors, and also to the federal government. Federal patents are only about 3% of the universe of domestic patents. We followed a conservative strategy in selecting federal and NASA patents with respect to finding differences between the two groups.
6. There are about 400 such classes. The mapping from patent classes to the five broad fields is available in the supplemental material for this chapter posted on the *Journal* editorial web page.

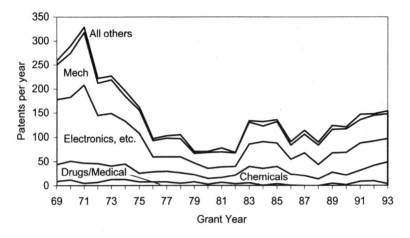

Figure 1A
NASA patents by field over time

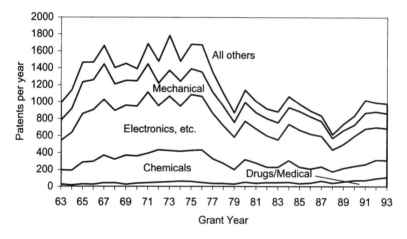

Figure 1B
Other federal patents by field over time

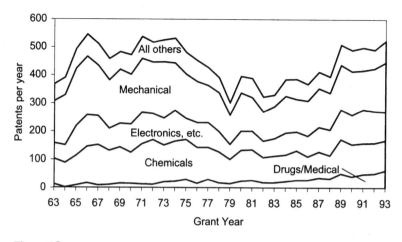

Figure 1C
Random sample patents by field over time

other hand, NASA has the right to deny the waiver and seek a patent in its own name, in which case our data would include a "NASA" patent that was funded by NASA money, but which did not come out of research performed at a NASA facility.

In principle, therefore, our NASA sample is a mixture of unknown proportions between patents from research performed at NASA facilities, and patents from NASA contracts or grant research where waivers were denied. We were told that the waiver policy became increasingly lenient through the 1970s. This resulted in a situation by the early 1980s where waivers were essentially automatically granted.[7] All else equal, this would produce some decline in the number of patents in our NASA sample, as patents from contract research where waivers were denied gradually disappear.[8]

"Other federal" patents remained approximately flat at about 1600 per year from 1965 through 1976, and then fell significantly, to the rate of about 1000 per year, and continued drifting downward to a low of fewer than 600 in 1988. Since then, the rate has risen again, to about 1000 per year. Unlike NASA, the Defense Department, the

---

7. Personal communication with Sylvia Kraemer, NASA Special Studies Division.

8. The need to apply for waivers was eliminated by statute in 1980 in cases where the contractor is a university or other non-profit entity. Note that the NASA Jet Propulsion Lab is owned and operated by Cal Tech; this means that there might be some JPL inventions before that date in our NASA sample (if a waiver was denied), but JPL patents are presumably not in our sample after 1980.

Department of Energy, and DOE's predecessor, the Atomic Energy Commission, do not require waivers before their contractors can patent inventions derived from funded research. This means that the "other federal" sample is not likely to be significantly contaminated by patents that do not originate at the labs. On the other hand, it also means that many patents originating at FFRDCs (including the large National Labs) may appear in the name of the operator of the facility rather than the government. This difference has to be considered when comparing NASA patents to other federal patents.

The historical pattern of total patents granted per year, as indicated by our random sample, is similar to that for federal labs other than NASA: a plateau through the late 1970s, followed by a decline and then leveling off. Note that all three series show an increase in patenting some time around the late 1980s. However, the exact timing differs somewhat in each case.[9]

The rate of patenting is determined by the scale of research effort, the success of that effort, and the "propensity to patent" whatever research outputs have been produced. Often, economists assume that the propensity to patent is stable over time. This assumption allows data on patent totals to be interpreted as measures of inventive output; combined with data on research inputs, they can then be used as measures of research productivity. If the statutory activity regarding technology transfer has been successful, however, one effect should have been an increase in the propensity to patent, as the labs increased their interest in and focus on commercial applications. Hence the series in Figures 1A and 1B confound the effects of changes in inventive output and changes in the propensity to patent.

These effects cannot be completely separated. We can characterize what has been happening, however, by examining the ratio of patents to R&D effort, proxied by expenditure. If the invention productivity of research effort is constant, this ratio is a proxy for the propensity to patent.

Figure 2 shows patents per million dollars of R&D expenditure for the three samples over time. In order to make broad movements more visible, and allow for the lag of one to three years between patent application and patent grant, each point in Figure 2 takes a moving

---

9. Year-to-year movements in these series can be artifacts of patent office operations. For example, the sharp dip in 1979 in all series is due to the fact that the patent office ran out of money for examiners in that year [Griliches, 1989].

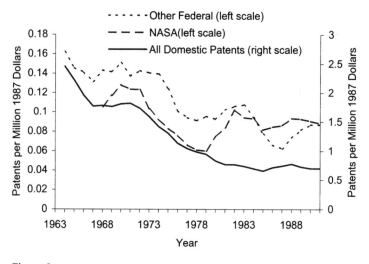

Figure 2
Patents per dollar of R&D over time

average of lab research expenditures and divides that research number into a moving average of the number of patents, moved forward two years.[10] Figure 2 implies that the propensity to patent for all domestic patents declined steadily up until about 1981. It has been roughly constant since. For non-NASA federal patents, the decline continues until about 1986. Then there has been steady growth.

Because of their mission-oriented R&D, federal labs have a lower propensity to patent than the private sector—many fewer patents per dollar of R&D—roughly one-fifteenth in the 1960s and 1970s. However, the difference narrowed to one-eighth by the early 1990s. NASA's patents-per-research-dollar figure was less than that of other federal agencies until the 1980s, but is now about the same.[11]

---

10. The denominator for NASA is fiscal year budget obligations for intramural facilities. For other federal labs, we divide by total R&D expenditures of federal facilities and FFRDCs. The "all domestic patents" series is estimated by taking the random sample patents, multiplying by 100, and dividing by total industry R&D. All R&D dollars are deflated to 1987.

11. This pattern is similar to that of university patents—which were more important and more general than the random sample in the late 1970s. For university patents, the decline in relative quality seems to have been driven by a reduction in the standards for patenting as incentives changed and many more patents were taken out in the 1980s [Henderson, Jaffe and Trajtenberg, forthcoming]. The NASA pattern—rising quality as numbers decline in the 1970s, followed by declining quality when the numbers recover in the 1980s—is consistent with a similar phenomenon, but we have not explored this issue in detail.

Though the rise in the propensity to patent since 1986 is consistent with the policy mandate for increased commercial relevance, it is worth noting that by the early 1990s, labs' propensity to patent had only returned to what it was in 1978.

Figure 2 shows that the steep decline in NASA patenting represented in Figure 1A over the 1970s can be interpreted as a combination of declining NASA research spending *and* declining propensity to patent at a rate approximately comparable to that for both "other federal" and all domestic patents.[12] Throughout this period, NASA's propensity to patent is somewhat below that for other federal labs. In the early 1980s there was a significant increase in NASA patents per dollar of research expenditure, up to approximately the level of the other federal labs. Since then, NASA patenting has moved in approximate proportion to research expenditures, leaving the ratio approximately constant.

Thus if we interpret increased propensity to patent as evidence of increased commercial orientation, there is evidence of such a reorientation for the federal labs other than NASA, but not for NASA. If the increased propensity to patent is brought about by a systematic increase in patenting of marginal inventions, then the rise in the number of patents would be accompanied by a decline in their average importance or impact. This is precisely what Henderson, Trajtenberg and Jaffe found to be occurring in university patents in the 1980s, measuring importance or impact using the citations received by the university patents.

Henderson, Trajtenberg and Jaffe used two citation-based measures of impact: the total number of citations received (dubbed "importance") and 1 minus the Herfindahl index of concentration of the citations across the 400 patent office patent classes (dubbed "generality"). Because importance and generality vary systematically with the age of a patent and its patent class, they cannot be measured absolutely, but only relatively. In this case, it is possible to use the random sample of all patents, controlling for year and patent class, as a baseline against which to measure the importance and generality of the federal patents. What we find is that, relative to the random sample, NASA patents were significantly (both quantitatively and statistically) more important and more general than the random sam-

---

12. The fact that NASA's patents per research dollar declined in the 1970s at about the same rate as both the rest of the government and patents as a whole suggests that the disappearance from our sample of contractor patents denied waivers may not have been quantitatively significant.

ple until the late 1970s, after which they suffered a precipitous decline to become indistinguishable from the random sample by the
early 1980s (importance) or late 1980s (generality).[13] In contrast, the
average importance of other federal patents was significantly and
persistently less than the random sample up until the late 1980s, but
has approached parity since then. The generality of the other federal
patents has generally not been distinguishable from the random
sample.

Hence the patterns of these citation-based measures of impact do
not tell a simple story regarding the best interpretation of the changing patent intensities. For NASA, the nature of patenting activity
underwent a transformation in the late 1970s and early 1980s, but it
is difficult to say exactly what happened, and how much it may have
been affected by the change in waiver policy. For the *other* federal
agencies, the one thing we can say is that, based on citation measures,
there is no evidence that the increase in patents per R&D dollar since
1988 has been associated with any decline in average quality. This
suggests that the increased propensity to patent has played out more
or less across the quality distribution, with potentially significant inventions that were previously unpatented now being patented.

Drawing firmer conclusions about how any increase in commercial
orientation has affected these agencies will require data beyond the
patent series. Therefore, in the second half of the paper, we turn to a
micro-qualitative analysis of one NASA research group to try to get
a deeper understanding of these issues.

IV Qualitative Evidence on NASA Patents and Patent Citations

Our analysis of NASA's patents provides some intriguing evidence
on technology spillovers from federal labs. The analysis rests, however, on the explicit assumption that patent citations reflect flows of
knowledge, and that citations received tell us something about the
technological significance of patents and the underlying inventions.
In this section we explore qualitatively the relationships among patents, patent citations and technology spillovers. We have three main
purposes for this part of the paper: (1) use the qualitative information gained from interviews to improve quantitative analyses of federal lab commercialization using patent data; (2) develop a deeper

---

13. The regression results underlying these statements can be found in the supple-
mentary materials for this article on the *Journal*'s web site.

understanding of the pathways through which federal lab research influences firm performance (in this case, innovation by firms); and (3) validate the use of patent citations for analyzing knowledge flows.

To achieve these objectives, we undertook a detailed analysis of the invention and patenting of the Electro-Physics Branch (EPB) of the NASA-Lewis Research Center located in Cleveland, Ohio, which is directed by one of the authors. In addition to having Banks' intimate knowledge of the inventions, patents, and technology transfer activities of the EPB, we also talked with a number of other people with knowledge about patenting and technology transfer involving government labs.[14] EPB is involved in the development of high performance durable power materials and surfaces technology to meet NASA, national, and US industrial needs.

(i) Evaluating EPB's Patents and Patent Cites

We began by identifying EPB's 38 patents as of October 1996. These patents had received 160 citations through 1994, of which 139 are from other organizations. Seven EPB patents received more than ten citations, representing nearly 70% of all citations. One stood out with 33 citations (#4 490 229: "Deposition of Diamondlike Carbon Films"). Two of EPB's patents have been licensed: patent #4 620 898 has been licensed to J.P. Technologies (long-life sputter masks), and #4 560 577 was licensed to Air Products and then assigned to Diamonex, Inc. (dual beam deposition of diamond-like carbon films).

We analyzed in detail citations made to the seven EPB patents that received ten or more citations overall.[15] We limited the analysis to

---

14. Interviews for this chapter included: EPB's branch chief, EPB personnel, selected firms working with EPB, NASA-Lewis' patent attorney, TRW's patent attorney, BF Goodrich's director of Corporate Technology (Specialty Chemicals Division), Picker International's patent attorney and Director of Technology Marketing, Owens–Corning's R&D Director, and a former R&D director of GE's engine division. Except for interviews of EPB personnel, these interviews were conducted by two of the authors, Fogarty and Jaffe, during 1996. A series of 38 interviews of EPB personnel, selected companies having contact with EPB, and local technology transfer organizations were conducted by Christine Williams in the summer of 1993 under the guidance of Michael Fogarty and Mohan Reddy. Williams was a research assistant and MBA student in the Center for Regional Economic Issues. Mohan Reddy is Professor of Marketing at Case-Western Reserve University.

15. Our analysis of the seven patents is not affected by a regime change in 1980 resulting from changes in federal policy permitting federal contractors to receive exclusive rights to any resulting patent. The seven patents were issued between 1980 and 1986. The general pattern of citation to each of the EPB patents is indistinguishable from that of citations to corporate patents.

citing patents that themselves received four or more citations (patents which themselves passed a minimum threshold of "importance"). Given the extensive time required for assessing each patent, it was not possible to analyze all EPB patents and all citing patents. This produced 53 citing patents.

The relationship between these 53 citing patents and the EPB patent that they cite was analyzed along three dimensions. First, Banks determined whether the inventors or the organization associated with the citing patent had ever had personal communication contact with EPB.[16] This characterization was made based on Banks' lab notebook records. To further explore the relationship between citations and communication, we identified 18 additional patents which were assigned to organizations known by Banks to have had extensive contact with EPB, and whose subject area was closely related to those of EPB patents.

Second, in order to get a sense for the extent to which citations truly correspond to our concept of inventions building upon one another, Banks characterized the *technological relationship* between the inventions captured in the citing and cited patents. This characterization took the form of determining whether the technologies embedded in the two patents were the same, related or unrelated, and whether the application to which the technology was put was the same, related or unrelated. In other words, each citing/cited patent pair was placed in a 3×3 matrix indicating whether the technology and its application were the same, related or unrelated. The resulting distribution of the 53 citing patents is shown in Figure 3. Approximately four of five citing patents involve some degree of technological relationship to the cited patent (the same or related technology and/or the same or related application of the technology).

Finally, irrespective of communication or lack thereof, Banks characterized the likelihood that each invention described in a citing patent had benefited from any kind of knowledge spillover from the cited invention. He categorized each cite on a scale of 1 through 5 (1 = spillover highly unlikely and 5 = spillover certain). This was done on the basis of such evidence as parallel citations to related

---

16. Banks has kept a personal lab notebook with information about his external contacts for over two decades. Additional data is maintained from all phone contacts with EPB researchers.

scientific papers and details of the invention that seem to indicate influence Figure 4.[17,18]

Technological Relationship between Inventions Connected by Citation
These qualitative results indicate considerable diversity of technological connections underlying citations. First, approximately one-fifth (11/53) of citations are cases where neither the technology nor the application is clearly related to the cited patent. The source of these apparently spurious citations is not entirely clear, although some views on their origin from industry participants is discussed below. Second, at the other extreme, there are a handful of citations (5/53, or 9%) where *both* the technology and the application are essentially the same as the cited patent. In theory, an invention that uses an existing technology for an existing application should not be patentable; these citations appear to represent the margin of patentability where minor variations in approach or features suffice to achieve the novelty or "non-obviousness" required for patenting.[19]

The remainder of cases (36/53, or 68%) correspond to situations in which citing patents utilize the same or related technologies in

17. While patent citations can be inserted by the patent attorney or the patent examiner in cases where the inventor was unaware of the earlier invention, citations to scientific papers are much less likely to appear in this way.

18. The micro-level analysis of one R&D lab's patents requires the lab director's intimate knowledge of both technologies and the lab's relationships with citing organizations. Although this methodology could potentially introduce bias if the director's incentive is to find spillovers, we believe the problem is insignificant in this case for several reasons. First, Bruce Banks essentially treated his assessment of EPB's patents in the same manner as he performs his research. For example, following good scientific practice, he has maintained record books on all external contacts since the mid-1960s. Second, independently he systematically analyzed a subset of firm contacts with EPB, tracing each contact according to origin (e.g. the contact occurred because an individual read a NASA paper) through each step of the decision process to ultimate result. This was done to improve the technology transfer process, but also out of curiosity about the process. Third, we view this type of analysis as an essential step in designing the next stage of work on patent citations, which will be a national survey of inventors. The national survey will further examine the meaning of patent citations, mechanisms at work, etc., as a way to study knowledge flows and technology spillovers.

19. It is particularly surprising to find so many apparently marginal patents, given that we limited ourselves to cases where the cited patents received ten or more citations and citing patents received four or more cites. As the median patent gets only one citation, these should be considerably better than average. Our finding supports the generally held view among practitioners that the "obviousness" standard for patenting is quite low and is applied with a great deal of variability.

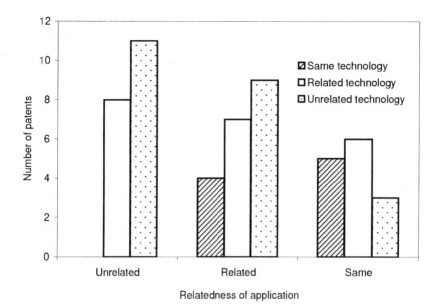

Figure 3
Relatedness distributions for citing patents

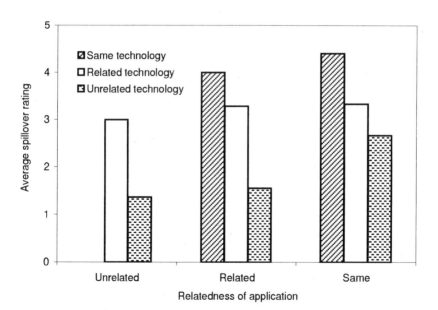

Figure 4
Average spillover rating for citing patents, by "relatedness"

unrelated applications, or conversely, apply unrelated technologies in similar applications. We believe these partially related inventions, which comprise the majority of all citations, correspond reasonably well to our conception of citations as indicating some form of cumulative technological impact.

Evidence of Influence or Knowledge Spillover from Cited to Citing Inventions

In order to better understand the extent to which citations can be used as a proxy for flows of knowledge between inventors, Banks examined evidence of explicit communication between EPB scientists and the inventors on patents that cite EPB patents. In addition, Banks provided a list of firms that he knew had learned from and utilized EPB research, and a systematic search was made to determine if the patents of such known "spillover recipients" contained evidence of that spillover in the form of citation to EPB patents. In other words, we looked for both "Type 1" error (citations occur but spillovers do not) and "Type 2" error (spillover occurs without citation) in the identification of citations with knowledge spillovers.

It is clear from these data that citation occurs without there having been known, direct communication; only 9/53 citations (17%) involved known contact. If we take "3" or better as evidence of spillover, then 51% (27/53) of all cites appear to involve technology spillovers. This also suggests that most spillovers result from indirect rather than direct communication. For example, this occurs when the citing inventor reads papers or patent documents, or learns from attending a presentation by the cited inventor—even without identifying herself to the inventor.

If we exclude the obvious "spurious" citations (those 11 citations involving both unrelated technology and unrelated application), then two-thirds of cites were evaluated as producing spillovers. Suggesting that contact matters, two-thirds of cites associated with direct contact were evaluated as producing spillovers; this contrasts with 48% of all cites in which no apparent direct contact occurred.

It is also clear that contact can occur and not generate any citations: 18 patents were found in the general area of EPB's research by organizations that had had significant contact with EPB but that did not cite the EPB patents. It is interesting, however, that in only two of the 18 patents where contact occurred but there was no citation does Banks conclude the evidence of spillover is fairly strong; in the other cases, the patented inventions are not directly related to EPB's, and there is little evidence of spillover. The average spillover rating for non-citing patents with related technology and the same application equals 4.0; in contrast, the average spillover rating for non-citing patents where both the technology and application were unrelated equals 1.125. The difference in estimated spillover between citing and non-citing patents is statistically significant (a t-statistic testing for a difference of means equal to zero between the two distributions is $t = 4.2$).[20]

Suffice it to say that citations are clearly a noisy indicator of spillovers. The overwhelming majority of citations do not appear to have involved known contact with EPB personnel. On the other hand, in many cases there is indirect evidence that the citing inventors knew about and apparently benefited from EPB research. Such evidence includes citations to scientific papers authored by EPB or related people, or details of the invention specification that strongly suggest prior knowledge of the EPB invention. Conversely, contact does not always lead to citation. In most cases the lack of citation appears to result from a lack of direct spillover benefit from the contact, at least to date. In a few cases apparent spillovers occurred despite no known communication and the absence of citation.

(ii)   Insights from Participants in the Patenting and Technology Transfer Processes

Our interviews with EPB and various companies point to a lot going on below the surface of patent citations. In interpreting patent citations, we have talked with three kinds of participants in the patenting process: the inventor, the R&D director, and the patent attorney. While each participant contributes important information about citations, our interviews have made it quite clear that it is the inventor who knows whose technology has been most important in the invention and the pathways by which the knowledge traveled (consulting, reading of papers, hiring of graduates, etc.).

At the broadest level, our discussions with practitioners confirm that quantity of citations to a patent is a valid indicator of an

---

20. The following are the statistics for citing, non-citing patents: number of patents (53, 18); means (2.68, 1.44); variance (0.967, 1.067); standard error of the estimated mean (0.176, 0.239); difference of means is 1.235 (assuming the two distributions are independent).

invention's importance.[21] While there will be exceptions in individual cases, it is clear that there is a systematic relationship between the depth and breadth of an invention's technological impact and the number and diversity of citations it receives. However, participants in the process are less convinced that citations are a strong proxy for the actual path of knowledge flow (i.e. if A cites B, it doesn't always mean that A learns directly from B.). Because many parties potentially play a role in the decision to include a citation, it is difficult to get a clear picture of the likelihood that citations occur in cases where the inventor had no knowledge of the technology underlying the cited patent.

It is clear that citations don't always represent what we typically think of as knowledge flow. Some of what we see represents noise. The reason is that citations get included for various reasons, which can be several types: cites involving recent knowledge flow (the inventor actually learned something important from another researcher either directly or indirectly); strictly legal cites (the patent attorney clouds the picture by acting in a risk-averse manner to avoid any hint of infringement, opting to include a citation even when the inventor doesn't consider it as prior art); after-the-fact cites (knowledge of a related technology is gained after the invention); teaching cites (patents that everyone considers basic, even if they are old); and cites added by the patent examiner. Unfortunately, at present we have no way to determine the frequencies attached to each category, although it appears from interviews that knowledge content increases more than in proportion to the quantity of citations as the number of cites increases.

On the decision to include a cite or not, the attorney will typically win out—in other words, opt to include the cite to be safe. (Interviews with patent attorneys at NASA and with private companies indicate the seriousness of the disclosure process. For instance, a common practice is to require the inventor to sign a form signifying that all known state-of-the-art work has been cited, including patents and non-patent sources.)

---

21. The patent law literature refers to "pioneer" patents. See Lawrence B. Ebert, "If a Patent Is Highly Cited, Is It a Pioneering Patent?," in *The Law Works* [June 1996], 5, 28–29. Our interviews indicate that although pioneer patents are acknowledged by patent lawyers as having special status, their status is somewhat informal and derived from legal cases. For a discussion of patent citations in litigation, see Anthony Brietzman and Francis Narin, "A Case for Patent Citation Analysis in Litigation," *The Law Works* [May 1996], 10–11, 26–27.

Not surprisingly, there is general agreement that patent citations are more indicative of patterns of knowledge flow at the level of organizations than at the level of individual patents. A number of organizations have begun to use patent citation information to identify centers of related technological activity around the world. Other firms who have not investigated citation patterns were clearly captivated when we showed them who was citing their patents. Typically, they quickly recognized most citing organizations' involvement in the technologies, particularly if the citing party is toward the top of the citing patents list based on number of cites to the cited patents (i.e. organizations responsible for a high percentage of citations to their patents).[22] What seems true is that organizations *frequently* citing a firm or federal lab are typically well known by the cited party, acknowledging their mutual technological dependence. Also, companies appear to be far more attuned to citing assignee activity than either government labs or universities. Of course, this shouldn't be surprising given their focus on profit and strategic advantage.

Interviews indicate that some firms have begun to pay increasing attention to external sources of technology and are more closely scrutinizing the technology capabilities of federal labs. It's clear from an examination of the patent files that a fairly prominent set of large R&D-performing companies appear to have technology that is closely connected to federal lab technology. (This is shown by there being a relatively short list of firms responsible for the lion's share of patent citations to federal lab patents.)

The incentives to patent and aggressively seek ways to commercialize EPB technology is influenced by factors similar to those operating in academic institutions. Like academics, NASA researchers' careers are significantly shaped by publication record. So increased pressure to commercialize can conflict with publishing goals.[23] One way this shows up is in attitudes among NASA researchers toward

---

22. Inventors and R&D directors typically know whom they cite because citing is part of the application process. However, they typically have not examined citations to their patents, even though in all cases they express considerable interest in knowing them. In one interview involving a large R&D-performing firm, the R&D director assessed the top 26 citing assignees based on the number of times firms had cited the interviewee firm's patent: he quickly went down the list noting which were customers, suppliers and competitors. In other words, customer, supplier and competitor relationships involved in patent citations seems to be a basic dimension of the technology relationship captured by citations.

23. If a tradeoff exists, it's interesting that NASA-Lewis' publishing increased over the past ten years, which is the same period in which NASA's patents increased in numbers and in quality.

research focused on fundamental problems versus research directed at commercial, non-aerospace products. However, NASA researchers have some incentive to pursue commercialization because inventors receive one-fourth of any royalties from licensed patents. One major difference is that there appear to be fewer opportunities for consulting with private firms by NASA researchers—a major avenue available to university researchers for technology transfer.

According to interviews, patent citations to NASA-Lewis patents significantly underestimate the influence of EPB research for two possible reasons: (a) NASA may seek patents only when the technology relates to a government purpose (which would mean that contracting firms can acquire technology that would not involve a citation to EPB since no patent was applied for); and (b) NASA may not aggressively pursue litigation to prevent infringement on NASA patents if they view the technology as having been supported by the public and, therefore, not to be treated in the same way as a private company's technology. It is possible that companies may thus feel less compelled to cite NASA technology. Of course, citations would exist if the patent examiner at the USPTO is aware of NASA's technology, whether in patent form or in another form of disclosure, such as in a publication.

Finally, EPB's experience confirms the importance of geographic proximity, as well as the role of the larger "complex" of NASA states found in the geographic regression results. Using patent citations as the gauge, 20% of cites to EPB's patents come from Ohio. Indeed, patent citations appear to understate the role of geography in EPB's commercial impact. EPB has analyzed its relationships with private firms via collaborative arrangements such as Space Act agreements between July 1993 and July 1996. About 28% of these (25/90) were from Ohio, a rate somewhat higher than the fraction of citations, and roughly two-thirds of these were from EPB's immediate region in Northeast Ohio.[24]

---

24. Some federal labs explicitly encourage geographic spillovers by offering more favorable licensing arrangements to firms who agree to locate in the state or region around the federal lab and by participating in technical assistance for local industry through local or regional technology assistance or extension networks. See Robert K. Carr, "Menu of Best Practices in Technology Transfer," http://milkern.com/rkcarr/flpart2.html, August 2, 1996. In reviewing labs in Huntsville, Alabama, and Oak Ridge, Tennessee, Carr found that geographic concentration of high-technology companies in these areas was primarily associated with lab procurement practices rather than technology transfer. (Labs subcontract a lot of their R&D, creating an incentive to locate nearby.)

More generally, technology transfer and knowledge transfer occur through many different mechanisms. Most citations to EPB patents did *not* involve what we have identified as direct contact, although there is somewhat more evidence of indirect communication. This is consistent with EPB's findings when it asked firms that had contacted it how they learned of EPB; the answers were: through word of mouth (64%), by reading EPB publications (22%), and through EPB presentations (6%).

There is some evidence that technology intermediaries may increase the efficiency of commercialization involving federal labs. Particularly where the technology is dual-use, a separate organization specializing in matching federal lab technology and industry need may be necessary to maximize economic benefits. For example, NASA has created six federally-funded Regional Technology Transfer Centers (RTTCs) to facilitate contact between business and the federal laboratory system.[25] The RTTCs provide contact with all government labs and state and local science and technology organizations. The RTTC for NASA Lewis is the Great Lakes Industrial Technology Center (GLITeC). As an indication of its potential for influencing commercial innovation from federal lab technology, EPB has maintained records of contacts with approximately 400 companies over the past three years, the bulk of which initiated contact with EPB. In comparison with a previously-analyzed five-year period, during the last three years EPB submitted 90 proposed collaborative arrangements, which have resulted in 43 awarded activities. The ratio of sharing of need and capabilities to initiating a proposed effort has increased by a factor of three from 30 : 1 to 9.3 : 1. The primary reason for the change has been GLITeC, which screens prospects and only encourages those companies representing a high probability of a good match between need and capability.

---

25. Another form of intermediary is the National Technology Transfer Center (NTTC), which plans to assist NASA by becoming the only contact between the NASA technology transfer system and national industry and R&D organizations (such as EPRI). NTTC intends to analyze the generic technology needs of particular industries and use its knowledge of the federal laboratory system to locate potential sources of these technologies. Apparently, intermediary organizations are developing to facilitate commercialization from other federal labs as well. For example, the Argonne Chicago Development Corporation (ARCH) is a non-profit corporation affiliated with the University of Chicago and Argonne National Laboratory. Through contract with the University of Chicago, DOE contractor with Argonne, ARCH can assume title of intellectual property coming from the University and ANL R&D, and pursue various modes of commercialization, including startups, licensing and joint ventures.

V Conclusions and Implications

We draw several broad conclusions from the quantitative analysis of federal lab patents and the case study of NASA-Lewis' Electro-Physics Branch. First, the evidence we've presented is consistent with increased effort to commercialize federal lab technology generally and NASA specifically since 1980. We do not find evidence that the increase in federal patenting in the late 1980s was accompanied by any decline in their average quality. It is clear, however, that a deeper knowledge of institutional factors can be essential for interpreting quantitative findings based on patent citation data. Differences in the application of a waiver policy involving patents produced by firms using NASA research or procurement funds is one example.

Second, our qualitative evidence provides some support for the use of patent citations as proxies for both technological impact and knowledge spillovers. But, not surprisingly, the picture is somewhat messy. A significant number of citations, maybe something like one-fourth, appear to be essentially noise, even when we limit the analysis to "important" patents. Nonetheless, aggregate citation patterns are indicative of technological impact; this conclusion is supported by both Banks' detailed analysis of citing patents and the perceptions and actions of technology managers in firms. If the obvious "spurious" patents are excluded, two-thirds of citing patents were deemed to represent likely knowledge spillovers. In most cases the spillover was indirect rather than resulting from known communication. Finally, a test for difference of means in the spillover assessment between EPB's citing and non-citing patents is significantly different from zero and thus supports the use of citations to indicate technology spillover.

In addition, the evidence based on the Electro-Physics Branch is consistent with the general finding in the literature that geographic proximity fosters spillovers. The EPB data suggest that contact increases the likelihood of spillovers and, furthermore, that geographic spillovers are underestimated by patent citations.

There are also many cases in which such spillovers occur without generating patent citations. One reason for this is that firms working with federal labs primarily seek know-how or tacit knowledge rather than the transfer of a specific technology. There is ample evidence that such tacit knowledge is important to the commercial innovation process,[26] and it may be a particularly important part of the social return to public research.[27] It is difficult to conceive of how this tacit knowledge transfer could be measured systematically. It would be nice to think that the rate of such transfer from a given organization would be highly correlated with technology flows as indicated by citations, but it is not yet clear that this would be the case.

Finally, our study has identified a number of important issues worth further research.

(1) Interviews suggest that firms are focusing more resources on acquiring technology from external sources. If so, this trend has interesting implications for the commercial impact of public research. It should also increase the utility of patent citations for analyzing knowledge flows and technology interdependence.

(2) One hypothesis worth exploring is that there exists a core of firms whose technology is closely connected with federal lab R&D and, consequently, who play a central role in diffusion of federal lab technology. In particular, aerospace firms are the first to cite NASA patents and are more likely to commercialize the technology. Are firms that are most closely connected to federal lab technology better performers? A more general question worth study is: How does the three-way interdependence of universities, government labs, and firms, revealed through patent citations, affect innovation? Within this complex, do organizations that act as technology intermediaries have a measurable impact on knowledge flows?

(3) Future research should focus more micro-level attention on the mechanisms involved in knowledge flows. Our interviews have convinced us that the best source of information for interpreting patent citations is the inventor. Of the four types of individuals involved in deciding patent citations on particular inventions (patent attorney, R&D lab director, inventor, and the patent examiner at the USPTO), the inventor clearly has the best knowledge of cites involving knowledge flows and the mechanisms at work. Inventors are the best source

---

26. See Arora [1995] and Roessner and Bean [1990]. Chatterji [1996] points out the increasing interest in external sources of technology. In fact, the Industrial Research Institute has formed a working group to identify and document "best practices" being used by companies to acquire external knowledge (p. 48).

27. Mansfield [1995] indicates that the overall impact of consulting by university researchers with private firms probably exceeds the impact of explicit transfer of university-developed technology.

for validating the use of patent citations in the study of technology spillovers. We plan to pursue this approach in future work.

References

Almeida, P. and Kogut, B., 1996, "The Economic Sociology of the Geographic Localization of Ideas and the Mobility of Patent Holders," mimeo.

Arora, A., 1995, "Licensing Tacit Knowledge: Intellectual Property Rights and the Market for Know-How," in *Economics of Innovation and New Technology*.

Brietzman, A. and Narin, F., "A Case for Patent Citation Analysis in Litigation," *The Law Works*, May 1996, pp. 10–11, 26–27.

Caballero, R. and Jaffe, A., 1993, "Standing on the Shoulders of Giants: An Empirical Assessment of Knowledge Spillovers and Creative Destruction in a Model of Economic Growth," in Blanchard, O. and Fischer, S. (eds.), *NBER Macroeconomics Annual, 1993* (MIT Press, Cambridge).

Carr, R. K., August 2, 1996, "Menu of Best Practices in Technology Transfer," http://milkern.com/rkcarr/flpart2.html.

Chatterji, D., 1996, "Accessing External Sources of Knowledge," *Research and Technology Management*, 39, pp. 48–56.

Ebert, L. B., "If a Patent is Highly Cited, is it a Pioneering Patent," *The Law Works*, June 1996, pp. 28–29.

GAO, "National Laboratories: Are Their Activities Related to Commercial Product Development?," GAO/PEMD-95-2, November 1994.

Griliches, Z., 1990, "Patent Statistics as Economic Indicators," *Journal of Economic Literature*.

Griliches, Z., 1989, "Patents: Recent Trends and Puzzles," Brookings Papers: Microeconomics (Washington, D.C.: The Brookings Institution), pp. 291–330.

Griliches, Z., 1984, *R&D, Patents and Productivity* (University of Chicago Press).

Henderson, R., Jaffe, A. and Trajtenberg, M., forthcoming, "University Patenting Amid Changing Incentives for Commercialization," *Review of Economics and Statistics*.

Jaffe, A., 1986, "Spillovers of R&D: Evidence from Firms' Patents, Profits and Market Value," *American Economic Review*.

Jaffe, A., Trajtenberg, M. and Henderson, R., 1993, "Geographic Localization of Knowledge Spillovers as Evidenced by Patent Citations," *Quarterly Journal of Economics*.

Jaffe, A. and Trajtenberg, M., 1996, "Flows of Knowledge from Universities and Federal Labs," *Proceedings of the National Academy of Sciences*.

Mansfield, E., "Academic Research Underlying Industrial Innovations: Sources, Characteristics, and Financing," *The Review of Economics and Statistics*, February 1995.

Podolny, J. and Shepard, A., 1997, "When Are Technological Spillovers Local?: Patent Citation Patterns in the Semiconductor Industry," mimeo.

Roessner, D. and Bean, A. S., 1990, "Industry Interactions with Federal Laboratories," *Technology Transfer*.

Schmookler, J., 1966, *Invention and Economic Growth* (Harvard University Press, Cambridge).

Trajtenberg, M., 1990a, "A Penny for Your Quotes," *Rand Journal of Economics*.

Trajtenberg, M., 1990b, *Economic Analysis of Product Innovation: The Case of CT Scanners* (Harvard University Press, Cambridge).

Trajtenberg, M., Jaffe, A. and Henderson, R., 1997, "A Window on the Basicness of Invention," *Economics of Innovation and New Technology*.

10

Reinventing Public R&D:
Patent Policy and the
Commercialization of
National Laboratory
Technologies

Adam B. Jaffe and
Josh Lerner

1 Introduction

The United States government is by far the single largest performer and funder of research and development in the world. Between 1941 and 1997, the U.S. government spent $5.4 trillion (in 1997 dollars) on R&D, just under one-half of the total amount undertaken in the United States (see Figure 1). In 1993, the government's R&D expenditures represented about 18% of the total funding of R&D in the major industrialized countries (National Science Board, 1998).

These expenditures, despite their magnitude and their potentially profound impact on productivity and growth, have attracted surprisingly little scrutiny by economists. Although one environment in which federally funded research takes place, the research university, has been studied extensively,[1] it accounts for a relatively small percentage of overall funding. (Between 1955 and 1997, only 24% of the total federally funded R&D performed in noncorporate settings took

We thank Alper Afya and especially Petia Topaloya for excellent research assistance. Helpful comments were provided by Linda Cohen, Rosemarie Ham Ziedonis, Ariel Pakes (Editor), Sam Petuchowski, participants in the 1999 NBER Conference on Patent Policy and Innovation and the 2000 American Economic Association annual meeting, seminar participants at the Federal Reserve Bank of Boston and New York University, and an anonymous referee. Numerous officials at the DOE and the laboratories assisted in accessing data and contributed helpful insights, but especial thanks should go to Ray Barnes, Victor Chavez, Paul Gottlieb, Toni Joseph, Karena MacKinley, Gib Marguth, Ronald Meeks, Jeff Mobley, Bill Shepard, Warren Siemens, Claire Sink, and Walter Warnick. Thanks should go as well to Buddy Beck, Clyde Frank, and Thomas Widmer. We appreciate Linda Cohen's help in accessing CRADA data. Funding was provided by the NBER Project on Industrial Technology and Productivity with support from the Alfred P. Sloan Foundation and by Harvard Business School's Division of Research. All errors are our own.

1. Examples include Nelson (1959), Jaffe (1989), and Henderson, Jaffe, and Trajtenberg (1998). See also Stephan (1996) and the references cited therein.

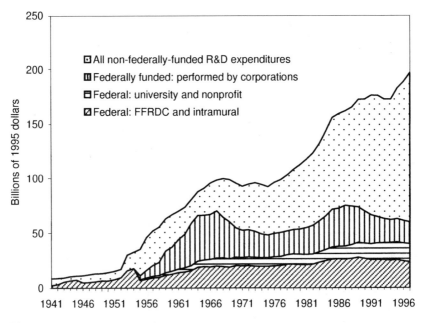

Figure 1
Federally funded and total U.S. R&D expenditures, 1941–1997. Prior to 1955, the performers of federal expenditures are not tabulated.

place in academic institutions.) The majority of these activities took place in laboratories owned by such agencies as the Departments of Defense and Energy, the National Aeronautics and Space Administration, and the National Institutes of Health. R&D activities in this arena have attracted little academic scrutiny.[2]

Lending particular urgency to such research is the interest shown by policy makers, both in the United States and abroad, in increasing the role of government-owned laboratories in the technology commercialization process. Beginning in 1980, a series of legislative initiatives and executive orders in the United States have sought to encourage the patenting and the licensing of federally owned technologies, as well as the formation of cooperative arrangements between laboratories and private firms. These challenges have been

2. Most of the academic literature has consisted of case studies of particular facilities (two thoughtful examples are Markusen and Oden (1996), and Ham and Mowery (1998)) and surveys of potential or actual users of laboratories (for example, Bozeman and Crow (1991), Roessner and Wise (1993), and Berman (1997)).

particularly pressing at the laboratories devoted to national defense, whose primary historical mission of designing and testing nuclear weapons has been rendered largely obsolete by world events. Similar efforts have been launched in many other nations.

We examine whether the statutory changes of the 1980s have had a significant impact on technology transfer from the national laboratories. We study the subset of federally funded research and development centers (FFRDCs) owned by the U.S. Department of Energy (DOE). These include some of the largest R&D laboratories in the country, such as the Lawrence Livermore, Los Alamos, and Sandia facilities. We undertake case studies of two particular facilities, and then we employ a series of databases developed by DOE not hitherto examined by academics. Both analyses explore how patenting, the utilization of these patents by industry, and other technology-transfer activities have shifted in response to these legislative changes.

In addition to examining shifts in the overall level of technology-transfer activities, we explore how the heterogeneous features of these facilities affect their success in commercialization. These laboratories differ from each other in at least three critical respects. First, the quality of the laboratories' technology may differ. This may partially reflect the nature of the laboratories' missions: those specializing in basic science or defense-related technologies, for instance, may have fewer technologies ripe for commercialization. It may also reflect the breadth of the laboratories' activities. Second, the facilities differ in the nature of the political problems that commercialization efforts are likely to face. The conditions under which contractors should be permitted to patent and license federally funded technologies remains highly controversial.[3] Across the laboratories, the relationships between the contractors assigned to run the facilities and the Department of Energy differ significantly. Finally, the locations of the facilities are highly disparate. Some FFRDCs are located

---

3. One example is the 1998 controversy that stemmed from a reexamination proceeding by the U.S. Patent and Trademark Office concerning two patents covering low-power radar. One patent had been awarded to a small Alabama company, the other to Lawrence Livermore National Laboratory. Before the patent hearing was even held, Alabama Representative Robert "Bud" Cramer requested investigations of Livermore's technology-transfer activities by three congressional committees. Cramer also proposed legislation that would have restricted future collaborations between DOE FFRDCs and the private sector. Similar controversies have emerged over the years at a number of other laboratories.

near population centers with extensive innovative and entrepreneurial activities, while others are in highly remote areas. An extensive literature has documented the regional aspects of knowledge spillovers, which might suggest that laboratories differ a great deal in their ability to have commercial impacts.

The results challenge some of the conventional wisdom about these laboratories, as reflected in government studies and press accounts. Both the case studies and empirical analyses suggest that the policy changes of the 1980s, far from having no effect, appear to have had a substantial impact on the patenting activity by the national laboratories. At the beginning of this period the laboratories had considerably fewer patents per R&D dollar than the average university, but today they are about equal. Even more impressive is the evidence from the citations in other patents, a proxy for their importance. While the recent increase in university patenting has been accompanied by a substantial decline in the quality of the awards (as measured by the number of citations they receive), the quality of the laboratory patents has remained constant or has increased slightly. These results suggest the organizational structure of the government-owned contractor-operated model used at DOE laboratories may be far more credible than critics have suggested.

The relatively small number of DOE laboratories, combined with limited variation over time for each lab, makes it difficult to draw strong conclusions about how the different laboratory environments and organizational structures affect the technology-transfer process. But several findings can be highlighted. First, consistent with claims that the diversification led to a degradation of the quality of the laboratories' R&D, it appears that the greatest commercial activity has derived from laboratories that have remained focused. Second, facilities with a turnover of contractors, when pressures from parties resistant to exclusive licensing are likely to have been lowest, have had greater success in accelerating their rate of commercialization. The case studies also present evidence consistent with these conclusions.

The plan of this chapter is as follows. In Section 2 we provide some background information on government patent policy and the national laboratories. Section 3 presents two brief case studies of particular laboratories. Section 4 describes the construction of the dataset and presents the analysis. Section 5 concludes.

2 Patent Policy and the National Laboratories

Patent Policy and Federally Funded R&D

A substantial literature discusses federal policies toward the patenting and commercialization of the innovations whose development it has funded (Cohen and Noll, 1996).[4] Even a casual review of these works, however, makes clear how little the debate has changed over the decades. Many advocates have consistently called for government to take title to innovations that it funds, to ensure the greatest diffusion of the breakthroughs. Others have argued for a policy of allowing contractors to assume title to federally funded inventions or, alternatively, allowing the exclusive licensing of these discoveries.

Questions about the federal government's right to patent the results of the research it funded were the subject of litigation and congressional debate as early as the 1880s, but the debate assumed much greater visibility with the onset of World War II. The dramatic expansion of federal R&D effort during the war raised questions about the disposal of the rights to these discoveries. Two reports commissioned by President Franklin D. Roosevelt reached dramatically different conclusions, and they framed the debate that would follow in the succeeding decades.

The National Patent Planning Commission, an ad hoc body established shortly after the Pearl Harbor attack to examine the disposition of the patents developed during the war, opined:

It often happens, particularly in new fields, that what is available for exploitation by everyone is undertaken by no one. There undoubtedly are Government-owned patents which should be made available to the public in commercial form, but which, because they call for a substantial capital investment, private manufacturers have been unwilling to commercialize under a nonexclusive license (U.S. House of Representatives, 1945; p. 5).

A second report, completed in 1947 by the Department of Justice, took a very different tack. Rather, it argued that "innovations financed with public funds should inure to the benefit of the public, and should not become a purely private monopoly under which the

---

4. This issue was the topic of over forty congressional hearings and reports and four special commissions between 1940 and 1975 (U.S. Energy Research and Development Administration, 1976). Three historical overviews of the debates are Forman (1957), Neumeyer and Stedman (1971), and Hart (1998).

public may be charged for, or even denied, the use of technology which it has financed" (U.S. Department of Justice, 1947, Vol. 1, p. 2). The report urged the adoption of a uniform policy forbidding both the granting of patent rights to contractors and exclusive licenses to federal technology in all but extraordinary circumstances. Over the ensuing 30 years, federal patent policy vacillated between these two views (Forman, 1957; Neumeyer and Stedman, 1971).

Beginning in the 1980s, policy seemed to shift decisively in favor of permitting exclusive licenses of publicly funded research to encourage commercialization. The Stevenson-Wydler Technology Innovation Act of 1980 (P.L. 96-480) explicitly made technology transfer a mission of all federal laboratories and created a variety of institutional structures to facilitate this mission. Among other steps, it required that all major federal laboratories establish an Office of Research and Technology Applications to undertake technology transfer activities. At about the same time, the Bayh-Dole Act allowed academic institutions and nonprofit institutions to automatically retain title to patents derived from federally funded R&D. The act also explicitly authorized government-operated laboratories to grant exclusive licenses on government-owned patents.

These two acts were followed by a series of initiatives in the 1982–1989 period that extended and broadened their reach. In 1986, the Federal Technology Transfer Act allowed government-operated facilities to enter into cooperative R&D arrangements (CRADAs) with industry (P.L. 99-502), as well as to grant outside collaborators the title to any invention that resulted. In 1989, the National Competitiveness Technology Transfer Act of 1989 (P.L. 101-189) extended the 1986 legislation enabling the formation of CRADAs to government-owned contractor-operated facilities. See Table 1 for a summary of relevant legislation.

This wave of legislation did not resolve the debate over how much ownership of government-funded R&D ought to be transferred to private-sector entities. Congressional and agency investigations of inappropriate behavior during the commercialization process—particularly violation of fairness of opportunity and conflict of interest regulations during the spin-out and licensing process—continued to be commonplace. CRADAs and other efforts to allow government to work with large companies have remained controversial. Nonetheless, this set of legislation represented a decisive shift in the long debate on government patent policy.

Table 1
Key federal technology policy initiatives related to national laboratory technology transfer

Year	Title	Description
1945	National Patent Planning Commission	Proposed that agencies be allowed to set disparate policies regarding technology.
1947	U.S. Department of Justice Investigation of Government Policies and Practices	Urged adoption of uniform policy in which the government took title to almost all federally funded technologies.
1950	Executive Order 10096	Established centralized Government Patent Board to decide upon patent ownership.
1961	Executive Order 10930	Allowed agencies to set separate patent policies, and to sometimes grant nonexclusive licenses.
1980	Stevenson-Wydler Technology Innovation Act	Made technology transfer a goal of all federal laboratories; required each to set up technology-transfer office.
1980	Patent and Trademark Laws Amendment (Bayh-Dole) Act	Allowed academic and nonprofit institutions to retain title to federally funded R&D.
1984	Trademark Clarification Act	Extended many, but not all, provisions of Bayh-Dole Act to contractor-operated laboratories.
1986	Federal Technology Transfer Act	Allowed government operated laboratories to enter into cooperative R&D agreements (CRADAs) with industry.
1989	National Competitiveness Technology Transfer Act	Allowed contractor-operated laboratories to enter into CRADAs.

The DOE FFRDCs

Many of the DOE FFRDCs,[5] also known as national laboratories, had their origins in the Manhattan Project during World War II. The development of the atomic bomb required the establishment of a number of specialized facilities, many of which were located in remote areas because of concerns about safety and security. After the war, these facilities were placed under the control of outside contractors, a mix of universities and private firms. It was hoped that these government-owned contractor-operated facilities (GOCOs) would be insulated from political pressures and would be better able to attract and retain talented personnel because they did not have to

---

5. This abbreviated history is based in part on Branscomb (1993), U.S. Office of Technology Assessment (1993), and U.S. General Accounting Office (1998). The interested reader is referred to these sources for more detailed accounts.

conform to civil service rules. From the launch of these facilities until today, however, the overwhelming majority of the funding for the programs has come from the federal government. In particular, almost all of the funds have come from the primary energy agency (first the Atomic Energy Commission, then the Energy Research and Development Administration, and finally the Department of Energy) and the units of the Department of Defense responsible for nuclear weapons design and procurement.

A series of reports over the past several decades have highlighted the limitations of the GOCO model.[6] They have repeatedly highlighted the same problems with the management of the laboratory system: (1) the desired political independence has never been achieved, with DOE imposing extensive regulatory guidelines that limit contractor flexibility; (2) there is duplication and redundancy across the laboratories; and (3) the diversification of the facilities into new activities lacks focus, particularly after funding for the core nuclear activities declined. As noted by a recent synthesis of these studies by the U.S. General Accounting Office (1998, p. 15), "despite many studies identifying similar deficiencies in the management of DOE's laboratories, fundamental change remains an elusive goal."

Patent Policy and the DOE FFRDCs

Prior to 1980, the laboratory contractors were assigned few patents and exclusive licenses were rare (see Table 2).[7] Although DOE policy began to change after the legislative changes of the 1980s, a number of accounts (e.g., U.S. Office of Technology Assessment, 1993) suggest that DOE's response was delayed until the period between 1986 and 1989.

Many observers also suggest that DOE's implementation of the 1980s reforms was problematic. Critics have attributed this to two factors:

---

6. These critiques date back at least as far as the "Bell Report" prepared by the Office of Management and Budget in 1963. Two clear expositions of these problems are found in the "Packard Report" (White House Science Council, 1983) and the "Galvin Report" (Task Force, 1995).

7. It should be acknowledged that within even the earliest contracts granted by the Manhattan Engineer District during the war was a recognition that contractors should control nonatomic innovations that were only tangentially related to the government's mission. In practice, however, the government made very little use of this right to grant ownership to national laboratory contractors or to license its patents on an exclusive basis. (For a discussion, see U.S. Energy Research and Development Administration (1976).)

First, the problems with the laboratory structure in general noted above led to resistance to these reforms. One illustration is the process through which proposed cooperative agreements with industry were evaluated. Although in many agencies laboratory directors were allowed to implement CRADAs with limited headquarters oversight or regulatory requirements, DOE introduced a three-part review process. CRADA proposals were reviewed at the laboratory level, followed by a centralized screening by the headquarters program offices (typically on an annual basis), followed by the negotiation of a contract and a work statement (which involved laboratory, field office, and program office personnel). Not surprisingly, during the period when DOE was actively seeking new CRADAs, the level of activity was lower than in other agencies and the time from inception to signing much longer (U.S. General Accounting Office, 1993).

Second, the fundamental conflict between the commercial need for clear private property rights in the form of exclusive licenses and the broader goals of public research seemed particularly acute at these facilities. In many cases, spin-out firms or cooperative partners were not able to obtain exclusive licenses to DOE patents, or were able to do so only after delays of many years. Some licenses were subsequently challenged as violations of conflict-of-interest or fairness-of-opportunity rules in lawsuits by competitors or in congressional hearings (see Markusen and Oden, 1996). DOE radically scaled back its CRADA program in 1995 and 1996 after Republican congressmen questioned whether it represented "corporate welfare" (Lawler, 1996).

These difficulties had a negative impact on corporations' or venture capitalists' willingness to invest in these projects. Reviews of technology-transfer activities at the national laboratories have almost universally highlighted the lack of progress, particularly when contrasted to universities.[8] This appears to have been a general problem that affected technology transfer at all the laboratories.

---

8. For instance, U.S. Office of Technology Assessment (1993) compares the technology-licensing revenues of the Massachusetts Institute of Technology to DOE FFRDCs. While MIT in 1996 had less than 12% of the collective R&D expenditures of the thirteen leading FFRDCs, it had nearly three times the revenues from its licensing activities in 1997 ($21.2 million versus $7.5 million). It should be noted, however, that licensing revenues is a "lagging indicator": much of the licensing revenues may be generated by technologies licensed a decade or longer ago.

Table 2
R&D spending and technology transfer at DOE FFRDCs

Fiscal year	Energy agency-funded R&D at DOE FFRDCs (billions of 1995 dollars)	Total R&D at DOE FFRDCs (billions of 1995 dollars)	DOE licensing revenues (millions of 1995 dollars)	Invention disclosures from DOE FFRDCs (number)	Exclusive licenses from DOE FFRDCs (number)	Nonexclusive licenses from DOE FFRDCs (number)	Active CRADAs at DOE FFRDCs (number)
1955	1.0						
1956	1.6						
1957	2.0						
1958	2.2						
1959	2.5						
1960	2.7						
1961	2.9						
1962	3.0						
1963	3.2			1,627			
1964	3.7			1,724			
1965	3.6			1,649			
1966	3.4			1,271			
1967	3.5			1,257	0	28	
1968	3.6			1,138	0	41	
1969	3.5			1,235	0	85	
1970	3.4			1,420	0	127	
1971	3.2			1,502	0	102	
1972	3.2			1,129	0	66	

1973	3.3			1,228	0	56	
1974	3.1			1,170	0	38	
1975	3.4			1,125	0	70	
1976	3.5			1,533	1	31	
1977	4.5						
1978	4.7						
1979	4.7						
1980	4.5						
1981	4.5	5.0					
1982	4.2	4.9					
1983	4.3	4.8					
1984	4.5	5.0					
1985	4.8	5.3					
1986	4.5	5.1					
1987	4.4	5.6	.4	857	14	23	
1988	4.4	5.6	.7	1,003	18	25	
1989	4.6	5.5	1.8	1,053	25	32	
1990	4.4	5.4	2.9	1,335	30	58	1
1991	4.3	5.2	3.5	1,665	29	96	43
1992	4.3	5.1	2.5	1,698	24	191	250
1993	3.7	4.3	2.8	1,443	30	378	582
1994	3.4	3.7	3.0	1,588	37	470	1,094
1995	3.3	3.6	3.5	1,758	61	575	1,382
1996	3.1	3.2	4.0	1,886	82	662	1,677
1997	3.1	3.4	5.5		68	189	749

3   Two Case Examples

We briefly illustrate these challenges through a discussion of two laboratories, Lawrence Livermore National Laboratory (LLNL) and the Idaho National Engineering and Environmental Laboratory (INEEL). These facilities are in some respects very different. The former has DOE's Office of Defense Programs as its primary funder, has an academic institution as a prime contractor, and is located in the San Francisco Bay Area. The latter is funded primarily by DOE's Office of Environmental Management, has a private corporation as the prime contractor, and is located in a remote area of eastern Idaho. But both facilities have overcome considerable challenges to develop technology-transfer efforts that in many respects represent "best practice" among the DOE FFRDCs. LLNL and INEEL have led the laboratories in the level of licensing revenue and spin-out companies respectively.

While a variety of insights can be drawn from the analysis, three observations were particularly salient for this analysis:

(i) In contrast to the pessimistic conclusions of many studies, the DOE laboratories have the potential for real commercial impact. LLNL has a long tradition of informal collaboration with industry. The reforms at INEEL appear to have triggered a wave of spin-out activity commercializing technology at the laboratory.

(ii) The uncertainty associated with the ownership of laboratory technologies is a barrier to commercialization. Unlike universities, where the Bayh-Dole Act of 1980 created a clear understanding that universities could license their technology, for the laboratories the property rights remain unclear. Despite the reforms of the 1980s, substantial questions remain about the ability of laboratory contractors to freely license their technologies.

(iii) The reforms of technology-transfer practices have had a dramatic impact on commercialization activities. At INEEL, a change in the managing contractors and the adoption of an innovative incentive contract appear to have had a dramatic effect on technology transfer. At Livermore, although neither the policy shifts nor the alteration in the volume of technology-transfer activity were as dramatic, shifts in government patent policy appear to have had a substantial impact on the pace of activity.

Lawrence Livermore National Laboratory

Lawrence Livermore is one of the three very large DOE FFRDCs that has historically specialized in nuclear weapons research. LLNL was established in 1952 in Livermore, California. The University of California has operated this facility from its inception. From the first, LLNL had a strong emphasis not only on the engineering of thermonuclear weapons, but on related fundamental science. It was an aggressive user of the newest computational technology: for instance, the first facility at Lawrence Livermore was a building to house the thennew UNIVAC computer, which was needed for the complex calculations required by the weapons design process. As at other facilities, there has been a broadening of the laboratory's mission over time into such areas as nonnuclear energy, biomedicine, and environmental science.

The evolution of the technology-transfer function at the laboratory has similarly featured both continuity and change. At least since the 1960s, the laboratory has had strong relationships with the computer and laser industries. Advances in the state of the art developed at the laboratory were often transferred to private firms or developed by companies in response to laboratory requests, in order to generate a production-scale source of equipment, instrumentation, or components for the larger experimental facilities. In many cases, the prototypes were cooperatively developed by private-sector and laboratory researchers. A significant number of these innovations eventually found their way into the civilian market. The laboratory's motivation for engaging in this activity, however, had little to do with concerns about "technology transfer." Rather, the staff went to the private sector because it was often more efficient to procure equipment from outside vendors than to manufacture it at the laboratory. The relationships with vendors were highly informal. LLNL made virtually no effort to claim intellectual property holdings, and in many cases their partners did not seek to patent the discoveries either.

A formal technology-transfer office was established at LLNL after the DOE issued the implementing regulations for the Stevenson-Wydler Act in 1982. Initially the office was modestly funded, with little internal or external visibility. There was a dramatic increase in activity, however, after the passage of the National Competitiveness Technology Transfer Act of 1989. In particular, the DOE established a central program (later known as the Technology Transfer Initiative) primarily to fund CRADAs between the laboratories and companies. With this influx of funding—in 1994 alone, LLNL received $55 million for this purpose from the DOE—the technology-transfer office (now known as the Industrial Partnerships and Commercialization (IPAC) office) grew rapidly. During this relatively brief era, LLNL collaborated with industry partners to carry out almost 200 mostly small, jointly funded projects spanning a broad spectrum of technology areas. A great deal of effort was devoted to writing proposals, attending trade shows, and hosting visiting delegations.

This period left two key legacies. First, the laboratory established a few significant relationships, such as with semiconductor manufacturers, that would have ongoing importance. Second, an infrastructure was developed to better interact with industry, i.e., the ability to enter fairly quickly into agreements, to protect proprietary information, and to allocate the intellectual property generated in the agreements. As time progressed, however, laboratory officials felt that such a large number of partnerships in relatively unfocused technology areas were distracting personnel from the facility's primary programs.

In 1995, the U.S. Congress, whose control had just switched to the Republican Party, dramatically cut funding for the Technology Transfer Initiative. The DOE followed suit with additional cuts. This triggered a shift at LLNL back to its original focus on just undertaking industrial partnerships related to its mission. Projects with outside companies that were only tangentially related to the laboratory's mission were largely terminated. As a result, LLNL as of November 1998 had a few very large technology-transfer efforts, a vastly reduced number of smaller R&D projects, and a growing number of licenses. At one extreme was the CRADA at LLNL and two other laboratories to produce semiconductors through extreme ultraviolet lithography, to which Advanced Micro Devices, Intel, and Motorola were contributing $250 million over three years. At the other extreme were numerous licenses of laboratory technology, primarily with small high-technology firms. (See panel A of Table 3 for a summary of LLNL's technology-transfer activities.)

Lawrence Livermore's success in licensing relative to the other laboratories had been facilitated by its strong ties to the University of California, as well as its physical proximity to the companies and financiers in the Bay Area. The IPAC office frequently interacted informally with the licensing staff at the University's Office of Technology Transfer. At the same time, the office faced challenges that its university-based peers did not. In particular, the IPAC office did not automatically receive title to patents (as universities have since ·the passage of Bayh-Dole). Rather, the staff had to formally request waivers from the DOE on a case-by-case basis, which could be a lengthy process. Second, the office faced much greater scrutiny of its actions under rules governing fairness of opportunity and conflict of interest. As a result of this scrutiny, the IPAC extensively publicized potential licensing opportunities and took great care to avoid these problems, including often encouraging prospective licensees to accept nonexclusive licenses.

LLNL's licensing activities and revenues rose dramatically in the 1990s. But it faced a continuing challenge posed by its diffuse and changing mandate from the U.S. Congress. For instance, the directives to the laboratories to transfer technology in a way that benefits the U.S. economy, to ensure fairness of opportunity, and to avoid competition with the private sector were interpreted very differently by various members of Congress. Anticipating how these concerns would evolve over time, and which transactions might be seen as problematic in retrospect, was not easy. A compounding factor was that as the laboratory's technology-transfer effort became more visible, it was increasingly a target of complaints and scrutiny, as illustrated by the case described in footnote 3.

Idaho National Engineering and Environmental Laboratory

Shortly after World War II, the federal government sought an isolated location to test nuclear reactors. The predecessor to INEEL, the National Reactor Testing Station, was established in 1949 on an 890-square-mile site in the southeastern Idaho desert that had been used as a practice bombing range during World War II. Over the years, the laboratory undertook major research programs seeking to develop prototypes of and to test reactors for both naval vessels and (until 1961) airplanes. Another important activity was the reprocessing of the large amounts of uranium generated by these reactors. Unlike LLNL, which from its inception has had only one contractor, INEEL was managed over the years by a series of contractors. These included Aerojet Nuclear (a subsidiary of General Tire) and a consortium including EG&G and Westinghouse Electric (between 1977 and 1994).

As the Management and Operation Contract for the laboratory neared completion in 1994, it became clear that a major emphasis in selecting the next contractor would be a commitment to technology-transfer activities. INEEL was a major employer in the state of Idaho. Local politicians had argued that more efforts were needed to soften the impacts of employment and funding cutbacks at the laboratory by encouraging the creation of spin-out firms. The minimal level of technology-transfer activity in this period can be seen in panel B of Table 3: for instance, in fiscal year 1992, there were no spin-outs and

Table 3
Technology-transfer activity at two DOE FFRDCs

Panel A: Lawrence Livermore National Laboratory

	Fiscal year								
	1989	1990	1991	1992	1993	1994	1995	1996	1997
Invention disclosures filed	141	192	193	270	219	264	205	240	193
Patent applications filed	29	68	60	43	92	89	126	130	134
Patents received		37	44	48	60	75	90	100	71
New patent licenses		3	6	8	4	11	28	47	28
Licensing revenues (thousands of 1995 dollars)		313	462	437	373	575	1,118	1,310	2,067
New CRADAs formed				18	57	60	67	34	37
Startups formed from laboratory technology									0

Panel B: Idaho National Engineering and Environmental Laboratory

	Fiscal year						
	1992	1993	1994	1995	1996	1997	1998
Patent applications filed	11	14	24	38	46	57	61
New patent licenses		5	9	12	36	23	18
Licensing revenues (thousands of 1995 dollars)	7	16	97	86	207	343	386
Startups formed from laboratory technology	0	1	0	5	10	7	5

the laboratory generated only $7,000 in licensing revenue.[9] While EG&G rapidly increased its signing of CRADA and licensing agreements in response to these pressures, the new contract was awarded instead to a consortium led by a subsidiary of the Lockheed Corporation (the company's name was changed to Lockheed Martin in 1995). Among the participants in the consortium was Thermo Electron Corporation, a Massachusetts company with a history of spinning out new technology businesses into publicly traded entities.

The contract included a variety of features to help ensure that technology-transfer activities would be taken seriously. The contractors committed to provide entrepreneurial training to laboratory researchers who were prospective leaders of spin-out firms. Thermo Electron committed to establish a $10 million venture capital fund to be made available to finance new businesses spinning out from the laboratory. Perhaps most important, Lockheed signed a contract under which its reward would be a function of its technology-transfer activity. In particular, Lockheed agreed to forgo several millions of dollars from its annual fee for managing the laboratory. In return, it received a share of fees and royalties, which increased with the cumulative amount of payments received over the course of the five-year contract. Until the first $1 million of licensing payments was received, the firm would receive 20% of the revenue (the remainder being divided between the researcher and the federal government). For the next $1 million, Lockheed would receive 30%, and thereafter it would receive 35%.[10]

To implement this contract, the new contractor undertook a variety of changes to the structure of the technology-licensing office as well. Lockheed recruited individuals who had held senior business development positions with companies such as General Motors and

---

9. INEEL did not experience the same increase in CRADA activity in the late 1980s and the early 1990s that LLNL did, because much of the funding for these efforts was provided by DOE's Office of Defense Programs. Because INEEL received only very limited funding from Defense Programs, the impact of this initiative was much smaller than at LLNL.

10. While universities—which under the Bayh-Dole Act own the patents from federally funded research at their facilities—routinely receive royalties from licensing activities, this provision was a first among FFRDC management contracts. Although other contracts had linked the payments to the contractor to success in more general aspects of laboratory management (e.g., the reduction of the laboratory's operating costs or progress in major environmental cleanup projects), this was the first to make an explicit link between technology transfer and compensation (U.S. General Accounting Office, 1996a).

IBM, as well as licensing account executives with private-sector sales and marketing experience. In addition, the company organized industry focus teams, with the responsibility to establish relationships with and market INEEL capabilities and technologies to companies in specific industries. As seen in panel B of Table 3, both spin-out and licensing activity increased dramatically in response to these activities. The increase in spin-out activity was particularly noteworthy: in fiscal year 1997, INEEL accounted for 7 out of the 19 spin-outs from DOE FFRDCs.

At the same time, the implementation of this plan faced unexpected difficulties. One was the extent of the barriers to spinning out of technologies from INEEL. Laboratory researchers seeking to obtain an exclusive license to a technology they had worked on faced an exhaustive and slow review process. Even when the entrepreneurs overcame concerns about fairness and conflict-of-interest provisions, in some instances they believed that the laboratory's demands for payments and royalties were excessive, given the early stage of the technologies. Some felt that the management contract gave the contractor incentives to license technologies to large corporations that could offer larger upfront payments than startups could afford. As of the end of fiscal year 1997, Lockheed had received a total of about $130,000 from its share of the royalties, only a few percent of the amount forgone in fees. At the same time, it is important to acknowledge the dilemma that Lockheed officials faced when considering licensing to prospective startups. To assess whether a startup was the entity with the greatest chance of commercializing an INEEL technology, the technology-transfer officials typically asked it to provide a business plan and show proof of adequate financing. But in many cases, entrepreneurs found (particularly in a state like Idaho, where little financing of small high-technology firms was available) that obtaining a license to the technology was a prerequisite to be considered for financing. Another challenge was the difficulty of identifying people with the entrepreneurial business talents to complement the laboratory scientists and engineers in a spin-out. In addition, entrepreneurs faced barriers to raising financing once they had exhausted the seed capital that the small Thermo Electron fund and other local investors could provide.

Despite the considerable success of the INEEL effort, its future was in doubt at the end of 1998. The DOE decided in September 1998 not to renew Lockheed's contract, but rather to put the contract once again up for bid. While the DOE review rated Lockheed's technology-transfer effort highly, the agency raised concerns about the contractor's record in worker safety and its failure to undertake an environmental cleanup project at INEEL for an agreed-upon price. While the DOE made it clear that it expects the next contractor to be committed to technology transfer, whether that contractor will be as successful as Lockheed in growing those activities remains uncertain.

4 Statistical Analysis

The Dataset

A point raised in many assessments of the national laboratory system (e.g., Task Force (1995), Section VII.C.5) is the extreme difficulty in obtaining data, particularly with regard to technology-transfer activities. This is at least partially a reflection of the DOE's complex management structure discussed above. As a result, we have constructed a dataset from a wide variety of sources.

We constructed a sample of 23 FFRDCs owned by the DOE and active between 1977 and 1997, derived from Burke and Gray (1995)[11] and U.S. National Science Foundation (various years). Two of these organizations commenced operations as FFRDCs during this period, while six were decertified for various reasons.

General Information
Information collected for each facility included:

(i) Historical information such as dates of establishment or decertification, and identity of contractor over time (Burke and Gray, 1995; U.S. General Accounting Office, 1996b; facility Web sites; news stories in LEXIS/NEXIS).

(ii) Regional characteristics such as the distance to the nearest standard or consolidated metropolitan statistical area (SMSA or CMSA), the population and education level of that area, and venture capital activity in the state (U.S. Bureau of the Census; Venture Economics' Venture Intelligence Database (described in Gompers and Lerner, 1999)).

---

11. References to sources only cited in this subsection are included in Appendix B, not in the main References list.

(iii) Overall laboratory budget level and funding sources.[12]

(iv) Annual R&D expenditures at each FFRDC between 1981 and 1995 (National Science Board, 1996; U.S. National Science Foundation, 1998).

(v) The number of new CRADAs formed annually between 1991 and 1994 under the aegis of three program offices (Defense Programs, Energy Efficiency, and Energy Research), and all CRADAs formed in 1995 and 1997.[13]

(vi) Miscellaneous data about a variety of technology-transfer activities (U.S. Department of Energy, Office of Defense Programs, 1998; U.S. Department of Energy, Office of the General Counsel, 1998).[14]

Table 4 provides summary data on these facilities.

Measures of Patenting Activity
The final set of variables measures the number of and citations to patents derived from laboratory research. This subsection reviews the difficulties associated with measuring patenting activity at the FFRDCs, the DOE database that allows us to address these problems, and the issues associated with the use of the database.

Patent awards from DOE research are sometimes assigned to the department; at other times when waivers are granted, they are assigned to the contractors. There is no single identifier in the patent application that allows one to identify DOE-funded patents: e.g., it is difficult to distinguish from the text of a patent assigned to the University of California whether it was derived from work at the university's Berkeley campus or at Lawrence Livermore. To address

12. While the DOE does not prepare an annual yearbook of activities at the laboratories, we obtained general statistical data on their funding levels and sources in three fiscal years—1979, 1988, and 1995—from two special compilations (U.S. Department of Energy, 1990; U.S. Department of Energy, Laboratories Operations Board, 1996).

13. The sources of the CRADA data are U.S. Department of Energy (1995), Technology Transfer Business (1998), and U.S. Department of Energy, Office of the General Counsel (1998). The three program offices with complete data accounted for 94% of all DOE outputs related to commercial product development in fiscal year 1992 (U.S. General Accounting Office, 1994) and 82% of all DOE CRADAs between fiscal years 1990 and 1992 (U.S. Office of Technology Assessment, 1993).

14. In both cases, the project staff made efforts to employ consistent definitions across the various facilities, but inconsistencies may remain. Much of the data are available only for the most recent period.

this problem, we employ a database compiled by the DOE's Office of Scientific and Technical Information (1998) of all patents to emerge from DOE laboratories since 1978.

The database, which consists of 6,479 U.S. patents awarded by the end of 1996, contains all patents arising from laboratory-produced research, regardless of the entity to which the patent is assigned. In particular, it contains patents assigned to the contractor who operates a given laboratory. U.S. Patent and Trademark Office databases (as well as the NBER/Case Western Reserve database discussed below) identify patents assigned to the U.S. government and its agencies. They do not provide, however, any way to separate patents assigned to firms in their capacity as contractors operating government laboratories from those derived from the contractor's other research (see Jaffe, Fogarty, and Banks, 1998). Of the patents we have included in our analysis, 42% were assigned to nongovernmental entities.

The file also has two major drawbacks. First, it contains awards assigned to entities that have never operated a DOE FFRDC. It is likely that some of these are patents derived from CRADAs between a laboratory and another entity. Others are derived from other contractor-operated facilities that are not designated as FFRDCs. Some of the patents, however, are apparently not derived from DOE-funded research but are merely in an area of interest to the department. A second difficulty is that the database does not provide any direct means to connect the patents to particular FFRDCs. Most, though not all, of the patents in the database are identified with a contract number that corresponds to the Management and Operation contract at the originating facility at the time of the patent award. These are identified through a database maintained by DOE's Office of Procurement and Assistance Management (1998) as well as personal communication with officials of this office.

The list of DOE patents was then merged with the NBER/Case Western Reserve patent database. This allows us to determine the patent class, application year, and the address of the inventor for each patent. (We also identified all patents that cited these patents through the end of 1995.) Given these ambiguities, we followed the following procedure:

First, every patent whose contract number in the database corresponds to a known Management and Operation contract was attributed to that FFRDC.

Table 4
DOE FFRDC cross-sectional data

FFRDC	Contractor type	1997 licenses Number	1997 licenses Revenue ($M)	Patent class concentration	1995 R&D shares National security	1995 R&D shares Basic science	State share of venture capital (1988)	Contract competitively awarded	FY 1997 licenses No. per $MM R&D	FY 1997 licenses Royalties ($M) per $MM R&D	Successful patent applications 1977	Successful patent applications 1993	Overall citations per patent	CRA-DAs
Ames	Univ	5	.005	.15	.0%	79.0%	.61%	No	.24	.24	0	11	1.77	10
Argonne	Univ	13	.134	.11	3.3%	51.8%	1.78%	No	.05	.55	0	32	1.27	111
Bettis Atomic Power	Firm			.15	100.0%	.0%	4.05%	Yes			9	13	2.65	0
Brookhaven	Univ	40	1.342	.11	5.0%	91.0%	3.75%	No	.18	6.04	6	15	2.39	40
Lawrence Berkeley	Univ	56	.351	.11	.0%	78.0%	31.51%	No	.24	1.52	0	14	1.38	140
Lawrence Livermore	Univ	19	2.118	.08	61.6%	16.0%	31.51%	No	.03	3.76	26	103	2.44	237
Energy Technology Engineering Center	Firm			.12			31.51%	Yes			4	1	4.20	0
Fermi Accelerator	Univ	0	.001	.13	.0%	100.0%	1.78%	No	.00	.01	2	1	2.16	0
Hanford Engineering Development	Firm			.38			1.84%	Yes			0	1	.25	0
Idaho Engineering and Environment	Firm	16	.358	.14	12.0%	28.0%	.06%	Yes	.25	5.70	0	15	.50	55
Inhalation Toxicology	Other			.33			.37%	Yes			0	0	3.00	3
Knolls Atomic Power	Firm			.10	100.0%	.0%	3.75%	No			3	1	2.00	0

Los Alamos	Univ	4	.379	.08	76.0%	13.0%	.37%	No	.01	.67	11	20	2.94	238
Mound	Firm			.09			2.21%	Yes			1	5	1.43	NA
Renewable Energy Research	Other			.09	.0%	2.0%	3.13%	Yes			1	19	1.68	41
Oak Ridge National Laboratory	Firm	38	1.289	.09	5.0%	42.0%	1.78%	Yes	.16	5.51	0	37	1.50	238
Oak Ridge Institute for Science and Education	Univ			.22	9.0%	64.0%	1.78%	No			0	1	.17	1
Pacific Northwest	Other			.11	13.0%	14.0%	1.84%	No			0	10	1.60	54
Princeton Plasma Physics	Univ	1	0	.51	.0%	100.0%	3.50%	No	.02	.00	0	4	1.16	4
Sandia	Firm	59	1.3	.08	77.0%	3.0%	.37%	Yes	.09	1.98	0	34	.88	260
Savannah River	Firm	5	.021	.17	18.5%	.0%	.18%	Yes	.29	1.22	1	32	.96	17
Stanford Linear Accelerator	Univ	3	.2	.21	.0%	100.0%	31.51%	No	.03	1.69	1	12	2.04	2
Thomas Jefferson Accelerator	Univ			.20	.0%	100.0%	2.09%	Yes			0	2	.36	0
Unattributed											100	73	3.47	

Second, every patent without a contract number whose assignee was the DOE and whose primary inventor lived in a SMSA where there was a DOE FFRDC was assumed to come from that laboratory.

Third, every patent without a contract number whose assignee was a laboratory contractor, and whose primary inventor lived in a SMSA where there was a DOE FFRDC run by that contractor, was assumed to come from that FFRDC.

Fourth, patents that could not be attributed to a specific FFRDC, but which most likely derived from DOE laboratory research, were used for aggregate analysis but were not included in the laboratory-specific analyses. These include patents with unidentified contract numbers, patents assigned by the patent office to DOE with inventors residing in SMSAs with multiple laboratories, and patents assigned to contractors with multiple laboratories in a given SMSA, with inventors residing in that SMSA.[15]

All other patents in the database were not used in the analysis below.

Overall, of the 6,479 patents in the DOE database, 3,185 were attributed to particular DOE FFRDCs, 1,771 were determined to be laboratory patents but were not attributed to any particular facility,[16] and 1,523 could not be determined to be derived from laboratory research and hence were ignored. Our approach undoubtedly both includes some nonlaboratory patents and excludes some laboratory patents. Overall, we are probably undercounting laboratory patents. Many of the 1,523 ignored patents have inventors living in a SMSA in which there is a laboratory, but they are assigned to firms other than the contractor. It is likely that some of these derive from CRADAs, but we have no way to determine that and so have excluded them.

Throughout this article, we date patents by the year of application, since that is when the research was likely to have occurred and the decision made to apply for the patent. The DOE patents database

---

15. The most important example of the latter is the University of California, which operates both the Lawrence Livermore and Lawrence Berkeley laboratories in the Bay Area. The patents of these laboratories could be distinguished only when the contract number was reported. Approximately 100 patents assigned to the university, with inventors residing in the Bay Area, did not have contract numbers and so could not be attributed to either laboratory.

16. Because the number of unattributable patents is falling over time—i.e., the probability of successfully attributing a patent is greater later in the period—if one ignored these patents, then we would overstate the upward trend.

contains only those patents awarded through the end of 1996. Since it typically takes between one and two years to process a patent application, we seriously undercount applications made in the years after 1993.

Table 4 shows the patent totals for each of the 23 DOE FFRDCs. Many of the laboratories had no successful patent applications in 1977. By the end of the period, most made successful patent applications every year. (Note that four laboratories were decertified by 1992.) Not surprisingly, a handful of the larger laboratories contribute most of the patent applications filed in each year.

Analyses of Overall Technology Commercialization Patterns

As discussed above, the numerous statutory changes in the 1980s were intended to foster the commercialization of federally funded R&D. If successful, these changes should have increased the rate of patenting of laboratory discoveries and the utilization of these inventions by the private sector. To explore this question, we look at the time trend in patenting and the citations to these patents, as well as other measures.

Figure 2 shows that the number of successful DOE laboratory patent applications rose from about 200 in 1981 to over 450 by 1993. (As noted above, the latter number is a slight underestimate, because some applications will have been granted after 1996.) Furthermore, this sharp increase in patenting has occurred in the face of declining real R&D expenditures at the DOE FFRDCs. As shown in the figure, the increase began in 1988, shortly after the passage of the Federal Technology Transfer Act, and continued into the mid-1990s.

To put this increase in the "propensity to patent" in perspective, Figure 3 compares the patent-to-R&D ratio for the DOE FFRDCs to a similar ratio for universities.[17] In the early 1980s, patents per dollar of FFRDC R&D were considerably lower than in the universities, despite the fact that two-thirds of the university research was for basic research, which is presumably less likely to lead to patent awards. (The comparable figure for all federal FFRDCs is slightly over 40%. The source of these tabulations is National Science Board (1998).) University patenting rose strongly through the 1980s, at least

---

17. Total university research expenditures are from National Science Board (1998). University patent totals are from the NBER/Case Western Reserve patents database.

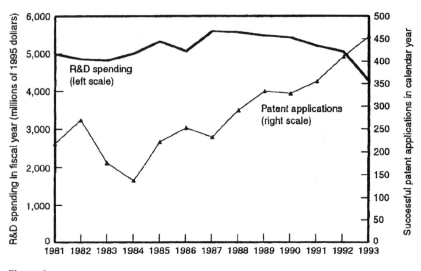

Figure 2
Overall successful patent applications and R&D at DOE FFRDCs

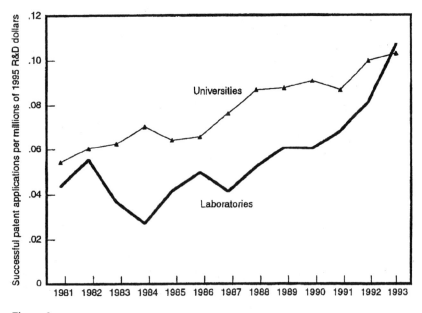

Figure 3
Patents per R&D dollar at DOE FFRDCs and universities

partially in response to the Bayh-Dole Act of 1980. But by the late 1980s, patenting (relative to R&D spending) at the DOE FFRDCs was rising even faster. By 1993, the two sectors were comparable in terms of patents per R&D dollar. While the lower share of basic research at the laboratories makes this a somewhat unfair comparison, the relative performance of the DOE FFRDCs in the late 1980s and early 1990s was nonetheless remarkable.[18]

It has been shown that the dramatic increase in university patenting in the 1980s was accompanied by an equally sharp decline in the quality of those patents, as measured by the citations they received relative to all patents with the same technological characteristics and award year (Henderson, Jaffe, and Trajtenberg, 1998). Before about 1985, university patents on average were much more highly cited than other patents. This difference had disappeared by the late 1980s. The increase in university patenting appears to have come about largely by "lowering the threshold" for patent applications, resulting in many more patents of marginal significance.

To explore whether similar changes occurred at the DOE FFRDCs, we construct the "normalized" citation intensity for each laboratory in each year. To do this, we calculate the difference between the actual number of citations received per patent and the "reference" citation intensity. The reference citation intensity is the expected number of citations per patent that a portfolio of patents with the same technological classifications as those of the laboratory would receive, based on the citations received by *all* patents in a given technology class in a given year. This normalized intensity controls for differences across technology classes and time in the "propensity to cite," as well as for the impact of the truncation imposed by our lack of knowledge of citations that will occur after 1995.

We also report in Figure 4 the trend in patenting. Here we employ not the aggregate count of patents derived from DOE FFRDCs, but rather a normalized series that controls for the shift in the overall "propensity to patent." In each technology class and in each year, we compute the ratio of the number of patents derived from the DOE laboratories to the total number of awards. The changes in this value, which is normalized to be 1.0 in 1981, are plotted over time. During

---

18. Unlike the declining trend of real R&D expenditures in the DOE FFRDCs, university research spending was rising rapidly during this period. Thus, while the laboratories were "catching up" in terms of patents per dollar of research spending, the absolute number of patents was rising faster in the university sector.

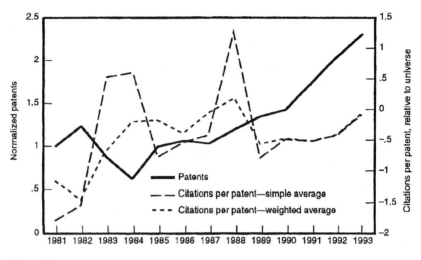

Figure 4
Patents and citations over time (15 FFRDCs with >50 patents)

periods when the overall number of patent applications is falling, this normalization will make an increase in DOE patenting appear more dramatic, and vice versa.

Figure 4 shows a citation pattern in conjunction with increased patenting for laboratories that is very different from that found for universities. First, note that in contrast to the university patents, laboratory patents have historically been slightly *less* highly cited than other patents.[19] It is striking, however, that the laboratory citation intensity did not decline in conjunction with the large increase in the propensity to patent after 1987. Whether we look at a simple average across the laboratories or an average weighted by the number of patents, the trend in citation intensity is upward. This trend, however, is not statistically significant. Thus, the kind of "digging deeper into the barrel" that characterized the increase in university patenting does not seem to have occurred at the DOE FFRDCs. While this clearly merits more study, the citation data are consistent with a process in which the laboratories produced more patents by reorienting their

---

19. Jaffe, Fogarty, and Banks (1998) examined the citation intensity of patents assigned at issuance to the U.S. government. As noted above, their analysis excluded patents from the laboratories assigned to the contractors but did include other agencies besides DOE. In that article, the citation "inferiority" of federal patents was even more pronounced, but it also showed some tendency toward reduction in the late 1980s.

research toward new areas with greater commercial applicability, in keeping with the intent of the statutory changes.

The pattern is also similar if we look only at "non-self-citations." Non-self-citations exclude those citations in patents that are assigned either to the DOE or to the contractor that operates the laboratory from which the cited patent originated. The non-self-citation measure is "normalized" as well, following a procedure similar to that described above but only using non-self-citations to construct the reference portfolio. The fact that the normalized non-self-citation pattern over time is so close to the normalized total citation pattern means that the rate of self-citation to laboratory patents is similar, on average, to the rate of self-citation for all patents.

It would also be desirable to look at other indicators of technology transfer. Unfortunately, we have only extremely limited and inconsistent data on other indicators of technology transfer and very few measures, particularly over time, of laboratory policies and behaviors. Below we explore other measures of technology transfer in panel and cross-sectional analyses of the laboratories. Before turning to that, however, we undertake panel data regression analyses using patents and citations.

Cross-Sectional Analyses Using Patent Data

We now turn to examining the differences across facilities. But before doing so, it makes sense to catalog the theoretical suggestions about which factors should affect the relative success of such a policy shift across different laboratory environments.

First, some kinds of research are inherently more difficult to commercialize. Laboratories that are particularly tied to national security issues or devoted to fundamental scientific research are less likely to have commercialization opportunities.

Second, laboratories that have pursued unfocused diversification efforts may have lower-quality research; this echoes the literature on adverse effects of diversification in the corporate setting (Lang and Stultz, 1994; Scharfstein and Stein, 1997). If diversification reduces research quality, it would lead to less "product" to transfer.

Third, organizational factors are also likely to matter. As discussed above, the 1980 Bayh-Dole reforms gave a great degree of flexibility to universities to license and spin out new technologies. Many academic institutions exploited these changes by building up technology-licensing offices and aggressively marketing new technologies (Henderson, Jaffe, and Trajtenberg, 1998). FFRDCs whose prime contractors were universities may have benefited from this know-how to make their technology transfer activities more effective.

Fourth, the nature of the contractor and its relationship with the DOE might have had an important influence. It might be thought that political direction was more difficult at organizations where the prime contractor had a long-standing presence at the laboratory. Efforts to encourage exclusive licensing have been highly controversial within the DOE. A particular source of resistance has been the DOE field offices, where in many cases the staff has questioned the desirability of senior management's efforts to change technology-transfer policies. (One motivation for these concerns may be the loss of control inherent in the delegation of a great deal of discretion to contractors' technology-licensing offices.) A new contractor typically brings in new staff when it receives an award to run a facility. Over time, however, this staff may develop close working relationships with DOE officials in the local field office. Consequently, resistance to residual efforts to assert control by DOE staff may be the greatest in a setting where there is a new contractor.[20]

Of course, it may be that poor performance on the part of the laboratory contributes in turn to the probability of contractor turnover. An example of this type of "reverse causality" may be the INEEL case discussed above: EG&G's poor performance in technology transfer appears to have been a contributing factor in its loss of the management contract. In other cases, the replacement of the contractor appears to have been driven by outside events, and to have been largely exogenous. An example was AT&T's decision to cease managing Sandia in 1992, after the divestiture of its regional operating units and the scaling back of much of the basic research at Bell Laboratories.

Finally, one might expect that geographic location would affect the success of technology transfer. Recent work has shown that knowledge spillovers tend to be geographically localized, particularly within geographic areas (Glaeser, et al., 1992; Jaffe, Trajtenberg, and Henderson, 1993). This concentration of knowledge spillovers has

---

20. This would be consistent with the evidence concerning the decision to contract out municipal services: in settings where municipal unions have greater influence (e.g., when public employees are not restricted from participating in political activities), there is much greater resistance to privatizing government services (López-de-Silanes, Shleifer, and Vishny, 1997).

implications for the relative level of technology transfer at the national laboratories because these facilities are located in very different areas. Some facilities are located far from any major metropolitan area, while others are near a major metropolis. If it is easier to transfer technologies to nearby firms, the laboratories located in remote areas will have more trouble finding recipients. This disadvantage could be amplified by the concentration of venture capital, the primary mechanism for funding for privately held, high-technology companies. Venture organizations are highly geographically concentrated, with over half the funds based on California and Massachusetts. (Gompers and Lerner (1999) provide a detailed description.) Furthermore, venture capitalists tend to be highly localized in their investment patterns: over half the venture-backed firms have a venture investor who serves as a board member based within 60 miles of the firm (Lerner, 1995). Thus, even if laboratories in remote areas with little venture capital activity do generate spillovers to nearby companies, the local firms may be unable to access the needed financial and other resources to profit from them.[21]

The regression analysis covers the period from 1981 to 1993. The first year of the analysis is determined by the availability of R&D spending data. The final year of the analysis is determined by the problem of lengthy patent-pending periods discussed above.

As dependent variables, we employ either the count of patent applications or the citations per patents at each DOE FFRDC in each year. Both the count of patents and the citations per patents are normalized to control for differences across technological classes, as described above. Because we believe that the "patent production function" at the laboratories will be multiplicative rather than additive—e.g., the policy shifts of the 1980s should have led to a more dramatic absolute increase in patenting at the larger laboratories—we employ the logarithm of normalized patenting as the dependent variable.[22] We employ both normalized total citations per

21. Some supporting evidence for this claim is found in Lerner's (1999) analysis of the federal Small Business Innovation Research program, an award program for small high-technology companies. Awardees that were located in regions with substantial venture capital activity did significantly better than a matching set of nonawardees. The awards had no effect, however, in regions without venture capital activity.

22. Because some laboratories had no patents in certain years, we add one to the total normalized count of patents before computing the logarithm of the dependent variable. We do not employ observations in the citation regressions when laboratories are without any patents.

patent and the normalized ratio excluding self-citations as dependent variables.

We employ a variety of independent variables. To capture the shifting regulatory environment, we employ a dummy variable that denotes whether the annual observation is from 1987 or after. This is roughly when numerous accounts suggest that there was a substantial shift in how seriously the DOE took its mandate to implement technology transfer. Second, we identify the periods when the contractor was changed. As suggested by the Idaho case study, such changes may provide the stimulus to focus real effort on objectives such as technology transfer. We arbitrarily hypothesize that the effect of such changes—both the dislodging of bureaucratic inertia and the incentive to improve performance—might be seen from two years before the change through two years after. There is a total of fifteen lab-years in the data that fall into such windows, about 8% of the data points used in the regression.

We also include in the regression a few characteristics of the laboratory or its environment. We employ the R&D of the lab in the patent equation, and the R&D and patenting rates in the citation equation. These variables control for the scale of the research enterprise, and they also allow the citation intensity to be different as the rate of patenting *relative* to R&D effort changes.

We also include a variety of time-invariant measures. First, as discussed above, a strong orientation toward national security or basic science may lead to less technology commercialization. We thus include as independent variables the shares of the laboratories' expenditures classified as related to national security and basic science. (Due to data limitations, we use 1995 values, but these measures appear to be quite constant.) Second, we indicate whether the contractor was a university, and likely to be more familiar with the transfer of early-stage technologies, by employing a dummy variable that assumes the value of unity when this was the case. Third, many reports have claimed that the laboratories' efforts to diversify away from their traditional areas of expertise have led to poor performance. To examine this suggestion, we construct from the patent data a measure of technological "focus": the Herfindahl index of concentration of patenting across technology classes.[23] We include both the measure of

---

23. The Herfindahl index is the sum of the squared shares of patenting in technology classes. Thus it is unity for a laboratory whose patents are all in one class, and a small fraction for laboratories whose patents are distributed across many classes.

focus as well as the *change* in our focus measure between the second and first half of the sample period.[24]

Estimation results are presented in Table 5. Columns 1–3 present the results of the patent regressions, and columns 4–7 are for citation intensity. Our data are in the form of a panel, in which the patenting or citation intensity for a given lab in each year depends upon lab variables that change over time, observable lab characteristics that do not vary over time, and (most likely) unobservable lab characteristics that are also correlated with both the time-varying regressors and the observable time-invariant lab characteristics. In this context, OLS on the pooled panel data produces potentially biased estimates, because of the correlation of the unobserved lab effect with the regressors. A "fixed effects" regression, or, equivalently, a regression including a set of lab dummy variables, yields unbiased estimates of the effect of the time-varying regressors.

The time-invariant regressors drop out of the fixed-effects regression. Indeed, in the absence of additional data and identifying assumptions, their causal impact on the dependent variable is inextricably mixed up with that of the unobserved fixed effect. We can, however, ask to what extent the overall "lab effect"—which combines the effect of the observable characteristics and that of unobservable characteristics in an unknown way—is associated with the observable characteristics. We do this by first estimating the regression with dummy variables for each lab, and then projecting the estimated dummy coefficients on the observable lab characteristics and the mean for each lab of the time-varying regressors. The results of this projection tell us the "effects" of the characteristics on the dependent variables, estimated in a way that takes into account an unbiased estimate of the effect of the time-varying regressors, though we cannot really say whether this effect is causal or due to a common correlation with the unobserved lab characteristics.[25]

Looking first at patenting, column 1 shows the results of simple OLS on the pooled panel data, and column 2 shows the results of the fixed-effects regression. The dramatic increase in patenting associated with the policy shifts of the late 1980s is apparent in the large

---

24. We also tried a variety of geographic variables in unreported regressions, but these are consistently insignificant.

25. See Mundlak (1978). The coefficients for the time-varying regressors in the second-stage regression indicate the partial correlation between the lab mean for these variables and the unobserved fixed effect. Since this does not have a structural interpretation, we do not report these coefficients.

Table 5
Panel regression results—patents and citations

Independent Variables	Dependent variable						
	Logarithm of patents[a] (1)	Logarithm of patents[a] (2)	Estimated fixed lab effect from column (2)[b] (3)	Total citations per patent[c] (4)	Non-self-citations per patent[c] (5)	Non-self-citations per patent[c] (6)	Estimated fixed lab effect from column (6)[b] (7)
Year = 1987 or later	.515 ***(.098)	.514 ***(.081)		.783 **(.373)	.444 (.330)	.666 *(.341)	
Logarithm of R&D in fiscal year	.223 ***(.089)	-.139 (.181)		-.175 (.254)	-.130 (.229)	-1.696 **(.772)	
Logarithm of patents[a]				-.568 **(.278)	-.524 **(.241)	-.900 ***(.312)	
"Competition"[d]	.019 (.222)	.172 (.229)		1.687 **(.750)	1.437 **(.663)	.970 (.743)	
"Focus"[c]	1.471 **(.598)		1.696 (1.828)	-1.045 (2.443)	-1.555 (2.259)		-2.801 (2.543)
Change in "focus"[c]	1.804 ***(.331)		1.116 (.834)	2.815 **(1.311)	2.282 **(1.087)		.916 (1.134)
National security share of R&D (FY 1995)	-.192 (.202)		-.477 (.734)	-.840 (.819)	-.913 (.784)		-.228 (.987)
Basic science share of R&D (FY 1995)	-1.801 ***(.335)		-1.722 **(.744)	-2.326 **(1.129)	-2.182 **(1.019)		-1.173 (.937)

University contractor	1.023 ***(.228)		.795 (.687)	1.119 *(.645)	.952 (.578)		1.025 (.584)
Lab fixed effects	Excluded	Included significant	NA	Excluded	Excluded	Included significant	NA
Number of observations	238	238	17	205	205	205	17
R^2	.495	.687	.831	.096	.096	.170	.969

a. Logarithm of (DOE FFRDC patents + 1)/(weighted average number of all patents by field) (see text for more detail).

b. Projection of estimated fixed effect on lab characteristics and means for time-varying regressors (see text).

c. Normalized for truncation and variation in propensity to cite as described in the text.

d. Dummy equal to unity from 2 years before through 2 years after change in contractor.

e. Herfindahl Index of concentration of patents across technology classes. The change is the difference between the second and first half of the sample period.

Heteroskedasticity-consistent standard errors in parentheses; *, **, *** convey statistical significance at the 90%, 95% and 99% levels, respectively.

and statistically significant coefficient on the period commencing in 1987. All else equal, patenting after 1986 is approximately 50% greater than patenting before 1987, in both the OLS and fixed-effects versions. The results also show that patenting is related to R&D in the panel as a whole, although this relationship is not present in the "within" or time-series dimension. This is not surprising, given that we know overall patenting has been rising while R&D has been falling. The estimated effect of the competition variable on the rate of patenting is small and statistically insignificant.

Turning to the lab characteristics that do not vary over time, the OLS results in column 1 suggest that facilities with a greater basic science share have less patenting; the national security share is also negative but not statistically significant. More focused laboratories get more patents, all else equal, and those that decreased their focus the most have fewer patents.[26] These effects are quantitatively as well as statistically significant. Consistent with the benefits that Livermore derived from its association with the University of California's technology-transfer offices, facilities run by universities have almost twice as many patents, *ceteris paribus*, an effect that is statistically significant.

As noted, these estimates for the time-invariant characteristics are potentially biased, and we cannot control for unobserved lab characteristics as column 2 does for the time-varying regressors. The best we can do is, in effect, to purge them of bias due to the mutual correlation among the time-invariant characteristics, the time-varying regressors, and the fixed effect. This is done via a cross-sectional regression of the estimated fixed lab effects on the characteristics and the lab means for the time-varying regressors. These results are shown in column 3. They are qualitatively consistent with the OLS results in column 1, but the standard errors are much larger, and hence only the basic science share effect is statistically significant. Thus, overall the results for these characteristics are consistent with our conjectures, but we cannot confirm the direction of causality from these data.

For citations, columns 4 and 5 present simple OLS results for all citations, and also for data limited to non-self-citations. Column 6 presents the fixed-effects results (for the non-self-citations), and col-

---

26. Most of the laboratories decreased their focus between the two subperiods. Overall, the average Herfindahl fell from .27 to .15.

umn 7 shows the projection of the fixed effects from this regression on the lab characteristics. The regressions have low explanatory power. Even with laboratory dummies, the R^2 is only .17. The dummy variable indicating that the observation is from 1987 or thereafter is positive but significant at the 95% level only for citations inclusive of self-citations. This is consistent with Figure 4, which showed a slight but uneven upward trend in normalized citations.

The R&D and patent variables have an interesting pattern of effect on citations. The patent variable has a significantly negative coefficient in both the OLS and fixed-effect regressions, providing some evidence that the "lower threshold" for patentability over time decreased the quality of patent applications. At the same time, R&D, which is essentially uncorrelated with citations (after controlling for patents) in the OLS, also has a significant negative coefficient in the fixed-effects regression. Taken together with the result for the patent variable, this says that years with above-mean patents have fewer citations, and years with above-mean R&D *relative to* patents also have fewer citations. Recall from Figure 2 that R&D was declining on average in the later years during which patenting was rising. Thus it is not clear whether the R&D and patent fixed-effect coefficients are telling us something "real" about the relationships among R&D, patent intensity, and citation intensity, or whether they are simply capturing a time pattern of policy changes that is more complex than our simple 1987-or-after dummy variable.

The competition variable has a positive and significant impact in the first two regressions. The point estimate of the magnitude is large, implying that patents applied for during the period of competitive pressures get an additional citation or so relative to what would otherwise be expected. This effect becomes smaller and statistically insignificant in the fixed-effects regression, which is not surprising given that the variation of the competition variable is mostly across laboratories rather than across time.

In the citation equations, the effect of "focus" is statistically insignificant. There is, however, a strong positive effective of the *change* in focus, at least in the simple OLS regressions in columns 4 and 5. That is, those laboratories whose focus decreased substantially saw a significant decline in their (normalized) citation intensity. We also find a statistically significant negative effect of basic science share, again in the OLS versions. None of these time-invariant characteristics have statistically significant impacts in the projection of the fixed effects, and, although none of them changes signs, some have significantly reduced magnitude. This makes it difficult to determine to what extent these factors are driven by correlations with R&D and patenting as distinct from a direct effect on citations.

Overall, the statistical results paint an interesting if slightly ambiguous picture of the technology-transfer process. There was a statistically significant increase in patenting, with no overall decrease in citation intensity. Within each lab there was an association between higher patenting and lower citations, and also between lower R&D and more citations. It is unclear whether these correlations are real or spurious. In the OLS regression there is a large, significant effect of university association on patenting, and a similarly large negative effect of diversification on both patenting and citation intensity; we cannot test for these effects in a way that controls for the presence of fixed effects. Finally, we find a suggestion in the panel of a positive effect associated with contractor turnover. It is unclear to what extent this is a selection effect, an incentive effect, or simply a "Hawthorne effect" in which management interest leads to an improvement in productivity even though nothing fundamental has changed.

Corroboratory Analyses

One concern with the analyses above is that the patenting patterns may not reflect those in technology commercialization more generally. In particular, the cross-sectional patterns in patenting and citations to these patents may potentially not provide a complete depiction of the relative growth of technology-transfer activities at these facilities.

To address the concern, we undertook a similar regression analysis, using another measure of technology commercialization: the number of new CRADAs approved annually at each laboratory. We used observations between fiscal years 1991 (the first year with a significant number of CRADAs at DOE) and 1997 (with the exception of 1996, for which we had no data). Another possibility would have been to examine the dollar volume of corporate spending associated with these CRADAs. We rejected this approach for two reasons. First, the data on these expenditures were less complete. Second, laboratories and DOE subagencies differ dramatically in how the total expenditures associated with these transactions are compiled. In particular, while in some cases the corporation's in-kind contributions of time and facilities are included, in other cases only the direct financial payments to the laboratory are compiled.

To normalize the data, we employed in all regressions a dummy variable for each fiscal year. In this way, we hoped to control for DOE senior management's shifting emphasis on the importance of CRADAs (as discussed above, this was a major policy focus until the shift in congressional control to the Republican Party). Otherwise, the independent variables were the same as those in the patent equation. Because of the relatively small number of new CRADAs at each facility in a given year, we also tested whether the results were similar in a maximum-likelihood Poisson model, which explicitly treats the dependent variable as a nonnegative integer.

The results of the CRADA regressions, presented in Table 6, are largely consistent with the patent analyses. Not surprisingly, larger labs (as measured by R&D expenditure) have more CRADAs (columns 1 and 4). When controlling for fixed effects, the OLS finds no significant effect of R&D (column 2), but the Poisson formulation does find a significant R&D effect even with fixed effects (column 5). Labs that changed contractors ("competition") are labs with more CRADAs (column 1), but there is no significant connection within labs over time between CRADA activity and when the laboratory turnover occurred (columns 2 and 5).

The diversification ("change in focus") variable is significant in the OLS regressions but not the Poisson one; the coefficient on focus is negative (in contrast to its positive coefficient in the patent equation) and statistically significant in the Poisson formulation. Both basic-science and national-security orientations have clearly negative associations with CRADA activity. Finally, the OLS indicates a positive association between CRADAs and having a university as lab contractor (statistically significant after removing the effect of the correlation between the fixed effect and R&D), but this is not significant in the Poisson formulation.

In addition to the patent and CRADA data, we obtained data on new licenses granted and total license revenues for 13 of the 23 laboratories in 1997. Not surprisingly, the largest laboratories dominate these absolute measures: Lawrence Livermore, Brookhaven, Oak Ridge, and Sandia. When we normalize licenses and license revenue per dollar of R&D, the standouts are much less clear. For instance, if we use the criterion of above-average performance in both the licensing and patenting dimensions, the winners are Ames, Livermore,

Table 6
Panel regression results—CRADA formation

Independent variable	Specification and dependent variable				
	OLS logarithm of new CRADAs formed[a] (1)	OLS logarithm of new CRADAs formed[a] (2)	OLS estimated fixed lab effect from column (2)[b] (3)	Poisson (ML) new CRADAs formed (4)	Poisson (ML) new CRADAs formed (5)
Logarithm of R&D in fiscal year	.897 ***(.123)	−.009 (.151)		1.045 ***(.216)	.768 **(.373)
"Competition"[c]	.649 **(.320)	−.058 (.267)		.401 (.340)	−.232 (.213)
"Focus"[d]	−1.822 *(.996)		−.986 (1.344)	−7.492 **(3.765)	
Change in "focus"[d]	−.855 **(.399)		−1.081 **(.500)	.295 (.594)	
National security share of R&D (FY 1995)	−1.430 ***(.463)		−2.220 ***(.339)	−1.495 ***(.428)	
Basic science share of R&D (FY 1995)	−1.680 **(.700)		−2.499 **(.829)	−.805 (.624)	
University contractor	.694 (.453)		1.352 ***(.408)	.227 (.377)	
Lab fixed effects	Excluded	Included significant	NA	Excluded	Included significant
Number of observations	95	104	19	95	104
R^2 or pseudo R^2 (for Poisson)	.744	.872	.876	.736	.823

a. Logarithm of (New CRADAs Formed + 1) (see text for more detail).
b. Projection of estimated fixed effect on lab characteristics and lab means for time-varying regressors (see text).
c. Dummy equal to unity from 2 years before through 2 years after change in contractor.
d. Herfindahl Index of concentration of patents across technology classes. The change is the difference between the second and first half of the sample period.
Heteroskedasticity-consistent standard errors in parentheses; *, **, *** convey statistical significance at the 90%, 95% and 99% levels, respectively.
All columns also include year dummies.

Idaho, Oak Ridge, and Savannah River. Los Alamos and the Stanford Linear Accelerator are relatively poor performers. (The data indicate essentially no licensing activity for two of the laboratories, Fermi and Princeton.)

Despite the small number of observations, we ran a few diagnostic regressions with these data. Each of the licensing-based indicators was regressed on the change in the technological focus measure, a competition measure, the national security share, and a dummy for being in a modestly large metropolitan area.[27] In the unreported results, the coefficient on the competition variable is positive but never statistically significant. The change in the focus variable has an effect that is positive for all indicators but is at best marginally statistically significant. The national security share is negative in all regressions but not statistically significant. Location in a metropolitan area has no significant effect. These results are at least broadly consistent with the patent- and CRADA-based measures, and they address some of the concerns about the generality of these measures.

5 Conclusions

This chapter has examined the commercialization of publicly funded research that is pursued in a little-studied but important environment, the national laboratory. The empirical and case study analyses suggest that the policy reforms of the 1980s had a dramatic and positive effect on technology commercialization. Patenting increased sharply. Although within labs there is some evidence of an association between greater patenting and a decline in patent quality, the overall increase in patenting does not seem to have been associated with an overall decline in quality, as was the case for universities.

Case studies suggest that the degree of technology-transfer success depends on bureaucratic factors, with beneficial effects of a university licensing office connection in one lab and a change in lab contractor in the other. The positive impact of a university connection is confirmed by the statistical analysis. There is some statistical evidence of an effect due to contractor turnover, but it cannot be pinned down

27. For the cross-sectional analysis, the "competition" dummy is set to unity if the laboratory contract has ever been subject to competition, even if such competition occurred outside the period of our analysis. The "metropolitan" dummy was set to unity for laboratories near SMSAs or CMSAs with a population of one million or more.

precisely or modelled explicitly given the relatively few observations of contractor change.

These findings challenge the general picture of failure painted by earlier assessments of technology transfer at the national laboratories. The striking improvement in the measures of commercial activities at the laboratories, especially when compared to the experience of the universities, stands in contrast to the negative tone in many discussions such as the "Galvin Report" (Task Force, 1995). The apparent importance of limiting the distortionary effects of political interference has also not been heavily emphasized in many of the government studies. We do seem to confirm the adverse effect of diluting a laboratory's focus through extensive technological diversification.

We believe that these findings represent a first step toward a better understanding of the federal technology-transfer process. At the same time, it is important to acknowledge this article's limitations, which in turn suggest a variety of avenues for future research. First, the act of technology transfer from the national laboratory only begins the process of incorporating this technology into commercial innovation. To understand the impact on innovation and move toward estimates of rates of return, we need to look at the receipt or pickup of transferred technology in the private sector. While such an analysis presents conceptual and data challenges, the survey responses collected and analyzed by Adams, Chiang, and Jensen (1999) represent a promising first step in this direction. Ideally, we would like to know the private rates of return earned by companies seeking to commercialize national laboratory technology, and to compare these private rates of return with the social returns.

Second, the relative social costs and benefits from efforts to encourage technology-transfer activities remain unclear. National laboratories play a number of roles, of which producing technology for the commercial sector is only one. To what extent do efforts that encourage the licensing of new technologies and the spin-out of entrepreneurial businesses affect other laboratory activities negatively, by distracting researchers from their key missions? To what extent does the increase in commercial interactions actually inform and enhance more traditional R&D efforts? To answer these questions, it would be helpful to analyze the evolution of a broader range of measures of laboratory activities over time and across facilities. We found it surprisingly difficult to get data of this sort, and it seems that many performance measures are simply not tabulated systematically across laboratories. These questions are likely to be answerable only through in-depth case studies such as those of Mansfield et al. (1977).

Third, it would have been helpful to examine the incentives of laboratory researchers in more detail. An extensive literature (reviewed in Stephan (1996)) has documented how "career concerns"—e.g., monetary and nonmonetary awards—affect the behavior of researchers in universities. We know far less about the types of formal and informal incentive schemes present within government-owned laboratories. To what extent do formal reward schemes shape behavior? Are employment opportunities outside the laboratory important motivators? These questions are likely to be answerable only though detailed field research at particular laboratories.

Finally, we have analyzed only the contractor-operated laboratories at one agency, the U.S. Department of Energy. One of the consequential econometric issues that we faced in the article was the limited cross-sectional variation due to the modest number of laboratories and the lack of variability within our panel along possibly important dimensions. Comparing the experiences of facilities operated by different agencies, employing different organizational structures, and in different countries would all be logical extensions of this work. Such studies would also allow us to compare the relative effectiveness of a wide variety of initiatives to encourage technology transfer.

Appendix A

Sources for the figures and tables found in the text follow.

Table 1 These are identified from a wide variety of historical accounts, especially Branscomb (1993), U.S. Office of Technology Assessment (1993), and U.S. General Accounting Office (1998). (References to sources cited only in this section are included in Appendix B, not in the main References list.)

Table 2 Data on energy agency-funded R&D (which includes spending by the U.S. Atomic Energy Commission, the U.S. Energy Research and Development Administration, and the DOE) at DOE FFRDCs between fiscal years 1970 and 1997 and on total R&D at DOE FFRDCs between fiscal years 1987 and 1995 are from National Science Board (1996, 1998). Data on energy agency–funded R&D at DOE FFRDCs between fiscal years 1955 and 1969 are from U.S. National Science

Foundation (various years) and are obligations (not actual spending, as elsewhere in the table). Data on total R&D at DOE FFRDCs between fiscal years 1981 and 1986 and in fiscal years 1996 and 1997 are from National Science Foundation (1998). Data on technology-transfer activities in fiscal year 1997 are from U.S. Department of Energy, Office of the General Counsel (1998). Data on technology transfer activities between fiscal years 1987 and 1996 are from U.S. Department of Commerce, Office of Technology Administration (various years). Data on technology-transfer activities between fiscal years 1963 and 1976 are from Federal Council for Science and Technology (various years). No technology-transfer data are available between fiscal years 1977 and 1986. No CRADAs were signed by DOE FFRDCs prior to fiscal year 1990. Licensing and CRADA data between fiscal years 1987 and 1996 include some activity by facilities operated by the DOE. Definitions of various technology-transfer activities may be inconsistent across different years and facilities.

Table 3 The technology transfer data are compiled from U.S. Department of Energy, Office of Defense Programs (1998), *http://www.llnl. gov/IPandC/About/ipacAnn.html*, and personal communications with DOE officials. The data series on the two FFRDCs have been selected to be as comparable as possible, but differences remain. For instance, the count of INEEL licenses includes only those transactions where royalties or fees have been collected by INEEL by the end of fiscal year 1998.

Table 4 Information on the dates of certification and decertification as a FFRDC, the contractors who managed the facilities, and the periods for which they were responsible for the facilities was gathered from Burke and Gray (1995), U.S. General Accounting Office (1996b), the historical information on many facilities' Web sites, and a variety of news stories in LEXIS/NEXIS. The Herfindahl index of patent class concentration is computed using patent applications between 1977 and 1995 awarded by the end of 1996, and it is based on a database compiled by the DOE's Office of Scientific and Technical Information (1998), as described in Section 4. The fractions of R&D at each FFRDC in fiscal year 1995 devoted to national security and basic science were from U.S. Department of Energy, Laboratory Operations Board (1996). The share of all U.S. venture capital disbursements in 1988 going to companies in the state (calculated using the number of companies funded) is based on a special tabulation of Venture Economics' Venture Intelligence Database. We determine whether the contract for the facility was ever competitively awarded from U.S. General Accounting Office (1996b). Data on new licenses and licensing revenues for DOE FFRDCs in fiscal year 1997 are based on U.S. Department of Energy, Office of the General Counsel (1998). Data on R&D at DOE FFRDCs in fiscal year 1995 are from National Science Board (1998). Data on successful patent applications (awarded by the end of end of 1996) derived from DOE FFRDCs are based on a database compiled by the DOE's Office of Scientific and Technical Information (1998), as described in Section 4. Data on citations to the patents are based on a tabulation of the NBER/Case Western Reserve patents database. The count of CRADAs in fiscal years 1991 through 1994 (which includes only awards made under the aegis of the Defense Programs, Energy Efficiency, and Energy Research program offices) is from U.S. Department of Energy (1995). The fiscal year 1995 and 1997 data, which include all DOE FFRDC CRADAs, are from Technology Transfer Business (1998) and U.S. Department of Energy, Office of the General Counsel (1998) respectively.

Table 5 See sources for Table 4. In addition, data on R&D at DOE FFRDCs between fiscal years 1987 and 1993 are from National Science Board (1998) and between fiscal years 1981 and 1986 are from U.S. National Science Foundation (1998). The information used to normalize patents and citations is based on a tabulation of the NBER/Case Western Reserve patents database.

Table 6 See sources for Table 4. In addition, data on R&D at DOE FFRDCs between fiscal years 1991 and 1995 are from National Science Board (1998) and in fiscal years 1997 from U.S. National Science Foundation (1998).

Figure 1 Data on federal and total R&D between 1960 and 1997 are from National Science Board (1996, 1998). Federal R&D data between 1955 and 1959 are from U.S. National Science Foundation (various years) and are obligations (not actual spending, as elsewhere in the figure) for each fiscal year (instead of calendar years). Federal R&D for 1953 and 1954 and total R&D between 1953 and 1959 are from U.S. Department of Commerce, Bureau of the Census (1975). All data before 1953 are from National Academy of Sciences (1952). Data from 1953 and before is less precise than in later years.

Figure 2 Data on R&D at DOE FFRDCs between fiscal years 1987 and 1993 are from National Science Board (1998) and between fiscal years

1981 and 1986 are from U.S. National Science Foundation (1998). Data on successful patent applications at DOE FFRDCs are based on a database compiled by the DOE's Office of Scientific and Technical Information (1998), as described in Section 4.

Figure 3 Data on R&D at DOE FFRDCs between fiscal years 1987 and 1993 and academic R&D between 1981 and 1993 are from National Science Board (1998). Data on R&D at DOE FFRDCs between fiscal years 1981 and 1986 are from U.S. National Science Foundation (1998). Data on successful patent applications derived from DOE FFRDCs are based on a database compiled by the DOE's Office of Scientific and Technical Information (1998), as described in Section 4. Data on successful patent applications derived from universities are based on a tabulation of the NBER/Case Western Reserve patents database.

Figure 4 Data on successful patent applications derived from DOE FFRDCs are based on a database compiled by the DOE's Office of Scientific and Technical Information (1998), as described in Section 4. The analysis is restricted to the fifteen FFRDCs with at least 50 successful patent applications filed between 1977 and 1993 (and awarded by the end of 1996). Data on citations to the patents and the information used to normalize patents and citations are based on a tabulation of the NBER/Case Western Reserve patents database.

Appendix B

Data sources not found in the References follow.

Burke, M. V. and Gray, J. R. "Annotated List of Federally Funded Research and Development Centers." *http://www.nsf.gov/sbe/srs/s4295*, 1995.

Federal Council for Science and Technology. *Annual Report on Government Patent Policy* (also known as *Report on Government Patent Policy*). Washington, D.C.: Government Printing Office, various years.

National Academy of Sciences. *Applied Research in the United States*. Washington, D.C.: National Academy Press, 1952.

National Science Board. *Science and Technology Indicators—1996*. Washington, D.C.: Government Printing Office, 1996.

Technology Transfer Business. "Federal Research & Development Laboratories." *http://www.ded.state.ne.us/fedlabl.html*, 1998.

U.S. Department of Commerce, Bureau of the Census. *Historical Statistics of the United States*. Washington, D.C.: Government Printing Office, 1975.

U.S. Department of Commerce, Office of Technology Administration. *Technology Transfer Under the Stevenson-Wydler Innovation Act*. Washington, D.C.: Government Printing Office, 1995.

U.S. Department of Energy. *Multiprogram Laboratories: 1979 to 1988, A Decade of Change*. Washington, D.C.: U.S. Department of Energy, 1990.

————. "List of CRADA Activity." Mimeo, 1995.

U.S. Department of Energy, Laboratory Operations Board. *Strategic Laboratory Missions Plan—Phase I*. Washington, D.C.: U.S. Department of Energy, 1996.

U.S. Department of Energy, Office of Defense Programs. "Licensing of Intellectual Property at Defense Program Laboratories and Plants in Fiscal Year 1997." Mimeo, 1998.

U.S. Department of Energy, Office of Procurement and Assistance Management. "DOE Procurement and Assistance Data System (PADS) On-Line Database." *http://www.pr.doe.gov/pads.html*, 1998.

U.S. Department of Energy, Office of Scientific and Technical Information. "DOE Patents Database." Mimeo, 1998.

U.S. Department of Energy, Office of the General Counsel. "Technology Transfer Activities, Fiscal Years 1997 through 1999." Mimeo, 1998.

U.S. General Accounting Office. *National Laboratories: Are Their R&D Activities Related to Commercial Product Development?* GAO/PMED-95-2. Washington, D.C.: U.S. General Accounting Office, 1994.

————. *Department of Energy: Contract Reform is Progressing, but Full Implementation Will Take Years*. GAO/RCED-97-18. Washington, D.C.: U.S. General Accounting Office, 1996b.

U.S. National Science Foundation. *Federal Funds for Research and Development*. Washington, D.C.: Government Printing Office, various years.

————. "Federal Obligations for Research and Development to Federally Funded Research and Development Centers (FFRDCs), by Individual FFRDC: Fiscal Years 1980–1997." Mimeo, 1998.

References

Adams, J., Chiang, E., and Jensen, J. "Federal Laboratory R&D and the Performance of Industrial Laboratories." Mimeo, University of Florida and Federal Reserve Bank of Cleveland, 1999.

Berman, E. M. "Cooperative Research and Development Agreements." In Y. S. Lee, ed., *Technology Transfer and Public Policy*. Westport, Conn.: Quorum Books, 1997.

Bozeman, B. and Crow, M. "Technology Transfer from U.S. Government and University R&D Laboratories." *Technovation*, Vol. 11 (1991), pp. 231–246.

Branscomb, L. M. "National Laboratories: The Search for New Missions and New Structures." In L. M. Branscomb, ed., *Empowering Technology: Implementing a U.S. Strategy*. Cambridge, Mass.: MIT Press, 1993.

Cohen, L. R. and Noll, R. G. "The Future of the National Laboratories." *Proceedings of the National Academy of Sciences*, Vol. 93 (1996), pp. 12678–12685.

Forman, H. I. *Patents: Their Ownership and Administration by the United States Government*. New York: Central Book Company, 1957.

Glaeser, E. L., Kallal, H. D., Scheinkman, J. A., and Shleifer, A. "Growth in Cities." *Journal of Political Economy*, Vol. 100 (1992), pp. 1126–1152.

Gompers, P. A. and Lerner, J. *The Venture Capital Cycle*. Cambridge, Mass.: MIT Press, 1999.

Ham, R. M. and Mowery, D. C. "Improving the Effectiveness of Public-Private R&D Collaboration: Case Studies at a U.S. Weapons Laboratory." *Research Policy*, Vol. 26 (1998), pp. 661–675.

Hart, D. M. *Forged Consensus: Science, Technology, and Economic Policy in the United States, 1921–1953*. Princeton, N.J.: Princeton University Press, 1998.

Henderson, R., Jaffe, A. B., and Trajtenberg, M. "Universities as a Source of Commercial Technology: A Detailed Analysis of University Patenting, 1965–1988." *Review of Economics and Statistics*, Vol. 80 (1998), pp. 119–127.

Jaffe, A. B. "Real Effects of Academic Research." *American Economic Review*, Vol. 79 (1989), pp. 957–990.

———, Fogarty, M. S., and Banks, B. A. "Evidence from Patents and Patent Citations on the Impact of NASA and Other Federal Labs on Commercial Innovation." *Journal of Industrial Economics*, Vol. 46 (1998), pp. 183–205.

———, Trajtenberg, M., and Henderson, R. "Geographic Localization of Knowledge Spillovers as Evidenced by Patent Citations." *Quarterly Journal of Economics*, Vol. 108 (1993), pp. 577–598.

Lang, L. H. P. and Stulz, R. "Tobin's q, Diversification, and Firm Performance." *Journal of Political Economy*, Vol. 102 (1994), pp. 1248–1280.

Lawler, A. "DOE to Industry: So Long, Partner." *Science*, Vol. 274 (October 4, 1996), pp. 24–26.

Lerner, J. "Venture Capitalists and the Oversight of Private Firms." *Journal of Finance*, Vol. 50 (1995), pp. 301–318.

———. "The Government as Venture Capitalist: The Long-Run Impact of the SBIR Program." *Journal of Business*, Vol. 72 (1999), pp. 285–318.

López-de-Silanes, F., Shleifer, A., and Vishny, R. W. "Privatization in the United States." *RAND Journal of Economics*, Vol. 28 (1997), pp. 447–471.

Mansfield, E., Rapoport, J., Romeo, A., Wagner, S., and Beardsley, G. "Social and Private Rates of Return from Industrial Innovations." *Quarterly Journal of Economics*, Vol. 91 (1977), pp. 221–240.

Markusen, A. and Oden, M. "National Laboratories as Business Incubators and Region Builders." *Journal of Technology Transfer*, Vol. 21 (1996), pp. 93–108.

Mundlak, Y. "On the Pooling of Time Series and Cross Section Data." *Econometrica*, Vol. 46 (1978), pp. 69–86.

National Science Board. *Science and Technology Indicators—1998*. Washington, D.C.: Government Printing Office, 1998.

Nelson, R. R. "The Simple Economics of Basic Scientific Research." *Journal of Political Economy*, Vol. 67 (1959), pp. 297–306.

Neumeyer, F. and Stedman, J. C. *The Employed Inventor in the United States: R&D Policies, Law, and Practice*. Cambridge, Mass.: MIT Press, 1971.

Roessner, J. D. and Wise, A. "Patterns of Industry Interaction with Federal Laboratories." Working Paper no. 9302, School of Public Policy, Georgia Institute of Technology, 1993.

Scharfstein, D. and Stein, J. "The Dark Side of Internal Capital Markets: Divisional Rent-Seeking and Inefficient Investment." NBER Working Paper no. 5969, 1997.

Stephan, P. E. "The Economics of Science." *Journal of Economic Literature*, Vol. 34 (1996), pp. 1199–1235.

Task Force on Alternative Futures for the Department of Energy National Laboratories. *Alternative Futures for the Department of Energy National Laboratories*. Washington, D.C.: U.S. Department of Energy, 1995.

U.S. Department of Justice. *Investigation of Government Patent Practices and Policies: Report and Recommendations of the Attorney General to the President*. Washington, D.C.: U.S. Government Printing Office, 1947.

U.S. Energy Research and Development Administration. *The Patent Policies Affecting ERDA Energy Programs*. ERDA-76-16. Washington, D.C.: U.S. Energy Research and Development Administration, 1976.

U.S. General Accounting Office. *Technology Transfer: Implementation of CRADAs at NIST, Army, and DOE*. GAO/T-RCED-93-53. Washington, D.C.: U.S. General Accounting Office, 1993.

———. *Federal Research: Information on Fees for Selected Federally Funded Research and Development Centers*. GAO/RCED-96-31FS. Washington, D.C.: U.S. General Accounting Office, 1996a.

———. *Department of Energy: Uncertain Progress in Implementing National Laboratory Reforms*. GAO/RCED-98-197. Washington, D.C.: U.S. General Accounting Office, 1998.

U.S. House of Representatives. *The Second Report of the National Patent Planning Commission*. Document no. 22. 79th Congress, 1st Session, January 9, 1945.

U.S. Office of Technology Assessment. *Defense Conversion: Redirecting R&D*. OTA-ITE-552. Washington, D.C.: Government Printing Office, 1993.

White House Science Council, Federal Laboratory Review Panel. *Report of the Federal Laboratory Review Panel*. Washington, D.C.: White House Science Council, 1983.

11 Innovation in Israel 1968–1997: A Comparative Analysis Using Patent Data

Manuel Trajtenberg

1 Introduction

In the aftermath of the 6-day war, Israel embarked on an ambitious course aimed at developing "high-tech" industries, as a means to exploit its perceived comparative advantage in world-class academic resources and highly skilled labor (contrasted to its relatively poor endowment in natural resources). The government undertook to actively support industrial R&D aimed primarily at export markets, in addition to harnessing the spillovers from a sophisticated defense R&D sector. And indeed, the last two decades have seen a surge of activity in high-tech fields in Israel, ranging from computer software to communications equipment to advanced medical devices to biotechnology. As a consequence, Israel is widely regarded as one of the few Silicon Valley type of technology centers outside the US, and has turned into an attractive location for R&D operations of leading multinationals.

We intend in this chapter to provide a close-up portrait of the Israeli high-tech sector with the aid of highly detailed patent data, drawn from all patents granted in the US to Israeli inventors, and to US patents granted to other countries. We shall address questions such as: How does Israel fare vis-à-vis other countries in terms of patenting activity? What is the technological composition of its innovations? Who actually owns the intellectual property rights, and to what extent can the local economy expect to benefit from the

Prepared for the Forum Sapir Conference, Tel Aviv, January 21, 1999. Special thanks to Adi Raz, Avi Rubin and Gal Steinberg for excellent research assistance, and to Liran Einav for helping out at earlier stages. Gal contributed greatly also in developing software tools that made possible the extraction of up-to-date patent data from the Internet.

innovations done by Israeli inventors? How do Israeli innovations compare to those of other countries in terms of their "importance" as reflected in patent citations? In addressing these questions we hope not only to shed light on the case of Israel, but also to demonstrate the power of this type of data for studying innovation in great detail and, in particular, for examining in a comparative fashion the innovative performance of countries and regions.

The reason for focusing on Israeli-held patents granted in the US is clear: if innovations are pursued primarily for export, it is the property rights in the *target* countries that have to be protected. True, Israel exports a great deal also to Europe, but it is usually the case that patents are sought first and foremost in the US (where the standards for patentability are more stringent than in most european countries).[1] Thus, one can hopefully learn a great deal about export-oriented technologies by analyzing the Israeli patents granted in the US. From the early 1960s through 1998 Israel-based inventors received about 7000 patents in the US. This is a large (absolute) number, and it placed Israel as the 14th largest foreign recipient of US patents, ahead of some OECD countries such as Norway and Spain.

Adam Jaffe and I have developed in recent years a methodological approach that allows one to study innovation in great detail with the aid of patent data, and not just to rely on patent counts.[2] In particular, building both on detailed information contained in patents and on patent citations, we can compute for each individual patent quantitative indicators of notions such as the "importance," "generality," and "originality" of patents (see Trajtenberg et al., 1997). We can also trace the "spillovers" stemming from each patent, and analyze their geographical and temporal patterns (e.g. are spillovers geographically localized? see Jaffe et al., 1993). Moreover, we have constructed a large data bank containing information on all US patents granted from 1963 to 1996[3] that allows us to compute this sort of measures for any subset of patents. This is a powerful capability that greatly enhances our ability to do empirical research in the area of the Economics of Technical Change.

---

1. In any case, casual evidence indicates that there is a strong correlation between patenting in the US and patenting in Europe.
2. Rebecca Henderson of MIT also participated in the initial stages of this endeavor, and Bronwyn Hall of Berkeley and Oxford has been involved in it for the past few years.
3. With the assistance of Michael Fogarty and his team at Case Western University.

The chapter is organized as follows: beginning with a concise discussion of the data in Section 2, we then examine in Sections 3 and 4 the main trends in Israeli patenting, both in itself and in comparison to three groups of countries: the G7, a group of countries with GDP per capita similar to Israel (Finland, Spain, Ireland and New Zealand), and the "Asian Tigers" (Taiwan, South Korean, Hong Kong and Singapore). Section 5 deals with the technological composition of Israeli innovations, relative to that of the US. In Section 6 we look in detail at the distribution of Israeli assignees, in an attempt to elucidate the all important issue of who really controls the rights to the intellectual property embedded in these patents, and hence who can expect to benefit from it. Section 7 undertakes to examine the relative "importance" or "quality" of Israeli patents vis-à-vis other countries, in terms of citations received. Section 8 offers concluding remarks.

2   Data

A patent is a temporary monopoly awarded to inventors for the commercial use of a newly invented device. For a patent to be granted, the innovation must be non-trivial, meaning that it would not appear obvious to a skilled practitioner of the relevant technology, and it must be useful, meaning that it has potential commercial value. If a patent is granted, an extensive public document is created. The front page of a patent contains detailed information about the invention, the inventor, the assignee, and the technological antecedents of the invention, all of which can be accessed in computerized form (see Fig. 1).

These extremely detailed and rich data have, however, two important limitations: first, the range of *patentable* innovations constitutes just a sub-set of all research outcomes, and second, patenting is a *strategic* decision and hence not all *patentable* innovations are actually *patented*. As to the first limitation, consider an hypothetical distribution of research outcomes, ranging from the most applied on the left to the most basic on the right. Clearly, neither end of the continuum is patentable: Maxwell's equations could not be patented since they do not constitute a device (ideas cannot be patented). On the other hand, a marginally better mousetrap is not patentable either, because the innovation has to be non-trivial. Thus, our measures would not capture purely scientific advances devoid of immediate applicability, as well as run-of-the-mill technological improvements that are too trite to pass for discrete, codifiable innovations.

Help   Welcome   Boolean   Advanced   Sales   PTDLS

◀ ▶ ▲   [USPTO] [CNIDR]   (4 of 5)

United States Patent	4,203,158
Frohman-Bentchkowsky, et. al.	May 13, 1980

Electrically programmable and erasable MOS floating gate memory device employing tunneling and method of fabricating same

Inventors: **Frohman-Bentchkowsky; Dov** (Haifa, IL); **Mar; Jerry** (Sunnyvale, CA); **Perlegos; George** (Cupertino, CA); **Johnson; William S.** (Palo Alto, CA).

Assignee: **Intel Corporation** (Santa Clara, CA).

Appl. No.: 969,819

Filed: **Dec. 15, 1978**

Related U.S. Application Data

Continuation-in-part of Ser No. 881,029, Feb. 24, 1978, abandoned.

Intl. Cl. :	G11C 11/40
U.S. Cl.:	365/185; 307/238; 357/41
Current U.S. Class:	365/185.29
Field of Search:	365/185, 189; 307/238; 357/41, 45, 304

References Cited | [Referenced By:]

	U.S. Patent Documents		
3,500,142	Mar., 1970	Kahng	365/185
4,051,464	Sept., 1977	Huang	365/185

Primary Examiner: Fears; Terrell W.
Attorney, Agent or Firm: Blakely, Sokoloff, Taylor & Zafman

Abstract

An electrically programmable and electrically erasable MOS memory device suitable for high density integrated circuit memories is disclosed. Carriers are tunneled between a floating conductive gate and a doped region in the substrate to program and erase the device. A minimum area of thin oxide (70 A-200 A) is used to separate this doped region from the floating gate. In one embodiment, a second layer of polysilicon is used to protect the thin oxide region during certain processing steps.

16 Claims, 14 Drawing Figures

Figure 1
United States patent

The second limitation is rooted in the fact that it may be optimal for inventors *not* to apply for patents even though their innovations would satisfy the criteria for patentability. For example, until 1980 universities in the USA could not collect royalties for the use of patents derived from federally funded research. This limitation greatly reduced the incentive to patent results from such research, which constitutes about 90% of all university research in the USA. Firms, on the other hand, may elect not to patent and rely instead on secrecy to protect their property rights.[4] Thus, patentability requirements and incentives to refrain from patenting limit the scope of analysis based on patent data. It is widely believed that these limitations are not too severe, but that remains an open empirical issue.

Our working hypothesis here is that, whereas these limitations may affect *level* comparisons across fields/industries and perhaps also across countries *at a point in time*, they do not affect the analysis of trends and changes over time. In other words, if we observe for example a big surge in the *share* of Israeli patents in the field of Computers and Communications and a concomitant decline in the share of Chemicals, it is hard to believe that these changes are due to underlying changes in the relative propensity to patent in these two sectors. Rather, the assumption is that these trends reflect true changes in the amount of innovation done in those fields.

The data that we use here were assembled from various sources. First, from our own massive data bank, which consists as said of all US patents and their citations, granted form 1965 through 1996, we extracted the following subsets: (1) all patents granted during that period to Israel, to the four countries in the Reference Group (Finland, Ireland, New Zealand and Spain), and a random sample of 1/72 of US patents; (2) for all those patents (over 30,000) we added all the patent citations that they received over the same period (about 110,000); (3) patent counts by application year for all the other comparison countries (the G7 and the Asian Tigers). Second, we extracted from the US Patent Office site in the Internet, all Israeli patents granted in 1997 and 1998 (up to December 15, 1998).[5] Third, we extracted from a related site data on "raw applications" for all these countries. We

---

4. There is a large variance across industries in the reliance on patents versus secrecy: see Levin et al, 1987.

5. The site is not geared towards massive data extractions, and hence we had to develop special software tools to extract the data. This turned out to be a rather complex and difficult endeavor.

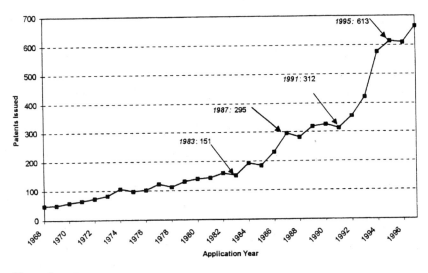

Figure 2
Israeli patents in the US—1968–1997

then added data on population for the comparison countries and Israel, data on R&D for the G7, and a variety of other data from the National Science Foundation (1996) and other sources.

3   Basic Facts about Israeli Patenting in the US

Fig. 2 shows the number of successful Israeli patent applications in the US over time, starting in 1968.[6] The growth in the annual number of patents has been very impressive, starting from about 50 in the late 1960s, to over 600 in the late 1990s (i.e. they grew by a factor of 12). However, as Table 1 reveals, the process was not smooth, but rather it was characterized by big swings in growth rates. Particularly striking are the two big jumps that occurred in the second half of the period: from 1983 to 1987 the number of patents doubled (in just 4 years!), and then they doubled again from 1991 to 1995. Notice that in between these two periods (i.e. 1987–1991) the annual flow of patents barely grew. We have to be careful with the timing though: patent applications reflect (successful) R&D conducted *prior* to the filing date, with lags varying greatly by sector. Thus, the number of

---

6. There were about 300 earlier patents, but we chose to conduct the analysis for the post 6-Day-War period, since concerted efforts to develop an innovative sector in Israel started only then.

Table 1
Israeli patents in the US—basic figures

Year	"Raw" applications	Patents issued, by appl. year	Rate of success	Patents issued, by grant year	Growth rate, %	Industrial R&D (1990) US$)
1960–1967		305		177		
1968	73	48	0.66	38	29.7	
1969	87	49	0.56	61	2.1	
1970	90	58	0.64	46	18.4	
1971	120	64	0.53	54	10.3	
1972	143	72	0.50	55	12.5	68.3
1973	155	82	0.53	84	13.9	74.5
1974	165	106	0.64	89	29.3	76.0[a]
1975	158	97	0.61	96	−8.5	77.5
1976	175	102	0.58	106	5.2	91.3
1977	206	122	0.59	92	19.6	150.7
1978	202	112	0.55	99	−8.2	153.8
1979	235	131	0.56	81	17.0	181.2
1980	253	140	0.55	113	6.9	205.8
1981	317	143	0.45	122	2.1	186.3
1982	316	159	0.50	114	11.2	242.9
1983	307	151	0.49	110	−5.0	275.5
1984	376	193	0.51	159	27.8	385.0[a]
1985	377	184	0.49	182	−4.7	495.4
1986	427	231	0.54	187	25.5	550.3
1987	503	295	0.59	244	27.7	423.2
1988	490	281	0.57	238	−4.7	396.6
1989	624	318	0.51	324	13.2	418.9
1990	608	325	0.53	298	2.2	468.6
1991	633	312	0.49	304	−4.0	510.7
1992	780	355	0.46	335	13.8	559.3
1993	803	421	0.52	314	18.6	574.7
1994	1,040	576	0.55	349	36.8	631.3
1995	1,072	613[b]	0.57	384	6.4	614.4
1996	1,042	609[b]	0.58	484	−0.7	668.6
1997	1,185	664[b]	0.56	529	9.0	
1998				741		
Total[c]	12,962	7,013	0.54	6,432	10.8	

a. Estimates, interpolation.
b. Estimates, based both on the average application-grant lag, and on the "success ratio."
c. For 1968–98 (i.e. does not include 1960–67).

patents in a particular year should be attributed to investments in R&D carried out in the previous 1–2 years at least, and in some sectors further back.[7]

What accounts for the observed path of Israeli patenting over time? I shall not attempt here to conduct a systematic analysis of the factors underlying such trajectory, but rather I'll content myself with, (i) enumerating key economic developments that coincided in their timing with turning points in patenting, suggesting that they may account at least in part for the observed pattern; and (ii) comparing the time series of patents to R&D expenditures. The first big jump in patenting (1983–1987) represents the very emergence of the high-tech sector in Israel, prompted inter alia by explicit policies designed to support industrial R&D, primarily through the establishment of the Office of the Chief Scientist of the Ministry of Industry and Trade. The in-between "flat" period of 1987–1991 (which represents R&D activity done circa 1985–1989) presumably reflects the big macro adjustment and micro restructuring that followed the stabilization program of 1985. That was also the period that saw the end of the "Lavi" program of the Israel Aircraft Industry (to develop a first-class jet fighter), and the beginning of the downsizing of defense-related industries. Both of these developments freed large numbers of qualified scientists, engineers and technicians, that were to play a key role in the subsequent second big jump of 1991–1995 (again, reflecting R&D activity circa 1989–1993). Notice that the single largest jump occurred in 1994, when the number of patents grew by a whooping 37%. It is likely that this dramatic increase incorporates, among other factors, the impact of the mass immigration from the former Soviet Union.

Fig. 3 shows industrial R&D expenditures (in constant 1990 US$) along with patents (see also Table 1).[8] There is clearly a (lagged) co-movement of the two series, as manifested for example in the simple Pearson correlations of Table 2. Thus, patents lead R&D by 2–3 years,

---

7. Notice for example the figures for the mid seventies: the number of patents grew substantially in 1973 and in 1974, but then declined in 1975 and barely grew in 1976. Moving back these figures 1–2 years would provide the right picture in terms of the impact of the Yom Kippur War.

8. The R&D figures are from Griliches and Regev (1999), Table 1. Since these refer to *industrial* R&D, it may be more appropriate to relate them to Israeli corporate patents (see Section 6 below) than to total patents. In practice the two patent series move pretty much in tandem, and hence the correlations with R&D of either series are virtually the same.

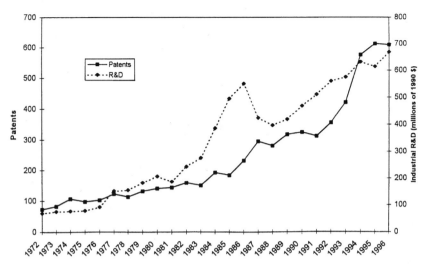

Figure 3
Israeli patents and industrial R&D

Table 2
Correlations of R&D expenditures with number of patents

		(−1)	(−2)	(−3)
Patents	0.850	0.877	0.884	0.883
Log patents with log R&D	0.890	0.901	0.922	0.928

and the correlation is stronger in rates (i.e. when using logs) than in levels. Looking in more detail, there is the striking run up in R&D from 1981 to 1986 (in particular, R&D expenditures more than doubled between 1980/81 and 1984/85), followed by the doubling of patents between 1983 and 1987. As said, this is the period that saw the emergence of the high-tech sector, and that is well reflected in both series. In 1986–1988 we see a decline in the level of R&D spending, and the concomitant flattening of patenting in 1987–1991, and then again a sustained increase through the early-mid 1990s that anticipates the second big jump in patenting. It is clear then (and reassuring) that industrial R&D expenditures are closely linked (with a reasonable lag) to patents, but further research is needed to understand the joint dynamics, integrating at the same time the sort of qualitative factors mentioned before.

The above cursory description carries a warning sign (or at least a serious question mark) for the future. Given the high rates of obsolescence of "Knowledge Capital" (K) that characterize high-tech sectors, a steady stream of innovations (here in the form of the annual flow of patents, P_t) is needed just to maintain current levels of K_t. Faster obsolescence (as may be happening in some areas of computers and communications) thus requires a *growing* P_t, and the same applies if we want to see a steadily growing stock of K_t. As we have seen, the big jumps in P_t are likely to have occurred, to a significant extent, as a consequence of big "shocks" to the system (e.g. in policy, availability of relevant inputs, etc.), including of course the jumps in R&D expenditures. The question is then how we expect to bring about/ support a sustained increase in P_t in the future, absent further (positive) shocks of that sort. Perhaps the attainment of "critical masses" in several dimensions of the high-tech sector will generate by itself the required future growth, but that remains to be seen.

Table 1 shows also the number of "raw applications," that is, the overall number of patent applied for in the USA by Israeli inventors. Of these, only those under "patents issued, by application year" (which is the figure we shall use all along) were actually granted, the rest did not pass the rather stringent tests of the US Patent Office (novelty, usefulness, etc.). The average "success rate" over the whole period was 54%, with no clear trend over time (except for the fact that it was clearly higher in the first decade, 1968–1977). We shall return to this datum in the context of international comparisons, but it is worth pointing out now that a 54% success rate suggests that there are margins for improvements even within this (narrow) context. That is, close to half of the innovations that were good enough to merit a costly application to the US Patent Office[9] do not seem to bear fruit, in the sense that they are not worthy of a US patent. Perhaps there is room for low-cost policies/actions that would target the R&D efforts underlying the unsuccessful 46% and channel them into more fruitful directions.

4   International Comparisons

Whereas the detailed analysis of Israeli patenting is revealing in itself (as we shall see in subsequent sections), we resort to international

---

9. That already constitutes a high standard.

comparisons in order to put in perspective the overall level and trend over time in Israeli patenting. We have chosen for that purpose 3 different groups of countries, as follows:

1. The G7: Canada, France, Germany, Italy, Japan, UK and USA.

2. A "Reference Group": Finland, Ireland, New Zealand and Spain.

3. The "Asian Tigers": Hong Kong, Singapore, South Korea and Taiwan.

The Reference Group was chosen according to their GDP per capita in the early 1990s, that is, we chose the four countries that had at that time a level of GDP per capita closest to that of Israel (in ppp terms). Notice that, except for Spain, the other three countries in this group are very similar to Israel also in terms of population.

Appendix A contains detailed patent figures for each country, and Figs. 4–6 show the time patterns of patents per capita for Israel ver-

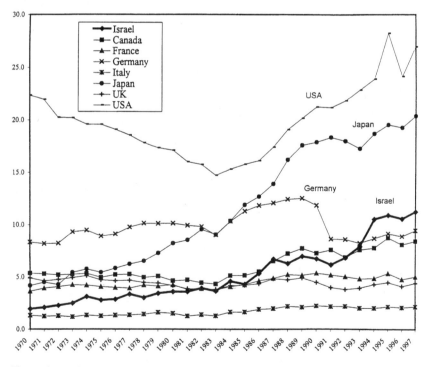

Figure 4
Patents per capita: Israel vs. the G7

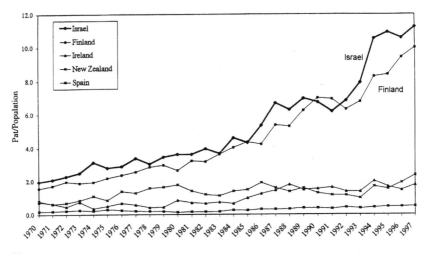

Figure 5
Patents per capita: Israel vs. the reference group

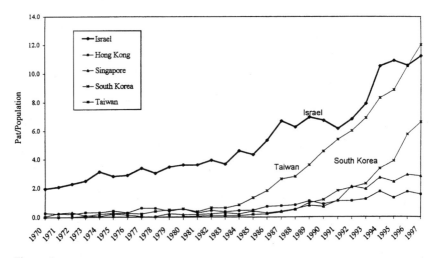

Figure 6
Patents per capita: Israel vs. the NIC

sus each of the above groups of countries. We chose to normalize the number of patents by population, simply because this is a widely available and accurate statistic that provides a consistent scale factor. Another normalization of interest would be R&D expenditures, but except for the G7, the figures for the other countries are far from satisfactory. Fig. 4 reveals that Israel started virtually at the bottom of the G7 (together with Italy), but by 1987 it had climbed ahead of Italy, UK, and France and was in par with Canada. In the early-mid 1990s it moved ahead of Canada and (the unified) Germany,[10] thus becoming 3rd after the USA and Japan. Using civilian R&D as deflator for these countries shows a similar result. Thus, there is no question that Israel had surged forward and placed itself in the forefront of technological advanced countries, at least in terms of (normalized) numbers of patents. It is interesting to note also that, other than Israel, the only country that grew all along since 1970 was Japan. The others were either stagnant or declined (as the USA did) until the early 1980s. The fact that 1983 proved to be a turning point for *all* of the largest countries at the same time (USA, Japan, Germany, and to a lesser extent also for Canada) is interesting in itself, but remains to be explained.

The comparison with the Reference Group shows a very clear picture: the only country that is "game" is Finland, which has followed a pattern virtually identical to Israel, both in levels and in the timing of fluctuations (this striking resemblance deserves further scrutiny—see below). The other three countries are well behind, and have remained at the bottom without any significant changes over time. The one surprise there is Ireland, which has pursued for over a decade active policies to attract foreign investments in advanced technologies. As for the Asian Tigers, we can see immediately that Taiwan has grown extremely rapidly since the early 1980s, actually surpassing Israel as of 1997.[11] And indeed, Taiwan is widely regarded today as a high-tech powerhouse, after being associated with low-tech, imitative behavior for a long time. South Korea seems to be embarked on a similar path. By contrast, Hong Kong and Singapore remain well behind.

---

10. Had Germany remained divided, Israel would probably reach parity with west Germany by 1998–1999.

11. The number of patents *granted* to Taiwan inventors reached 4045 in 1998, almost doubling that of 1997 (this figure is not incorporated in our statistics) and hence it is clear that the trend is accelerating. See, however, Table 3 for the peculiar composition of assignees for Taiwan.

Table 3
Country statistics: averages by 5- and 30-year periods

Country	Patents per year		Patents per capita		Success rate		Annual growth rate	
	1968–1997	1992–1997	1968–1997	1992–1997	1968–1997	1992–1997	1968–1997	1992–1997
Israel	234	577	5.3	10.2	54%	56%	10.1%	13.3%
G7								
Canada	1525	2401	6.1	8.1	56%	55%	3.4%	5.5%
France	2423	2896	4.5	5.0	66%	63%	1.9%	0.5%
Germany	6338	7250	9.8	8.9	65%	63%	2.3%	2.4%
Italy	937	1197	1.7	2.1	59%	58%	2.8%	−0.4%
Japan	13,226	23,847	11.5	19.0	65%	61%	8.4%	2.8%
UK	2547	2494	4.4	4.3	55%	51%	−0.2%	3.1%
USA	46,913	66,325	19.8	25.2	62%	59%	1.6%	5.3%
Reference group								
Finland	214	438	4.5	8.6	57%	58%	8.6%	10.0%
Ireland	35	60	1.0	1.7	49%	48%	6.8%	5.5%
New Zealand	42	61	1.3	1.7	42%	42%	4.9%	16.9%
Spain	105	173	0.3	0.4	49%	50%	4.2%	3.1%
Asian tigers								
Hong Kong	39	95	0.7	1.5	49%	46%	12.5%	9.6%
Singapore	22	83	0.8	2.6	55%	52%	16.5%	10.3%
South Korea	443	1989	1.1	4.4	61%	62%	27.7%	27.9%
Taiwan	554	2006	2.8	9.3	44%	47%	33.8%	15.7%

For all their limitations, these comparisons correspond quite well to what we know about these countries, only that this way we get a much more detailed and precise picture of the underlying trends. The observed patterns for Finland, Ireland and Taiwan are particularly revealing, and exemplify the power of patent statistics to uncover phenomena that otherwise are hard to detect.

Table 3 summarizes the main statistics for all these countries, including their "success rates" and growth rates in patenting, over the whole period (1968–1997) and for the past 5 years. Notice that, in terms of recent patents per capita, Israel stands third after the USA and Japan, in comparison to *all* the 15 countries, and in terms of growth rates it also ranks third, after South Korea, Taiwan and New Zealand (the latter not yet an important player). This is no doubt a remarkable achievement. The picture is less flattering in terms of success rates: Israel ranks 8th, after most G7 countries, Finland and South Korea. The average for those countries ahead of Israel is 61%; if Israel were able to reach this mark from the present 56%, that would represent an increase of about 10% in the annual number of patents granted. This would be like an increase in the productivity of the R&D process, rather than an increase in the overall level of resources devoted to inventive activity. As to growth rates, Israel grew faster than both the G7 and the reference group over the whole period, with wide fluctuations in growth rates over time. The Asian Tigers display much higher rates, but we have to remember that they started from very low levels, and hence these rates should be seen primarily as "catch up."

Lastly, it is important to note that in the present context the *absolute* number of patents remains key (similarly to the absolute level of R&D expenditures, rather than its ratio to GDP). In order to establish a viable, self-sustaining high-tech sector, a country has to achieve a critical mass in terms of pertinent infrastructure, skills development, managerial experience, testing facilities, marketing and communication channels, financial institutions, etc. Similarly, it is clear by now that spillovers, and in particular *regional* spillovers, are extremely important in fueling the growth of this sector. Once again, the amount of spillovers generated, and the ability to capture external spillovers is a function of absolute, not relative size. If we take the number of patents as indicative of the absolute size of the innovative sector, then Israel has still a long way to go: it stands well below all the G7 countries, and is about 1/4 the size of Taiwan and South Korea. In order to get to the (absolute) level as of today of, say, the lower tier G7 countries (Canada, France, UK) and the leading Asian Tigers (Taiwan and South Korea), Israeli patenting would have to grow at a rate of about 30% per year over the next 5 years! At present growth rates (of 13.3% per year), it would take 10 years to get there. That's too long, by all accounts.

5   The Technological Composition of Israeli Patented Innovations

The US Patent Office has developed over the years a very elaborate classification system by which it assigns patents to technological categories. It consists of some 400 main patent classes, and over 150,000

patent subclasses. The 400 or so classes have been aggregated traditionally into four fields: chemical, mechanical, electrical and other.
We have developed recently a new classification scheme, by which
we assigned these 400 patent classes into 35 technological "sub-
categories," and these in turn are aggregated into six categories:
Computers and Communications, Electrical and Electronics, Drugs
and Medicine, Chemical, Mechanical and Other.

Fig. 7a and 7b shows the breakdown of Israeli patents by these
six technological categories (in percentages) over time. Fig. 8 does
the same but for US patents,[12] thus providing us with a standard of
comparison. Let us start from the latter, which is supposed to reflect
the main world-wide trends in technology itself. The pattern is quite
clear: from 1968 and up to about 1980 all series were pretty much
flat, i.e. the relative shares of each of the six categories remained virtually constant. The shares of Mechanical and Other were highest
(over a quarter each), then came Chemical (21–23%), and further
down Electrical and Electronic (15%). Both Drugs and Medicine and
Computers and Communications accounted for a tiny fraction back
then, up to 5% each. Starting in the early 1980s this static picture starts
to change, as follows: the three top fields decline (Mechanical decline
the most), Electrical and Electronics does not change at all, and the
two bottom ones surge forward, with Computers and Communications accounting in 1994 for over 15% of all patents.

As Fig. 9 reveals, the pattern for Israel is similar, except that the
changes are much more abrupt (and the initial levels are also quite
different). The most striking development is the surge of Computers
and Communications from about 5% in the 1970s (as in the US), to a
full 25% by 1994 and beyond. Likewise, Drugs and Medicine doubles
its share from 10% to 20%. Electrical and Electronics oscillates around
15% (exactly as in the US), increasing recently to 20%. The flip side
is the much more pronounced decline in the traditional categories,
with Chemicals exhibiting by far the sharpest drop, from 40% at the
beginning of the period, to less than 10% by 1996. Thus, the "big
story" in Israeli patenting is the growth in Computers and Communications and Drugs and Medicine at a significantly faster pace than
in the US, and the even faster decline in Chemicals. The composition
of innovations has thus changed dramatically in Israel, and seem-

---

12. This distribution is based on the sample of 1/72 of US patents (over 20,000 in
total).

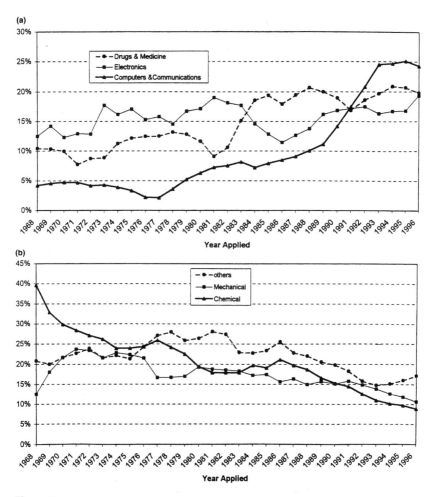

Figure 7
(a) Israeli patents by Tech categories: rising fields. (b) Israeli patents by Tech categories: declining fields

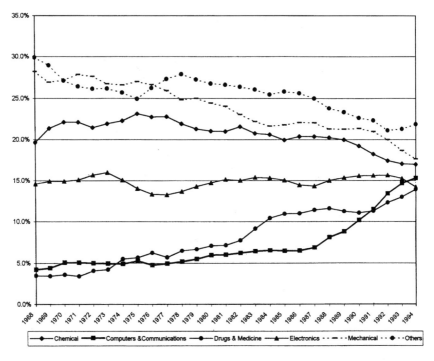

Figure 8
Distribution of US patents by Tech categories

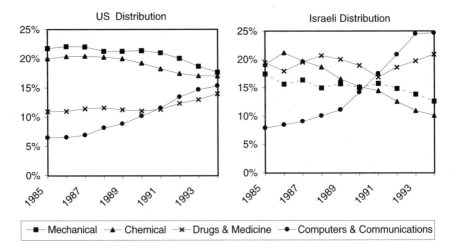

Figure 9
US vs. Israel Tech categories—1985–1994

ingly in a healthy way, in the sense that we are in tandem with world-wide changes in technology, but we experience them at an accelerated rate. Finally, Appendix B shows the actual number of patents in each subcategory, sorted by the cumulative number in the past 5 years.

6   Who Owns What? A View at the Distribution of Israeli Patents Assignees

By way of introduction, we need to describe the different "players" related to any given patent. First, there are the inventors, that is, those individuals directly responsible for carrying out the innovation embedded in the patent. Second, there is the assignee, that is, the legal entity (corporation, government agency, university, etc.) that owns the patent rights, assigned to it by the inventor(s). However, there are individual inventors that work on their own and have not yet assigned the rights of the patent to a legal entity at the time of issue, in which case the patent is classified as "unassigned" (or "assigned to individuals").[13] For most patents, the inventors are typically employees of a firm, in which case the assignee is the firm itself.

According to the conventions of the US Patent Office, the "nationality" of a patent is determined by the address (at the time of application) of the *first inventor*. That is, if a patent has many inventors and they are located in a variety of countries, the location of the first inventor listed on the patent determines to which country it is deemed to belong. Likewise, if the assignee is located in a country different from that of the first inventor, it is once again the location of the latter that determines the nationality of the patent. Thus, in the patent shown on Fig. 1, the first inventor has an Israeli address, whereas the other three inventors listed have addresses in the USA, and the patent was assigned to Intel of Santa Clara, CA; nevertheless, the patent is formally classified as Israeli.[14]

The data that we have presented so far (e.g. number of patents by countries) were compiled according to this convention: Israeli patents are those for which the address of the first inventor was in Israel, regardless of the identity and location of the assignees or of the other inventors, and similarly for the other countries. The

---

13. That is, the inventor herself may appear as the legal entity that owns the patent rights.

14. Clearly, this convention is completely inconsequential for anything but the compilation of statistics about international patenting activity.

important question now is, who actually owns the rights to these inventions? Keeping in mind that for patents labeled "Israeli" it was indeed Israeli scientists and engineers that were responsible for the "innovative act" that led to these patents (they certainly provided the "brain power"),[15,16] the question is: which entity, commercial or otherwise, is in a position to reap the economic benefits from these inventions?

At the upper level of aggregation there are three possibilities: (i) that there is no assignee (i.e. the inventor herself retains the rights to the patent), and hence it is not clear if and when the patent will be commercially exploited; (ii) that the assignee is also Israeli, that is, that the location of the entity owning the rights to the patent is in Israel; (iii) that the assignee is foreign. Even the seemingly sharp distinction between (ii) and (iii) is not quite as clear. There are on the one hand Israeli corporations that have established subsidiaries or otherwise related firms in other countries, and they may choose to assign the patents (done is Israel) to their "foreign" subsidiaries (but in fact we should regard them as Israeli). On the other hand, there are multinational corporations that have established subsidiaries in Israel, and some may choose to assign the locally produced patents to the Israeli subsidiary, even though the multinational retains effective control over the property rights. We have dealt as well as we could with the first difficulty, by examining the names of the assignees, and spotting those cases that were designated as foreign assignees but were clearly Israeli firms (e.g. Elscint US, Ormat, etc.). By contrast we have not addressed the second difficulty, but rather taken on face value the address of the assignee, e.g. Motorola Hertzlia will appear as an Israeli assignee, Motorola US as a foreign assignee.

The distinction between these three categories, unassigned, Israeli ("local") and foreign, is then telling of the extent to which the country can expect to benefit from "its" patents. The unassigned patents

---

15. We ignore for the moment the issue of the possible variety of nationalities of inventors, that is, we assume that for Israeli patents all inventors reside in Israel and not just the first, and the same for other countries.

16. The reason we have to be careful with the wording here is as follows: suppose that an Israeli scientist goes to a sabbatical to MIT in Cambridge, MA, and carries out a project in a lab there that results in a patented invention (there are quite a few of these in the data). Such a patent would be labeled as Israeli, but the assignee would be MIT. Now, the invention was made possible not only by the ideas and efforts of the Israeli scientist, but also by the facilities, physical and otherwise, of the host institution. The end result is no doubt a function of both.

may of course find their way to successful commercial applications (and many do), but they typically face much higher uncertainty than corporate assignees that own from the start the patents issued to their employees. Moreover, corporations are in a better position to capture internally the spillovers generated by those innovations. Thus, the higher is the percentage of unassigned patents, the less would be the economic potential of a given stock of patents. The distinction between foreign and local assignees is presumably informative of the probability that the *local economy* would be the prime beneficiary of the new knowledge embedded in the patent. One can draw various scenarios whereby foreign ownership may be as good if not better in that respect than local ownership of the patent rights (e.g. the foreign multinational offers marketing channels for the innovation that would be inaccessible to local firms). Still, we are rapidly moving in many technological areas to an era where the prime asset is the effective control of intellectual property, and presumably that is correlated with the ownership of patent rights. However, we do not need to take a strong stand in this respect, only to agree that this distinction is informative and quite likely important for understanding the potential value for a country of its stock of patents.

A further distinction for assigned patents, whether Israeli or foreign, is according to the "type" of assignee, and in this context we consider three main categories (although we have made actually finer distinction in the data): corporate, government and universities (including hospitals and related research institutions). The working hypothesis is that the likelihood of down-the-line commercial application of a patent would be higher if owned by a corporation, and lower if owned by the Government or by Universities.

Fig. 10 shows the distribution of Israeli patents among different types of assignees for the whole period, at the two levels of aggregation. Just slightly over half of the total number of patents received during the past 30 years is owned by designated *Israeli assignees*. Almost a third are unassigned, and the remaining 17% belong to foreign assignees. Of the 53% owned by Israeli assignees, a full third went to Israeli Universities and to the Israeli Government, the latter mostly to Defense-related institutions (primarily to "Rafael" and to "Taas," the Military Industry). Thus, the percentage of all Israeli patents that belong to Israeli corporate assignees is just over a third: $0.53 \times 0.67 = 0.355$. This percentage is very low by any standard (see below): it

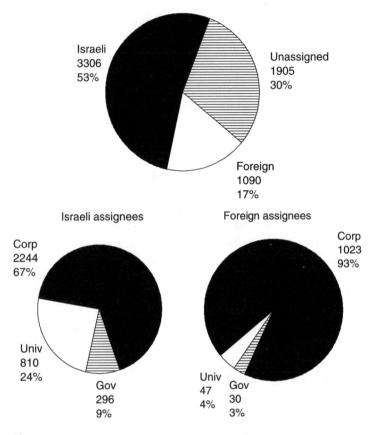

Figure 10
Distribution of Israeli patents by type of assignees (totals)

implies that only a third of all patents generated by Israeli *inventors* have a relatively high chance to bring in economic benefits to the Israeli economy. To repeat, this is only a probabilistic statement: for sure many of the patents granted to Universities, to Rafael, or to private individuals eventually resulted (or will result in the future) in commercially successful innovations for Israeli firms. Still, unassigned patents, patents granted to foreign assignees, or to Universities and the Government presumably offer lower *expected local returns* than those assigned to Israeli corporations.

Table 4 puts these figures into perspective (see below for a more detailed comparison).

Table 4
Distribution of assignee types[a]

	USA (1963–1993)	All other countries (1963–1993)	Israel (1968–1997)
Corporations	71%	84%[b]	43%
Unassigned	24%	15%	37%
Government	3%	1%	6%
Universities	2%	na	16%

a. Percentages out of total number of patents issued to assignees or individuals of a given country, thus not including those assigned to foreign assignees.
b. Including universities, but these account for a tiny percentage.
Source: National Science Foundation. Science and Engineering Indicators, 1996, appendix table 6–7, p. 275, in addition to our data.

The differences between Israel and both the USA and all other countries are startling: Israel has much higher percentages of the three bottom types, Unassigned, Government and Universities, particularly so for Universities. As a consequence, the percentage of corporate patents, those that have the highest ex ante chance of finding commercial applications, is just 43%, almost half the corresponding percentage for all other countries except the USA, and 40% lower compared to the USA. These figures mimic the distribution of R&D by sector: in 1995 just 45% of civilian national R&D in Israel was conducted by the business sector, as opposed to 72% in the US, and a median of 62% for OECD countries (Central Bureau of Statistics, 1998, table 17).

Table 5 offers a more detailed (if slightly different) perspective. In it we show comparative figures for the upper "pie" of Fig. 10, that is, the distribution between unassigned, "local" and foreign assignees.[17] As we can see, the percentage of local assignees is much lower than that of all G7 countries except for Canada. As to the reference group, Finland has a much higher share of local assignees than Israel, the other three (with few patents each) have lower percentages. In the

---

17. These figures are not strictly comparable to those presented so far, for the following reasons: (1) The number of patents assigned to a country in table 3 include all patents in which *any* of the inventors resides in that country; (2) the period covered in table 3 is 1976–1998 for granted patents, as opposed to 1968–1997 for applied patents in all other tables. Both are due to limitations of the search capabilities in the Internet site of the US Patent Office.

Table 5
Distribution of assignee types—international comparison 1976–1998

Country	Number of patents				Percentages		
	Unassigned	Foreign	Local	Total	Unassigned	Foreign	Local[a]
Israel	1815	1807	3443	7065	26%	26%	49% (52%)
G7							
Canada	15,756	8614	21,175	45,545	35%	19%	46% (50%)
France	6567	8883	49,500	64,950	10%	14%	76% (75%)
Germany	13,147	17,060	117,660	147,867	9%	12%	80% (77%)
Italy	3957	3904	19,293	27,154	15%	14%	71% (72%)
Japan	9003	6950	341,854	357,807	3%	2%	96% (95%)
UK	5812	15,698	37,693	59,203	10%	27%	64% na
USA	296,191	19,546	887,308	1,203,045	25%	2%	74% (76%)
Reference group							
Finland	834	422	4739	5995	14%	7%	79% (81%)
Ireland	259	512	385	1156	22%	44%	33% (32%)
New Zealand	614	224	685	1523	40%	15%	45% (52%)
Spain	1048	784	1503	3335	31%	24%	45% (51%)
Asian tigers							
Hong Kong	688	760	1824	3272	21%	23%	56% (55%)
Singapore	110	488	274	872	13%	56%	31% (43%)
South Korea	1154	531	10,666	12,351	9%	4%	86% (92%)
Taiwan	13,296	991	6362	20,649	64%	5%	31% (44%)

a. Numbers in parenthesis: the percentages for 1998.

case of the Asian Tigers, the two large patent holders stand at opposite extremes: Taiwan has a very low percentage of local assignees (due to an extremely high share of unassigned, 64%), whereas South Korea has an extremely high share (topped only by Japan). These differences are clearly related to the industrial organization of these countries (e.g. Taiwan has a very large number of small enterprises, and an extremely high rate of turnover of firms, whereas South Korea is dominated by huge, stable *chaebol*), but it is a topic worth of further investigation. The contrast between the latest figures (for 1998) and those for the whole period 1976–1998 reveal that the G7 countries are quite stable, whereas most of the others increased the share of local assignees, some of them very significantly such as Taiwan, Singapore, New Zealand and Spain. Thus, the world-wide trend

Table 6
Israeli patents assigned to large foreign corporations

Time period	Average annual number of patients
1968–1986	2
1987–1989	6
1990–1991	18
1992–1993	36
1994–1995	70

is towards an increase in the share of local assignees. What characterizes Israel vis-à-vis other countries is that *both* the shares of unassigned and of foreign are relatively high (the only other countries for which that is true are all minor players: New Zealand, Spain and Hong Kong).

6.1 Foreign Assignees—A Further Look

We have referred extensively to the fact that Israel has a very high percentage of foreign ownership of patents received by Israeli inventors, compared to other countries. Who are these foreign assignees? The largest foreign patent holders of Israeli patents are: Motorola (112 patents), Intel (95), IBM (75) and National Semiconductors (57). Of course, these are the familiar names that have had a strong presence in Israel for quite a while now. Table 6 shows the annual number of Israeli patents taken by these corporations. Clearly, the number of Israeli patents assigned to large foreign corporations grew extremely fast, from less than 10 prior to 1990 to about 70 in the mid 1990s, whereas in the course of the same period the overall number of Israeli patents barely doubled.

As already suggested, we have to be very careful in how to judge this phenomenon. On the one hand the fact that these multinationals have established a foothold in Israel is extremely important in terms of the (positive) externalities that they generate, as well as in opening foreign markets for Israeli technology. On the other hand they may be competing for the one key resource that Israel has, namely, innovative talent in cutting edge technologies (see below). It is this talent that they seek in opening R&D labs in Israel, and in so doing they acquire control over the intellectual property generated there.

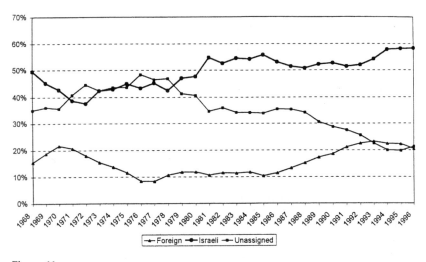

Figure 11
Distribution of assignees—all Israeli patents

Whatever the normative stand that one takes on this issue, it is imperative to know well the facts, and this is what we have attempted here.[18]

6.2   Trends in the Distribution of Assignees

So far we have looked at the distribution of assignees for the whole stock of Israeli patents of the past 30 years, and the picture is rather bleak; however, the picture brightens significantly when we examine time trends. Fig. 11 shows the distribution over time of the unassigned-local–foreign percentages: there is a slow increase in the share of Israeli assignees, approaching now 60% (from about 45% in the 1970s), a marked decline in the share of unassigned (from about 40% in the 1970s to 20% in the mid 1990s), but also a significant increase in the share of foreign patents from about 10% in the 1980s to over 20% in the 1990s. The sharp and persistent decline in the share of unassigned patents (we are now in that respect at the level of the USA) is certainly very good news; the remaining (and still open) question is how to relate to the increase in the share of foreign assignees.

18. The wider issue (not addressed here) is how to formulate R&D policies in the era of globalization, whereby brainpower and spillovers flow freely across national boundaries. The figures presented here offer partial evidence on these flows.

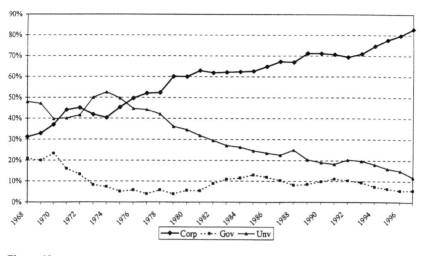

Figure 12
Distribution of Israeli assignee types

Fig. 12 displays the distribution of Israeli assignees among the various types: corporate, universities, and government. Here the main trends are very encouraging: the share of corporate-owned patents has risen steadily from a low of 30% at the beginning of the period, to a high of 83% in 1997. This rise came mostly from the corresponding dramatic drop in the share of universities: from a high of about half of all patents at first, to 12% in 1997. The share of government patents has fluctuated quite a bit around the 10% mark, but seems to be decreasing steadily as of the early 1990s (to 6% in 1997). Still, a total of 18% for Government and Universities combined is very high compared to all other countries, and we expect that this percentage will continue to shrink to internationally acceptable levels of less than 10%.

Fig. 13 summarizes these trends into one figure, the share of Israeli corporate patents out of the total number of Israeli patents. As already suggested, these are the patents with the highest expected payoff for the Israeli economy, and hence the focus on them. Once again, the overall trend here is certainly encouraging: Israeli corporate patents accounted for a dismal 15% at the beginning of the period, and now account for almost half (48%) of all Israeli patents. As we can see, the rise was not smooth, and actually throughout the 1980s it hovered around the 35% mark. It is only since 1992 that it has

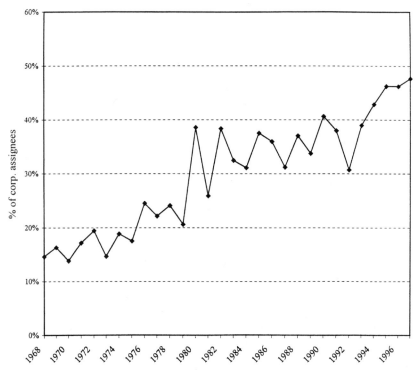

Figure 13
Percentage of Israeli Corporate assignees

climbed steadily up to today's level. Of course, there is still a very long way to go: in order to take full advantage of the potential embedded in Israeli inventions to the benefit of the Israeli economy, this percentage would have to increase steadily (to, say, the 70–80% mark). That would require a continuous reshuffling of inventive resources, away from all other competing players and towards the Israeli corporate sector.[19]

6.3   Competing for Talent?

As already suggested, the identity of the assignees may be informative not only of who owns what, but of who competes for the limited

_____

19. We do *not* see so far such reshuffling in the distribution of R&D expenditures by sector—see Central Bureau of Statistics, 1998, table 1.

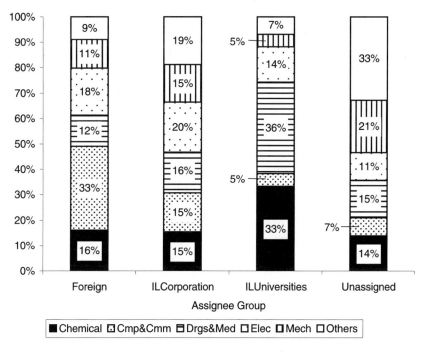

Figure 14
Technological distribution by assignee types

pool of skills, scientific and technological talent and entrepreneurial drive that Israel has. One way to approach this issue is through the information displayed in Fig. 14, that is, the distribution of patents by technological categories, for each type of assignee. Thus, foreign and Israeli corporations look quite similar in that respect, except that foreign assignees are much more active than Israelis in Computers and Communications (the share of foreigners in that field is 33% versus 15% for Israeli assignees). By contrast, both Universities and individual inventors operate in rather different technological areas than corporations: Universities primarily in Chemistry and Drugs and Medicine, individual inventors in Mechanical and "Other." In short, foreign and local corporations do seem to compete for the same sort of human capital, universities and individual inventors do not.

7   The Relative "Importance" of Israeli Patents

Simple patent counts are a very imperfect measure of innovative activity, simply because patents vary a great deal in their technological and economic "importance" or "value," and the distribution of such values is extremely skewed. Recent research has shown that patent citations can effectively play the role of proxies for the "importance" of patents, as well as providing a way of tracing spillovers (see Trajtenberg, 1990; Jaffe and Trajtenberg, 1996; Henderson et al., 1998). By citations we mean the references to previous patents that appear in the front page of each patent (see Fig. 1).

Patent citations serve an important legal function, since they delimit the scope of the property rights awarded by the patent. Thus, if patent 2 cites patent 1, it implies that patent 1 represents a piece of previously existing knowledge upon which patent 2 builds, and over which 2 cannot have a claim. The applicant has a legal duty to disclose any knowledge of the prior art, but the decision regarding which patents to cite ultimately rests with the patent examiner, who is supposed to be an expert in the area and hence to be able to identify relevant prior art that the applicant misses or conceals.[20]

We use data on patent citations here in order to examine the "quality" of Israeli patents vis-à-vis US patents, and patents of the reference group of countries. That is, we ask to what extent Israeli patents are more or less frequently cited than the patents of these other countries, controlling for various effects. Moreover, we analyze how these differences vary over technological categories, and over time. We regress the number of citations received by each patent (ncites), on control variables (dummies for five technological classes as well as for grant years), a dummy for the US and another for the group of reference countries. The sign and magnitude of the coefficients of these two latter dummies are telling of the extent to which Israeli patents receive more or less citations on average than these other countries, controlling for technological composition and age of patents. The results for the benchmark regression are as in Table 7.

---

20. Because of the role of the examiner and the legal significance of patent citations, there is reason to believe that patent citations are less likely to be contaminated by extraneous motives in the decision of what to cite than other bibliographic data such as citations in the scientific literature (Van Raan, 1988; Weingart et al., 1988). Moreover, bibliometric data are of limited value in tracing the *economic* impact of scientific results, since they are not linked to economic agents or decisions.

Table 7
Benchmark regression

Number of obs = 37,313
$F(7, 37,272) = 196.21$
Prob > F = 0.0000
R-squared = 0.1330
Adj R-squared = 0.1321
Root MSE = 5.0211

ncites	Coefficient	Std. err.	t	P > |t|
usa	0.6954136	0.0793592	8.763	0.000
refer	−0.6985195	0.0855526	−8.165	0.000
chemical	0.335095	0.0773475	4.332	0.000
cmpcmm	2.372321	0.1090868	21.747	0.000
drgsmed	1.61299	0.107602	14.990	0.000
elec	0.3790388	0.0845855	4.481	0.000
mech	−0.2321834	0.0745865	−3.113	0.002
_cons	2.988059	0.0842784	35.455	0.000
gyear	$F(33, 37,272) = 142.390$ (34 categories)			0.000

Thus, US patents are "better" than Israeli patents by about 25% (the coefficient of 0.695 for the US divided by the constant term of 2.98), but Israeli patents are of significantly better quality than the patents of the reference countries. Next we ask what happened to these differences over time, that is, are Israeli patents getting better or worse relative to other countries? Just interacting the coefficients of interest in the above regression with time won't do, because as time advances (i.e. as we get closer to the present, which necessarily truncates future citations) the number of citations received declines. One way to go about it is to define the dependent variable in logs, which in principle should be immune to truncation (since the coefficients on the dummies for countries are in percentage terms).[21] In the regressions in Tables 8 and 9 we compare in that fashion the relative standing of Israeli patents in the last 10 years versus the previous 20 years (dummies for tech categories are included in both but not shown):

---

21. The only remaining difficulty is what to do about observations with zero citations, which account for about 1/3 of all patents. A number of standard procedures are at hand, here we chose to assign the value of 0.1 to the observations with 0 citations, but the results are pretty much the same if one resorts to other means.

Table 8
Israeli patents prior to 1986

Grant year < 1986
Number of obs $= 20{,}287$
$F(7, 20{,}257) = 54.69$
Prob $> F = 0.0000$
R-squared $= 0.0859$
Adj R-squared $= 0.0846$

lncite01	Coefficient	Std. err.	t	P $> |t|$
usa	0.1928575	0.0384885	5.011	0.000
refer	−0.2633523	0.0427346	−6.163	0.000
_cons	0.5544518	0.0402906	13.761	0.000
gyear	$F(22, 20{,}257) = 76.064$ (23 categories)			0.000

Table 9
Israeli patents after 1986

Grant year > 1986
Number of obs $= 17{,}026$
$F(7, 17{,}008) = 128.21$
Prob $> F = 0.0000$
R-squared $= 0.3667$
Adj R-squared $= 0.3661$

lncite01	Coefficient	Std. err.	t	P $> |t|$
usa	0.1751703	0.029623	5.913	0.000
refer	−0.266625	0.031084	−8.578	0.000
_cons	−0.4513321	0.032458	−13.905	0.000
gyear	$F(10, 17{,}008) = 935.922$ (11 c tegories)			0.000

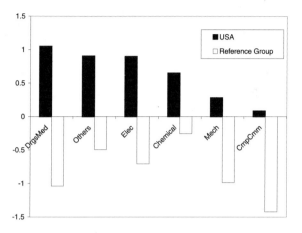

Figure 15
Relative "importance" of Israeli patents by Tech category

Thus, whereas in the pre-1986 period US patents were about 19% better than Israeli patents, in the post-1986 period that advantage seems to have decreased slightly (to 17%). The relative standing of Israeli patents vis-à-vis the reference group of countries did not change. We also run similar regressions for the whole period whereby time is interacted with the dummies for the US and reference countries, and the results are pretty much the same, except that their significance is rather fragile.[22] In any case, it is quite clear that the converse is not true, that is, one can easily reject the null hypothesis that the quality of Israeli patents has *declined* over time, in the wake of the rapid growth in their numbers.

In Fig. 15 we show graphically the results of the analysis for each technological class. The columns represent the value of the respective dummies, e.g. the coefficient of the USA dummy in a (separate) regression just for Drugs and Medicine was 1.01, whereas the coefficient of the reference group dummy in that same regression was −1.06, and so forth.[23] Thus, Israeli patents are particularly good in Computers and Communications (in that category we are on par with the US, and much better than the reference countries), whereas

---

22. The coefficient of (time × USA) is negative but borderline significant, and moreover its significance does depend on how we treat the observations with zero citations.
23. We don't show there the s.e. (or *t* values): most coefficients are significant, not all, but the qualitative results are well represented in the figure.

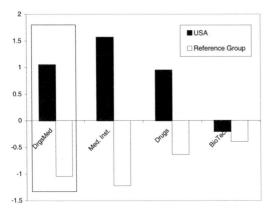

Figure 16
Relative "importance" of Israeli patents in drugs and medical

the biggest disadvantage vis-à-vis the US resides in Drugs and Medical.

In Fig. 16 we look into Drugs and Medical in more detail, and the picture that emerges is as follows. We stand at a large disadvantage vis-à-vis the US both in Surgery and Medical Instrumentation and in Drugs, but we are actually at a small advantage in Biotechnology and Molecular Biology. The reason for the disadvantage in Drugs is clear: the Israeli pharmaceutical industry has focused for the most part on generics, which by definition are not break-throughs and therefore do not receive many citations, whereas the pharmaceutical industry in the US is by far the most advanced in the world. The disparity in Medical Instrumentation is more puzzling and requires further scrutiny, given the relatively high standards of that sector in Israel. The very good news resides in Biotechnology, whereas said Israeli patents are of comparable importance to those of the US.[24]

Thus, Israeli patents are on par with the US in terms of the "importance" or "quality" of its innovations in two technological fields that stand at the forefront of technology worldwide, Computers and Communications and Biotechnology. The former is also Israel's fastest growing field, the latter is still very small but growing. This is a very reassuring finding, and speaks of the great potential that resides with the high-tech sector in Israel.

---

24. But we have to remember that there are still relatively few Israeli patents in Biotechnology (see Appendix B): just 196 for the whole period.

8   Concluding Remarks

Before summing up, it is important to emphasize once again that the forgoing analysis was conducted entirely on the basis of data contained in Israeli and other patents issued by the US Patent Office. Clearly, not all Israeli innovations are reflected in those patents (the same is true for the comparison countries), and hence the results should be qualified accordingly. However, given that the high-tech sector in Israel is overwhelmingly export-oriented, and that the US is a prime destination for those exports, there is reason to believe that Israeli patents issued in the US are indeed representative of the main technological trends and patterns in Israel.

Israeli patenting in the US has grown very rapidly for the past 3 decades (the growth rate averaging over 10% per year), placing Israel as the 14th largest foreign recipient of US patents. There is a close statistical association between the annual flow of Israeli patents and Industrial R&D expenditures in Israel. Moreover, the time path of patents seems to have been strongly influenced by major "supply shocks" such as the termination of the project to build a jet fighter (which freed a large number of engineers and technicians), and the mass immigration from the former Soviet Union. This raises the question of whether such the rapid growth in innovative outputs is sustainable, given the recent stagnation (and even cuts) in Government support to R&D, and the lack of significant foreseeable additions to the pool of highly skilled workers.

Israel fares very well in international comparisons (vis-à-vis the G7, a Reference Group of countries with similar GDP per capita, and the "Asian Tigers"), both in terms of patents per capita, and in growth rates of patenting. Thus, in recent years it holds third place among these countries in patents per capita (after the US and Japan), and third again for growth rates (after Taiwan and South Korea). However, many aspects of the innovation process require a "critical mass," and for those purposes it is the *absolute* size of the innovative sector that counts, as proxied here by the (absolute) number of patents. Israel has still a long way to go in those terms: it stands well below all of the G7 countries, and is about 1/4 the size of Taiwan and South Korea. Once again, the question is whether there are forces in the Israeli economy capable of keeping the momentum going for the high-tech sector, bringing it up to the size required to ensure its long-term viability. This remains to be seen.

The technological composition of Israeli patents has changed dramatically over time: traditional fields such as Chemical and Mechanical have declined steeply (in relative terms), whereas Computers and Communications rose from a mere 5% of patents to 25% by the late 1990s. These changes are in tandem with worldwide trends in technology, except that Israel is experiencing them at an accelerated rate. Israeli patents are inferior to US patents in terms of "importance" as measured by citation rates, but better than patents issued to the Reference Group of countries. In terms of technologies, Israeli patents are particularly "good" (i.e. highly cited) in the key fields of Computers and Communications and Biotechnology.

The analysis so far indicates that Israel's innovative performance has been quite impressive. However, the question arises as to whether the Israeli economy can take full advantage of the innovations generated by Israeli inventors, in view of the composition of the patent assignees, i.e. of the owners of the intellectual property rights to those innovations. In fact, just about half of all Israeli patents granted in the last 30 years are owned by Israeli assignees (corporations, universities or government): the rest belongs to private inventors ("unassigned" patents) or to foreign assignees. This percentage is lower than most of the comparison countries, certainly much lower than the corresponding figure for the G7 countries except Canada (local assignees made 74% of patents in the US, 96% in Japan). The presumption is that (local) economic gains from innovation are correlated with this figure, and furthermore, that they are correlated with the percentage of patents owned by local *corporations* (just 35% in Israel). The trend is encouraging though: the percentage of patents that belong to Israeli corporations has been raising steadily, and stands now at close to 50%.

The overall picture is thus mixed: on the one hand Israel exhibits a rapidly growing and vibrant innovative sector, that has achieved an impressive international standing. On the other hand, the Israeli economy has still a way to go in order to fully realize the economic benefits embedded in those innovations.

Appendix

Table 10
Patents for selected countries, 1968–1997 by application year

Country	1968–1972	1973–1977	1978–1982	1983–1987	1988	1989	1990	1991	1992	1993	1994	1995	1996	1997
Israel	58	102	137	211	281	318	325	312	355	421	576	613	609	664
G7														
Canada	1106	1180	1147	1345	1876	2029	1933	2049	1955	2180	2270	2583	2419	2555
France	1929	2164	2199	2397	2940	2925	3044	2968	2885	2795	2832	3107	2787	2957
Germany	4874	5745	6167	6660	7621	7759	7487	6880	6909	6669	7063	7469	7278	7772
Italy	660	718	819	971	1267	1232	1282	1249	1260	1141	1159	1242	1204	1237
Japan	4062	6385	9359	13,979	19,866	21,650	22,072	22,701	22,342	22,515	23,357	24,474	24,252	25,637
UK	2764	2709	2357	2429	2704	2811	2584	2320	2227	2305	2517	2628	2421	2600
USA	45,150	41,894	38,222	37,990	46,968	50,190	53,130	53,451	55,741	58,990	62,216	74,249	64,026	72,144
Reference group														
Finland	70	103	143	212	262	310	349	349	318	344	421	429	482	513
Ireland	20	18	21	36	63	52	54	57	49	49	72	60	53	64
New Zealand	17	33	47	49	45	52	43	39	39	34	59	55	70	85
Spain	67	87	63	99	124	146	146	133	163	146	162	183	184	190
Asian tigers														
Hong Kong	11	17	23	30	46	62	50	64	65	72	106	81	111	103
Singapore	4	2	4	8	14	21	19	31	60	56	80	81	99	98
South Korea	4	9	20	74	205	409	509	787	892	1019	1497	1747	2632	3049
Taiwan	1	33	87	279	557	725	931	1116	1256	1460	1778	1924	2262	2607

The figures for the four 5-year periods between 1968 and 1987 are yearly averages.

Table 11
Distribution of patents by tech sub-categories[a]

Sub-category	5 years (1990–1994)	Total (1968–1997)
Communications	198	417
Computer Hardware and Software	197	409
Drugs	140	391
Surgery and Med Inst	135	424
Miscellaneous—chemical	104	389
Miscellaneous—Others	102	362
Power Systems	86	266
Biotechnology	77	196
Mat Proc and Handling	76	238
Measuring and Testing	63	230
Miscellaneous—Mechanical	56	187
Furniture, House Fixtures	55	168
Nuclear and X-rays	54	158
Organic Compounds	50	244
Optics	46	116
Electrical Devices	43	125
Miscellaneous—Elec	41	111
Fluid Sprinkling, Spraying, and Diffusing	41	175
Transportation	40	100
Liquid Purification or Separation	40	162
Agriculture, Husbandry, Food	37	150
Resins	32	125
Miscellaneous—Drgs and Med	26	90
Heating	26	109
Semiconductor Devices	23	58
Electrical Lighting	22	69
Refrigeration	20	76
Amusement Devices	20	101
Motors and Engines + Parts	20	110
Computer Peripherals	18	40
Receptacles	17	60
Fluid Handling	17	91
Information Storage	16	55
Apparel and Textile	15	57
Metal Working	10	50
Pipes and Joints	9	38
Agriculture, Food, Textiles	7	47
Earth Working and Wells	6	57
Coating	5	41
Gas	3	11
Total	1993	6304

a. Sorted by last 5 years total.

References

Central Bureau of Statistics, 1998. State of Israel, "National Expenditure on Civilian Research and Development 1989–97." Publication No. 1086, May 1998.

Griliches, Zvi and Haim Regev, 1999, "R&D, Government Support and Productivity in Manufacturing in Israel, 1975–94." Mimeo, presented at the Forum Sapir Conference, January 1999.

Henderson, R., Jaffe, A., Trajtenberg, M., 1998. Universities as a source of commercial technology: a detailed analysis of university patenting 1965–1988. Review of Economics and Statistics 80(1), 119–127, February 1998.

Jaffe, A., Henderson, R., Trajtenberg, M., 1993. Geographic localization of knowledge spillovers as evidenced by patent citations. Quarterly Journal of Economics, 577–598, August 1993.

Jaffe, A., Trajtenberg, M., 1996. Modeling the flows of knowledge spillovers. Proceedings of the US National Academy of Sciences 93(99), 12671–12677, November.

Levin, R., Klevorick, A., Nelson, R. R., Winter, S. G., 1987. Appropriating the returns from industrial research and development. Brookings Papers on Economic Activity 3, 783–820.

National Science Foundation, 1996. Science and Technology Data Book. NSF, Washinton, DC.

Trajtenberg, M., 1990. A penny for your quotes: patent citations and the value of innovations. The Rand Journal of Economics 21(1), 172–187, Spring.

Trajtenberg, M., Jaffe, Henderson, R., 1997. University versus corporate patents: a window on the basicness of invention. Economics of Innovation and New Technology 5(1), 19–50.

IV

The Patents and Citations Data: A Close-up

12

The Meaning of Patent Citations: Report on the NBER/Case-Western Reserve Survey of Patentees

Adam B. Jaffe, Manuel Trajtenberg, and Michael S. Fogarty

1 Introduction

It is well understood that the nonrival nature of knowledge as a productive asset creates the possibility of "knowledge spillovers," whereby investments in knowledge creation by one party produce external benefits by facilitating innovation by other parties. At least since Griliches's seminal paper on measuring the contributions of R&D to economic growth (1979), economists have been attempting to quantify the extent and impact of knowledge spillovers. One line of research of this type has utilized patent citations to identify a "paper trail" that may be associated with knowledge flows between firms.[1]

Very little of this research has attempted to determine the modes or mechanisms of communication that actually permit knowledge to flow. Further, most of the work has simply assumed that citations or other proxies are sufficiently correlated with knowledge flows to allow statistical analysis of the proxies to be informative regarding the underlying phenomenon of interest.[2]

This chapter reports on a preliminary attempt to improve this situation. We undertook a small but systematic survey of inventors to

Helpful comments from Sam Kortum (including the suggestion to describe the "control" patent in the survey as a "placebo") are gratefully acknowledged. Financial support was provided by the Alfred P. Sloan Foundation, via the Project on Industrial Technology and Productivity at NBER. The views expressed and responsibility for all errors lie with the authors.
1. Patent citations or references appear on the front page of a granted patent. They serve the legal function of identifying "prior art" upon which the current invention builds. For more detail, see Jaffe, Trajtenberg, and Henderson 1993.
2. A partial exception is Jaffe, Fogarty, and Banks 1998, in which a limited number of interviews with inventors were used to shed light on the relationship between citations and knowledge flows.

try to learn about the extent and modes of their communication with earlier inventors and about the extent to which the appearance of citations in their patents is indicative of this communication. The results suggest that such communication is important, and that patent citations do provide an indication of communication, albeit one that also carries a fair amount of noise.

2 Survey Design

The idea for the survey emerged from a series of interviews with patent attorneys, R&D directors, and inventors for a project on commercializing federal lab technology.[3] We quickly learned that each brought a different perspective and a different willingness to discuss patent citations. Patent attorneys were least willing to share information about citations; R&D directors represented the organization's broader strategic perspective; and the inventor clearly had the best knowledge of R&D spillover mechanisms. These discussions suggested to us that patent citations are a noisy but potentially valuable indicator of both the importance of the technology as well as the extent of knowledge spillovers. But it also became clear that the inventors were an underexploited source of insight into these issues. Since inventors are all identified on the computerized patent records, we decided to undertake a systematic survey of inventors to learn their views about knowledge flows, patent citations, and the relationship between them.

We began by first developing questions to explore the validity of patent citations for analyzing the technological and commercial importance of patents as well as for evaluating knowledge spillovers. After developing draft questions, we tested the survey on a sample of inventors. The test group consisted of twenty inventors drawn from four types of institutions: universities, government labs, research hospitals, and industry. The draft survey was then revised to incorporate the inventors' numerous comments and suggestions.

---

3. These interviews were conducted by two of the authors during 1996. See Adam B. Jaffe, Michael S. Fogarty, and Bruce A. Banks, "Evidence from Patents and Patent Citations on the Impact of NASA and other Federal Labs on Commercial Innovation," *Journal of Industrial Economics* 46 (1998), no. 2: 183–205. The interviews included the Electro-Physics Branch (EPB) chief, EPB personnel, selected firms working with EPB, NASA's and Lewis's patent attorney, TRW's patent attorney, BF Goodrich's director of corporate technology (Specialty Chemicals Division), Picker International's patent attorney, Picker's director of technology marketing, Owens-Corning's R&D director, Owens-Corning's patent attorney, and a former R&D director of GE's engine division.

Selection Criteria and Qualifying 1993 Patents

Our goals for the survey were to learn about the mechanisms and pathways by which inventors learn of previous work and to test or measure the extent to which citations are a useful proxy for knowledge flows and/or the technological significance of patents. We surveyed two groups, one in which we asked inventors about citations *made* in their patents to previous patents (the *"citing inventor"* survey), and one in which we asked inventors about citations *received* by their patents from subsequent patents (the *"cited inventor"* survey). Our expectation, based on the interviews we had conducted with a small number of inventors and other research personnel, was that citing inventors would be inclined to understate their reliance on the work of prior inventors, while cited inventors would tend to overstate the extent to which they had influenced those who came after. By surveying both groups, we hoped to "triangulate" (Helper 2000) and get a more robust picture of the knowledge flows.

Since communication or knowledge flows are inherently difficult to measure quantitatively, the best we could hope to get from inventors were qualitative rankings on a Likert scale. This means that, whatever answers we got about the extent of communication, it would be hard to say whether the reported communications between citing and cited inventors was significant or not. To overcome this problem, we introduced into the citing-inventor surveys "placebo" patents. That is, we asked inventors about their communications with the inventors of several previous patents, some of which were cited by the surveyed inventor's patent, and some of which were not. Of course, the citing inventors were not told that any of the previous patents were placebos. All of the previous patents were referred to in the survey as "cited patents." The placebo patents were chosen to match the cited patents by technology class and date. Our basic strategy, then, is to *compare* the rankings of the citation and placebo patents, and look for statistically and economically significant differences between the responses for the citations and the responses for the placebo patents.

Because tens of thousands of patents are granted to American inventors every year, there is a large universe from which to pick a sample for a survey of patentees. From this universe, we selected samples of *citing* and *cited* inventors. We designed the samples to be unbiased along the important dimensions, while taking into account cost constraints, and we focused on inventions recent enough that the inventors had good recall of the events surrounding them. At the same time, we wanted patents that were old enough so that there would be significant citation information related to them. In balancing these considerations, we chose 1993 patents for the *citing* inventor survey. For the *cited* inventor survey, we identified patents cited by 1993 patents, which were issued in 1985 or later. To allow the citing-inventor survey to cover older citations too, we included in the survey questions about other citations going back to 1975.

To select the patents for the citing-inventor survey, we began by identifying all U.S. patents granted in 1993 that meet the following criteria:

1. The principal (first listed) inventor should have a U.S. address.[4]

2. The patents should contain 3 or more citations made to patents issued 1985 or later, which themselves meet the following criteria:

   a. There should be no inventor on a cited patent that is the same as the inventor on the 1993 citing patent.

   b. The assignee on the cited patent should not be the same as the assignee on the 1993 citing patent.

3. In addition to the 3 post-1985 citations, patents should have 1 or more additional citations to patents issued in 1975 or later.

The selection criteria produced 14,762 citing patents. On the basis of desired sample size, expected response rates, and resource constraints, we decided on an initial stratified target sample of approximately 600 citing inventors to be surveyed. A stratified sample was called for because we believe that the patterns of knowledge flows (as well as inventors' ability to recall) might be different for more "important" patents, and we know from previous research that most patents are relatively "unimportant" (at least as measured by citation counts). Thus, the sample was designed so as to oversample from more highly cited (and hence presumably more important) patents. First, we included *all* of the 100 most cited 1993 patents that otherwise met our criteria. (Each of these had at least 10 citations.) In addition, we drew a random sample of those patents with 4 or more citations and a separate random sample of those that received 1–3 citations. We did not survey any patents that themselves received 0 citations.

---

4. This requirement was meant to maximize the chances of actually finding the inventor.

Each of the citing inventors was queried about 3 earlier patents: two actual citations that appeared on their patent (one granted after 1985, and the other after 1975) and a placebo that does not appear among the citations on their patent but that matches the second cited patent by technology class and grant year. For the *cited* inventor survey, we identified the primary inventor of the first citation about which the citing inventor was queried (the cited patent granted after 1985). This inventor was queried about her patent, the citing patent, and the relationship between the two (that is, there were no "placebos" in the cited inventor surveys.)

We then undertook the time-consuming task of searching for addresses and telephone numbers, both in Internet directories (Yahoo, Excite, Lycos) and in other sources such as the 1998 edition of CD ROM 88 Million Phone Book. In the end, 1,306 surveys were mailed to inventors, approximately equally divided between citing and cited inventors. Of these, 165 were returned as undeliverable. After the initial mailing, a reminder postcard was sent, and inventors who had not responded within about two months were sent a second copy of the survey. In addition, about 150 inventors who had not responded but whose counterpart citing/cited inventor had responded were contacted by telephone to encourage their participation. On the basis of these calls, we estimate that at least 10% of the *remaining* possible respondents never received copies of the survey. Therefore, the actual number of possible respondents came down to slightly over 1,000.

In the end, we got 166 partial or complete responses to the *citing* survey and 214 partial or complete responses to the *cited* inventor survey. Of these, 72 represent matched pairs. The combined gross return rate is about 30%, and the return rate adjusted for the likely undelivered surveys is about 37%.

The mailing included a cover letter describing the purpose of the survey, the survey questionnaire, and abstracts of the relevant patents. Each abstract and associated information was copied from the USPTO and Community of Science web sites. These were then combined with the standard questionnaire format.[5] The *citing* inventors were thus sent information on 4 patents (theirs plus the 2 citations and the placebo), whereas the *cited* inventor was sent information on two patents (theirs and the citing patent).

---

5. A number of inventors said that patent claims would have provided more useful information on the patent than the abstract. Consequently, any future survey should probably also include the patent claims.

The questions asked fall into 3 broad categories. First are questions that ask each inventor about her patent, without regard to its relationship to other patents (questions 1–6 in both the citing- and cited-inventor surveys). Second are questions that focus on the extent, timing, and nature of any learning that the citing inventor may have gotten from the cited invention (questions 7–10 in the citing-inventor survey and 7–9 in the cited-inventor survey). Finally, we asked 2 questions about the technological relationship between the cited and citing inventions. Despite their placement at the end of the survey, we begin by examining the answers regarding the technological relationship between the inventions. We then turn to the communication questions, including the issue of whether the citing and cited inventors differ in their assessment of the extent of communication that may have occurred. Finally, we examine for all of the surveyed inventors whether their perceptions regarding the economic and technological significance of their inventions is correlated with the number of citations the patents received.

3   Citations and the Technological Relationship between Inventions

The decision by the patent examiner that patent X must cite patent Y is supposed to indicate that patent Y represents prior art upon which patent X builds. On the basis of conversations with inventors and patent attorneys, it seemed to us that the nature of the technological relationship that this represents could take two generic forms. It could be that patent X represents an alternative way of doing something that patent Y did before. (For example, you built a better mousetrap by using titanium in the spring; I built a better mousetrap by using zirconium in the spring.) Alternatively, it could be that patent X does something different than what patent Y does but utilizes a similar method to that used by patent Y, albeit for a different purpose. (You built a better mousetrap by putting titanium in the spring; I built a better jack-in-the-box by putting titanium in the spring.)[6] We refer to the first of these possibilities as "related application" and the second as "related technology." As a first indication of the meaning of citations, we explore the extent to which the inventors perceive that patents linked by citation are related along these two dimensions.

---

6. In principle, the case where X does the same thing as Y, and does it in the same way, should not be observed, as in that case X is not novel and should not be patentable.

Figures 1a and 1b show the distribution of responses for the citing inventors (combining their answers to the two patents that they cited) and for the cited inventors. Figure 1a presents the perceived relatedness in technology, and figure 1b the perceived relatedness in application. Overall, 44% of the citations did not rank above 2 on either relatedness dimension. This suggests a fair amount of noise in the citations, a theme that will recur throughout this paper. At the other extreme, only 14% of the citations were rated at 4 or greater on either relatedness dimension. In addition, the two dimensions of relatedness are highly correlated, with a correlation coefficient of 0.62.

As expected, the cited inventors tend to see a much higher degree of relatedness between the citing and cited patents than do the citing inventors. From their perspective, only 25% of the pairs score 2 or less on both relatedness dimensions, while 37% score 4 or more on at least one dimension. Overall, the mean relatedness in application is 2.6 as perceived by the citing inventors and 3.3 as perceived by the cited inventors; the corresponding means for relatedness of technology are 2.6 and 3.2. Further, for the 56 citation pairs where these questions were answered by both the citing and cited inventors, the correlation between the different inventors' answers is not very high (.14 for related application and .33 for related technology). Indeed, the correlation between the *citing* inventor's rating on relatedness of *technology* and the *cited* inventor's rating on relatedness in *application* is higher (.37) than the correlation of their answers to the same questions. This, combined with the high correlation across questions for a given respondent leads us to believe that the respondents were not quite able to distinguish clearly between these two dimensions. For this reason, we combined the two answers to form a composite relatedness score that runs from 2 to 10. Figure 2 shows the distribution of this composite score for the cited patents (using the answers of both the citing and cited inventors) and for the placebo patents. Despite the apparent ambiguity in the meaning of the questions and the relatively low consistency of answers for the matched pairs, it does seem that the citations are clearly different from the placebos. Fully two-thirds of the placebos were judged unrelated on *both* dimensions (composite Likert score = 2), and only 10% merited a composite score of 5 or more, in contrast to 50% of the citations meriting composite scores of 5 or more, even as judged by the citing inventors.

The conclusion that we draw from these questions is that a cited patent is significantly more likely to be perceived as related by tech-

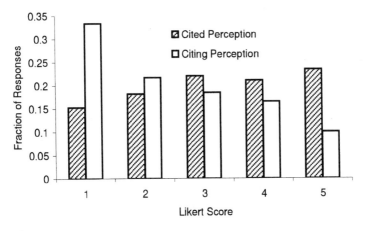

Figure 1a
Perceived similarity of technology between citing and cited patents

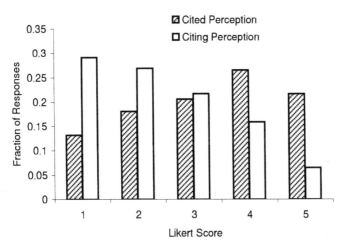

Figure 1b
Perceived similarity of application between citing and cited patents

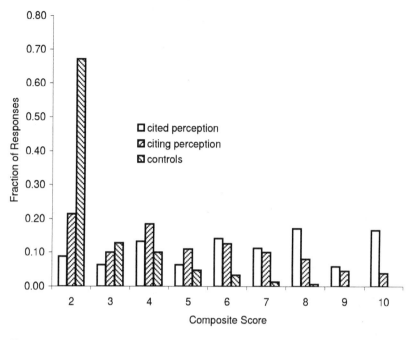

Figure 2
Distribution of composite "relatedness" index

nology and application than a contemporaneous uncited patent in the same technology field. It does appear, however, that a significant fraction of citations are to patents judged by the inventors themselves to be unrelated, even if the judgment is made by the cited inventor. Further, the concepts of related application and related technology do not seem to have been successfully distinguished by the questionnaires. It is unclear whether this is because they are not effectively distinct concepts or because the questionnaires were not sufficiently clear about the distinction between them.

4   Results Regarding Extent, Timing and Nature of Communication

General Responses on Sources of Invention

Question 6 in both surveys asked the inventors to check off one or two "significant influences on the development of your invention." Figure 3 shows the fraction of respondents who selected each of the

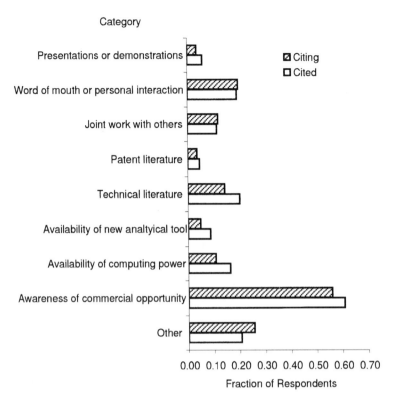

Figure 3
Significant influences on the development of inventions

named influences. Not surprisingly, by far the most frequently noted influence is "awareness of commercial opportunity," noted by almost 60% of all respondents. "Technological opportunity," in the form of availability of computing power or new analytical tools, is cited by perhaps one-fifth of the inventors.[7] Influences that bear some connection to spillovers or communication are also frequently noted: word of mouth, personal interaction, or viewing a presentation or demonstration (about 25%); joint work with others (about 10%); and technical or patent literature (about 20%). The distribution of responses for the citing and cited inventors are generally similar, although the cited inventors (patents granted between 1985 and 1992) more often

---

7. A majority of the comments supplied in the "other" category also pertained to specific technical developments that facilitated the invention.

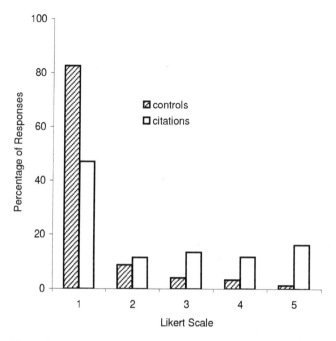

Figure 4
Distribution of answers to, How familiar are you with the previous invention?

noted technical literature, new analytical tools, and computing power than did the citing inventors (patents granted in 1993). Overall, the answers are generally consistent with expectations and confirm a significant role for spillovers.

Citing Inventor Responses

Figures 4–7 show the distribution of responses of the *citing* inventors to questions 7–10 regarding their communication with the cited inventors. Figure 4 gives responses on a 5-point Likert scale to a question regarding the overall degree of familiarity of the citing inventor with the cited invention. For the patents that were in fact cited, 28% of the responses indicated a 4 or 5 on the Likert scale, indicating high familiarity; just under half of the respondents rated their familiarity at the low end of the scale. In contrast, over 80% of the respondents rated their familiarity with the placebo patent at the lowest possible level.

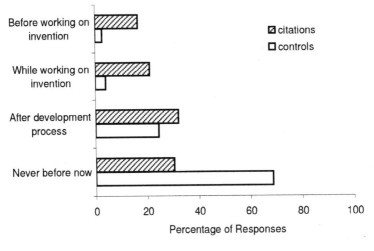

Figure 5
Distribution of answers to, When did you learn about the previous invention?

Figure 5 indicates the inventors' responses to a question regarding *when* they learned about the cited invention.[8] For the true citations, about 38% of respondents indicated that they had learned about the cited invention either before or during the development of their own invention. About one-third indicated that they had learned about it after essentially completing their invention. Partially on the basis of the responses to the next question, we believe that this includes a significant number of cases where they learned about the cited invention during the preparation of their own patent application. A little less than one-third indicated that, despite the presence of the patent citation, they had not learned about the cited invention before receiving our survey. This is not surprising, because citations to inventions unknown to the inventor can be generated by the inventor's patent attorney or the patent office examiner.

Figure 6 relates to a question regarding the mode of knowledge spillover. Even for the true citations, only about 18% indicated that they had had either direct communication or had been exposed to some kind of presentation or demonstration of the cited invention.

---

8. Specifically, the question asks when the inventor learned about the "research or work underlying the patented invention," in order to include the possibility that the inventor knew about the work without being familiar with the specific embodiment of that work captured in the cited patent.

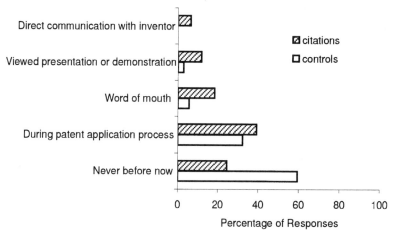

Figure 6
Distribution of answers to, How did you learn about the previous patent?

Another 18% indicated that they learned through "word of mouth" or had read the patent document itself. Consistent with the answers regarding timing, almost 40% indicated that the process of their own patent application had caused them to learn of the previous invention.

Figure 7 presents the distribution of answers to a question that, perhaps ambitiously, tried to get at the nature of assistance that the citing inventor may have received from the cited invention. Respondents were given a set of choices that we thought possible, and also invited to "write in" their own responses. About 60% of the respondents indicated some specific way in which they had benefited from the "cited" invention; the single most common response was that the cited invention represented a concept that could be improved upon. The "other" responses stated by the inventors provide some insight into the nature of possible interactions. Examples include the following:

"The technology from patent 1 was incorporated in the product which used my invention."

"New market for our new technology!"

"The other patents gave credibility to our idea—they showed our ideas were 'feasible' to the people not intimately involved in our idea."

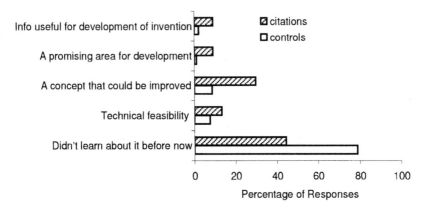

Figure 7
Distribution of answers to, What did you learn from the previous invention?

Other explanations confirmed that many citations derive from the patent process and probably are not related to any spillover:[9]

"Did not learn of patents before filing—therefore these patents were not a factor in our work."

"A patent cited by the patent examiner with no direct ties to my patent"

If these responses can be taken at face value (an issue we return to below), they suggest that a significant, but not preponderant, fraction of the links indicated by patent citations correspond to some kind of spillover. Across the different aspects captured by each of these questions, typically one-quarter of the responses correspond to a fairly clear spillover; perhaps one-half of the answers indicate no spillover, and the remaining quarter indicate some possibility of a spillover. It appears that addition of citations by the inventor's patent lawyer or the patent examiner is the primary reason for citations to patents unknown to the inventor.

Figures 4–7 strongly suggest that the extent of perceived spillover is greater for the cited patents than for the placebos. To explore this issue further, we constructed a composite spillover index for each

---

9. All of the quoted comments relate to the true citations. Interestingly, several of the inventors told us that the placebo patent, which we had described as a citation in order not to bias their responses, was a mistake, i.e., that they had not cited it. It is not possible for us to know if they knew this from memory or if they took the trouble to go back and check their actual patent document.

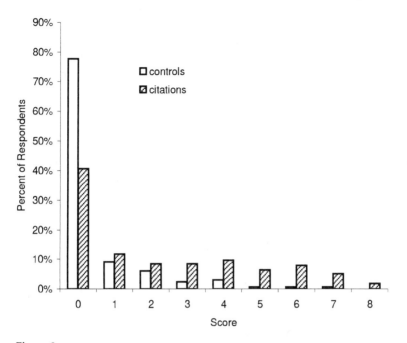

Figure 8
Distribution of composite spillover score

cited patent, using the answers to all 4 questions. This index was constructed by consolidating the possible answers to each question to produce a score of 0, 1, or 2, and then adding these scores across the 4 questions. The distribution of this composite spillover index for both the true citations and the placebos is shown in figure 8. Not surprisingly, the distribution of the composite index is more skewed than that of the individual questions. Figure 8 confirms the general pattern that the upper tail of the distribution for the true citations is much thicker than that for the placebos, and that about half of the citations are not distinguishable from the placebos.

Table 1 presents the results of an ordered probit analysis of this score, using as regressors variables that would seem likely to foster communication between the cited and citing inventors, variables that might foster the inventor's *remembering* that communication occurred, other controls, and a dummy variable for whether the score pertains to a true citation as opposed to a placebo. Columns 1 and 2 include the combined sample of citations and placebos. Column 3 looks only at the placebos, and columns 4 and 5 only at the citations.

Table 1
Ordered probit for spillover index

	All answers	All answers	Placebos only	True citations only	True citations only
True cited patent	0.861 **(.145)	0.511 **(.160)			
"Cited" grant year	0.016 (.012)	0.008 (.013)	−0.048 *(.024)	0.036 **(.014)	0.028 (.014)
Log of total citations received by cited patent	0.187 **(.071)	0.104 (.076)	0.202 (.153)	0.186 *(.081)	0.08 (.087)
Same state	0.414 *(.189)	0.418 *(.201)	0.196 (.461)	0.43 *(.210)	0.421 (.219)
Total citations made by citing patent	−0.0086 *(.0040)	−0.0072 (.0042)	−0.019 (.012)	−0.007 (.004)	−0.006 (.005)
Chemicals and Drugs	0.258 (.169)	0.375 *(.177)	−0.208 (.370)	0.383 *(.194)	0.465 (.202)
Electronics, Computers and Communication	−0.503 **(.128)	−0.451 **(.135)	−0.288 (.265)	−0.558 **(.147)	−0.508 (.154)
Technology relatedness		0.174 **(.061)			0.141 *(.064)
Application relatedness		0.264 **(.056)			0.248 **(.059)
Dependent mean	1.68	1.77	0.53	2.21	2.3
No. of observations	467	429	148	319	297

Excluded technology group is Mechanical and Other. Figures in parenthese are standard errors.
* = significant at 0.95 level; ** = significant at 0.99 level.

Overall, the results confirm that citations can be interpreted as providing a (noisy) signal of spillovers. The difference in spillover score between the citations and placebos is quantitatively and statistically significant. The other variables generally have plausible and often significant effects. Overall, the spillover score is higher if the cited patent is more recent. Interestingly, columns 4 and 5 show that this combined effect mixes a significantly positive effect for the citations with a significantly negative effect for the placebos. For the citations, this is consistent with more recent patents being more useful and older citations being more likely to be nonspillovers included by the lawyer or examiner. It could also reflect the possibility that the inventor's memory of actual communication is better with respect to more recent technology. Conversely, for the placebos, the spillover index is *lower* the more recent the cited invention. Since these represent patents that *were not* cited, there should not have been communication. Thus the negative coefficient for the placebos is consistent with the inventors' giving more accurate answers with respect to more recent patents and more often mistakenly indicating communication with respect to older patents.

We included the (log of) total citations received by the cited patent to control for the overall importance of that patent. Its positive effect means that more important patents are perceived to have generated greater spillovers, either because the spillovers are truly greater or because these patents are more likely to be remembered by the respondent. Similarly, cited patents whose inventors reside in the same state are perceived to have generated greater spillovers. We interpret the *lack of* a significant effect for these two variables when looking only at the placebos as further confirming that citations are meaningful, in the sense that the perceived extent of spillovers is correlated with variables that *ought* to be linked with spillovers for the true citations but is uncorrelated with these same variables for the placebos. We also included the total number of citations *made* by the citing (i.e., responding) patent, to control for the possibility that the inventor would have difficulty remembering or sorting out the effect of any one cited patent, if many were cited. And indeed, citations made has the predicted negative effect.

The effects for technology fields are reasonably large and statistically significant within the citations group. There are two slightly different interpretations of this result. One is that spillovers are simply greater, on average, in Chemicals and Drugs, and less in Electronics and Computers and Communications (C&C), with the Mechanical and Other group being intermediate. A slightly different interpretation is that what varies by field is the extent to which patent citations are a good indicator of spillovers. Under this latter interpretation, the results would be consistent with the conventional wisdom that the general importance or centrality of patents in the innovation system is highest in Chemicals and Drugs and lowest in Electronics and C&C.

Finally, columns 3 and 6 add to the regressors the inventors' perceptions regarding the relatedness of the patent pair, as reflected in the answers to questions 11 and 12 discussed above. Both of these have a significant positive association with the perceived extent of

spillovers, whether looked at in the combined sample or for the citations alone.[10] Again, there are two possible interpretations to this result. One is that related patents are more likely to generate spillovers.
The other is that these concepts are not clearly distinguished in the
respondents' minds, or their memories are hazy, so that they are
more likely to indicate the presence of spillovers if the inventions are
related, or more likely to indicate relatedness if they remember
communication.

Comparison of Citing and Cited Inventors' Perceptions

By definition, the acknowledgement of a spillover from a cited inventor to a citing inventor diminishes to some extent the perceived
accomplishment of the latter and augments the accomplishment of
the former. For this reason, we would expect that the citing inventors
would tend to underestimate the extent of spillovers and the cited
inventors would tend to overestimate it. By asking both the citing
and cited inventors to evaluate the likelihood of spillover, we hoped
to probe the extent to which the citing inventors' admissions of spillover might understate their true dependence on the cited inventions.

Overall, the results for the *cited* inventors do indeed suggest a
greater degree of perceived spillovers. In particular, question 9 of the
cited-inventor survey ("What is the likelihood that the citing inventors were aware of or relied upon knowledge of your work?") is
qualitatively symmetric to question 7 in the citing inventor survey
("Indicate the degree to which you were familiar with the research
being conducted by [the cited research lab]"). As expected, the mean
Likert response by the cited inventors was 3.2, compared to 2.5 for
the citing-inventor responses shown in figure 4. Of course, it is impossible to determine the extent to which the difference is due to
understatement by the citing inventors or overstatement by the cited
inventors, or possibly connected to the slightly different wording of
the two questions.

In addition to comparing the means, we can examine the correlation between the evaluations of the cited and citing inventors for
those cases where both responded with respect to a given citation
link. Unfortunately, we have only 72 such matched pairs, and only

---

10. These variables are also significant within the placebo group (results not
reported).

61 of these contain responses to all of the questions discussed in this section. For these pairs, the correlation between the cited inventor's answer to question 9 with the citing inventor's answers to the various spillover questions is typically about .25. While this correlation is high enough to suggest that the survey responses are consistent at least in this sense, it reminds us that the responses are themselves only noisy indicators of the true underlying process.

Two other questions in the cited inventor survey provide some insight into the extent of spillovers, as perceived by their presumed "source." Question 7 asks about the cited inventors' knowledge of the research of the citing inventors. About 14% of the cited inventors indicated that they knew that the citing inventor was engaged in this kind of research. About 10% either knew that research of this sort was underway but didn't know who was doing it, or knew of the citing inventor but not that they were working on the citing invention. Approximately three-fourths indicated knowledge of the citing inventors or their research. Question 8 asks about memory of communication with the citing inventor. About 80% of the cited inventors indicated that they had no knowledge of communication with the citing inventor, 9% did remember communication, and 9% were not sure.

In comparing these responses to those of the citing inventors, there are presumably two offsetting effects. While the cited inventors may generally have a greater tendency to indicate communication than the citing inventors, some forms of communication (e.g., reading the cited inventor's papers) occur without the knowledge of the cited inventor. In figure 6 about 6% of citing inventors reported "direct communication" with the cited inventor, and another 12% indicated that they had viewed a presentation or a demonstration. Since the citing inventor's viewing a demonstration or presentation might or might not be something that the cited inventor would know about, this seems quite consistent with both the 14% of cited inventors who knew the citing inventors and their work, and the range of 9%–18% for the fraction of cited inventors who believe that communication occurred.

5   Citations and Perceived Importance

In addition to the use of individual citation links as possible evidence of knowledge flow, a number of authors have utilized the total number of citations received by a patent as an indicator of the relative significance of patents.[11] Both our citing-inventor and cited-inventor surveys asked the inventors to rate the "technological significance" and the "economic importance" of the inventions, and also asked whether the patent had been licensed and whether it had been commercialized. Table 2 examines the extent to which each of these different concepts of importance are associated with highly cited patents. In addition, we constructed a composite index of importance by adding up scores on each of the 4 questions in a manner similar to what was described above for the spillover questions.

Each column reports the regression of the log of total citations received on a particular indicator of importance. For this purpose, the citing and cited responses were combined into one data set. To control for variations in citation practice by field and changes in propensity to cite and extent of truncation over time, all regressions include technology-field and grant-year dummy variables. In addition, because of the findings of Lanjouw and Schankerman (1999), we also included the log of the number of claims made by each patent, to allow for the possibility that patents containing more claims are more highly cited.

The results do provide some evidence that citations are correlated with significance or importance as perceived by the inventors themselves. Each of the indicators is positively correlated with log citations, with the coefficients achieving t-statistics that vary from just below to just above 2, depending on the question. Not surprisingly, use of the composite index slightly increases the significance of the correlation. There is no particular indication as to whether citations are more associated with technological or economic significance. The claims variable is strongly significant, though its elasticity of about .25 suggests strong diminishing returns with an increasing number of claims, as distinct from the constant-returns relationship suggested by Lanjouw and Schankerman (1999). If the number of claims is excluded from the regression (column 6), the effect of the perceived-importance variable increases, which suggests that importance, as perceived by the inventor, reflects both the "size" of the patent, as indicated by the number of claims, and the importance or significance of each of the claims.

---

11. See, for example, Trajtenberg 1990 and Henderson, Jaffe, and Trajtenberg 1998. For a discussion of citations as one of several indicators of patent importance, see Lanjouw and Schankerman 1999.

Table 2
Citations received as a function of inventors' perception of importance

	Technological significance[a]	Economic importance[b]	Licensed[c]	Commercialized[d]	Composite index[e]	Composite index[e]
Importance indicator	0.073	0.076	0.098	0.089	0.041	0.05
	(.038)	*(.035)	(.051)	(.051)	*(.019)	*(.020)
Log of claims	0.241	0.239	0.243	0.251	0.25	
	**(.054)	**(0.054)	**(.053)	**(.053)	**(.052)	
No. of observations	367	364	368	344	380	380
R^2	0.237	0.24	0.237	0.262	0.242	0.195
Indicator mean	3.6	3.3	0.86	2.3	4.8	4.8

Dependent variable is log of citations received. All equations also include dummies for each year and technology field (6 fields). Figures in parentheses are standard errors.
* = significant at 0.95 level; ** = significant at 0.99 level.
a. Likert scale (5 point).
b. Likert scale (5 point).
c. "No" = 0, "maybe" = 1, and "yes" = 2.
d. "Not incorporated in any product or process" = 0; "Incorporated in commercially unsuccessful product or process" = 1; "Incorporated in product or process; too soon to tell if successful" = 2; "Incorporated in a commercially successful product or process" = 3.
e. Sum of technological significance, economic importance, licensed, and commercialized.

6 Concluding Remarks

Many of the important concepts in the economics of technological change are fundamentally unobservable. We therefore routinely rely on proxies or indicators for the concepts of interest. Often our only test of the validity of these measures is the extent to which the correlation of the proxies with other variables matches the pattern of correlations predicted by theory. In this chapter we provide an additional kind of evidence about the unobservable process of knowledge flow and the relationship of patent citations to that process. While survey evidence has its own limitations, including small sample sizes and the biases of the survey respondents, it allows us to get "inside the black box" and potentially achieve a richer and deeper understanding of the processes that we are studying.

The results suggest a "cup half full" with respect to the validity of patent citations as indicators of knowledge spillovers. If we take the responses at face value, the likelihood of knowledge spillover, if there is a patent citation, is significantly greater (in both the statistical and quantitative senses) than the likelihood without a citation. Nonetheless, a large fraction of citations, perhaps something like one half, do not correspond to any apparent spillover. We believe that these results are consistent with the notion that citations are a noisy signal of the presence of spillovers. This implies that aggregate citation flows can be used as proxies for knowledge-spillover intensity, for example, between categories of organizations or between geographic regions. Further work is needed, however, to refine our understanding of the mechanisms by which these flows move and the relationship of those mechanisms to the citation process.

More generally, our results provide some context for the widely held view that invention is a cumulative process where inventors build in important ways on the work that came before them. They suggest a possibly significant role for direct communication between inventors as part of this cumulative process. Clearly, more work is needed in this area, both to assess the importance of communication and to understand its determinants. In particular, our survey says nothing about what attributes of inventors or technologies influence the extent to which different kinds of communication are used or are effective. For future work, consideration should be given to collecting more information about the inventors themselves, so that these relationships can begin to be explored.

References

Griliches, Zvi. 1979. "Issues in Assessing the Contribution of R&D to Productivity Growth." *Bell Journal of Economics* 10: 92–116.

Helper, Susan. 2000. "Economists and Field Research: 'You Can Observe a Lot Just by Watching'." *American Economic Association Papers and Proceedings*, forthcoming.

Henderson, Rebecca, Adam B. Jaffe, and Manuel Trajtenberg. 1998. "Universities as a Source of Commercial Technology: A Detailed Analysis of University Patenting, 1965–1988." *Review of Economics and Statistics* 80: 119–127.

Jaffe, Adam B., Manuel Trajtenberg, and Rebecca Henderson. 1993. "Geographic Localization of Knowledge Spillovers as Evidenced by Patent Citations." *Quarterly Journal of Economics* 108: 577–598.

Jaffe, Adam B., Michael S. Fogarty, and Bruce A. Banks. 1998. "Evidence from Patent Citations on the Impact of NASA and Other Federal Labs on Commercial Innovation." *Journal of Industrial Economics* 46: 183–206.

Lanjouw, Jean O., and Mark Schankerman. 1999. "The Quality of Ideas: Measuring Innovation with Multiple Indicators." National Bureau of Economic Research, working paper no. 7345.

Trajtenberg, Manuel. 1990. "A Penny for Your Quotes: Patent Citations and the Value of Innovations." *Rand Journal of Economics* 21: 172–187.

13   The NBER Patent-Citations Data File: Lessons, Insights, and Methodological Tools

Bronwyn H. Hall, Adam B.
Jaffe, and Manuel Trajtenberg

1   Introduction

The goal of this chapter is to describe the data base on U.S. patents
that we have developed over the past decade, so as to make it widely
accessible for research. In so doing, we discuss key issues that arise
in the use of patent-citation data and suggest ways of addressing
them. We also present some of the main trends in patenting over the
last 30 years, including a variety of original measures constructed
with citation data, such as indices of "originality" and "generality,"
self-citations, backward and forward citation lags, etc. Many of these
measures exhibit interesting differences across the six main technological categories that we have developed (comprising Computers
and Communications, Drugs and Medical, Electrical and Electronics,
Chemical, Mechanical, and Others).

Broadly speaking, the data comprise detailed information on almost 3 million U.S. patents granted between January 1963 and December 1999, all citations made to these patents between 1975 and
1999 (over 16 million), and a reasonably broad match of patents to
Compustat (the data set of all firms traded on the U.S. stock market).
As it stands now, the data file is fully functional and can be used
with relative ease with standard software such as SAS or Access. We
hope that the availability of patent data in this format will encourage
researchers to use these data extensively, and thus make patent data
a staple of research in economics.

This represents the culmination of a long-term research and data-
creation effort that involved a wide range of researchers (primarily
the present authors, Rebecca Henderson, and Michael Fogarty), institutions (NBER, REI at Case-Western, Tel-Aviv University), program-
mers (Meg Fernando, Abi Rubin, and Adi Raz), research assistants

(notably Guy Michaels and Michael Katz), and financial resources (primarily from various NSF grants). We hope that the contribution of these data to present and future research in economics will justify the magnitude of the investment made.

Patents have long been recognized as a very rich and potentially fruitful source of data for the study of innovation and technical change. Indeed, there are numerous advantages to the use of patent data:

• Each patent contains highly detailed information on the innovation itself, the technological area to which it belongs, the inventors (e.g., their geographical location), the assignee, etc. Moreover, patents have very wide coverage (in terms of fields, types of inventors, etc.). And during the last three decades U.S. patents increasingly reflect not only inventive activity in the U.S. itself, but also around the world.[1]

• There are a very large number of patents, each of which constitutes a highly detailed observation: the stock of patents is currently in excess of 6 million, and the flow comprises over 150,000 patents per year (as of 1999–2000). Thus the wealth of data potentially available for research is huge.

• Patents have been granted in the U.S. continuously since the late eighteenth century. The current numbering and reporting system dates to the 1870s, which means that there are (in principle) over 100 years of consistently reported data.

• In contrast to other types of economic information, the data contained in patents are supplied entirely on a voluntary basis, and the incentives to do so are plain and clear. After all, the whole idea of patents is that they constitute a "package deal," namely, the grant of temporary monopoly rights in exchange for *disclosure*.

• Patent data include citations to previous patents and to the scientific literature. These citations open up the possibility of tracing multiple linkages between inventions, inventors, scientists, firms, locations, etc. In particular, patent citations allow one to study spillovers and to create indicators of the "importance" of individual patents, thus allowing one to capture the enormous heterogeneity in the value of patents.

---

1. The percentage of U.S. patents awarded to foreign inventors has risen from about 20% in the early sixties to about 45% in the late 1990s.

There are also serious limitations to the use of patent data, the most glaring being the fact that not all inventions are patented. First, not all inventions meet the patentability criteria set by the U.S. Patent and Trademark Office (USPTO): the invention has to be novel, to be nontrivial, and to have commercial application. Second, the inventor has to make a strategic decision to patent, as opposed to rely on secrecy or other means of appropriability. Unfortunately, we have very little idea of the extent to which patents are representative of the wider universe of inventions, since there is no systematic data about inventions that are not patented. This is an important, wide-open area for future research. Another problem that used to be a serious hindrance stemmed from the fact that the patent file was not entirely computerized. Furthermore, until not long ago it was extremely difficult to handle those chunks that were computerized, because of the very large size of the data. In fact, the whole feasibility of this data-construction project was called into question (certainly at the beginning of this endeavor, in the early 1990s), because of these problems. However, rapid progress in computer technology has virtually eliminated these difficulties, so much so that at present all the data reside in personal computers and can be analyzed with the aid of standard PC software.

The idea of using patent data on a large scale for economic research goes back at least to Schmookler (1966), followed by Scherer (1982), and Griliches (1984).[2] The work of Schmookler involved assigning patent counts to industries (by creating a concordance between patent subclasses and Standard Industrial Classifications [SICs]), whereas Griliches' research program at the NBER entailed matching patents to Compustat firms. In both cases the only data item used, aside from the match itself, was the timing of the patent (the grant or application year), so that in the end the patent data available for research consisted only of patent counts by industries or firms, by year. Of course, what make these data valuable is their being *linked out* to other data, so that patents could then be related to the wealth of information available on the industries/firms themselves. The project that Scherer undertook involved classifying a sample of 15,000 patents into industry of origin and industries of use, by the textual

---

2. This is by no means a survey of patent-related work. Rather, we just note the key data-focused research projects that put forward distinctive methodologies and had a significant impact on further research. For a survey of research using patent data, see Griliches (1990).

examination of each patent. The result was a detailed technology-flow matrix that again could be linked to other data, such as R&D expenditures and productivity growth.

One of the major drawbacks of these and related research programs, extremely valuable as they were, was that they relied exclusively on simple patent counts as indicators of some sort of innovative output. However, it has long been known that innovations vary enormously in their technological and economic importance, significance, or value and, moreover, that the distribution of such values is extremely skewed. The line of research initiated by Schankerman and Pakes (1986) using patent renewal data clearly revealed these features of the patent data (see also Pakes and Simpson 1991). Thus, simple patent counts were seriously and inherently limited in the extent to which they could faithfully capture and summarize the underlying heterogeneity (see Griliches, Hall, and Pakes 1987). A related drawback was, of course, that these projects did not make use of any of the other data items contained in the patents themselves, and could not do so, given the stringent limitations on data availability at the time.

Keenly aware of the need to overcome these limitations and of the intriguing possibilities held by patent citations, we realized that a major data-construction effort was called for. Encouraged by the novel finding that citations appear to be correlated with the value of innovations (Trajtenberg 1990), we undertook work aimed primarily at demonstrating the potential usefulness of citations for a variety of purposes: as indicators of spillovers (Jaffe, Trajtenberg, and Henderson 1993; Caballero and Jaffe 1993), and as ingredients in the construction of measures for other features of innovations, such as "originality" and "generality" (Trajtenberg, Jaffe, and Henderson 1997). For each of these projects we used samples of patent data that were acquired and constructed with a single, specific purpose in mind. As the data requirements grew, however, we came to the conclusion that it was extremely inefficient if not impossible to carry out a serious research agenda on such a piecewise basis.

In particular, the inversion problem that arises when using citations received called for an all-out solution. The inversion problem refers to the fact that the original data on citations come in the form of citations *made* (i.e., each patent lists references to previous patents), whereas for many of the uses (certainly for assessing the importance of patents) one needs data on citations *received*. The trouble is that to obtain the citations received by any *one* patent granted in year t, one needs to search the references made by *all* patents granted after year *t*. Thus, any study using citations received, however small the sample of patents is, requires in fact access to all citation data in a way that permits efficient search and extraction of citations. This means being able to invert the citations data, sorting it not by the patent number of the *citing* patent but by the patent number of the *cited* patent. This inherent indivisibility led us to aim for a comprehensive data-construction effort.[3]

The paper is organized as follows: Section 2 describes the data in detail and presents summary statistics (primarily via charts) for each of the main variables. Since these statistics are computed on the basis of *all* the data, the intention is both to provide benchmark figures that may be referred to in future research, as well as to highlight trends and stylized facts that call for further study. Section 3 discusses the problems that arise with the use of citation data, because of truncation and other changes over time in the citation process. We outline two ways of dealing with these issues: a "fixed-effects" approach and a structural-econometric one.

2 Description of the Data

Scope, Contents, and Sources of the Data

The main data set extends from January 1, 1963, through December 30, 1999 (37 years), and includes all the *utility* patents granted during that period, totaling 2,923,922 patents;[4] we shall refer to this data set as PAT63_99. This file includes two main sets of variables: those that came from the Patent Office ("original" variables) and those that we created from them ("constructed" variables). The citations file, CITE75_99, includes all citations made by patents granted in 1975–

---

3. It is interesting to note that in the early 1990s this enterprise seemed rather far-fetched, given the state (and costs) of computer technology at the time: the patent data as provided then by the Patent Office occupied about 60 magnetic tapes, and the inversion procedure (of millions of citations) would have necessitated computer resources beyond our reach. However, along the way both computers and data availability improved fast enough to make this project feasible.

4. In addition to utility patents, there are three other minor patent categories: design, reissue, and plant patents. The overwhelming majority are utility patents: in 1999 the number of utility patents granted reached 153,493, versus just 14,732 for design patents, 448 reissue patents, and 421 plant patents. Our data do not include these other categories.

1999, totaling 16,522,438 citations. In addition, we have detailed data on inventors, assignees, etc. The patent data themselves were procured from the Patent Office, except for the citations from patents granted in 1999, which come from MicroPatent. The PAT63_99 file occupies less than 500 MB (in Access or in SAS), the CITE75_99 about 260 MB. The contents of these files are as follows:

PAT63_99
Original Variables[5]

1. Patent number

2. Grant year

3. Grant date[6]

4. Application year (starting in 1967)

5. Country of first inventor

6. State of first inventor (if U.S.)

7. Assignee identifier, if the patent was assigned (which started in 1969)

8. Assignee type (i.e., individual, corporate, or government; foreign or domestic)

9. Main U.S. patent class

10. Number of claims (which started in 1975)

Constructed variables

1. Technological category

2. Technological subcategory

3. Number of citations made

4. Number of citations received

5. Percent of citations made by this patent to patents granted since 1963[7]

---

5. We also have the patent subclass and the SICs that the Patent Office matched to each patent. However, we have not used these data so far, and they are not included in the PAT63_99 file.

6. Number of days elapsed since January 1, 1960.

7. That is, for each patent we compute the following ratio: number of citations made to patents granted since 1963 divided by the total number of citations made. The point is that older citations are not in our data, and hence for purposes such as computing the measure of originality, the actual computation is done only on the basis of the post-1963 citations. However, one needs to know to what extent such calculations are partial.

6. Measure of generality

7. Measure of originality

8. Mean forward citation lag

9. Mean backward citation lag

10. Percentage of self-citations made, upper and lower bounds

CITE75_99

1. Citing patent number

2. Cited patent number

The "Inventors" file

This file contains the full names and addresses of each of the multiple inventors listed in each patent (most patents indeed have multiple inventors, the average being over 2 per patent). The names of the inventors and their geographical locations offer a very rich resource for research that has yet to be fully exploited.

The "Coname" file

1. Assignee identifier (numerical code, as it appears in PAT63_99)

2. Full assignee name

The Compustat match file

See below.

Dating of Patents, and the Application-Grant Lag

Each patent document includes the date when the inventor filed for the patent (the *application* date) and the date when the patent was granted. Our data contains the grant *date* and the grant *year* of all patents in the file (i.e., of all utility patents granted since 1963) and the application *year* for patents granted since 1967.[8] Clearly, the actual timing of patented inventions is closer to the application date than to the (subsequent) grant date. This is so because inventors have a strong incentive to apply for a patent as soon as possible following the completion of the innovation, whereas the grant date depends upon the review process at the Patent Office, which takes on average about 2

---

8. Actually, the grant year can be retrieved from the patent numbers, since these numbers are given sequentially along time. Moreover, the Patent Office publishes a table indicating the first and last patent number of each grant year.

years, with a significant variance (see table 1). Indeed, the mode of operation of the Patent Office underwent significant changes in the past decades, thereby introducing a great deal of randomness (which has nothing to do with the actual timing of the inventions) into any patent time series dated by grant year.

Thus, and whenever possible, the application date should be used as the relevant time placer for patents.[9] On the other hand, one has to be mindful in that case of the *truncation* problem: as the time moves closer to the last date in the data set,[10] patent data timed according to the application date will increasingly suffer from missing observations consisting of patents filed in recent years that have not yet been granted. Table 1 shows the distribution of application-grant lags for selected subperiods, as well as the mean lag and its standard deviation.[11] Overall, the lags have shortened significantly, from an average of 2.4 years in the late 1960s to 1.8 years in the early 1990s, as the number of patents examined (and granted) more than doubled. Notice, however, that the trend was not monotonic: during the early 1980s the lags in fact lengthened, but shortened again in the second half of the 1980s and early 1990s. Notice also that the percentage granted 2 years after filing is about 85% (for recent cohorts), and after 3 years about 95%. Thus, it is advisable to take at least a 3-year "safety lag" when dating patents according to application year, and/or to control for truncation, for example by including dummies for years.

Number of Patents

Figure 1 shows the annual number of patents granted by application year, and figure 2 the number of patents by grant year. The extent of the truncation problem can be clearly seen in figure 1 for the years 1996–1999: the sharp drop in the series is just an artifact reflecting the fact that the data include patents granted up to the end of 1999, and hence for the years just before that we observe only those patent applications that were granted relatively fast, but not all those other patents that will be granted afterwards. The series in figure 1 are

---

9. The series for the patent variables that we present below are indeed mostly by application year and include data up to 1997. Because we have patents granted only up to December 1999, truncation leaves too few applications for 1998 and 1999.

10. For our data this date is December 1999.

11. The figures presented there may still suffer slightly from truncation: there probably are patents applied for in 1990–1992 that still were not granted by December 1999.

Table 1
Application-grant lag distribution by 3-year subperiods

Lag (years)	Application years							
	1967–69	1970–72	1973–75	1976–79	1980–82	1983–85	1986–89	1990–92
	Distribution of lags (in %)							
0	0.4	0.1	1.0	1.0	0.2	1.0	1.8	2.6
1	11.3	19.9	40.1	32.5	18.0	26.6	40.4	40.4
2	48.7	59.8	48.2	51.0	51.1	49.4	43.6	42.0
3	32.0	16.2	8.0	11.9	24.1	16.7	10.6	11.1
4	5.6	2.4	1.5	2.0	4.0	3.7	2.5	2.3
5	1.0	0.9	0.6	0.8	1.2	1.5	0.7	0.7
6	0.4	0.3	0.2	0.4	0.7	0.7	0.2	0.4
7+	0.5	0.3	0.3	0.3	0.7	0.4	0.2	0.4
Total	100.0	100.0	100.0	100.0	100.0	100.0	100.0	100.0
Mean and standard deviation of the lag (years)								
Mean	2.39	2.08	1.74	1.88	2.25	2.05	1.76	1.76
S.d.	1.02	0.93	0.91	0.93	1.02	1.02	0.90	0.95

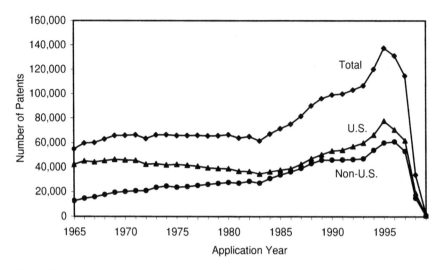

Figure 1
Number of patents by application year

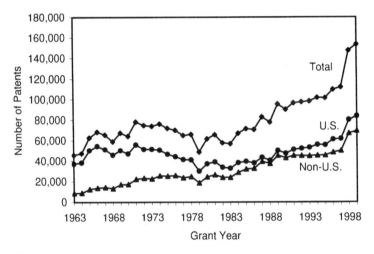

Figure 2
Number of patents by grant year

Table 2
Types of assignees by which the USPTO classifies patents

1	Unassigned	18.4%
Assigned to		
2	U.S. nongovernment organizations (mostly corporations)	47.2%
3	Non-U.S. nongovernment organizations (mostly corporations)	31.2%
4	U.S. individuals	0.8%
5	Non-U.S. individuals	0.3%
6	U.S. federal government	1.7%
7	Non-U.S. governments	0.4%

smoother than those in figure 2, reflecting the changing length of the examination process at the Patent Office, which causes the series dated by granting date to vary from year to year in a rather haphazard way.

Figure 1 shows that the total number of successful patent applications remained roughly constant up to 1983, oscillating around 65,000 annually, and then took off dramatically, reaching almost 140,000 in the mid 1990s. In terms of patents granted, the single most pronounced changed occurred between 1997 and 1998, when the number of patents granted increased by almost 1/3 (from 112K to 148K). In terms of composition, the number of patents granted to U.S. inventors actually declined up to 1983, but this decline was almost exactly compensated for by the increase in the number of patents granted to foreigners. Despite these differences for the pre-1983 period, the acceleration that started in 1983 applies to both U.S. and foreign inventors (see Kortum and Lerner 1998). Note in figure 2 that the turning point there (according to grant year) would appear to have occurred in 1979, but this just reflects the application-grant lag (and changes in that respect) and not a real phenomenon.

Types of Assignees

The USPTO classifies patents by type of assignees, into the seven categories in table 2 (the figures are the percentages of each of these categories in our data).

"Unassigned" patents are those for which the inventors have not yet granted the rights to the invention to a legal entity such as a corporation, university, or government agency, or to other individuals.

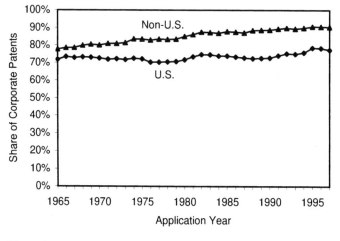

Figure 3
Share of patents assigned to corporations

These patents were thus still owned by the original inventors at the time of patenting, and they may or may have not transferred their patent rights at a later time (we do not have data on transfers done after the grant date). By far the vast majority of patents (78.4%) are assigned to corporations,[12] and another 18.4% are unassigned. Of the remaining ones, 2.1% are assigned to government agencies, and 1.1% to individuals. This later category is thus unimportant, and for practical purposes can be regarded as part of the "unassigned" category. As figure 3 shows, the percentage of corporate patents for U.S. inventions increased slightly over the period from 72% to 77%, whereas for foreign patents the increase was much steeper, from 78% in 1965 to 90% in 1997. The increase in the share of corporate inventions reflects the long-term raising dominance of corporations as the locus of innovation and the concomitant relative decline of individual inventors.

Technological Fields

The USPTO has developed over the years a highly elaborate classification system for the technologies to which the patented inventions belong, consisting of about 400 main (3-digit) patent classes,[13] and

12. The category refers to "nongovernment organizations," which consists overwhelmingly of business entities (i.e., corporations), but also includes universities.
13. There were 417 classes in the 1999 classification, which is the one we use.

over 120,000 patent subclasses. This system is continuously being updated, reflecting the rapid changes in the technologies themselves, with new patent classes being added and others being reclassified and discarded.[14] Each patent is assigned to an "original" classification (class and subclass) and to any number of subsidiary classes and subclasses. For the vast majority of uses one is likely to resort only to the original 3-digit patent class, and hence we include only it in the PAT63_99 file.

Furthermore, even 400 classes are far too many for most applications (such as serving as controls in regressions), and hence we have developed a higher-level classification, by which the 400 classes are aggregated into 36 two-digit technological sub-categories, and these in turn are further aggregated into 6 main categories: Chemical (excluding Drugs); Computers and Communications (C&C); Drugs and Medical (D&M); Electrical and Electronics (E&E); Mechanical; and Others (see appendix 1). Of course, there is always an element of arbitrariness in devising an aggregation system and in assigning the patent classes into the various technological categories, and there is no guarantee that the resulting classification is right or adequate for most uses. For example, we found that within the category Drugs and Medical there is a high degree of heterogeneity between subcategories in some of the dimensions explored: the subcategory Drugs (no. 31) exhibits a much higher percentage of self-citations than the others, and Biotechnology (no. 32) scores significantly higher in terms of generality and originality. Thus, we suggest that while convenient, the present classification should be used with great care and critically reexamined for specific applications.

Figure 4 shows the number of patents in each of the six technological categories over time by application year. Figure 5 expresses these numbers as shares of total patents. The changes are quite dramatic: the three traditional fields (Chemical, Mechanical, and Others) have experienced a steady decline over the past 3 decades, from about 25% to less than 20% each. The big winner has been Computers and Communications, which rose steeply from 5% in the 1960s to 20% in the late 1990s, and also Drugs and Medical, which went from 2% to over 10%. The only stable field is Electrical and Electronics, holding

---

14. From time to time the Patent Office reassigns patents retroactively to patent classes according to the most recent patent classification system. Therefore, one has to be careful when jointly using data files created at different times or when adding recent patents to older sets.

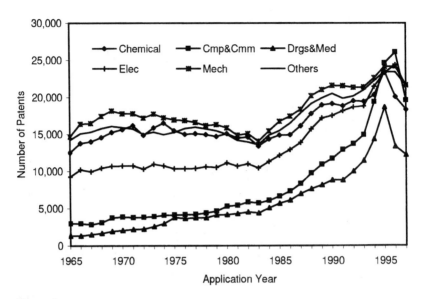

Figure 4
Distribution of patents by technological categories (absolute numbers)

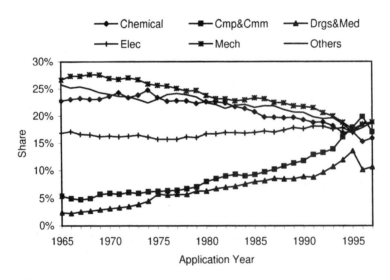

Figure 5
Distribution of patents by technological categories (shares)

steady at 16%–18%. All told, the 3 traditional fields dropped from 76% of the total in 1965 to 54% in 1997. (Their share of 1999 grants was just 51%.) This clearly reflects the much-heralded "technological revolution" of our times, associated with the rise of information technologies and the growing importance of health care technologies.

Figure 4 reveals yet another aspect of these changes: the *absolute* number of patents in the traditional fields (Chemical, Mechanical, and Others) declined slightly up to 1983 (certainly during the late seventies) and then increased by 20%–30%. By contrast, the emerging fields of Computers and Communications and Drugs and Medical increased throughout the whole period, with a marked acceleration after 1983. All told, the absolute number of patents in C&C experienced a *5-fold* increase since 1983, and similarly for those in D&M. This makes clear both the fact that there was indeed a sharp turning point in the early 1980s (across the board) and the fact that there were dramatic changes in the rates of growth of innovations in emerging versus traditional technologies. When we compare patents of U.S. versus non-U.S. inventors, the only significant difference is that the field of D&M grew significantly faster in the U.S.: by the mid 1990s the share of D&M for U.S. inventors was 12%, versus 8% for non-U.S. inventors.

Citations Made and Received

A key data item in the patent document is "References Cited—U.S. Patent Documents" (hereafter we refer to these as just "citations"). Patent citations serve an important legal function, since they delimit the scope of the property rights awarded by the patent. Thus, if patent *B* cites patent *A*, it implies that patent *A* represents a piece of previously existing knowledge upon which patent *B* builds, and over which *B* cannot have a claim. The applicant has a legal duty to disclose any knowledge of the "prior art," but the decision regarding which patents to cite ultimately rests with the patent examiner, who is supposed to be an expert in the area and hence to be able to identify relevant prior art that the applicant misses or conceals. The presumption is thus that citations are informative of links between patented innovations. First, citations made may constitute a paper trail for spillovers, i.e., the fact that patent *B* cites patent *A* may indicate knowledge flowing from *A* to *B*. Second, citations *received* may be telling of the importance of the cited patent.[15] The following quote provides support for the latter presumption:

> The examiner searches the ... patent file. His purpose is to identify any prior disclosures of technology ... which might be similar to the claimed invention and limit the scope of patent protection ... or which, generally, reveal the state of the technology to which the invention is directed. If such documents are found ..., they are "cited." ... If a single document is cited in numerous patents, the technology revealed in that document is apparently involved in many developmental efforts. Thus, the number of times a patent document is cited may be a measure of its technological significance. (Office of Technology Assessment and Forecast, USPTO, 1976, p. 167)

Beyond that, one can construct citation-based measures that may capture other aspects of the patented innovations, such as "originality," "generality," "science-based," etc. (see Trajtenberg, Jaffe, and Henderson 1997). We discuss some of these measures below.

Our data include citations made starting with grant year 1975, and to the best of our knowledge, there are no computerized citation data prior to that.[16] Figure 6 shows the mean number of citations made and received over time. Notice the steep rise in the number of citations made: from an average of about 5 citations per patent in 1975 to over 10 by the late 1990s.[17] This increase is partly due to the fact that the patent file at the USPTO was computerized during the 1980s, and hence patent examiners were able to find potential references much more easily.[18] Beyond that, we cannot tell the extent to which some of the rise may be real as opposed to being purely an artifact that just reflects changing practices at the USPTO. Thus, one has to be very careful with the time dimension of citations and use appropriate controls for citing years.

---

15. See chapter 12 for evidence from a survey of inventors on the role of citations in both senses.

16. Citations were made before 1975 and may have resided within the Patent Office in some computerized form. However, we have not been able to establish precisely when the current citation practices started at the USPTO, and moreover, no publicly available electronic data of which we are aware contains pre-1975 (grant year) citations.

17. The decrease in the mean number of citations made after 1995 in the series plotted by *application* year is somewhat puzzling, in view of the fact that the series keeps rising when plotted by *grant* year. The divergence may be due to the fact that patent applications that make fewer citations are less complex, and hence are granted relatively quickly.

18. Another reason may be the steep rise in the number of patents granted since 1983, which means that there are many more patents to cite.

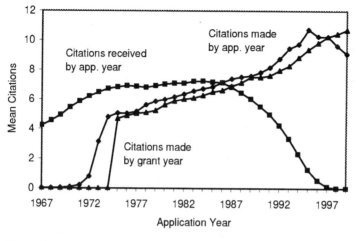

Figure 6
Mean citations made and received by application year and grant year

The decline in the number of citations received in recent years as shown in figure 6 is a result of truncation: patents applied for in, say, 1993 can receive citations in our data just from patents granted up to 1999, but in fact they will be cited by patents in subsequent years as well, only we do not yet observe them. Obviously, for older patents, truncation is less of an issue. In general, the extent to which truncation is a problem depends on the distribution of citation lags, which we examine below. Notice that patents applied for prior to 1975 also suffer from truncation, but in a different way: a 1970 patent will have all the citations received from patents granted since 1975, but none of the citations from patents granted in 1970–1974. Truncation thus reinforces the need to use appropriate controls for the timing of citations, beyond the aforementioned problem of the rising number of citations made.

Figure 7 shows the number of citations made, by technological categories, and figure 8 does the same for citations received. Clearly, patents belonging to different technological categories diverge far more in terms of citations *received* than in terms of citations *made*. In general, the traditional technological fields cite more and are cited less, whereas the emerging fields of C&C and D&M are cited much more but are in-between in terms of citations made. Thus, the category Others displays the highest number of citations made, Electrical and Electronics the lowest, Computers and Communications makes

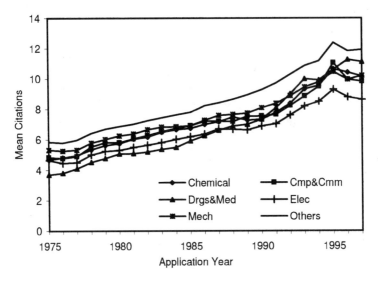

Figure 7
Mean citations made by technological categories

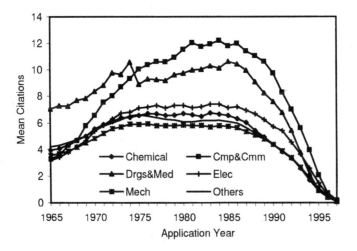

Figure 8
Mean citations received by technological categories

as many citations as Chemicals, whereas Drugs and Medical went from making the lowest number of citations to making the second highest.

On the receiving side, the distinction between traditional and advanced fields is clear-cut, and the differences are very large. Thus, C&C received up to 12 citations per patent (twice as many as Mechanical), D&M about 10, E&E over 7, whereas the traditional fields received about 6. Once again, we do not know whether the differences in citations *made* reflect a real phenomenon (e.g., fields citing less are truly more self-reliant and perhaps more original) or different citation practices that are somehow artifactual. On the other hand, the differences in citations received are more likely to be real, since it is hard to believe that there are widespread practices that systematically discriminate between patents by technological fields when making citations.

Citation Lags

There are two ways to look at citation lags: backward and forward. Backward lags focus on the time difference between the application or grant year of the *citing* patent and that of the *cited* patents. For patents granted since 1975 we have the complete list of citations *made*, we know their timing, and therefore we can compute for them the entire distribution of backward citation lags. When we look at citations received and hence at forward lags, the situation is very different, because of truncation: for patents granted in 1975, the citation lags may be at most 24 years, and for more recent patents, the distribution of lags is obviously truncated even earlier.

Figure 9 shows the frequencies of backward citation lags up to 50 years back, and separately the remaining tail for lags higher than 50. Figure 10 shows the cumulative distribution up to 50 years back.[19] A striking fact that emerges is that citations go back very far into the past (some even over a hundred years!) and to a significant extent

---

19. These distributions are computed by taking each citation to be an observation, rather than by taking the average lag for each patent. The backward lags are computed from the grant year of the citing patent to the grant year of the cited patent: we do not have the application year for patents granted prior to 1967, and we hence could not compute the lags from application year to application year. For the forward lags we do have the application year for both citing and cited patents (starting with the 1975 cited patents), and hence they are computed from application year to application year.

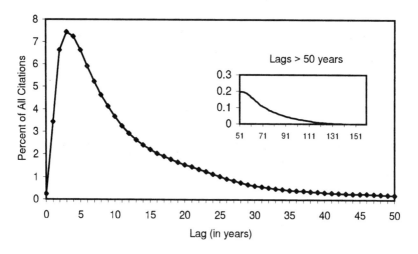

Figure 9
Distribution of backward citation lags

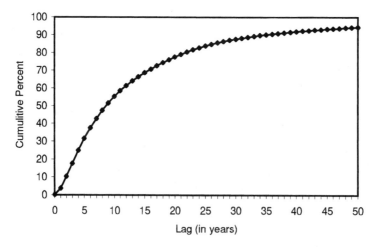

Figure 10
Cumulative distribution of backward citation lags (up to 50 years back)

Table 3
Mean backward lag (in years)

Cohort	By citations	By citing patents
1975–1977	15.22	14.30
1983–1985	16.44	15.22
1989–1991	15.96	14.52
1997–1999	14.08	12.66

patents seem to draw from old technological predecessors. Thus, 50% of citations are made to patents at least 10 years older than the citing patent, 25% to patents 20 years older or more, and 5% of citations refer to patents that are at least 50 years older than the citing one! To reverse the perspective, if this distribution and the number of patents granted were to remain stable over the long haul, patents granted in year 2000 will receive just half of their citations by 2010, 75% by 2020, and even by 2050 they will still be receiving some. Of course, we know very little about the stability of the lag distribution (strictly speaking, it is impossible to ascertain it), but there is some indication that the lags have been shortening lately, as evidenced by the figures in table 3 for various cohorts of citing patents.[20] Thus, starting in the early 1980s the backward citation lag has shortened significantly (by over 2 years). As discussed further below, however, this trend could simply be due to the fact that the rate of patenting has accelerated since then, meaning that the target population for citing is, on average, younger than it used to be.

To turn now to forward citation lags, figure 11 shows the frequency distribution of lags for patents from selected application years. An interesting feature of these distributions is that they are quite flat, particularly those for the earlier years. This is simply the result of the steep rise both in the number of citations *made* per patent and in the number of patents granted (and hence in the number of citing patents). Take the distribution for 1975 patents: after the first 3–4 years and as time advances, these patents should have been getting fewer citations. In fact, though, the number of citations that the 1975 patents received did not fall, because the number of citations made

---

20. The mean lag by citation is computed by taking the lag of each citation to be an observation and computing the mean for all of the citations. The mean lag by citing patent means that we first compute the mean lag for each citing patent and then take the mean for all citing patents.

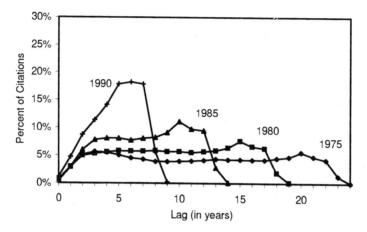

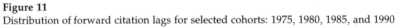

Figure 11
Distribution of forward citation lags for selected cohorts: 1975, 1980, 1985, and 1990

by later patents kept rising (and among others, they were citing 1975 patents) and the number of citing patents kept growing. These trends compensated for the fact that the 1975 patents were getting older and hence becoming less likely to be cited. Of course, as the distribution approaches the maximum lag possible (of 24 years for the 1975 patents), the number of citations has to fall because of truncation.

Another feature of interest is that it took over 10 years for the 1975 patents to receive 50% of their (forward) citations. Thus, even with truncation, it is clear that the citation process is indeed a lengthy one, however one looks at it. It is therefore imperative to take quite a wide time window to get significant coverage of forward citations. This does not imply that citation analysis has to be confined to old patents, but that one needs to carefully control for timing in using citations.

Self-Citations

One of the interesting issues in this context is whose patents are cited and, in particular, to what extent patents cite previous inventions patented by the same assignee (we refer to these as "self-citations"), rather than patents of other, unrelated assignees. This has important implications, *inter alia*, for the study of spillovers: presumably, citations to patents that belong to the same assignee represent transfers of knowledge that are mostly internalized, whereas citations to patents of others are closer to the pure notion of (diffused) spillovers.

We compute the percentage of self-citations made as follows: for each patent that has an assignee code, we count the number of citations that it made to (previous) patents that have the same assignee code, and we divide the count by the total number of citations that it made.[21] This is in fact a lower bound, because the assignee-code variable starts only in 1969, and hence for citations to patents granted earlier we cannot establish whether they are self-citations or not.[22] We also compute an upper bound, dividing the count of self-citations by the number of citations that have an assignee code, rather than by the total number of citations.[23]

The mean percentage of self-citations made is 11% at the lower bound and 13.6% at the upper bound. However, there are wide differences across technological fields, as shown in figure 12 (computed for the lower bound). The fact that the percentages are much higher in Chemical and in Drugs and Medical corresponds well with what we know about these fields: innovation is concentrated there in very large firms, and hence the likelihood that they will cite internally is higher.[24] Others and Mechanical are at the other extreme: in these fields innovation is much more widely spread among highly heterogeneous assignees (in terms of size, types of products, etc.), and hence self-citations are on average less likely.

Self-citations occur much more rapidly than citations to other patents. For the cohort of patents granted in 1997–1999, the overall mean backward citation lag was of 14.1 years, and the median was 9 years. For self-citations the mean was just 6.5 years, and the median 5 years. These differences are part of a more general phenomenon:

---

21. We exclude from the computation citing patents that are unassigned (about 25% of patents), since by definition there is no match possible to any other assignee of the cited patents.

22. There is a further reason for this to be a lower bound: the assignee code is not consolidated, that is, the same firm may appear in different patent documents under various, slightly different names, one assignee may be a subsidiary of the other, etc. Thus if, for example, we were to compute the percentage of self-citations using the Compustat codes CUSIPs, rather than the assignee codes (after the match), we would surely find higher figures.

23. This is presumably an upper bound because we know that self-citations occur earlier on average than citations to unrelated assignees. Since patents with missing assignee codes are relatively old (i.e., granted prior to 1969), citations to them would be less likely to be self-citations. However, the issue raised in the previous footnote still remains open, and hence this is not an upper bound in that sense.

24. There is a huge difference between Drugs and Medical in this respect: the percentage of self-citations in Drugs is about 20%, that in the remaining D&M subcategories is just 8%.

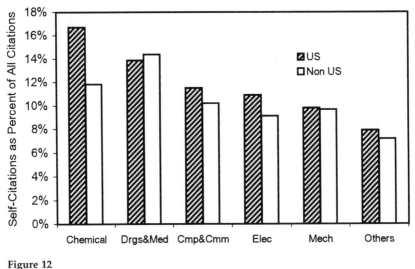

Figure 12
Self-citations made, by technological category

citations to and from patents that are closer in terms of geography, technology, or institutional belonging occur earlier than citations to and from patents that are further removed along these dimensions (see Jaffe, Trajtenberg, and Henderson 1993).

Figure 13 examines how the fraction of self-citations made has varied over time. There was a gradual increase over the 1970s. After 1980 there are some movements up and down but no clear trend. This may reflect some kind of increase in competition in invention in the last two decades, but that is pure conjecture at this point. More detailed examination of these variations in self-citation rates might provide valuable insights into the cumulative and competitive aspects of dynamic innovation.

Just as we have looked at the fraction of self-citations *made*, so we can examine the fraction of the citations *received* by a given patent that come from the same assignee. Self-citations received are, however, potentially distorted by the truncation of our data series, in interaction with the phenomena that self-citations come sooner. That is, because they come sooner, self-citations are less affected by truncation than non-self-citations, which causes the calculated percentage of self-citations received for recent cohorts to be biased upward. This is clearly seen in figure 14, which is analogous to figure 13 but calculated on the basis of percent of self-citations received. It shows

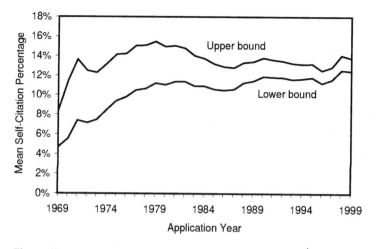

Figure 13
Self-citations made as a percentage of total citations made, by application year

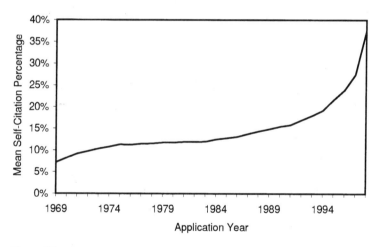

Figure 14
Self-citations received as a percentage of total citations received, by application year

the same slight upward trend in the 1970s, followed by a leveling off, and then a rapidly rising rate as we approach the truncation of the data in the 1990s.

Measures of Generality and Originality

A wide variety of citation-based measures can be defined and computed to examine different aspects of the patented innovations and their links to other innovations. We have computed and integrated into the data two such measures, generality and originality, as suggested in Trajtenberg, Jaffe, and Henderson 1997:[25]

$$Generality_i = 1 - \sum_{j}^{n_i} s_{ij}^2$$

Here s_{ij} denotes the percentage of citations received by patent i that belong to patent class j, out of n_i patent classes (note that the sum is the Herfindahl concentration index). Thus, if a patent is cited by subsequent patents that belong to a wide range of fields, the measure will be high, whereas if most citations are concentrated in a few fields, it will be low (close to zero). If we think of forward citations as indicative of the impact of a patent, a high generality score suggests that the patent had a widespread impact, in that it influenced subsequent innovations in a variety of fields (hence the "generality" label). "Originality" is defined the same way, except that it refers to citations made. Thus, if a patent cites previous patents that belong to a narrow set of technologies, the originality score will be low, whereas citing patents in a wide range of fields would render a high score.[26]

These measures tend to be positively correlated with the number of citations made (for originality) or received (for generality): highly cited patents will tend to have higher generality scores, and likewise, patents that make lots of citations display on average higher originality. In effect, where there are more citations, there is a built-

---

25. Note that these measures depend, of course, on the patent classification system: a finer classification would render higher measures, and conversely for a coarser system.
26. As indicated earlier, we included in the data a variable indicating the percentage of citations made by each patent to patents granted since 1963, which in the present context means the percentage of cited patents that have a patent class. Since originality was computed on the basis of these patents only (rather than on the basis of the total number of citations made), this is an indicator of the extent to which the computation is accurate.

in tendency to cover more patent classes. How one thinks about this tendency is to some extent a matter of interpretation. To some degree, the tendency of highly cited patents to also have a more general impact is presumably real. It can, however, lead to potentially misleading inferences, particularly when comparing patents or groups of patents that have different numbers of citations because they come from different cohorts and are therefore subject to differing degrees of truncation. If one views the observed distribution of citations across patent classes as a draw from an underlying multinomial distribution, then it can be shown that the observed concentration is biased upward (and hence the generality and originality measures are biased downward), due to the integer nature of the observed data. In effect, it is likely that many of the classes in which we observe zero citations do have some nonzero expected rate of citation. The resulting bias will be particularly large when the total number of citations is small. Appendix 2 (by Bronwyn Hall) shows how to calculate the magnitude of the bias, and hence some bias-adjusted measures, under fairly simple assumptions about the structure of the process.

Figure 15 shows the averages over time for both generality and originality. The rise in originality is quite likely related to the increase in the average number of citations made, and likewise, the decline in generality after 1990 is at least partly due to truncation.[27] Figures 16 and 17 present these measures over time by technological fields. The traditional fields Mechanical and Others are at the bottom in terms of generality, whereas Computers and Communications is at the top, with Chemical and Electrical and Electronics in between. Surprisingly, perhaps, Drugs and Medical is also at the bottom, in terms of both generality and originality. However, a closer look reveals that the subcategory of Biotechnology stands much higher than the rest of D&M in both generality and originality, and hence that the aggregation in this case may be misleading in terms of these measures. Also somewhat surprisingly, Chemical (which we regard as a traditional field) stands high in both measures, being second to C&C in generality, and even higher than C&C in originality.

---

27. The slight decline in mean originality during 1996–1997 may also be due to truncation, in the sense that the number of citations made may be indicative of the complexity of the patent, and hence patents that are granted relatively fast probably make fewer citations. Since originality is correlated with number of citations made and for those years we have only those patents that were granted relatively quickly (by application year), we should indeed observe a decline in originality for recent years.

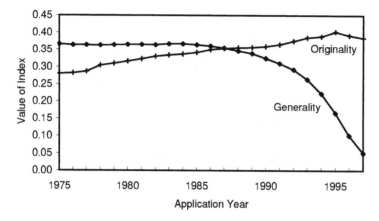

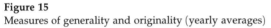

Figure 15
Measures of generality and originality (yearly averages)

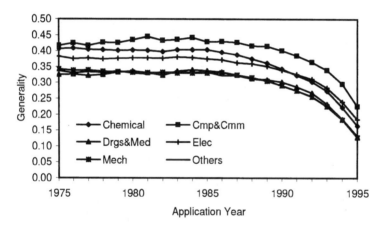

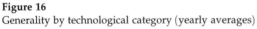

Figure 16
Generality by technological category (yearly averages)

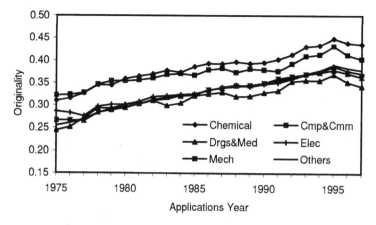

Figure 17
Originality by technological category (yearly averages)

The fact that Computers and Communications scores highest in terms of generality fits well the notion that this field may be playing the role of a general-purpose technology (see Bresnahan and Trajtenberg 1995), and its high originality score reinforces the view that it is breaking traditional molds even within the realm of innovation. Likewise, the low scores of Mechanical and Others correspond to our expectations of low innovativeness and restricted impact in those fields. In that sense, this constitutes a sort of validation of the measures themselves. At the same time, we should be aware of the fact that both originality and generality depend to a large extent on the patent classification system, and hence there is an inherent element of arbitrariness in them. Thus a finer classification within a field, in terms of the number of 3-digit patent classes available, will likely result, ceteris paribus, in higher originality and generality measures, and one may justly regard this as just an artifact of the classification system (this may be the case, for example, with Chemicals). In terms of field averages, there is the further issue of degree of heterogeneity within fields, as for example with Drugs and Medical. Further exploration of these issues, and the possible role played by the calculation bias in them, is a fruitful area for future research.

Number of Claims

A further item in our data is "number of claims," as it appears on the front page of each patent. The claims specify in detail the

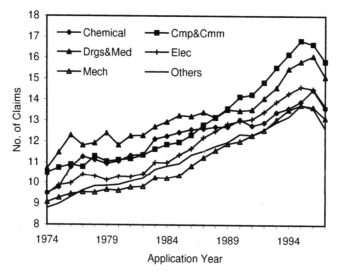

Figure 18
Claims made by technological categories (yearly averages)

"components," or building blocks, of the patented invention, and hence their number may be indicative of the "scope" or "width" of the invention (see, for example, Lanjouw and Schankerman 1999). The average number of claims made has risen substantially over time, from 9.3 in 1974 to 14.7 in 1996. Figure 18 shows the averages by technological field over time: traditional fields make fewer claims than advanced fields, with Chemical crossing from high to low in the 1990s. The differences are substantial: in 1995 the average for Computer and Communications (the top field) was 16.8, the average for Others (the lowest) just 13.7.

Match to Compustat

To take full advantage of the wealth of information contained in patent data, one needs to be able to link patents to outside data of various sorts. Otherwise, the analysis would be self-contained, with all the limitations that this implies. Thus, for example, the information on the location of inventors (state/city/counties for U.S. inventors, country/city for foreign ones) allows one to place each patent in geography space, and hence to link out with location-specific data. Similarly for data items such as technological field, time, and institutional belonging.

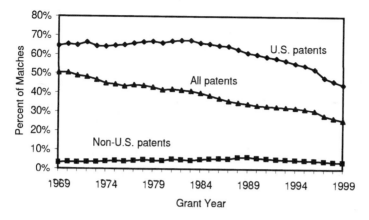

Figure 19
Percentage of patents matched to Compustat (out of assigned patents)

One of the potentially most fruitful linkages is through the identity of the assignee: if one could relate each patent to the corporation that owns it and bring together data about the corporations and about the patents, the scope of analysis would be greatly expanded. This is indeed what Zvi Griliches envisioned in setting up the NBER R&D, patents, and productivity project in the early 1980s (see Griliches, 1984). At that time, though, the only data item available about patents was patent counts by assignees, which were then attached to Compustat. Linking out our data allows one to use *all* the patent data fields, not just their count.

As already mentioned, about 80% of patents are assigned to nongovernment organizations, which are in fact mostly corporations, and our data contains both the name of the assignee and an assignee code. The trouble is that there are about 150,000 such names, and their corresponding codes are internal to the patent system, with no outside linkages. We undertook to match these assignee names to the names of corporations as they appear in Compustat, which comprises all firms traded on the U.S. stock market (about 36,000 of them). This was one of the most difficult and time-consuming tasks of the entire data-construction project.

Figure 19 shows the percentage of patents matched, out of the total number of *assigned* patents. Not surprisingly, the percentage of foreign patents matched is very small, since the overwhelming majority of foreign assignees are not traded on the U.S. stock market and hence do not appear in Compustat. For U.S. patents, though, the percentage is quite high up to the early 1980s, hovering around 70%. The steep decline from then on probably reflects both the fact that the match was done for the 1989 Compustat file and the rapidly changing composition of patents. Indeed, as mentioned above, the technological composition of patents has changed quite drastically since the mid 1980s, with traditional fields declining to less than 50% of all patents. It is quite likely that these changes have been accompanied by a large turnover in the composition of assignees, with many of the new entrants not yet traded by 1989, the year of the match.

3   "Benchmarking" of Citation Data

Overview

Although the previous sections have demonstrated intriguing trends and contrasts visible in the data on patent citations, it must be acknowledged that there is no natural scale or value measurement associated with citations data. By itself, the fact that a given patent has received 10 or 100 citations does not tell you whether that patent is highly cited. Information on patent citations is meaningful *only* when used comparatively. That is, the evaluation of the patent intensity of an invention, an inventor, an institution, or any other group of patents can only be made with reference to some benchmark citation intensity.

Determining the appropriate benchmark is complicated by several phenomena inherent to the patent-citation data. First, as already mentioned, the number of citations received by any given patent is truncated in time because we only know about the citations received so far. More important, patents of different ages are subject to differing degrees of truncation. For example, it is not obvious whether a 1990 patent that received 5 citations by 1999 should be thought of as more or less highly cited than a 1985 patent that received 10 citations by 1999. Second, differences in Patent Office practices across time or across technological areas may produce differences in citation intensities that are unrelated to the true impact, for which we use citations as a proxy. As shown above, the average patent issued in 1999 made over twice as many citations as the average patent issued in 1975 (10.7 versus 4.7 citations). At first blush, this would seem to imply something about the meaning or value of a given number of citations.

The problem created by the increase in the number of citations made *per patent* is exacerbated by the fact that the number of *patents* issued has also been rising steeply since 1983. Even if each patent issued made the same number of citations as before, the increase in the universe of citing patents would increase the total number of citations made. The combination of more patents making more citations suggests a kind of citation "inflation," which may mean that later citations are less significant than earlier ones. As a result, if we compare the citations received by a 1994 patent 5 years forward (i.e., up to 1999) with those received by a 1975 patent up to 1980, we cannot be sure that these totals are comparable. Thus even such "fixed-window" comparisons, which do not suffer from truncation bias, may be hard to make.

In addition to varying over time, the number of citations made per patent varies by technological field (see figure 7). Thus, one might suspect that a given number of citations received from patents in Computers and Communications (which typically *make* fewer citations than those in other fields) is indicative of a larger impact than the same number of citations received from other fields. On the other hand, differences in citations *received* per patent (across time, fields, etc.) could be indicative of real differences in technological impact (see figure 8).

How we treat any of these systematic differences in citation intensities when developing appropriate benchmarks for analyzing citation data will depend on our hypotheses as to which of them are real and which are artifacts. For example, we might believe that the increase in the rate of patenting represents a real increase in the rate of invention, so that the latter's contribution to changes in the number of citations received by patents is part of the real technological impact of the cited patents. At the same time, we might believe that the increase in the number of citations made *per patent* is a pure artifact of changes in patent-examination practices, so that the best measure of real technological impact would be citation intensity purged of any differences due to changing citation propensity. If so, we would want to control for the latter, but not make any adjustment for changes in the rate of patenting. Or we may be agnostic and try to infer the nature of these effects by constructing citation-based impact measures with and without first purging the citation data of these effects, and then examine which measures are more highly correlated with nonpatent indicators of technological or economic impact.

This discussion implicitly assumes that it is possible to identify and quantify the changes in citation intensity that are associated with the different effects. But this is actually harder than it may seem. Consider, for example, the increase in the average number of citations made per patent. It might seem that if each patent is making twice as many citations, that means each citation is worth half as much. But since the stock of patents available to be cited has been growing at a rapid (and accelerating) rate, this is not clear. Since there are so many potentially cited patents competing for the citations, you might think that getting one means as much as it did before, not withstanding the increase in the flow of citations.

To begin to think systematically about this set of issues, consider the following stylized facts that hold in our data: (i) the average number of citations received by patents in their first 5 years has been rising over time; (ii) the average number of citations *made* per patent has been rising over time (see figure 6); and (iii) the observed citation-lag distributions for older cohorts have fatter tails than those of more recent cohorts (see figure 11). Considering the first fact in isolation, one might conclude *either* that more recent cohorts are more fertile, *or* that the citation-lag distribution has shifted to the left (citations are coming sooner than they used to.) Considering the second fact in isolation, one might conclude that there has been an artifactual change in the propensity to make citations.[28] The last fact, taken by itself, seems to suggest that the citation-lag distribution has shifted to the right. Without further assumptions one cannot tell which of these competing scenarios is correct, and hence one cannot make any statistical adjustments to the citations data, including adjustments for truncation of lifetime citations.

In this section we discuss two generic approaches to these problems. The first, which we call the *fixed-effects* approach, involves scaling citation counts by dividing them by the average citation count for a group of patents to which the patent of interest belongs.[29] This approach treats a patent that received, say, 11 citations and belongs to a group in which the average patent received 10 citations as equivalent to a patent that received 22 citations but happens to belong to a group in which the average was 20. Likewise, such a patent would be regarded as inferior to a patent receiving just 3 citations but for

28. Another, more subtle interpretation could be that the rising propensity to cite is itself merely a reflection that more recent cohorts have been more fertile.
29. Empirical analyses based on this approach include Henderson, Jaffe, and Trajtenberg 1998 and Jaffe and Lerner 2001.

which the group average was only 1. The advantage of this approach is that it does not require one to make any assumptions about the underlying processes that may be driving differences in citation intensities across groups. The disadvantage is that, precisely because no structure is assumed, it does not distinguish between differences that are real and those that are likely artifactual.

The second, *quasi-structural*, approach attempts to distinguish the multiple effects on citation rates via econometric estimation.[30] Once the different effects have thereby been quantified, the researcher has the option to adjust the raw citation counts to remove one or more of the estimated effects. If the assumptions inherent in the econometric estimation are correct, this approach permits the extraction of a stronger signal from the noisy citation data than the nonstructural fixed-effects approach.

The Fixed-Effects Approach

The fixed-effects approach assumes that *all* sources of systematic variation over time in citation intensities are artifacts that should be removed before comparing the citation intensity of patents from different cohorts. That is, we rescale all citation intensities and express them as ratios to the mean citation intensity for patents in the same cohort.[31] If we want to compare a 1990 patent with 2 citations to a 1985 patent with 4 citations, we divide each by the average number of citations received in its cohort. This rescaling purges the data of effects due to truncation, effects due to any systematic changes over time in the propensity to cite, and effects due to changes in the number of patents making citations. Unfortunately, it also purges the data of any systematic movements over time in the importance or impact of patent cohorts. It is possible that the *typical* 1985 patent has more citations than the *typical* 1990 patent (partly) because it is indeed more fertile. Conversely, it could be that the 1990 patent is in fact better than the 1985 patent, once the effects of truncation are removed. Under the fixed-effects approach we do not attempt to separate real differences among cohorts from those due to truncation or propensity to cite, so any real effects that may be there are lost.

---

30. An example of analysis based on this approach is Hall, Jaffe, and Trajtenberg 2001.
31. Henderson, Jaffe, and Trajtenberg (1998) compared the citation intensity of university patents to the citation intensity of corporate patents from the same year. Since most patents are corporate patents, this is similar in effect to comparing the university patents to the overall mean.

An issue arises as to how to treat technological fields in applying the fixed-effects correction. As with any fixed-effect approach, one can take out year effects, field effects, and/or year-field interaction effects.[32] As discussed above, there are systematic differences across fields in the frequency of citations made and received. If one believes that such effects are real, then it is not appropriate to remove them when rescaling. To the extent that they are artifacts of, for example, the disciplinary training of patent examiners in different fields, one may want to remove them. Further, the distribution of citation lags varies by technological field, which means that the extent of truncation of a patent of given vintage depends on its technological field.

Tables 4 and 5 show the average number of citations received by patents of each cohort in each technological field, as well as the overall means (table 4 according to application year and table 5 by grant year). To remove all year, field, and year-field effects, one can take the number of citations received by a given patent and divide by the corresponding year-field mean. Alternatively, to remove only pure year effects, one can divide by the yearly means (calculated without regard to field). Finally, one can also remove year effects and year-field interaction effects but *not* the main-field effect. This can be accomplished by dividing the entries in tables 4 and 5 by the overall mean for each technological category (bottom row). Each cell in the resulting matrix is then the year-field mean *relative* to the overall mean for the field. If actual citation counts are then divided by the appropriate entry from this adjusted matrix, overall differences in mean intensities across fields are *not* removed. This permits the correction for truncation to vary by field, while allowing the overall average differences in citation intensity by field to remain in the rescaled data.[33]

---

32. An obvious question to ask is why we propose to rescale the citations data rather than simply including the corresponding fixed effect in whatever regression or other statistical analysis we are going to use the citations in. The reason is that such analyses typically have as a unit of observation entities that in any given year hold patents from many different cohorts. Hence, the rescaling described here does not correspond to a simple fixed-effects regression.

33. Note that we have calculated these rescaling factors by the technological field of the cited patent. One could imagine constructing similar factors by technological field of the citing patent. Indeed, one might believe that variations by field of the citing patent are more likely to be pure artifacts than variations by field of the cited patent. As a practical matter, rescaling by the field of the citing patent is computationally much more difficult. The rescaling factors that we propose can be applied directly to the total citations received by a given patent. Rescaling factors tied to the field of the citing patent would have to be applied individually to each *citation* rather than simply to each cited patent.

Table 4
Citations received by application year and technological category

App. year	Chemical	Computers & Comm.	Drugs & Medical	Elect. & Electronics	Mechanical	Others	All
1967	4.35	4.30	7.27	3.80	3.87	4.52	4.24
1968	4.72	4.68	7.70	4.20	4.17	4.76	4.57
1969	5.00	5.80	7.84	4.66	4.50	5.03	4.94
1970	5.55	6.56	8.37	5.40	4.85	5.44	5.46
1971	5.90	7.55	8.82	5.82	5.22	5.78	5.87
1972	6.10	8.02	9.77	6.29	5.58	6.02	6.22
1973	6.39	8.70	9.64	6.73	5.70	6.26	6.50
1974	6.42	9.34	10.58	6.80	5.91	6.54	6.74
1975	6.58	10.06	8.90	7.12	5.90	6.61	6.85
1976	6.71	10.40	9.32	7.20	5.94	6.52	6.93
1977	6.69	10.63	9.26	7.30	5.79	6.39	6.89
1978	6.57	10.62	9.20	7.11	5.80	6.28	6.82
1979	6.59	10.96	9.63	7.32	5.79	6.23	6.92
1980	6.70	11.55	9.75	7.31	5.84	6.10	7.04
1981	6.62	12.06	9.99	7.15	5.80	6.10	7.10
1982	6.49	11.77	10.04	7.22	5.82	6.18	7.11
1983	6.77	11.96	10.30	7.40	5.70	6.17	7.24
1984	6.66	12.21	10.13	7.40	5.80	6.21	7.25
1985	6.56	11.82	10.64	7.15	5.74	6.12	7.19
1986	6.32	12.01	10.44	7.23	5.66	5.99	7.14
1987	6.05	11.42	9.95	6.94	5.34	5.65	6.84
1988	5.44	11.06	9.10	6.69	5.09	5.21	6.45
1989	4.93	10.63	8.26	6.24	4.78	4.80	6.03
1990	4.39	9.75	7.59	5.73	4.38	4.35	5.53
1991	3.82	8.29	6.79	5.40	3.89	3.91	4.98
1992	3.34	7.04	5.45	4.55	3.38	3.31	4.26
1993	2.59	5.62	3.77	3.66	2.67	2.62	3.35
1994	1.71	3.96	2.18	2.60	1.87	1.81	2.34
1995	0.93	2.08	0.95	1.49	1.10	1.03	1.28
1996	0.40	0.75	0.41	0.60	0.49	0.44	0.53
1997	0.11	0.18	0.10	0.16	0.14	0.13	0.14
All	4.62	6.44	5.99	4.75	4.17	4.46	

Table 5
Citations received by grant year and technological category

Grant year	Chemical	Computers & Comm.	Drugs & Medical	Elec. & Electronics	Mechanical	Others	All
1963	2.86	1.98	4.89	2.21	2.77	3.36	2.90
1964	3.08	1.99	5.35	2.30	2.93	3.43	3.01
1965	3.47	2.20	5.75	2.44	3.08	3.67	3.20
1966	3.63	2.47	5.21	2.72	3.24	3.90	3.40
1967	3.71	2.92	6.40	2.89	3.39	4.07	3.61
1968	3.85	3.25	6.57	3.24	3.62	4.23	3.82
1969	4.11	3.19	6.95	3.51	3.78	4.42	4.02
1970	4.41	3.93	7.72	3.82	4.07	4.73	4.35
1971	4.85	5.20	8.71	4.59	4.41	4.93	4.83
1972	5.41	6.74	8.03	5.42	4.85	5.45	5.45
1973	5.81	7.27	8.56	5.89	5.20	5.73	5.82
1974	5.92	8.03	9.27	6.40	5.51	6.06	6.16
1975	6.17	8.65	10.20	6.78	5.80	6.40	6.54
1976	6.44	9.25	9.59	6.82	5.97	6.58	6.73
1977	6.57	10.10	9.10	7.23	5.95	6.73	6.92
1978	6.75	10.64	8.56	7.27	5.87	6.57	6.91
1979	6.76	10.11	9.27	7.32	5.90	6.42	6.92
1980	6.46	10.62	9.30	7.17	5.75	6.24	6.81
1981	6.77	10.86	9.15	7.28	5.85	6.22	6.90
1982	6.63	11.28	10.02	7.21	5.91	6.26	7.05
1983	6.72	11.56	10.14	7.26	5.96	6.24	7.10
1984	6.72	12.66	10.14	7.24	5.70	6.13	7.08
1985	6.72	11.91	10.09	7.40	5.71	6.18	7.11
1986	6.67	11.75	10.91	7.27	5.80	6.07	7.17
1987	6.59	12.07	11.46	7.38	5.80	6.08	7.33
1988	6.27	11.81	10.40	7.12	5.63	6.00	7.09
1989	5.82	11.18	9.69	6.79	5.20	5.37	6.67
1990	5.33	11.18	9.20	6.63	4.97	4.97	6.34
1991	4.84	10.26	8.64	6.14	4.58	4.66	5.87
1992	4.43	10.06	7.83	5.69	4.24	4.23	5.48
1993	3.73	9.17	6.52	5.23	3.72	3.69	4.90
1994	3.17	7.92	5.47	4.37	3.13	3.08	4.22
1995	2.37	6.05	3.85	3.50	2.50	2.40	3.30
1996	1.61	4.43	2.40	2.47	1.74	1.63	2.34
1997	0.85	2.45	1.09	1.40	0.99	0.90	1.28
1998	0.32	0.87	0.33	0.51	0.39	0.34	0.48
1999	0.03	0.06	0.02	0.05	0.03	0.03	0.04
All	4.62	6.44	5.99	4.75	4.17	4.46	

To summarize, fixed-effects rescaling aims to increase the signal-to-noise ratio in the data and allow comparison of citation counts over time by removing from the data variance components associated with truncation and also with possibly artifactual aspects of the citation-generation process. Unfortunately, there is no way to do so without also removing variance components that might be real. The only way to tune this more finely is to put more structure on the problem, with a model that, under additional assumptions, allows separate identification of different sources of variation.

The Quasi-Structural Approach

If the citation-lag distribution, the fertility of different patent cohorts, and the propensity to cite all vary over time, there is no general way to identify separately the contribution of each of these to variations in observed citation rates. The fixed-effects approach accepts this reality and simply removes variance components that are likely to be contaminated to some degree. To go any further one must impose additional structure, and in particular one must commit to some identifying assumptions. The assumptions that we make here are as follows:

Proportionality The shape of the lag distribution over time is independent of the total number of citations received, and hence more highly cited patents are more highly cited at all lags.

Stationarity The lag distribution does not change over time, i.e., does not depend on the cohort application or grant year of the cited patent.

These assumptions accomplish two objectives. First, stationarity allows us to estimate a time-invariant citation-lag distribution, which tells us the fraction of lifetime citations that are received during any specified time interval in the life of the patent. With proportionality, the observed citation total at a point in time for any patent can then be corrected for truncation, simply by scaling up the observed citation total by dividing it by the fraction of the lifetime citations that are predicted to occur during the lag interval that was actually observed. Second, these assumptions allow us to estimate changes in the propensity to cite over time in a way that controls for the citation-lag distribution, as well as for changes in the fertility of the cited cohorts (at least to some extent). In principle, this allows a researcher who believes that the citing-year effects are artifactual but cited-year effects are real to remove the former but not the latter. In contrast, the fixed-effects approach implicitly takes out both.

Of course, we cannot know whether these identifying assumptions are really valid. As to proportionality, we found some (still weak) supporting evidence in the fact that there is virtually zero correlation between the average forward citation lag per patent and the number of citations received.[34] That is, the average citation lag for patents with few citations is virtually identically to the mean lag for patents that receive lots of citations. Stationarity is a more complex issue, since the observed citation-lag distribution could shift over time for different reasons, and without *other* identifying assumptions, it is difficult to test this in data while other things are also changing over time.

To implement this approach, let P_{ks} be total patents observed in technological field k in year s. Let C_{kst} be the total number of citations *to* patents in year s and technology field k coming *from* patents in year t. The ratio C_{kst}/P_{ks} is then the average number of citations received by each s-k patent from the aggregate of all patents in year t. Consistent with our proportionality assumption, we model this citation frequency as a multiplicative function of cited-year (s) effects, citing-year (t) effects, field (k) effects, and citation-lag effects. Denoting the citation lag $(t - s)$ as L, we can write this as follows:

$$C_{kst}/P_{ks} = \alpha_0' \alpha_s' \alpha_t' \alpha_k' \, \exp[f_k(L)]$$

Equivalently:

$$\log[C_{kst}/P_{ks}] = \alpha_0 + \alpha_s + \alpha_t + \alpha_k + f_k(L)$$

Here $\alpha_j = \log(\alpha_j')$, and $f_k(L)$ indicates some function, perhaps varying by technological field, that describes the shape of the citation-lag distribution. It could be a parametric function, such as the double exponential used by Caballero and Jaffe (1993) and Jaffe and Trajtenberg (1999), or it could be different proportions estimated for each lag. We impose the constraint that the summation of $\exp[f_k(L)]$ over L $(L = 1, \ldots, 35)$ is unity. We also normalize $\alpha_{t=1} = \alpha_{k=1} = 0$.[35]

---

34. The correlation coefficient is 0.03 for all patents, and 0.015 for patents with 5 citations or more.

35. Note that since $L = t - s$, all of the α_s and α_t may not be identified, depending on the functional form of $f_k(L)$. We discuss this further below.

This equation can be estimated by ordinary least squares, at least for some forms of $f_k(L)$, or by nonlinear methods, as in Jaffe and Trajtenberg 1999. The α parameters can be interpreted as the proportional difference in citation intensity for a given year or field relative to the base group. These parameters can therefore be used directly to adjust or normalize observed citations for these effects, if desired. The estimated $f_k(L)$ can be used to adjust patent totals for differential truncation across cohorts.

Implementation of this approach is illustrated in table 6, which updates through 1999 estimates originally presented in Hall, Jaffe, and Trajtenberg 2001. In this model, $f_k(L)$ is as follows:

$$f_k(L) = \exp(-\beta_{1k}L)(1 - \exp(-\beta_{2k}))$$

Here the parameter β_{1k} captures the depreciation or obsolescence of knowledge, and β_{2k} captures its diffusion.[36] Because this function is nonlinear, it is possible to identify distinct α_s and α_t effects, at least in principle. In practice, we found that estimation was difficult with a full set of unconstrained cited-year and citing-year effects. Because we believe that the true fertility of invention changes only slowly, we grouped the cited years and estimated separate α_s coefficients for five-year intervals. The α_t effects are allowed to vary every year.

The estimates in the first column constrain the diffusion parameter β_2 to be the same across different fields k, while allowing the obsolescence parameter β_1 to vary. The second column reverses this, holding obsolescence constant but allowing diffusion to vary. The column labeled "full model" allows both of these parameters to vary across fields. Although allowing the β coefficients to vary does not have a large effect on the overall fit, it does affect somewhat the estimated shape of the lag distributions; this can be seen in summary form in the variations in the simulated modal citation lags shown at the bottom of the table. We will focus herein on the full-model results in the last column.

The results show that the citing year effects are indeed significant.[37] After controlling for the effects of the lag distribution, the number of patents available to be cited, and cited-year fertility, the number of citations made roughly *tripled* between 1975 and 1995. Note that this

---

36. For the motivation of this parameterization, see Caballero and Jaffe 1993.
37. There is less variation in the cited-year effects, and there is no clear pattern over time.

Table 6
Estimation of citation probabilities

	Constant diffusion		Constant obsolescence		Full model	
	Coef.	S.e.	Coef.	S.e.	Coef.	S.e.
Tech-field effects (base = other)						
Chemicals exc. Drugs	1.004	0.026	0.867	0.020	0.526	0.030
Computers & Comm.	2.281	0.058	1.451	0.033	1.495	0.094
Drugs & Medical	1.295	0.035	1.818	0.051	0.724	0.042
Electrical & Electronics	1.374	0.035	0.896	0.021	0.678	0.038
Mechanical	0.937	0.026	0.742	0.019	0.444	0.025
Citing-year effects (base = 1975)						
1976	0.742	0.036	0.812	0.038	0.871	0.040
1977	0.764	0.037	0.828	0.038	0.878	0.039
1978	0.839	0.041	0.900	0.041	0.943	0.041
1979	0.905	0.044	0.962	0.043	0.997	0.042
1980	0.956	0.045	1.008	0.044	1.034	0.041
1981	0.967	0.048	1.010	0.047	1.026	0.043
1982	1.022	0.052	1.059	0.050	1.064	0.045
1983	1.010	0.055	1.037	0.051	1.030	0.045
1984	1.110	0.061	1.130	0.056	1.111	0.048
1985	1.230	0.070	1.243	0.063	1.209	0.053
1986	1.360	0.080	1.362	0.071	1.312	0.059
1987	1.545	0.094	1.530	0.083	1.459	0.069
1988	1.728	0.111	1.692	0.097	1.600	0.079
1989	1.855	0.123	1.800	0.106	1.684	0.085
1990	1.931	0.132	1.856	0.112	1.724	0.090
1991	2.018	0.143	1.919	0.120	1.769	0.096
1992	2.256	0.165	2.119	0.137	1.940	0.109
1993	2.551	0.195	2.365	0.159	2.151	0.127
1994	3.053	0.241	2.799	0.197	2.529	0.155
1995	3.947	0.321	3.583	0.261	3.218	0.205
1996	3.382	0.284	3.033	0.227	2.709	0.180
1997	2.816	0.246	2.495	0.193	2.217	0.152
1998	0.701	0.069	0.612	0.054	0.542	0.044
1999	0.030	0.003	0.026	0.002	0.023	0.002

Table 6 (continued)

	Constant diffusion		Constant obsolescence		Full model	
	Coef.	S.e.	Coef.	S.e.	Coef.	S.e.
Cited-year effects (base = 1963–64)						
1965–69	0.635	0.018	0.710	0.022	0.814	0.021
1970–74	0.637	0.018	0.741	0.022	0.886	0.029
1975–79	0.602	0.022	0.724	0.027	0.911	0.038
1980–84	0.555	0.027	0.700	0.033	0.926	0.049
1985–89	0.511	0.032	0.686	0.040	0.937	0.062
1990–94	0.433	0.033	0.624	0.046	0.866	0.068
1995–99	0.287	0.029	0.434	0.041	0.604	0.063
Beta1: obsolescence by technology field						
Chemicals exc. Drugs	1.007	0.020			0.689	0.025
Computers & Comm.	1.297	0.026			1.099	0.034
Drugs & Medical	0.760	0.018			0.503	0.024
Electrical & Electronics	1.235	0.025			0.850	0.027
Mechanical	1.040	0.022			0.653	0.025
Beta1 (base = other)	0.102	0.003	0.104	0.004	0.111	0.003
Beta2: diffusion by technology field						
Chemicals exc. Drugs			1.639	0.105	3.404	0.362
Computers & Comm.			2.358	0.156	2.200	0.203
Drugs & Medical			0.783	0.048	2.919	0.287
Electrical & Electronics			2.615	0.188	3.815	0.390
Mechanical			2.091	0.144	4.572	0.527
Beta2 (base = other)	0.436	0.016	0.225	0.012	0.162	0.011
R^2	0.950		0.941		0.956	
Standard error of regression	0.0595		0.0653		0.0561	
Simulated modal lag						
Chemicals exc. Drugs	3.81		4.10		3.82	
Computers & Comm.	3.35		3.41		3.83	
Drugs & Medical	4.34		5.62		4.75	
Electrical & Electronics	3.43		3.22		3.27	
Mechanical	3.74		3.63		3.26	
Other	3.82		5.11		5.55	

The dependent variable is citations (by citing year, cited year, cited field) divided by potentially citable patents (by cited year and cited field). Cited years run from 1963 to 1999, and citing years from 1975 to 1999, for a total of 3,600 observations [6 × (12 × 25 + (24 × 25)/2)].

is the combination of effects due to the increased number of citing patents and the increased rate of citations made per patent. The part due to the increased rate of citations made per patent, because it has been purged of other effects, can be thought of as a measure of changes in the pure propensity to make citations. To focus on this, table 7 takes the increasing citing-year effect and decomposes it into the rise in the number of citing patents and the pure propensity-to-cite effect. We see in column 2 that the number of citing patents *by application year* peaks in 1995 in our data at about twice the number in 1975.[38] Column 3 is just the α_t coefficients from table 6. Column 4 divides this series by the index of the number of potential citing patents by application year (column 2), which thus removes the effect due to the rising number of citing patents. We find that the pure propensity to cite was also rising until 1995, accounting for about a 50% increase in citations made.

In looking at totals of citations *made*, one could similarly divide the number made by the entry in the table that corresponds to the application year of the patent(s) of interest.

It is interesting to compare this estimated pure propensity-to-cite effect with the raw change in the average number of citations made by each patent. The latter increased by about 100% between 1975 and 1995 (from about 5 to about 10). Our estimates say that roughly half of this increase was due to the rising pure propensity to cite, and the other half was due to the fact that there were many more patents out there available to be cited.

After 1995, both the number of patents and the estimated overall citing-year effect decline. Indeed, the citing-year coefficients from the regression decline *faster* than the number of patents, causing the rise in the pure propensity to cite to reverse itself. Now, this latter effect *is not* due to truncation. It says that the patents issued in the late 1990s made fewer citations, after we controlled for the size and fertility of the stock of patents available to be cited, than those before.[39] This finding is consistent with the general notion that the patent of-

38. This was already seen in figure 1. To emphasize again, the decline in the application-year numbers in the late 1990s is due to the truncation in the application-year series owing to the cutoff in the grant-year series at the end of 1999. Once the rest of the applications from the late 1990s are processed, we will no doubt see a continued increase in successful applications per year.

39. This effect is even visible in the raw averages of citations made per patent, which also turn downward in the late 1990s after the earlier increases already noted.

Table 7
Potential "deflators" for citing patent totals

Application year	Total patents (1)	Index of patent total (1975 = 1) (2)	Citing year coefficient (from table 6) (3)	Pure propensity-to-cite effect [(3)/(2)] (4)
1975	65,888	1.000	1.000	1.000
1976	65,804	0.999	0.871	0.872
1977	65,978	1.001	0.878	0.877
1978	65,601	0.996	0.943	0.947
1979	65,726	0.998	0.997	0.999
1980	66,491	1.009	1.034	1.025
1981	63,910	0.970	1.026	1.058
1982	65,009	0.987	1.064	1.078
1983	61,563	0.934	1.030	1.103
1984	67,071	1.018	1.111	1.091
1985	71,442	1.084	1.209	1.115
1986	75,088	1.140	1.312	1.151
1987	81,458	1.236	1.459	1.180
1988	90,134	1.368	1.600	1.170
1989	96,077	1.458	1.684	1.155
1990	99,254	1.506	1.724	1.145
1991	100,016	1.518	1.769	1.165
1992	103,307	1.568	1.940	1.237
1993	106,848	1.622	2.151	1.326
1994	120,380	1.827	2.529	1.384
1995	137,661	2.089	3.218	1.540
1996	131,450	1.995	2.709	1.358
1997	114,881	1.744	2.217	1.271
1998	33,780	0.513	0.542	1.057

fice has been overwhelmed by the dramatic upsurge in patent applications in the last few years, with patent examiners having less time to review each application, and therefore being less thorough in finding prior art that should be cited.

The series presented in columns 3 and 4 of table 7 can be interpreted as deflators that can be used to purge citation totals of effects due to the rising tide of citations made. For a given patent or set of patents, one can divide the number of citations received from each application year by the appropriate entry in the table. Dividing counts of citations by the deflator in column 3 removes *all* citing-year effects.

Dividing by column 4 removes only the effect due to the changing propensity to cite, and thus implicitly treats the effect due to the rising patenting rate as real. Either way, the resulting deflated totals of citations received can be interpreted as real 1975 citations, just as nominal dollar amounts divided by a base year 1975 price index are interpreted as real 1975 dollars.[40]

If one were interested in deflating the number of citations *made* by a given patent or set of patents, one does not need to worry about effects due to the rising number of patents. But one might be interested in removing the pure propensity-to-cite effect. This could be accomplished by dividing the number of observed citations made by the entry in column 4 corresponding to the application year of the patent(s) of interest.

Analogous deflators derived from table 6 can be used across technology fields if one believes that the average difference in citation rates across technology fields is an artifact of field practices rather than a real difference across fields in knowledge flows. One can simply deflate citation totals by dividing by the α_k coefficients for the different fields. The interpretation of this is to convert citation totals into equivalent numbers of citations for the Other technology field (the base group, whose α-coefficient is normalized to unity). We have not employed such adjustments in our work, because we believe that field effects are likely to contain a significant real component. But this is a topic for further research. If field effects are real, then deflating citation totals by field effects ought to *decrease* the signal to noise ratio in citations data, which implies that the correlation of citations with other indicators of technology impact (e.g., market value) ought to be reduced by deflation. If the opposite is true, it would suggest that much of the variance in the citation intensity across fields is artifactual.

The estimates in table 6 can also be used to correct the citation totals of any given patent for truncation. As shown in figure 20, the estimates for β_1 and β_2 can be used to construct the citation-lag distribution by field (normalized to unity over 35 years), after removing cited-year and citing-year effects. The contrast between figure 20 and figure 11 illustrates the dramatic impact of the citing-year and cited-

40. Because it is purged of truncation effects, the deflator in column 4 applies (in principle) to citation totals no matter how derived. Column 3, however, reflects the truncation by application year in our data, and so is appropriate only for citation totals derived from within this data set.

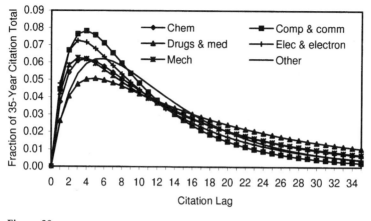

Figure 20
Simulated citation-lag distributions by field

year effects on the shape of the citation-lag distributions. The variations across field are also quite apparent. Citations in Computers and Communications come the fastest, followed by Electronics. Drugs and Medical, and Other are the slowest, with Chemicals and Mechanical falling in the middle. This has some effect on corrections for truncation. The estimates imply, for example, that if we have citation data truncated at 5 years after the initial application, we are seeing about 33% of the "lifetime" citation total (actually, the citation total for the first 35 years) for an average C&C patent, but only 22% of the "lifetime" citations for a Drug and Medical patent.

The yearly fractions underlying figure 20 are presented in cumulative form in table 8. These can be used to directly adjust citation totals on the basis of the observed interval, whether the truncated or unobserved portion is at the end, at the beginning (cited patents applied for before 1975), or both. For example, for a patent applied for in 1973, we observe only years 2 through 25 of the citation-lag distribution (1975–1999). If this were a Chemical patent, we see from table 8 that for the typical Chemical patent, 87% of the estimated or predicted "lifetime" citations occur in this interval (0.906–0.037), so we would divide the observed total by 0.87 to yield the truncation-adjusted total.

Finally, under the proportionality assumption, all corrections or adjustments are purely multiplicative. This makes it possible, in principle, to correct or adjust for any combination of effects. If, for

Table 8
Simulated cumulative lag distributions by technology field

Lag (yrs.)	Chem. exc. Drugs	Comp & Comm	Drugs & Medical	Electrical & Electronic	Mechanical	Other
1	0.037	0.045	0.026	0.048	0.043	0.026
2	0.091	0.112	0.067	0.115	0.101	0.069
3	0.152	0.188	0.114	0.187	0.164	0.123
4	0.214	0.266	0.165	0.259	0.226	0.182
5	0.275	0.342	0.216	0.327	0.285	0.244
6	0.333	0.413	0.265	0.390	0.341	0.306
7	0.387	0.479	0.314	0.448	0.393	0.366
8	0.438	0.538	0.360	0.502	0.442	0.424
9	0.485	0.592	0.404	0.550	0.487	0.479
10	0.529	0.640	0.446	0.594	0.530	0.530
11	0.569	0.683	0.486	0.635	0.569	0.578
12	0.607	0.721	0.524	0.671	0.606	0.622
13	0.642	0.755	0.560	0.705	0.640	0.662
14	0.674	0.785	0.593	0.735	0.671	0.699
15	0.704	0.812	0.625	0.763	0.701	0.732
16	0.732	0.835	0.656	0.788	0.728	0.763
17	0.758	0.856	0.684	0.811	0.753	0.790
18	0.782	0.875	0.711	0.832	0.777	0.815
19	0.804	0.891	0.737	0.851	0.799	0.837
20	0.824	0.906	0.761	0.868	0.820	0.858
21	0.843	0.919	0.784	0.884	0.839	0.876
22	0.861	0.930	0.806	0.898	0.856	0.892
23	0.877	0.940	0.826	0.911	0.873	0.907
24	0.892	0.949	0.845	0.923	0.888	0.920
25	0.906	0.957	0.864	0.934	0.902	0.932
26	0.919	0.964	0.881	0.943	0.916	0.942
27	0.931	0.970	0.897	0.952	0.928	0.952
28	0.942	0.976	0.913	0.960	0.939	0.961
29	0.952	0.981	0.928	0.968	0.950	0.968
30	0.962	0.985	0.941	0.975	0.960	0.975
31	0.971	0.989	0.954	0.981	0.969	0.981
32	0.979	0.992	0.967	0.986	0.978	0.987
33	0.987	0.995	0.978	0.991	0.986	0.992
34	0.994	0.998	0.990	0.996	0.993	0.996
35	1.000	1.000	1.000	1.000	1.000	1.000

example, one wants totals corrected for pure propensity-to-cite effects and for truncation, one would divide the number of citations received from each year by column 4 of table 7, and then take the resulting total for each patent and normalize using table 8. If one also wanted to remove technology-field effects, one could then divide by the estimated α_k reported in the last column of table 6. Of course, none of these adjustments should be taken as gospel or applied mechanically; we present them to illustrate the approach and to encourage further research on the best ways to maximize the signal-to-noise ratio in these data.

4 Conclusion

A major theme of the NBER since its inception is that good economic research depends on the generation of appropriate and reliable economic data. It is generally agreed that the twenty-first-century economy is one in which knowledge—particularly the technological knowledge that forms the foundation for industrial innovation—is an extremely important economic commodity. The inherently abstract nature of knowledge makes this a significant measurement challenge. We believe that patents and patent-citation data offer tremendous potential for giving empirical content to theorizing about the role of knowledge in the modern economy. We hope that by constructing the NBER Patent-Citations Data File, demonstrating some of the uses to which it can be put, and making it available to other researchers, we can provide a broader and deeper measurement base on which to build the economics of technological change.

Appendix 1

Table 9
Classification of patent classes into technological categories and subcategories[a]

Cat. code	Category name	Subcat. code	Subcategory name	Patent classes
1	Chemical	11	Agriculture, Food, Textiles	8, 19, 71, 127, 442, 504
		12	Coating	106, 118, 401, 427
		13	Gas	48, 55, 95, 96
		14	Organic Compounds	534, 536, 540, 544, 546, 548, 549, 552, 554, 556, 558, 560, 562, 564, 568, 570
		15	Resins	520, 521, 522, 523, 524, 525, 526, 527, 528, 530
		19	Miscellaneous—Chemical	23, 34, 44, 102, 117, 149, 156, 159, 162, 196, 201, 202, 203, 204, 205, 208, 210, 216, 222, 252, 260, 261, 349, 366, 416, 422, 423, 430, 436, 494, 501, 502, 510, 512, 516, 518, 585, 588
2	Computers & Communications	21	Communications	178, 333, 340, 342, 343, 358, 367, 370, 375, 379, 385, 455
		22	Computer Hardware & Software	341, 380, 382, 395, 700, 701, 702, 704, 705, 706, 707, 708, 709, 710, 712, 713, 714
		23	Computer Peripherals	345, 347
		24	Information Storage	360, 365, 369, 711
3	Drugs & Medical	31	Drugs	424, 514
		32	Surgery & Medical Instruments	128, 600, 601, 602, 604, 606, 607
		33	Biotechnology	435, 800
		39	Miscellaneous—Drugs & Medical	351, 433, 623
4	Electrical & Electronic	41	Electrical Devices	174, 200, 327, 329, 330, 331, 332, 334, 335, 336, 337, 338, 392, 439
		42	Electrical Lighting	313, 314, 315, 362, 372, 445
		43	Measuring & Testing	73, 324, 356, 374

Table 9 (continued)

Cat. code	Category name	Subcat. code	Subcategory name	Patent classes
		44	Nuclear & X-rays	250, 376, 378
		45	Power Systems	60, 136, 290, 310, 318, 320, 322, 323, 361, 363, 388, 429
		46	Semiconductor Devices	257, 326, 438, 505
		49	Miscellaneous— Elec.	191, 218, 219, 307, 346, 348, 377, 381, 386
5	Mechanical	51	Materials Processing & Handling	65, 82, 83, 125, 141, 142, 144, 173, 209, 221, 225, 226, 234, 241, 242, 264, 271, 407, 408, 409, 414, 425, 451, 493
		52	Metal Working	29, 72, 75, 76, 140, 147, 148, 163, 164, 228, 266, 270, 413, 419, 420
		53	Motors, Engines & Parts	91, 92, 123, 185, 188, 192, 251, 303, 415, 417, 418, 464, 474, 475, 476, 477
		54	Optics	352, 353, 355, 359, 396, 399
		55	Transportation	104, 105, 114, 152, 180, 187, 213, 238, 244, 246, 258, 280, 293, 295, 296, 298, 301, 305, 410, 440
		59	Miscellaneous— Mechanical	7, 16, 42, 49, 51, 74, 81, 86, 89, 100, 124, 157, 184, 193, 194, 198, 212, 227, 235, 239, 254, 267, 291, 294, 384, 400, 402, 406, 411, 453, 454, 470, 482, 483, 492, 508
6	Others	61	Agriculture, Husbandry, Food	43, 47, 56, 99, 111, 119, 131, 426, 449, 452, 460
		62	Amusement Devices	273, 446, 463, 472, 473
		63	Apparel & Textile	2, 12, 24, 26, 28, 36, 38, 57, 66, 68, 69, 79, 87, 112, 139, 223, 450
		64	Earth Working & Wells	37, 166, 171, 172, 175, 299, 405, 507
		65	Furniture, House Fixtures	4, 5, 30, 70, 132, 182, 211, 256, 297, 312

Table 9 (continued)

Cat. code	Category name	Subcat. code	Subcategory name	Patent classes
		66	Heating	110, 122, 126, 165, 237, 373, 431, 432
		67	Pipes & Joints	138, 277, 285, 403
		68	Receptacles	53, 206, 215, 217, 220, 224, 229, 232, 383
		69	Miscellaneous—Others	1, 14, 15, 27, 33, 40, 52, 54, 59, 62, 63, 84, 101, 108, 109, 116, 134, 135, 137, 150, 160, 168, 169, 177, 181, 186, 190, 199, 231, 236, 245, 248, 249, 269, 276, 278, 279, 281, 283, 289, 292, 300, 368, 404, 412, 428, 434, 441, 462, 503

a. Based on the Patent Classification System as of December 31, 1999. The list of patent classes as of that date includes 8 additional new classes that are not found in the data: 532, 901, 902, 930, 968, 976, 984, and 987.

Appendix 2: A Note on the Bias in Herfindahl-Type Measures Based on Count Data

Bronwyn H. Hall

Introduction

Measures based on citations obtained by patents in individual patent classes or held by individual firms often suffer from bias due to the count nature of the underlying data. The source of the bias lies in the fact that cells with small numbers of expected citations have a non-zero probability that no citations will actually be observed. When this happens, the cell is removed from the analysis, which implies that measures of diversification will be biased downward and measures of concentration will be biased upward. In the cases considered in the text, patent generality and originality measures take the form of diversification measures and will therefore be biased downward when the total number of citations to or from the patent are small. If the bias is not corrected for, patents with few forward or backward citations will be more likely to be considered less "general" or "original" than those with many.

This appendix suggests a method for correcting the bias that is valid under a set of simple but fairly general assumptions. The two key assumptions are the following:

1. Either we treat the total number of citations (or patents) on which the measure is based as given (that is, we condition on them), or the number is large enough relative to the individual cell counts so that it can be treated as nonrandom.

2. The probability that a given citation or patent falls in a cell is independent of the probability that it falls in another cell. That is, there is no causal connection between the deviation of the observed outcome from the expected outcome in a particular cell and what happens in another cell (other than the adding up constraint). We can therefore describe the probability distribution over a set of cells as a set of multinomial probabilities.

On these assumptions we are able to compute a simple correction for the bias that depends only on the total number of counts in the measure. This correction is large when the number of counts is small and quickly converges to zero as the number of counts increases.

Mathematically, the statement of the problem is the following: suppose a researcher uses a Herfindahl-type measure to describe the concentration of patents or cites across patent classes, patent holders, or some other set. Here we use patents as an example, but all the same arguments apply to citation counts. For a set of N patents falling into J classes, with N_j patents in each class ($N_j \geq 0, j = 1, \ldots, J$), the sample Herfindahl index (HHI) is defined by the following expression:

$$HHI = \sum_{j=1}^{J} \left(\frac{N_j}{N}\right)^2$$

However, the population Herfindahl is given by the following:

$$\eta = \sum_{j=1}^{J} \lambda_j^2$$

Here the λ_js are the multinomial probabilities that the N patents will be classified in each of the J classes. Under reasonable assumptions, $E[N_j/N] = \lambda_j$. Unfortunately, this does *not* imply that $E[HHI] = \eta$, because of nonlinearity. In fact, in general the measured HHI will be biased upward when N is small, owing to Jensen's inequality and the properties of the count distribution.

Computing and Adjusting for the Bias

Assume a multinomial distribution with parameters $(\lambda_j, j = 1, \dots, J)$ for the $\{N_j\}$. Then the expectation for each N_j^2 is the following (Johnson and Kotz 1969):

$$E[N_j^2] = N\lambda_j + N(N-1)\lambda_j^2$$

Conditional on the total number of patents N, this implies the following relation between the estimated and true Herfindahl measure:

$$E[\text{HHI} \,|\, N] = E\left[\sum_{j=1}^{J}\left(\frac{N_j}{N}\right)^2\right] = \sum_{j=1}^{J}\frac{E[N_j^2]}{N^2} = \sum_{j=1}^{J}\frac{N\lambda_j + N(N-1)\lambda_j^2}{N^2}$$

$$= \frac{1}{N} + \frac{N-1}{N}\sum_{j=1}^{J}\lambda_j^2 = \frac{1}{N} + \frac{N-1}{N}\eta$$

Note that as $N \to \infty$, $E[\text{HHI} \,|\, N] \to \eta$, as we would expect. The bias in this estimator is this:

$$E[\text{HHI} \,|\, N] - \eta = \frac{1-\eta}{N}$$

The bias declines at a rate N as the number of counts grows and as concentration increases. Both results are intuitive.

Under the assumptions given in the introduction, it is straightforward to correct for this bias. Consider the following estimator for the Herfindahl:

$$\hat{\eta} = \frac{N \cdot \text{HHI} - 1}{N - 1}$$

For a given N and under the assumption that the underlying process is multinomial with parameters $\lambda_j, j = 1, \dots, J$, this estimator is an unbiased estimator of η:

$$E[\hat{\eta} \,|\, N] = \frac{N \cdot E[\text{HHI} \,|\, N] - 1}{N - 1} = \frac{1 + (N-1)\eta - 1}{N - 1} = \eta$$

The Generality Index

For many problems, the measure used is $1 - \mathrm{HHI}$ rather than the Herfindahl itself. In particular, we define generality as follows:

$$G_i = 1 - \sum_{j=1}^{J} \left(\frac{N_{ij}}{N_i}\right)^2$$

Here N_i denotes the number of forward citations to a patent, and N_{ij} is the number received from patents in class j. We use a similar formula to measure originality on the basis of the distribution of citations made. Patents with a high G_i are cited across a broad range of patent classes.

This measure is also a biased estimate of the true measure $\gamma_i = 1 - \eta_i$:

$$E[G_i \,|\, N_i] = 1 - E\left[\sum_{j=1}^{J} \left(\frac{N_{ij}}{N_i}\right)^2 N_i\right] = 1 - \frac{1 + (N_i - 1)\eta_i}{N_i} = \frac{N_i - 1}{N_i}\gamma_i$$

The bias is the following:

$$E[G_i \,|\, N_i] - \gamma_i = -\frac{\gamma_i}{N_i}$$

Again, the absolute size of the bias declines as the sample size increases and as generality decreases. The generality index will be biased downward in general, and this effect is larger for small N. Figure 21 plots the bias versus the index for three values of N (3, 10, and 100). Clearly, the magnitude is largest when N is small or generality is high.

Once again, one can form an unbiased estimator of γ_i:

$$\hat{\gamma}_i = \frac{N_i}{N_i - 1}G_i$$

The same arguments as above apply to standard error estimates of the generality index. The true standard errors will be $N/(N-1)$ larger than the estimated standard errors. When the number of cites to a patent is small, generality will be underestimated, and it will be more likely that significant differences among generalities of

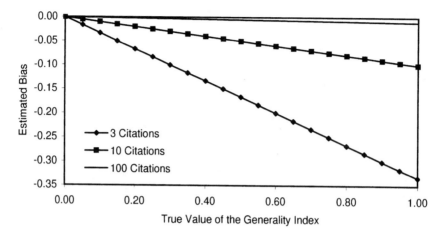

Figure 21
Bias of the generality index based on patent citations

different patents will be found. But as we have indicated, correcting for the bias is straightforward.

References

Bresnahan, T., and M. Trajtenberg. 1995. "General Purpose Technologies—Engines of Growth?" *Journal of Econometrics* 65(1): 83–108.

Caballero, R., and A. Jaffe. 1993. "How High Are the Giants' Shoulders: An Empirical Assessment of Knowledge Spillovers and Creative Destruction in a Model of Economic Growth." In O. Blanchard and S. Fischer, eds., *National Bureau of Economic Research Macroeconomics Annual*, vol. 8. Cambridge: MIT Press.

Griliches, Zvi. 1990. "Patent Statistics as Economic Indicators." *Journal of Economic Literature* 28: 1661–1707.

Griliches, Zvi, ed. 1984. *R&D, Patents, and Productivity*. NBER Conference Proceedings. Chicago: University of Chicago Press.

Griliches, Z., B. H. Hall, and A. Pakes. 1987. "The Value of Patents as Indicators of Inventive Activity." In P. Dasgupta and P. Stoneman, eds., *Economic Policy and Technological Performance*. Cambridge, England: Cambridge University Press.

Hall, B. H., A. Jaffe, and M. Trajtenberg. 2001. "Market Value and Patent Citations: A First Look." University of California, Berkeley, Dept. of Economics, working paper no. E01-304.

Henderson, R., A. Jaffe, and M. Trajtenberg. 1998. "Universities as a Source of Commercial Technology: A Detailed Analysis of University Patenting, 1965–1988." *Review of Economics and Statistics* 80: 119–127.

Jaffe, A., and J. Lerner. 2001. "Reinventing Public R&D: Patent Policy and the Commercialization of National Laboratory Technologies." *Rand Journal of Economics* 32(1): 167–198.

Jaffe, A., M. Trajtenberg, and R. Henderson. 1993. "Geographic Localization of Knowledge Spillovers as Evidenced by Patent Citations." *Quarterly Journal of Economics* 108: 577–598.

Jaffe, A., and M. Trajtenberg. 1999. "International Knowledge Flows: Evidence from Patent Citations." *Economics of Innovation and New Technology* 8: 105–136.

Jaffe, A., M. Trajtenberg, and M. Fogarty. 2000. "Knowledge Spillovers and Patent Citations: Evidence from a Survey of Inventors." *American Economic Review, Papers and Proceedings* 90: 215–218.

Johnson, Norman L., and Samuel Kotz. 1969. *Discrete Distributions*. New York: John Wiley and Sons.

Kortum, S., and J. Lerner. 1998. "Stronger Protection or Technological Revolution: What Is behind the Recent Surge in Patenting?" *Carnegie-Rochester Conference Series on Public Policy* 48: 247–304. Abridged version reprinted as "What Is behind the Recent Surge in Patenting?" *Research Policy* 28(1999): 1–22.

Lanjouw, Jean O., and Mark Schankerman. 1999. "The Quality of Ideas: Measuring Innovation with Multiple Indicators." National Bureau of Economic Research, working paper no. 7345.

Pakes, Ariel, and Margaret Simpson. 1991. "The Analysis of Patent Renewal Data." *Brookings Papers on Economic Activity, Microeconomic Annual*, pp. 331–401.

Schankerman, M., and A. Pakes. 1986. "Estimates of the Value of Patent Rights in European Countries during the Post-1950 Period." *Economic Journal* 96(384): 1052–1077.

Scherer, F. M. 1982. "Inter-industry Technology Flows and Productivity Growth." *Review of Economics and Statistics* 64: 627–634.

Schmookler, J. 1996. *Invention and Economic Growth*. Cambridge: Harvard University Press.

Trajtenberg, M. 1990. "A Penny for Your Quotes: Patent Citations and the Value of Innovations." *Rand Journal of Economics* 21(1): 172–187.

Trajtenberg, M., A. Jaffe, and R. Henderson. 1997. "University versus Corporate Patents: A Window on the Basicness of Invention." *Economics of Innovation and New Technology* 5(1): 19–50.

Sources

Chapter 2, Manuel Trajtenberg, "A Penny for Your Quotes: Patent Citations and the Value of Innovations." *RAND Journal of Economics* 20 (1990): 172–187.

Chapter 3, Manuel Trajtenberg, Rebecca Henderson, and Adam B. Jaffe, "University versus Corporate Patents: A Window on the Basicness of Invention." *Economics of Innovation and New Technology* 5 (1997): 19–50.

Chapter 4, Ricardo J. Caballero and Adam B. Jaffe, "How High Are the Giants' Shoulders: An Empirical Assessment of Knowledge Spillovers and Creative Destruction in a Model of Economic Growth." In O. Blanchard and S. Fischer, eds., *National Bureau of Economic Research Macroeconomics Annual*, vol. 8. MIT Press, 1993.

Chapter 5, Adam B. Jaffe, Manuel Trajtenberg, and Rebecca Henderson, "Geographic Localization of Knowledge Spillovers as Evidenced by Patent Citations." *Quarterly Journal of Economics* 108 (1993): 577–598.

Chapter 6, Adam B. Jaffe and Manuel Trajtenberg, "Flows of Knowledge from Universities and Federal Laboratories: Modeling the Flow of Patent Citations over Time and across Institutional and Geographic Boundaries." *Proceedings of the National Academy of Sciences* 93 (1996): 12671–12677.

Chapter 7, Adam B. Jaffe and Manuel Trajtenberg, "International Knowledge Flows: Evidence from Patent Citations." *Economics of Innovation and New Technology* 8 (1999): 105–136.

Chapter 8, Rebecca Henderson, Adam B. Jaffe, and Manuel Trajtenberg, "Universities as a Source of Commercial Technology: A Detailed Analysis of University Patenting, 1965–1988." *Review of Economics and Statistics* 80 (1998): 119–127.

Chapter 9, Adam B. Jaffe, Michael S. Fogarty, and Bruce A. Banks, "Evidence from Patents and Patent Citations on the Impact of NASA and Other Federal Labs on Commercial Innovation." *Journal of Industrial Economics* 46 (1998): 183–204.

Chapter 10, Adam B. Jaffe and Josh Lerner, "Reinventing Public R&D: Patent Policy and the Commercialization of National Laboratory Technologies." *RAND Journal of Economics* 32 (2001): 167–198.

Chapter 11, Manuel Trajtenberg, "Innovation in Israel 1968–1997: A Comparative Analysis Using Patent Data." *Research Policy* 30 (2001): 363–389.

Index

Absorption parameter, 100
Academic article citations and patent citations, 161
Aerojet Nuclear, 302
Aerospace firms and NASA patents, 283
Age, vs. importance, of patents, 33, 33 n., 45–46
Aggregation system, 415
Air Products, 272
Albany, in localization study, 167
Ames laboratory, 325
Antecedent, of research, 201
Appropriability, 51
  measures of, 52, 63, 83–84
    and larger corporations, 78
    patent data for, 53–56
    research design and data characteristics of, 66–70
    simple patent counts and, 84
    statistical analysis of, and results, 71, 72, 76
    statistical test of, 63–66
  and self-citation, 215, 215 n.
Argonne Chicago Development Corporation (ARCH), 281 n.
Argonne laboratories, 308
Arrow, Kenneth, 5
Articles in academic journals, 161
Asian Tigers and Israeli patents, 14, 347–357, 360
Assignees, 355
  of Israeli patents, 355–365
  types of, 413–414
Association of University Technology Administrators (AUTM), surveys of, 244
AT&T, 316

Attorneys and information about citations, 106 n., 380, 392

Backward-looking measures of basicness, 56, 62–63, 70–73, 75
  and forward measures, 81–83
Basicness, 51, 246. *See also* Generality; Importance of patents
  continuum of, 54, 55
  measures of, 52, 56–57, 83–84
    backward-looking, 56, 62–63, 70, 71, 72–73, 75, 81–83
    forward-looking, 56, 57–62, 70, 72, 73, 75, 81–83
    patent data for, 53–56
    research design for, and data characteristics of, 66–70
    simple patent counts and, 84
    statistical analysis of, and results, 70–83
    statistical test of, 63–66
Basic research, 162. *See also* Unpatentable research/innovation
Bayh-Dole Act (1980), 13, 243–244, 293
  and university incentives, 256
  and university licensing of technology, 298, 303 n., 315
  and university patenting, 313
  and university title to patents from federally funded R&D, 292, 293, 301, 303 n.
Bell Report, 294 n.
Benchmarking of citation data, 434–437
  fixed-effects approach to, 436, 437–441
  quasi-structural approach to, 437, 441–451
Bettis Atomic Power laboratory, 308